ROUTLEDGE LIBRARY EDITIONS:
AFGHANISTAN

Volume 2

ORAL NARRATIVE IN AFGHANISTAN

ORAL NARRATIVE IN AFGHANISTAN

The Individual in Tradition

MARGARET A. MILLS

Routledge
Taylor & Francis Group

LONDON AND NEW YORK

First published in 1990 by Garland Publishing

This edition first published in 2020
by Routledge
2 Park Square, Milton Park, Abingdon, Oxon OX14 4RN

and by Routledge
52 Vanderbilt Avenue, New York, NY 10017

Routledge is an imprint of the Taylor & Francis Group, an informa business

British Library Cataloguing in Publication Data
A catalogue record for this book is available from the British Library

ISBN: 978-0-367-14305-3 (Set)
ISBN: 978-0-429-29389-4 (Set) (ebk)
ISBN: 978-0-367-26513-7 (Volume 2) (hbk)
ISBN: 978-0-429-29386-3 (Volume 2) (ebk)

Publisher's Note
The publisher has gone to great lengths to ensure the quality of this reprint but
points out that some imperfections in the original copies may be apparent.

Disclaimer
The publisher has made every effort to trace copyright holders and would welcome
correspondence from those they have been unable to trace.

Oral Narrative in Afghanistan

Afghanistan

The Individual in Tradition

Margaret A. Mills

GARLAND PUBLISHING
NEW YORK & LONDON
1990

© 1990 by Margaret Ann Mills

Library of Congress Cataloging-in-Publication Data

Mills, Margaret Ann.
    Oral narrative in Afghanistan: the individual in tradition /
Margaret A. Mills.
    p. cm. — (Harvard dissertations in folklore and oral tradition)
Includes bibliographical references.
ISBN 0-8240-2871-6
    1. Tales—Afghanistan—History and criticism. 2. Oral
tradition—Afghanistan—History and criticism. 3. Folklore—
Afghanistan—Performance.   I. Title. II. Series.
GR302.5.M55   1990
398.2'09581—dc20   90-2960

All volumes printed on acid-free, 250-year-life paper.
Manufactured in the United States of America.

Design by Julie Threlkeld

Preface to the Garland Edition

Garland Publishing undertakes a community service in publishing dissertations which, to some extent, would now count as period pieces. That is certainly the case for this work, at least from the viewpoint of theory and method. Nonetheless, data on Afghan oral traditions being sadly sparse, I hope it will be of some interest to readers, who are asked for their indulgence regarding the now out-of-date aspects of the study. We do not know what the oral performance world of post-war Afghanistan will be like. Surely priorities and rhetorics have been radically influenced by ten years of war, and the war's end is not, in late 1989, yet in sight. It may be apparent in the coming years that the world of oral fiction entertainments in Afghanistan has been as radically changed as has the world of narrative theory and ethnographic representation, in the last decade.

The woman who is the main focus of this study guarded her privacy carefully in the years that I knew her, though she was quite happy to help with my research and especially to share her verbal artistry with me. She preferred that her name not be used in this study, nor her picture published, and I have complied with that preference. I have begun a book project to publish and analyze her story repertoire in more complete form, together with a fuller presentation and analysis of her biography and personal experience narratives in connection with her fictional narrative and poetic activities. That study should see print in four or five years' time.

—**Margaret A. Mills**
University of Pennsylvania
November 1989

To my mother and father,

for unfailing trust.

الصوت نصف العلم

"The voice is half the wisdom."

-apocryphal hadith

For the monetary support which made this project possible, I wish to thank the American Association of University Women's Education Foundation, Harvard University's Sheldon Fund, the Department of Health, Education and Welfare's Fulbright-Hays Dissertation Grants Program, and the National Science Foundation.

Many people have taught me, and to them I owe thanks, whatever misuse I have made of their ideas. To enumerate a few would slight the rest. I mention only three, whose gift of patient friendship has meant even more than their ideas and information: Aminollah Azhar, 'Madar Zaher', and first and last, Annemarie Schimmel.

TABLE OF CONTENTS

FIGURES AND DIAGRAMS

I. Theoretical Background

Since the turn of the century, folklorists' work on oral prose narrative has proceeded along two major lines, deriving respectively from historical philology and structural linguistics. The European scene was dominated, for the first half of the century, by the historical-geographical or Finnish school, which studied folktale texts as chains of detachable and to some extent interchangeable parts, designated 'motifs'.[1] The second line of inquiry, growing out of structural linguistics, attracted the interest of a variety of anthropologists and linguists. Structuralism is perhaps a misnomer for some of the branches which this line of inquiry has yielded,[2] but all the structuralist and formalist   theories have in common their treatment of narrative texts as wholes, and their search for meanings in the interrelationships of elements within a text.[3]

Each of these analytic approaches, in its way, confronts the

---

[1] The canonical reference works of the Finnish school are Aarne & Thompson, The Types of the Folktale (2nd recision, 1961), and Thompson's Motif Index of Folk-literature (Helsinki and Bloomington, IA, 1932-1936).

[2] Particularly in the last two decades, Russian formalist ideas have entered the thinking of many European 'structuralists', but the relationship of these two schools of thought exceeds the scope of the present discussion.

[3] Two case studies which illustrate the method of the most prolific of the structuralists, Claude Levi-Strauss, are "La Geste d'Asdiwal," Ecole Pratique des Hautes Etudes, Section des Sciences religieuses, Annual (1958-59), Paris, 1959, and "The Structural Study of Myth," Journal of American Folklore 68 (1955).

phenomenon of variants (story texts which are similar and whose geographical provenance suggests an historical relationship). The historical-
geographical school has traditionally been concerned with mapping differences in a cycle of tales (e.g. the 'tale of the lost husband,' of which
Text G, discussed below, is a variant), often with an eye to postulating
an historical/geographical origin point for a given story, on the basis
of the fact that differences between variants tend to be greater as time,
distance and linguistic and cultural barriers intervene between them. Differences are generally mapped in terms of details of content, particularly
in the choice of motifs (e.g. the tasks set for the hero(ine), which can
range from the retrieval of various objects to the answering of certain
questions, etc.), or, as in the Cinderella tale cycle, whether the main
character is a male, a female, or twins, and whether the magical helper is
a cow or other animal, or an anthropomorphic supernatural, etc.

Although the historical-geographic scholars are quite aware that
in the narrative framework of causes and effects, tasks set for the hero
or the like may take a number of different forms and still serve the same
narrative purposes, and conversely, that the same incidents may serve different narrative purposes in different tales, their main interest in the
problems of variation and transmission has been directed toward indexing
these component parts, and has not addressed the relations between 'motifs'
within a story. For this reason, the 'motif index' approach to folktale
study is dismissed as atomistic by the structuralists.

Structuralism emphasizes the relationship of component parts to
each other.[1] Simply put, the structuralist sees traditional narrative as

_____

[1] This is not to say that Levi-Strauss himself does not indulge in comparative techniques which are in fact atomistic, almost Fraserian, at

a limited set of conceptual categories, variously combined and opposed in
a series of interactions which comprises a narrative. The basic interactional pattern proposed by Levi-Strauss is dialectical. The thought process of myth and other traditional narratives, as Levi-Strauss describes
it, consists of postulating pairs of opposing categories, based on perceived natural phenomena (light-dark, wet-dry, male-female, up-down, etc.),
which are variously combined in the personages and locales of stories, such
that 'mediations' are effected between them: that is, combinations of categories or encounters or alliances between forces. Structural analysts see
each narrative as a series of transactions, proceeding toward a final
transaction which offers a possible resolution of conflicts between opposing ideas.

As might be imagined, category identification in structural analysis and the description of narratives as series of repeated transactions
are generalizing processes which can lead to extreme reductionism.[1] It
becomes unimportant whether a supernatural adversary is a cannibal spirit
on the Northwest coast of America or a flying horse in Central Asia. The
basis for the choice of particular objects to stand for conceptual categories is not of primary interest for structuralists: the objects are significant only as they reveal the categories. Thus the features chosen by
historical-geographical folklorists to distinguish variants may be insigni-

---

(footnote continued)

times. See E. Leach, Claude Levi-Strauss (N.Y.: Viking Press, 1970),
for a succinct criticism of Levi-Strauss's general methodology.

[1] For an extremely reduced, but interesting analytical model, see Alan
Dundes' The Morphology of American Indian Folktales, Folklore Fellows
Communications #195, Helsinki, 1964. This work also attempts a rapproche-
ment between structuralist and Russian formalist theory.

ficant from a structuralist point of view. Nonetheless, the choice of creatures, objects and personages to fill structural roles in folktale is to a high degree culturally determined. A difference in objects or creatures chosen may be as indicative of cultural differences as the design of a water pot, and may, like the design of the pot, imply major differences in social organization and technology. The structuralists' effort, and especially that of Levi-Strauss, has in recent years been directed toward describing universal, not culturally specific, aspects of narrative, and to that degree sacrifices particular cultural meanings in favor of these general configurations.

Thus the battle lines are drawn between the lumpers and the splitters, but because the methodologies and goals of the two schools really have no common ground, there has been virtually no fruitful dialogue between the camps. One thing the two do share, however, is a willingness to treat narrative texts as related if they share very general features of content and if their geographical provenance is somewhat contiguous. Once a relationship between texts is assumed on general linguistic or contentual grounds, the structuralists proceed to work out parallels in structure, and the historical-geographical people itemize differences in content. Neither school has been particularly at pains to find and work with narrative texts which have a known relationship to each other, in terms of actual steps of transmission through known individual narrators. Relations of transmission are simply assumed to exist between narratives which share some features and do not share others.

Although the assumptions made about the historical relations of narrative texts by both schools are not extravagant (and are rendered safer by their vagueness), each addresses the phenomenon of variation in folktale without much attention to the actual mechanics of how variants arise in transmission. This lack of attention is perhaps more surprising in the case of the Finnish school, whose main activity has been to inventory and map variants, but it is no less limiting to the structuralists, who have everything to say about the 'grammar' and 'syntax' of narrative, but (to extend their own linguistic analogy) relatively little to say about diction or the lexicon without which no 'language' is of much use for communication.

The following chapters discuss stories in a series of variants whose relationship, in terms of transmission, is known. Mār Čučeh and Afsāneh-e Garg were stories which one informant taught to another. I recorded performances by both the teacher and the learner, and in the case of Mār Čučeh, I was able to record the 'teaching' performance, at which the learner first heard the story from her teacher. The differences in the stories are significant, both from the structuralist and from the historical-geographical points of view. From the historical-geographical viewpoint, the 'distance' between these stories is minimal: it is a single step in the perennial transmission process, and therefore provides a base line for measuring the differences between variants whose 'distance' from each other, in terms of transmission, can only be hypothesized, such as those catalogued in Aarne and Thompson's Types of the Folktale. In a normally active oral tradition, storytellers and story learners hear near 'variants' of the same tale all the time. What do they make of their differences? Do they perceive stories to be related in the way that diffusionist folklorists do? Do they perceive analogies between 'motifs' or episodes in different stories? What part do these analogues play in their remembrance of stories? Do storytellers assimilate, conflating similar episodes, or do they distinguish analogous episodes as separate entities, and if so, on what basis?

From the structuralist viewpoint, the omission of an episode, or the substitution of one set of events for another, such as occurs in Mār Čūčeh and Afsāneh-e Garg, will alter the 'meaning' of the tale, if the conceptual categories presented by the tale are altered thereby. Is the variation observable in normal transmission significant at the structural level, or is it merely the substitution of conceptually equivalent objects, personages and events for each other? Is there evidence in the transmission events discussed below, that storytellers recognize or use 'structural' patterns to organize their storytelling? The structuralists assert that the 'grammar' they seek to describe is not just descriptive, but generative as well, that is, that it is used by people to formulate narratives. Is this assertion verifiable in the transmission process here documented? If structural analysis elucidates meaning (as it is supposed to do), then changes in structure, where they occur, signal changes in meaning. What does the structuralist concept of 'meaning' have to do with the changes that arise in transmission?

The main issue of the discussions which follow is whether the distinctions and constructions which the two main schools of folk narrative study make are useful in understanding the process of generation and transmission of traditional narrative, as exemplified in two instances of story learning, and in the instance of a story which a traditional narrator described as her own new composition (Šīr o Palang, Texts L and M). For the most part, observations are confined to the contents and structure of the narratives themselves. Where other information was supplied spontaneously, as in audience remarks, etc., recourse is made to the evaluations and opinions of people familiar with the tradition, to help understand the transmission process. In recording these performances, the author intentionally pursued a policy of non-intrusion, and the limits of this field strategy will also be discussed in the concluding remarks.

b)   Analytic Methodology

It is assumed that certain analogous episodes, or 'motifs' as they are designated by the historical-geographical school, will be intuitively obvious to the reader of the texts here discussed. (The concept of the motif was and is somewhat indeterminate, leaving one with the impression that the methods used by the Finnish school to isolate 'motifs' are, in the main, intuitive, anyway.) Examples of such analogues are the 'magic wedding' in texts A through B, or the 'Horse of Forty Colts' and 'Tree of Bells/Tree of Forty Voices' episodes in texts H, I and K. For all the discussion of 'motifs' over the last seventy years, the narrative unit so designated remains vague, and the idea of 'the same motif' is even harder to pin down. I have in fact avoided using the term 'motif', using instead the term 'episode' to describe a series of actions in which a problem or goal is set, actions result and some resolution is reached with regard to the problem or goal. Within an episode, component actions or events may also be seen to have analogues in other episodes. Individual characters, objects, events and actions, as well as whole episodes, have been given the status of motifs in the parlance of the Finnish school, if they can

be seen to occur independently from story to story within tradition.[1] I
have not yet devised a satisfactory, universally applicable unit of narrative (nor has anyone else that I know of), and so I resort to common-sense
terminology, with some trepidation.[2]

Some explanation is due for the type of structural analysis employed
in the discussions which follow to elucidate the relations of events within
single narratives. In essence, the process is simple. One describes, as
completely as possible, the conceptual categories used to define the physical setting and characters of each tale. As Olrik observed in the early
part of this century, the delineation of character proceeds by oppositions:
"This very basic opposition is a major rule of epic composition: young and
old, large and small, man and monster, good and evil." (Olrik, 1965:135).
The polarities used, and the roles of the dramatis personae in folktale
(which are always defined with reference to the main character) comprise a
very limited set. In general, the characters by and large do not undergo
development in their dramatic role: they are either a priori allies or
adversaries of the main character, or they are personages to be won over
to the main character's side by successful performance of prescribed tasks
and tests.

---

[1] Stith Thompson, The Folktale (1946:415): "A motif is the smallest element in a tale having a power to persist in tradition." Thompson further describes motifs as falling into three classes: actors, objects, and
"single incidents," the last comprising "the great majority of motifs."
(p. 416).

[2] Recently, linguists working in the field of semiotics have turned seriously to the task of defining narrative units, Hendricks (1973b) and
Mathiot (1972) being two. Their analytic method excises all descriptive
material, leaving only 'action' constructions (subj. + v.i. or subj. +
v.t. + obj.) and thus discards a great volume of information pertinent
to the transmission process, for much variation occurs at the level of
description, some of it important for the identification of conceptual
categories.

Likewise the geographical categories of folktale are an extremely limited set; there is 1) the home, where the main character has a recognized, established relationship to other characters, or 2) foreign territory, in which human social rules apply, but the main character's identity and social role are at first undefined, or 3) the other world, where the social and physical rules of human life as defined by the storyteller's society are suspended or inverted in various ways.[1]

Characters are defined by their belonging to one of the three geographical domains, by their age, their sex, their cleverness or stupidity, their physical weakness or strength, their human or non-human form, and by their status as allies or adversaries of the main character. Within a category such as 'malign male supernatural,' there may be further distinctions, such as 'dragon/$d\bar{\imath}v$/jinn', on the basis of human or non-human form, and so on. Each character, drawn up from an inventory of qualities which can be arrayed as sets of contrast pairs or complements, also has a characteristic repertoire of behavior. A story may or may not employ all the permutations of even the above limited set of terms. For a simple narrative, all that is needed is two adversaries (any type) and a contested issue or prize. From the point of view of variation in transmission, I will try to show, for each story performance discussed, which conceptual categories are used, in which combinations, and in particular, which combinations pertain to allies to the main character, and which to adversaries. Though often cast in a fantasy realm, all folktales concern power relation-

---

[1] In this connection it should be stressed that the fantasies of a culture derive from its real social forms, therefore the folklorist must be familiar with a society's view of 'normal' existence, social, technological, and physical, to understand the relationship of its fantastic creations to its general conceptual system.

ships and alliance patterns among anthropomorphically conceived personages;
they are essentially imaginative statements about real or potential social
problems and possibilities. The omission, substitution or reordering of
interactions between characters is a frequent phenomenon in transmission,
and in successive performances of one story by a single narrator. The effect of these changes on thematic structure, on the progressive presentation of conceptual categories, is a major concern of the textual analysis
which follows.

Besides the generic, classificatory nature of character description
in traditional storytelling, the other feature of oral style which strikes
(and often disappoints) the literate listener is its highly repetitive manner of presentation. Oral presentation is of necessity highly repetitive.
Major and minor series of events are presented more than once, so that the
audience can comprehend and remember the overall flow of events. The repetition patterns in the Herātī stories here translated (as in other traditional narrative) are of three major types:

a) Verbal repetitions. These include repetitive phrasings, such
as "He told her, anyway. He told her, and (then) morning came." (G.93-
94), or "The came and came and came," (G.61, and ubiquitous elsewhere in
journey themes). The former example is a 'stall' in that such a repeated
phrase allows the storyteller a moment to organize the next sequence of
events. Bruce Rosenberg (1975:76ff.) developed this term to describe the
chaining of phrases in black American folk preaching, which is identical
to the phenomenon here described. He emphasizes the utility of the manner-
ism to the speaker, allowing him to compose the next utterance without
interrupting the flow of speech. Equally important in narrative is the

mnemonic aid such repetition gives to listeners who might be learning the story, as a 'rehearsal' technique.[1] The second type a verbal repetition, "They came and came and came" and the like, though it may also serve as a stall, has another more immediate effect of the audience, emphasizing distance, elapsed time, or intense activity.

Another aspect of Dari style, which accounts for some repetitive patterns, is difficult to render in English translation because it is caused by the inherent ambiguity of the single pronoun u (ﻭ/), which is replaced in translation by he, she and it. In addition, /ū/ in colloquial speech replaces ān, 'that'. Ambiguities are generated in the narrative which would not arise in English, an example being the question of whether Mār Čūčeh lay down beside the vizier or his wife, (A.143), an ambiguity which in part facilitates later changes in the story (see discussion pp. below). In speech, this ambiguity is partly resolved by stress, ('she went this way, and he went that way'), and partly by context. Many references remain unclear, so that verbal repetitions arise in which the speaker is simply clarifying pronominal reference (e.g. "His heart burned. Xasteh Xomār's heart burned.", G.93).

A third type of verbal repetition frequent in the stories here translated, and in traditional prose narrative from many traditions,[2] is the fixed phrase formula, not to be confused with the 'formula' which is the basic compositional unit of oral improvisational verse. Fixed phrase

---

[1] Dennis Tedlock describes the same verbal technique in Zuni (1972:119ff). There is reason to consider it universal in oral narrative. Its presence in other narrative utterances besides folktale is observable from, e.g., Text N. See pp. 180-181 below.

[2] See, e.g., Basgöz (1975) or Boratav (1963).

formulas in the narratives discussed below occur at important transition points in the narrative. Rhymes, often short nonsense narratives in themselves, called by my informants /būd-nabūd/, "there was and was not's", open the folktale by transporting the listeners from a real into a fantastic world. The opening formulas of texts G and I are examples of Mādar Zāher's standard /būd-nabūd/ rhyme. The opening lines describe the real world of fruit-bearing and non-fruit-bearing plants. Succeeding verses describe a fanciful scene in which various vermin perform household chores, and a journey to a 'real' village (my informants told me that there actually is a village called *Hauz-e Palās*, 'Cotton Mat Pond', south of Herat), to a fictional person's home (Mulla 'Abbās), to an unlikely entertainment which is comically inadequate by local standards of hospitality (anti-clerical sentiment surfaces here), followed by a set of events whose causal relations are progressively more tenuous (a wall falls down, a water jar on the back of the speaker's donkey is broken, and a cow gives birth) and a final plea that the chain of events should end. Several such playful narratives may be strung together, each more fantastic than the last. A common final verse for the series is "And this evening the turn to tell lies is at my feet." The rhyme ends, and the story begins, "There was and was not . . ." Opening formulas locate *afsāneh* or fictional folktales firmly in the realm of fantasy. Other narrative genres have different opening formulas, which also establish truth values.

Within the narrative proper, fixed phrase formulas serve to indicate time passing, as in Mādar Zāher's prosaic "Some days and some while passed." More rarely in the Herātī stories I collected, a more elaborated rhymed formula for the passage of time was used. Major scene shifts are also indicated by fixed phrase formulas. Mādar Zāher's "Let that be and take up this" is commonly used by other narrators as well.

Closing formulas, like opening formulas, are highly elaborated in many of the stories I collected. Particularly where the story ends in a wedding, the wedding formula goes directly into a distancing formula, which emphasizes the discontinuity between the world of the narrative and that of the storyteller's audience:

> After that he went back to the vizier's house, with the vizier's wife, and for seven days and nights they hit the stick with the drum, and the drum with the stick, and
>
> They gave the Hindus raw food, and the Muslims cooked,
>
> And I didn't get one little burnt scrap from the bottom of the pot.

(C.179-181)

A simpler, detachable distancing formula, which may close stories which do not end in weddings or be appended to those which do, is simply, "And they stayed on that side of the stream, and I (we) on this," or its paraphrases, which was used by many of the storytellers who performed for me (e.g. Mādar Zāher, L.72).

The opening and closing formulas, which seem to be more developed and more commonly used in *afsāneh* than those used for internal transitions, are particular to the *afsāneh* genre, which is characterized by storytellers and audience alike as 'lies', and the formulas serve to emphasize the radical separation of the world of *afsāneh* from real life. The formulas commonly used for 'book' romances, both in print and in performance, provide a slightly different form of 'bracketing' for that genre, and sacred narrative uses still other forms of invocation. These elaborated speech elements in Dari prose narrative may be a key to indigenous genre classification, for different types of utterance are marked in different ways. Unfortunately, my collecting of genres of narrative performance other than *afsāneh* and 'book' romances was not systematic enough to provide an inventory of the different types of invocation used, or their full implications for genre definition.

b) Planning/execution/recapitulation scenes constitute the second major class of repetitive structure in Afghan oral narrative. Very often a character announces a plan or gives directions for a series of actions which are then carried out (e.g. the magic wedding, G.42-44). After the completion of a series of actions, there is often an opportunity for one or another of the characters to recapitulate, briefly or at length, the events which have gone before. Recapitulations frequently occur as components of recognition scenes, in which a character establishes his or her identity or legitimacy by demonstrating a knowledge of certain events. Recapitulations often occur at a structural point immediately before the final resolution of the story's major problem, the 'frame' episode. They may also appear at the conclusion of an episode within the story, and act as a preliminary to the next episode. The human bride's speech to Xasteh Xomār immediately after their wedding (G.50) is an example of the latter case, which serves to emphasize both the girl's loyalty to her family, and her sisters' callousness. Her husband's approval of her conduct (G.51) implies a negative judgment on her elder sisters, who assume the role of adversaries in the next section of the story (G.52-103).

c) Series of analogous events, or reiterative episodes, are the third major class of repetitive structure. These include the three sisters' responses to their father (G.23,30,39), or the five tasks which Xasteh Xomār's mother sets for the heroine (G.153,165,174,180), with their related causes and effects. Although these events seem very similar, even redundant in their contribution to the plot, they contain minimal differences which distinguish them in the minds of storyteller and audience. Their order of presentation is often hierarchical (in difficulty of accomplishment, or as in the heroine's tasks in Xasteh Xomār, in the degree of overt magical content), so that the succession of similar events creates an intensification of drama. This emphatic effect was recognized by many early students of oral traditional style, including Olrik (1965:133). Olrik, like others, however, was preoccupied with the similarities of episodes, not with their distinguishing features.[1] For the type of analysis undertaken here, the distinguishing features of similar episodes are of primary interest, because they define the conceptual relations between the events, which in turn may give significance to their order of presentation.

---

[1] Cf. R. Dorson, "Oral Styles of American Folk Narrators, "Folklore: Selected Essays, pp. 112-13: "No doubt this division [of the folktale 'The Master Thief'] into similar episodes, characteristic of Märchen, assists in the considerable feat of memorization; the narrator need keep firmly in mind only the six objects stolen." Dorson does not consider the distinctions between the objects, or their possible membership in a related class. Nor does he consider their contribution to story structure, apart from emphasis. Likewise Propp (1968:74-75) devotes only a brief comment to reiterative patterns of a single variety, which he calls 'trebling', but as Hendricks (1975:284) has pointed out, he treats such repetitious events like modifiers in a sentence, which can be excised without destroying sentence structure. The same criticism can be levelled at Propp's consideration of "transformations," the substitution of analogous events or personages from tale to tale (Propp, 1972). No consideration is given to nuances of meaning developed through multiple episodes, except as regards the emphatic power of repetition. A more illuminating approach to thematic repetition within a tale is presented by D.M. Segal (1972), despite a somewhat cumbersome notation system.

Their distinguishing features articulate different conceptual possibilities whose conjunctions and disjunctions may vary from performance to
performance, either by changes in the order of occurrence or by omission
or substitution of episodes. Related episodes establish the range of
dramatic interaction for one or more characters, through different responses to a related set of problems. I refer to series of analogous
events within a single narrative as reiterative patterns, because they
define the possibilities of one character or problem from several different perspectives. Among the repetitive features of narrative, they alone
are at once semantically, syntactically and mnemonically significant.
Repetitive phrasing, described above, is a device for pacing narration,
for rehearsal by speaker or audience, or for emphasis.[1] Recapitulations
may serve the same three purposes, may give the speaker a more extended
'breather' from narrative composition, and may also be so located as to
emphasize certain deeds and relationships over others (an important semantic function at times: see Šīr o Palang discussion, pp. 181-82, below),
but it is the reiterative patterns which permit the orderly exposition
of conceptual categories which is the heart of a story's meaning.

      The mnemonic value of reiterative patterns is more problematical
than that of repetitive phrasing and recapitulation, however. The meaning
of a story, as conveyed by the relations of its events and especially by
the final configuration of ideas with which its action resolves, is hardly rigid. The communicative value of stories lies in their fictional,
symbolic manipulation of shared human concepts and experiences. A symbol

---

[1] Cf. Dorson, op. cit., p. 116; Dorson describes the use of repetition in
brief anecdotes to "emphasize the salient points" in rapid-fire narration.

is distinguished from a sign by its metaphorical status, a disjunctive relationship with its referent which permits multiple interpretations. The indeterminacy of reference in stories is enhanced by the flexibility with which events, taken as symbols of human realities, are juxtaposed. In this regard, the semantic potential of the order of a story's events is in competition with its mnemonic function, for semantic power depends on flexibility of formulation and interpretation, whereas mnemonic utility depends on a stable pattern of associations.[1]

Mnemonic mechanisms are generally treated as conscious, intellectual activities (oral rehearsal and associative tricks of the 'one is a bun, two is a shoe' variety being prominent in psychologists' writings on the subject as well as the classical works on practical mnemonics[2]). The applications of psychological research on mnemonics to the learning of narrative are limited, because experimental tasks for testing serial memory have usually involved the learning of groups of related or unrelated items (numbers, words) in arbitrary order. In fact, a standard technique for remembering a random series is to construct a narrative to which the items to be remembered are attached by associations. One reviews the narrative to recall the items in their proper order. Thus narrative structuring aids memorization, rather than the reverse. In fact, reformulating or 'reconstructing' in recall, an activity which

---

[1] Cf. Lee Drummond's excellent critique of the static (because synchronic) nature of structural analysis (1977:842-46). I am wholly in agreement with his critique of the negative effect of separating narrative structure from narrative process, although I did not learn of his work on Arawak myth and cultural syncretism in time to incorporate his thinking into my own methodology.

[2] Cf. Bartlett (1932:50), Norman (1969:68).

experimenters on memory often try to filter out of experimental results, is of primary interest to the student of oral narrative. Bartlett, in his early experiments on the learning of narrative texts, remarked on his subjects' "constant effort to get the maximum possible of meaning into the material presented," (1932:84), which resulted in substantial reformulation of the Northwest Coast Indian tales they were asked to learn and recall, for which they lacked a frame of reference (such as shared concepts of the supernatural, etc.).[1]

Although narrative reformulation, with particular relevance for perceived meaning, is more dramatically evident in performance situations when the narrator is assimilating foreign material (either narrative material or real experiential data; cf. Drummond, 1977), it is a constant process in any active oral tradition. Only the most recent work on comparative mythology and other traditional performance forms has examined the connection between structure, process and meaning in any detail.[2]

The three tales (Mār Čūčeh, Afsāneh-e Garg, and Šīr o Palang) discussed below illustrate different aspects of the reformulation process in performance, but in one respect, they all lend themselves to a type of observation rarely made in oral narrative analysis. The individual texts here translated represent performances which occurred in a known temporal

---

[1] Cf. Norman (1969:138): "Experts in tasks often appear to have a better memory of what happened than other people...for the expert not only knows what he should concentrate attention on, but he also knows the basic constraints on the situations."

[2] On narrative structure and process, A.B. Lord's Singer of Tales (1960) was well ahead of the current attention to these issues. Other helpful contributions have since been made, some addressing the question of meaning more directly than does the Singer of Tales. Cf. Baumann (1975), Ben-Amos (1971), Da Matta (1971), Goldstein (1967), Hymes (1971).

order and relationship to each other. Most narrative texts studied as
variants of one 'tale' or 'tale type' are of diverse provenance, often collected decades apart from informants whose interrelationships, if any, are
difficult to trace. In the case of Mār Čūčeh, the first two performances
constitute learning occasions, on which performers in subsequent recordings learned the tale. The reformulations represented by texts C through
E were recorded from the two story learners soon after they heard the
story for the first time, and again several months later. Šīr o Palang
provides an example of a newly composed tale in the traditional mode, for
which the real events instigating its formulation are also known and can
be compared to the tale itself. The advantage of working with a series
of narrative performances with known relationships to each other, in studying reformulation and transmission, should be obvious. One avoids the aspect of indeterminacy which is present in all comparisons of texts whose
precise historical relations are unknown. Other types of indeterminacy
remain, which are harder to resolve (see Garg discussion, pp. 220 f. below), but the narratives discussed here nonetheless provide an opportunity
to observe the flexibility of tale structure (and meaning) at the minimal
level of a single transmission step, and to study composition and reformulation as the creative activities of a single narrator, from one performance to the next. Ultimately, I am attempting through structural analysis
to map and understand narrative process, for to be truly illuminating structural analysis must be made to reveal process; otherwise it remains a mere
descriptive model, and not a generative one.[1]

---

[1] Cf. Dell Hymes (1975:72): ". . . the validity of structural analysis
radically depends on interpretation of the praxis of those whose structure it is, and on self-awareness of the praxis of those who comprehend
that structure."

II. Background to Performance

A. The Setting

The city of Herat dominates, as it has for more than 2500 years, the fertile Harī Rud (Herat River) valley in western Afghanistan. Flowing out of the western extremity of the Hindu Kush (Paropamisus Range), the Harī Rud waters a wide, populous valley running east and west from the mountains to the present Iran-Afghanistan boundary, where it turns sharply northward. The border parallels the river northward to its intersection with the Afghan-Soviet border, and the river continues northward until it ends in an outwash plain at Tejin, west of Merv, in the Turkmen S.S.R.

Herat first appears in written documents in the Avesta (Vendidād), and in Old Persian as Haraiva. Arrian referred to the city as Artakoana and described it as the royal city of the people of Aria at the time of Alexander. The city was for centuries the dividing point of the two great east-west caravan routes, where the southern branch, leading to the Indian subcontinent, and the northern branch, the great Chinese Silk Road through Central Asia, came together in a single westerly route. Intermittently an independent political entity and a tributary of other cities, Herat has also been a seat of imperial power, most notably in the last 100 years of the Timurid dynasty founded by Timur (Tamarlane), from 1407 to 1506. Under Shah Rukh, the grandson of Timur (reigned 1407-1447), and his heirs, Timurid Herat was a center of arts, architecture and learning, a city of palaces, gardens, schools and thriving bazaars, despite a history of royal parricide and fratricide (Sykes, 1940, Vol. I:267-272; Malleson, 1880: 40-42).

Over the centuries, Herat was dominated by various powers centered to the east and west, but repeatedly survived military siege and destruction to rebuild as a center of commerce, as well as the urban center of a rich agricultural area. By the eighteenth century, the decline of the overland trade route between Europe and Asia had seriously undermined the city's economic base, but throughout the nineteenth century Herat remained the focus of English, Russian, Persian and Afghan political designs, in the so-called 'Great Game' for the control of Central Asia and the sub-continent. Independent for varying periods in the last century, the city last came under Persian domination in 1856, only to be taken by the Afghan Amir Dost Mohammed in May, 1863. The old Amir died 13 days after his victory at Herat, and his newly consolidated Afghanistan dissolved in fratricidal struggles among his numerous heirs (Alder, 1975).

The British in India continued to maneuver for a strong Afghan occupation of Herat, as a counter to Russian expansion in Central Asia (Gregorian, 1969:125). Amir Abd ur-Rahman finally succeeded in consolidating the state of modern Afghanistan in the latter part of the nineteenth century, by a combination of political and military actions, and by an aggressive program which resettled segments of his own Mohammedzai Pashtun and other tribes in the fertile steppe lands north of the Hindu Kush. These areas were formerly populated by Turkic groups, but had been depopulated in the early 1800's due to the extreme political instability of the region (Malleson, 1880:140,155,157). By the time of his death in 1901, Abd ur-Rahman had once again consolidated Mohammedzai Pashtun control over

Qandahar and Herat, and had occupied what is now Afghan Turkestan as well (Gregorian, 1969:133). Herat's economic stagnation was not alleviated by the stabilized political situation, however (Gregorian 1969:197). In recent years it has shared the relative isolation and slow economic growth of the rest of the country.

Herat province in western Afghanistan ranks sixth in land area and seventh in population in the country. The city of Herat has an estimated population of 73,700 people in 1969,[1] ranking eighth in size in the country, against a total provincial population of 706,100. The province contains over 970 villages (Ministry, 1350/1972:3-4). According to the Afghan Ministry of Planning's figures, 10.4% of the population was urban, 89.6% rural. This compares with a national average of 15/85% (Ministry, 1350/1972:Chart #1). The total population of the country was estimated at 17,086,300 in 1349/1971, but more recent estimates have ranged from 12,000,000 (SUNY team figures, unpublished 1974 census), to 19,000,000.[2] A severe two-year drought in the early 1970's had an undetermined effect of fertility and population growth. The U.N. Demographic Yearbook for 1970 estimated Afghanistan's annual birth rate at 39/1000, death rate at 16/1000, for a net growth of 23/1000. By comparison, the average growth rate of Iran, Turkey and Pakistan was 33.5/1000 (Ministry, 1350/1972:8). The growth rate for Soviet Central Asia is also probably substantially higher.

---

[1] Compare the fact that in 1219 A.D., just prior to Genghis Khan's arrival, the city was estimated to have 144,000 occupied houses! (Malleson, 1880: 49).

[2] The politics of foreign aid are such that the Republican Government of Afghanistan refused to accept the low figure, which was based in part on air surveys.

Herat province supported 1,025,000 sheep (the primary meat source in Afghanistan) in 1968/1346, or 7.3% of the national total (Ministry, 1350/1972:23-24). The province contained 3,776,000 hectares of arable land of which 682,000 hectares were irrigated, and a total of 2,503,000 hectares were under active cultivation. Of this total, 1,524,000 hectares were planted in grain. Herat's arable land represents 5.9% of the country's total (Ministry, 1350/1972:14-15). There were 90,000 landowners in the province, and the average size of holding was 27.8 *jerīb* (5.43 hectares), as compared with the national average of 18.1 *jerīb* (3.53 hectares) per landowner. Relatively speaking, Herat's population is slightly more rural than that of the country as a whole, and individual land holdings are 150% larger than the national average. This latter figure does not necessarily imply a more prosperous small land-owning class, however, since yields per hectare vary greatly, depending on available water and the length of the growing season. Until the Land Reform Decree of 1975, certain individual landowners held several thousand-hectare parcels. The 1975 act set a maximum individual holding of 100-150 *jerīb* (20-30 hectares), depending on water supply, but the effect of that legislation is uncertain. The new socialist regime which succeeded to the government in the past month (April, 1978) will doubtless attempt some type of land reform as well. The agricultural villages of the area are concentrated along the river and its tributary streams, from the mountains to the outwash plain in Soviet Turkmenistan. The outskirts of Herat City itself merge directly with surrounding villages, some of which are now on municipal power and transportation lines.

In 1974-76, the period of my stay in Afghanistan, commercial transport in and around Herat City was predominantly by truck, bus, and horse-drawn cart. The number of motor taxis operating in and around the city was probably less than 200, and private cars were few. Small farmers brought their excess produce to market by donkey, camel (occasionally), or space rented on private trucks which plied regular routes between villages and the bazaars of Herat City or its 12 satellite county seats (11 *woluswālī*, one *aliqadārī*). Commodities not produced in the village (fabrics and clothing, tea, sugar, vegetable ghee and certain other foodstuffs, manufactured products) are purchased primarily in the bazaars of the city and county seats, market days being held at least twice a week.[1]

Besides the numerous economic links between the villages and the town and city markets, the economic life of Herat province is marked by a great degree of mobility among sharecroppers and agricultural workers. Reidar Grønhaug, conducting a study of village economics during 1971-72 in the early period of the two-year drought, found that

> A striking feature of the average village in the Herat valley is the high and rapid turn-over in community membership. Only to a very limited extent is the little community here a 'cradle-to-the-grave arrangement,' . . . In a neighborhood of about twenty households, a third may have lived there two generations or more, another third a decade or two, the rest only a few years or less. Many households have come to the place in the past, stayed on for a couple of years, and then left. The villagers are living in tight complexes or blocks of residences, so that neighbours, living in the next room to each other, may, in many cases, not have seen each other before one, or both of them, arrived.
>
> The most mobile people are agricultural workers and share-croppers without land and oxen. Sharecroppers possessing one or two oxen are more stable, and if they also own a little land, they will belong to the old-timers of the place. Most villagers

---

[1] For a detailed study of an Afghan bazaar town, see P. Centlivres, Un bazar d'Asie Centrale, Wiesbaden: Reichert, 1972.

are sharecroppers, tilling the land of a resident or an absentee
landlord who frequently resides in the city of Herat. Some are
sharecroppers who at the same time own a small piece of land,
while a few are freeholders, utilizing mainly their own labour.
At some stage in the household development, members of freeholder
families will become sharecroppers themselves. In general, the
statuses of worker, sharecropper, and freeholder, constitute
stages in the development of the average peasant family over a
generation or two.   (Grønhaug, 1972:6-7)

The intra-provincial mobility of the agricultural labor force in
the Herat River valley is augmented by the steady drain of migrant labor
to Iran in the last decade or two, for urbanization and rapid growth in
Iran have caused a perennial labor shortage, both on the land and in the
cities, which peaks during the harvest season. During the summer of 1975,
my research assistant, Aminullah Azhar, a Kabul university economics student, observed that over 60% of the adult male labor force from his home
village of Taw Beryān (located about 8 miles east of Herat) had gone to
Iran to work, leaving mostly old men and young boys to bring in the crops.
People contemplated sending women into the fields, an extremity which the
village hoped to avoid.[1] The proximity of Herat to Mashhad in Iran, with
its direct links to other Iranian cities, has created an influx of capital
in the form of wages brought home by migrant workers. Luxury items such
as radios and fuel-saving pressure cookers are frequent booty from vil-
lagers' sojourns in Iran, where the daily wage (and basic commodity prices)
range to ten times what they are in Afghan cities. Prices of local commodities such as meat and staple grains are rising in Herat, due to increasing
exportation (including smuggling) to Iran.

---

[1] Women normally work in the fields in rural Iran and in certain parts of
Afghanistan (e.g. the Hazarajat, the central mountain area), but Heratis are proud of the fact that their women do not do agricultural field
work.

The combined effect of these economic trends is to give Heratis an increasingly cosmopolitan world view, after the last two or three centuries of isolation. Village elders listen to Kabul Radio and world news broadcasts, and discuss Afghan and international political policy.[1] Young men think in terms of migratory labor and the economic advantages of mobility. Movement between city and village, and village and village, causes a constant mixing of Herat's numerous ethnic groups. As Grønhaug observed,

> Even such a small neighbourhood [as the village] is heterogeneous in many ways. Most people speak Farsi, but one, two or more other languages may be present. Many persons are bilingual. People reckon themselves to belong to a series of 'tribal' categories - without any corporate organization, leadership or territory. In the little neighbourhood, 'Tadjik,' 'Afghan,' 'Timuri,' 'Taimenni,' 'Moghol,' 'Turkmen,' 'Jat,' or many other such categories, plus a multitude of sub-categories, may be represented; five or six different categories within a neighbourhood of twenty households is not rare. (1972:7)

In my limited experience, I found somewhat more village continuity and homogeneity than Grønhaug's description would lead one to expect, including a village which was characterized by its inhabitants as being entirely Turkish and settled by refugees from Merv in the early 1900's.[2] The more stable groups in many villages also seem to be more homogeneous, but mobility and inter-ethnic contact are universal in the Herat valley in recent years. In my collecting experience, this mobility and ethnic contact meant that the storytellers I met in villages were frequent visi-

---

[1] I was questioned about Viet Nam by several village elders. Most assumed that Viet Nam shares a border with the U.S., or else we would not have fought them.

[2] Certain villages near Herát City seemed, in my limited experience, to approximate his description quite closely.

tors in the city, and many lived there for varying periods. I met Ǧolām
Nabī 'Bīnawā,' one of my finest informants, in his home village of Nevīn,
an hour outside Herat, but later learned that he lived in Herat city,
about 10 minutes from my own residence. His career exemplifies the economic
possibilities of mobility: in young adulthood he ran a village oil mill
that had belonged to his father, but later he moved to the city to operate
a horse-taxi, as the oil mill had ceased to furnish his family a living.
Himself of Tajik and Said descent (two Persian-speaking groups), he moved
into a rented compound in the city, where his neighbours were a family of
Turkoman rug weavers. The carpet-manufacturing industry of Herat was and
is dominated by Turkomans, among whom the women are the traditional weavers. The Turkoman family agreed to take Ǧolām Nabī's oldest daughter as
an apprentice, and at age 16 she was a full-fledged rug weaver, weaving
carpets of medium good quality in the Turkoman style, and had her younger
sister and another neighbor girl as apprentices on her loom. Ǧolām Nabī
now has two daughters (his two eldest children) involved in the cash economy,
from which traditional women of his ethnic group are generally excluded
(with the exception of a few religious healers such as Mādar Zāher, whose
circumstances are described below).

The cultural amalgam of Herat city and village life makes for a
great deal of cross-fertilization in the oral tradition. Ethnic Turks and
Pashtuns in Herat province often speak Persian as their first language,
depending on their families' length of habitation in the area. Bilingual-
ism is common even among those who did not learn Persian as their first
language. Traditional narratives and songs are freely exchanged over
joint projects such as rug-weaving (in these women's case) or travel and
work on roads and irrigation projects, in the case of the men (cf. Baghban,

n.d.:7). Before the advent of the government cotton monopoly and the re-
quirement that everyone grow open-bole cotton for sale to the government,
the native cotton was a closed-bole variety, and parties were organized to
clean the cotton for home spinning, social occasions which brought neighbors together over long winter evenings when storytelling was the common
form of entertainment.

The government's policy of relocating men outside their native province for compulsory military service, a practice designed in part to
break down ethnic and regional prejudices and forge a national consciousness, also facilitates the sharing of traditional entertainment forms.
Ordinary soldiers, who have little or no schooling, are conscripted for
two years; the educated, who serve as officers, for only one, a circumstance which further favors contact and exchange between traditional people. Since ordinary soldiers receive only room and board and a pittance
for pocket money, even the 30-cent movie admission may be prohibitive,
forcing the soldiers to fall back on the free, traditional, do-it-yourself
entertainment forms of singing and storytelling. Men frequently cited
military service (and boarding high schools, in the case of my few educated informants), when asked about the sources of their stories.

Storytelling in Herat is not currently a professional activity.
Neither I nor Hafizullah Baghban could find a single person who earned a
living telling stories, though some of our informants remembered older
relatives who were attached to rich men's households and told stories as
part of their duties (Baghban, n.d.:8). I paid informants with whom I
worked on a regular basis, and several remarked that this was the first
time anyone had given them money for stories, although others told me of
relatives who had performed for personages such as Amir Abd ur-Rahman, or

for Kabul Radio music recording projects in former years (cf. text B.130).
Although professional storytelling has been common in Iran, and has been
reported from other parts of Afghanistan (Morgenstierne, 1975), it does
not seem to have been the practice in Herat in recent years.

Respect for learning and literacy is deep and strong in the history
of Herat and of Afghanistan in general. Afghans are keenly aware of their
numerous native poets, scholars and philosophers, among whom are many of
the giants of Persian and Indo-Persian learning and letters. Nonetheless,
90% of the population is probably functionally illiterate today (N.Y. Times,
Apr. 28, 1978:A6). Despite government efforts at education reform (dating
from the 1920's, and gaining momentum steadily since the early 60's), the
free, compulsory public education mandated by law is unevenly available,
especially in rural areas, and the education of women in particular is
lagging. The literary rate for women was recently estimated at 3%, but
this is probably optimistic (N.Y. Times, Apr. 28, 1978:A6). Girls' schools
in 1971 represented approximately 1/10-1/8 the number allotted for male
students, at elementary and middle levels. The ratio of girls' to boys'
middle and high schools fell significantly in the years 1962-71. In that
period, ten new high schools were built for girls, bringing the total to
16, while 101 new schools were built for boys, for a total of 117. In the
years between 1962 and 1971, the total number of students enrolled at all
levels almost trebled (Ministry, 1350/1972:115, 116), however, and despite
considerable recidivism, literacy is slowly gaining ground in both rural
and urban areas. In 1971, it was estimated that 22.8% of school-age children (between ages 7 and 12) were enrolled in Herat province. Rural children (90% of the school-age population) first attend 3-year village schools,
taught by village mullas, which teach literacy through rote recitation of

the Qor'ān and religious texts in Persian (Smith et al., 1973:135-136).
I questioned all my informants about their educational background, and
found no one who, as a graduate only of the three-year village school,
was functionally literate.[1]

Despite the fact that Afghanistan is still overwhelmingly illiterate,
the general population has had regular access to certain types of literature, through the public reading and preaching of its mullas and educated private citizens (Baghban, n.d.:9). Mullas and other literate people
read both religious and secular works, including the classical Persian Shah-
nameh of Ferdowsī (d. 1020) and mystical and didactic poetry (Jāmī is particularly popular in Herat, where that great 15th century mystic is buried).
Also popular are prose storybooks, such as Hamzanāmeh, Tuṭīnameh, or Najmā
Šīrāzī, whose topics range from religious pseudo-history and military adventures with human and supernatural adversaries, to purely fictional
tales of romantic adventure. Illiterate storytellers often cite a literate friend or relative from whom they have learned certain stories. Mādar
Zāher and Adī, the two women whose storytelling is discussed in the chapters
which follow, each boasted a grandfather who was 'besyār molla', 'very well
educated', and able to compose poetry as well as read books. Golām Nabī,
the fine storyteller and improvisational poet mentioned above (p.27),
first attracted my attention by his superb performance of Moġol Doxtar, a
lengthy romance which does not presently exist in written form in Persian.[2]

---

[1] The literacy picture is complicated by the fact that there are those who
can read, but do not consider themselves bā savād, 'lettered', because
they do not write. I met several older men in this category, all products
of the mosque schools.

[2] H. Baghban published a synopsis of the story in English in R. Dorson,
Folktales Told around the World, 1975,pp.209-221.

He also told me a number of stories which he identified as coming from
the 1001 Nights, which he said he had learned from a Persian edition of
that work. Later he accompanied me on a book-buying expedition to the
bazaar, where he identified a copy of 1001 Nights in Persian, which he believed to be identical with the one he had borrowed from a neighbor in
Nevin village, from which he had learned his stories. He offered to record as much *ketābxānî* ('book-reading') as I cared to hear, from whatever
book I chose, but I was never able to tear myself away from his oral storytelling to record his reading style. A substantial study of the connections between oral and literary narrative in Persian still needs to be
done (cf. Baghban, n.d.:1), and could be done fairly readily from materials
in my collection, or with a little supplementary field work. The present
study was conceived as the first half of a study of oral/literary connections, and simply outgrew the time and space available. I hope to be able
to pursue this line of inquiry in the near future.

B. Collecting

Oral narrative in Afghanistan is still, truly, an 'ocean of story,'
in which various flora and fauna flourish, and in which the collector must
learn to swim. My collection comprises 500 hours of tape, over 800 separate
items from almost 100 informants, including songs and interviews as well as
narrative items which vary in length from a minute or two to five hours.
I do not pretend to have taken the range of Herati oral tradition, much
less that of the whole of Afghanistan. In the study which follows, I have
abandoned hope of presenting an overview, and instead have focused on aspects of the oral narrative process which can be observed in individual
performances.

Intensive field recording of traditional material from a limited number of performers in a circumscribed geographical area, such as forms the basis for this study, is particularly suited to the study of performance, and still more, to the study of transmission process and repertoire formation. Yet despite one's best efforts at systematic collection, in the analytic stages every collector realizes and regrets a multitude of lacunae in the collection, and honesty demands that these lacunae be acknowledged. In my case, it seems obvious that the storytelling I recorded only partially resembles the normal storytelling event. A foreign woman with a tape recorder is hardly part of the normal storyteller's audience, and in many cases my tape recorder and I were the entire audience. This unusual circumstance directly affected the storytellers' performances. My understanding of the normal storytelling event and the processes of normal transmission is thus extrapolated from what informants have told me about storytelling as they experienced it, and from events at which I was present. Nonetheless, I could witness directly certain processes in performance which have general significance for the understanding of the form and style of prose narrative.

In the collecting process, I endeavored to question all my informants about their vital statistics (age, occupation, place of birth and residence history, education, marital status, number of children), and the sources of their stories. Apart from these questions, however, I intentionally exerted minimal influence on the performers, either in the selection or the performance of the material. I felt that the effect of my own foreignness could best be minimized by a non-intrusive style of collecting. I now wish that I had questioned or challenged various informants more directly on certain topics, especially regarding the meaning they found in their stories. I hope I have been accurate in interpreting the implicit contents of the performances I witnessed, but I am confident that a native observer could have gleaned a good deal more from the same experiences.

C. The People

To discuss oral narrative process, I have chosen two story-learning events and one instance of the composition of a new story, in hopes of describing some generative, creative aspects of variation in transmission. These recordings are the fruit of a personal friendship for which I shall be perpetually and wonderingly grateful. Every collector has his or her favorite informants, people whose skills and temperament make them particularly rewarding collaborators (cf. Asadowskij, 1926, or Dégh, 1969). In Mādar Zāher, however, I found a friend, a highly gifted woman whose total lack of formal education in no way inhibited her imaginative and resourceful participation in my work. A keen student of human nature, she had made it a point, over her husband's eight-year career as a Peace Corps cook, to meet and befriend his female employers and their friends. Her sensitivity to and patience with foreigners' needs and demands seemed unfailing. She was religiously conservative, yet endlessly curious about the values and beliefs of others. Toward the end of my stay in Herat, our candor had progressed to the point that she felt free to ask me my candid opinion on such subjects as the veil and my compatriots' sexual behavior and mores. Despite her strongly-held values, her interest in other people was based on a deep desire to understand their priorities and their ways of dealing with each other.

Mādar Zāher herself is unusually gifted in verbal arts, and has made unusual use of her gifts. She is an oral poet and a diviner, who diagnoses illnesses, locates lost people and objects, and prescribes religious charms to help people through various difficulties. Her clients are women, who come to her at home for diagnosis and advice, sometimes on behalf of their male relatives. Her eldest son, Zāher, who attends high school, writes the charms for her, out of a book of *ta'awīz* (charms and amulets) furnished to her by her religious patron, and she dispenses them to her clients. When I left Herat in 1976, Zāher had just received permission to dispense charms to male clients, under his mother's direction.

Mādar Zāher's diagnostic techniques include trance states induced by reciting with a *tasbīh* (rosary) or by inhaling the smoke of a burning paper charm (*dūdī*), during which she regularly speaks in tongues. I was present on two occasions when she entered such a trance state, once at the behest of three women clients, using a *tasbīh*, and on another occasion when she was preoccupied with questions about a dispute raging in her own family (described in Text N), using the smoke of a *dūdī*, recitation of the name of God (*Allāh*) and rhythmic bowing (*sejdeh*). On the latter occasion, when she abruptly returned to a normal state of consciousness after alternately reciting the name of God and speaking in tongues for over five minutes, she asked me whether I had understood what she said. I answered that I had heard a number of Persian words, but could not follow the whole of it. I asked her whether she understood it, and she said that she did not, "But you are a foreigner, and I thought you might know the language". When working with clients, she normally diagnoses their problems after returning to normal consciousness, with little or no direct reference to any of her trance-state utterances.

Madar Zaher came to her special skills through an initiation process which began with acute mental illness. After the birth of her third child (a daughter who died in infancy), when Madar Zaher was less than 20 years of age, she became self-destructive, lapsing into trance states and injuring herself. The family took her to various shrines for religious diagnosis and cure, and she finally became the patient of a famous religious healer in Herat City, Said Alī Shāh. He accomplished her cure by recitation and prayer (*xāndan*) over her, and after her cure she regarded him as her *pīr* or spiritual guide. She visited the shrine repeatedly with small gifts and offerings, and in the winter before I met her (1974-75), perhaps eight years after her cure, her *pīr* gave her religious sanction to become a healer in her own right, and furnished her with the book out of which her son copies the *ta'avīz* appropriate for the problems she diagnoses.[1] The day before my second visit to Mādar Zāher's house to record her stories, in the spring of 1975, her *pīr* died in his forties, of lung disease, and the religious leadership of his shrine passed to his son, who was not yet an adult.

The news of her patron's death was a great blow to Mādar Zāher, who told me, "He was like my father, because I lost my father, I was an orphan." (Mādar Zāher's father died in her early childhood, and her mother subsequently married his younger brother.) When I arrived to record stories, Mādar Zāher told me what had happened, and asked to record some verses she had composed in his memory. Her verse-making is another aspect of an extremely creative spirit. On other occasions she improvised

---

[1] This book, entitled Kollīyāt-e Majme' al-Da'vāt-e Kabīr, "Complete Compendium of the Great Prayers," is a lithograph published in Tehran by Mohammed Hassan 'Ilmī booksellers (n.d.).

lengthy eulogies for Henrietta Weibel, a former employer of her husband whom she remembered with great affection, and for me. She also composed *čārbeitī* (folk quatrains related to the literary *rubāī*) for inclusion in some of the stories she invented.

Mādar Zāher was the only informant I had who admitted to composing oral narratives in traditional style. She suspected that they would be inferior in my eyes, and at first concealed from me the fact that they were her own compositions (see pp. 177 f. below). Although I had found some of her tales to be structurally anomalous, different from the rest of her repertoire or stories I had heard from others, it was some time from her first performance of one of her own compositions (May 16, 1975) to her first admission that some of her narratives were original (June 9).

Mādar Zāher is totally uneducated. She was born in 1945 or 1946, married at puberty to her childhood fiance, a cousin, and bore her first child, Zāher, at age 14. She now has six living children from seven births, three sons and three daughters, the last daughter born in the early summer of 1977. Between the birth of her last son, Tīmur (now 5), and her seventh conception, she had taken birth control pills, but had abandoned the pills due to stomach pain of undetermined origin. Although her family has a history of TB, she is extremely healthy, a vigorous, hard-working woman of about 5 feet in height, slightly built, with attractive, regular features that reveal her Tajik ancestry.

Mādar Zāher was born in the village of Gušmī, very close to Herat in the southern district of Anjīl. She came to the city with her husband, who found a job as a Peace Corps cook in 1967 or 1968, and has been more or less continuously employed by Peace Corps and other foreigners since then. Reliable wage labor has meant that Xairuddīn, Mādar Zāher's husband, was able to let his share of village land to sharecroppers (some, of whom are relatives), and amass capital which ultimately allowed him to buy a small, traditional house in the new district of Herat where the small foreign community resides. While foreign employment lasts, Xairuddīn and his family are upwardly mobile, able to amass property. It is unclear what his strategy will be if that employment fails. During a 9-month period of unemployment last year, he rejected going to Iran as a migrant laborer, because of the physical danger of going (most workers skimp of their own food while in Iran, and return home sick and debilitated to recuperate every few months), and out of worry for his family if they were left behind. A few months ago he found a job with a foreign World Bank project member, at a salary subtantially better than what his Peace Corps employers were able to offer. Mādar Zāher supplements the family income with what she can earn from doing washing for foreigners, prescribing ta'awīz, and baking bread for the neighbors from time to time.

Adī, the other storyteller whose work is discussed below, is a Durrani Pashtun woman of 40 or 45 years of age, from the town of Anār Darreh, 60 km. northwest of Farah and about 200 km. south of Herat. Anār Darreh, like the larger town of Farah, has become a backwater since the relocation of the Herat-Qandahar highway in the early 1960's. The original road passed through Farah, and only about 30 km. east of Anār Darreh. Anār Darreh now consists of about 1000 houses, in a mountain valley which contains numerous fruit orchards and supports a good deal of livestock herding in the surrounding hills (Grötzbach, 1974:114). When I questioned Adī's relatives about her life style, they replied, "They live like nomads (māldār, 'pastoral nomads')". Adī is bilingual in Pashtu and Persian. She,

like Mādar Zāher, remembers a grandfather who was a storyteller and poet
as well as other relatives who taught her particular stories (B.130, A.174).
The people of Anār Darreh are only 90 km. from the Iranian border, and
enjoy a reputation for mechanical ability, especially applied to motor
transport (Grötzbach, 1974:117). Smuggling is also reputed to be a local
specialty.

True to their town's reputation, Adī's two sons came to Herat to
become, respectively, a motor mechanic and a 'klīnar' (ticket agent and
driver's assistant) on a truck service operating out of Herat. There they
met Mādar Zāher's family, and ultimately married Mādar Zāher's two eldest
half sisters. Adī's two sons now reside with their wives in Mādar Zāher's
stepfather's household, and when I left Herat they each had an infant son.
Adī came to Herat to visit her children and grandchildren bringing her
own youngest, a boy of 4, in the summer of 1975. I met her there, in
Mādar Zāher's house, a block from Mādar Zāher's parents' home where Adī
was staying. Adī's in-laws encouraged her to record several stories for
me. Different female members of the family joined the audience from time
to time, but Mādar Zāher, who had already worked with me extensively, was
her most avid listener. Mādar Zāher's oldest daughter Māhgol, nine years
old, also paid close attention to Adī's stories. Some of Adī's performances were recorded during the day, others at night. My women informants
were willing to tell stories during the day, if other work or the demands
of their children did not interfere, although Mādar Zāher preferred evenings or other times when her youngest children were asleep. No strong
superstitions governed my women informants' choice of times to tell stories, although one aged man did express a prohibition about daytime story-

telling, because it 'causes confusion' (*sargerdunî dāreh*) (cf. Baghban, n.d.:6-7). Adî's female in-laws encouraged her to tell stories, but she stipulated that her eldest son, Mesterî ('Mechanic'), not be told about our activities, as she feared his disapproval (A.53).

Adî, like Mādar Zāher, is totally uneducated, strong and vigorous for her age, with a ready wit and a charming speaking style. Her Persian is quite ungrammatical: the Afghan anthropologist Nazif Shahrani, hearing a tape, called it "the worst Persian I ever heard". Her style of narration is simple and straightforward, but vigorous and colorful in the use of dialogue (see Text H). Unfortunately, timing, pitch and emphasis are all lost in transcription, and all these are vital ingredients of effective oral presentation. The few descriptive 'stage directions' I have included in the translations are inadequate. I can only refer those who would appreciate the full vigor of Adî's and Mādar Zāher's performances, to the tapes themselves. Even in listening to them, one must imagine gestures and facial expressions which make storytelling a richly mimetic activity.

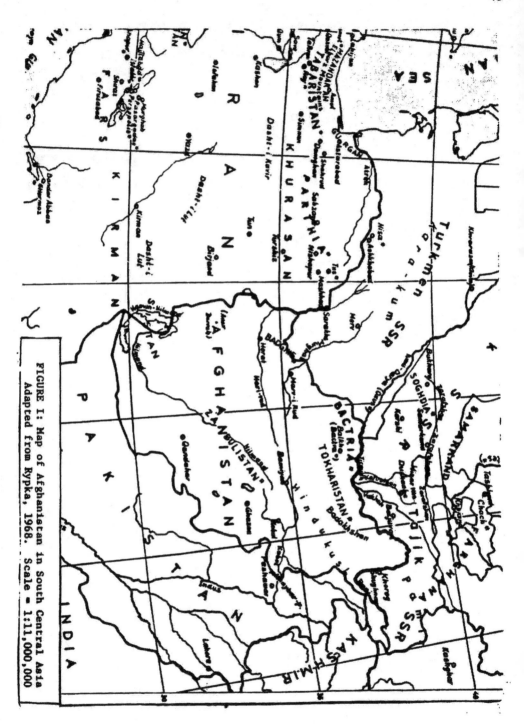

FIGURE I: Map of Afghanistan in South Central Asia
Adapted from Rypka, 1968.   Scale = 1:11,000,000

41

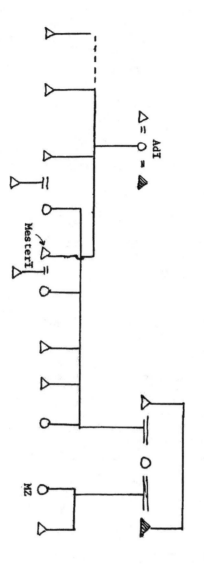

Figure II

Kinship Chart for Mādar Zāher and Adī

(MZ = Mādar Zāher)

III. MÃR ČUČEH: Story Learning and Story Patterns

The six performances of Mãr Čučeh (The Snake Chick)[1] which are discussed in this chapter are the product of a visit to my principal female
informant, Mãdar Zãher, by her half-sister's mother-in-law, Tãjwar, known
as Adī. The two women knew each other prior to this visit. Adī lives
with her second husband in the town of Anãr Darreh, six or more hours by
paved road and jeep track from Herat. (Travel time depends on weather,
with roads becoming impassable for varying periods during the winter.) Adī
could not count on making a second visit to Herat during the year I planned
to be there, so we tried during that two-month visit to record all of the
stories she could remember, a total of only ten.

While in Herat, Adī stayed with Mãdar Zãher's stepfather's family,
who are her own sons' in-laws, an extended family consisting of Mãdar Zãher's mother and stepfather, her three half-sisters (two of whom are married to Adī's two eldest sons), her two half-brothers and the young wife
of one of the half-brothers. Adī's two daughters-in-law each had an infant son and were pregnant with their second child.[2]

Most of these recordings were made in Mãdar Zãher's home, a five-

---

[1] Parts of this tale match episodes from Eberhardt and Boratav's Type #357,
"Keloghlan und der böse Köse", but the fit is not comprehensive. Friedl
(1975:41) has analyzed a similar story according to Thompson's Motif Index (1932-36), but was unable to assign it to a single Aarne-Thompson
tale type. She noted similarities between her two variants of this tale
and Aarne-Thompson Types 1003, 1007 and 1012. I leave the motif-index-
ing of these tales to those who are trained in it, as my primary interest is in internal structure and patterns.

[2] See kinship chart, p. 41 .

minute walk from her stepfather's. Adī felt that her sons, particularly

the elder, who is a truck mechanic and somewhat 'modern', would disap-

prove of story-telling and singing (see text, A.52), but felt safe from

interference at Mādar Zāher's, because Mādar Zāher observes purdah toward

her brothers-in-law, and they would not normally visit her compound. The

audience at Adī's two performances of Mār Čučeh consisted of Mādar Zāher,

her five children, and Adī's youngest son Azīzollah, about 3 1/2 years

old. Performance A occurred early one evening toward the end of a record-

ing session which stretched over most of a day, with intermissions and a

variable audience coming and going. B performance occurred late in the

evening about six weeks later, with Mādar Zāher's children also present

but extremely sleepy or asleep for portions of the performance.

Adī, like most of my female informants, had never been recorded be-

fore I met her, though she had seen and heard portable radio-cassette

tape recorders in her sons' and other households. Mādar Zāher had al-

ready recorded most of her active repertoire of stories for me prior to

Adī's visit, and she eagerly encouraged and listened to Adī's stories, in

one or two cases remarking on similarities to stories she had told me.[1]

Mādar Zāher said that she had never heard Mār Čučeh before Adī's perform-

ance of the story during A session. This seemed an excellent opportunity

to examine the assimilation of an item perceived as 'new' into an accom-

plished storyteller's repertoire. After Adī had left Herat, I encouraged

Mādar Zāher to tell me several of the stories she had heard from Adī.

Māhgol, Mādar Zāher's 9-year-old daughter, was present for both of Adī's

---

[1] Specifically, Adi's Afsāneh-e Garg, to be discussed in Chapter. IV,
below, which she likened to her own Alī Zarrīn (H.227).

performances of Mār Čučeh, as was Madar Zaher's 14-year-old son Zāher.
Both took a keen interest in Mādar Zāher's retelling of the story, as
their interjected comments (Texts C,F) indicate. Māhgol, in addition, was
eager to perform the story for me. Zāher refused; in general he was a reluctant story-teller (cf. I.337).

Although my recordings of child story-tellers were too sporadic
to reveal general patterns in their acquisition of storytelling techniques
and repertoire, Māhgol's two performances of Mār Čučeh offer some insights
into the transmission of stories in the family setting, into Mādar Zāher's
two performances, and into how people learn to tell stories. If my informants' statements are to be believed, much story-learning occurs in
late childhood and early adolescence, though children are exposed to storytelling from infancy and storytellers may go on adding to their repertoire
into old age. Māhgol, at nine years, was then entering what several of my
informants, including her mother, described as their most active period of
story-learning.

Adī's two performances of Mār Čučeh were separated by my absence
from Herat, from June 28 to August 1. When I returned, I asked Adī to
tell me Mār Čučeh, saying that I did not remember having recorded it, although she did. After Adī returned to Anār Darreh, I asked Mādar Zāher
several times if she remembered the story; she finally performed it for me
on September 11, 1975, just one day before I left Herat again for an extended absence. Her reluctance to perform the story was unusual enough to
arouse my attention, as she was normally a cooperative, enthusiastic informant.

When I returned to Herat in February, 1976, I immediately asked

Mādar Zāher whether she still remembered Adī's stories. I asked her in particular whether she could still tell Mār Čučeh; she answered that she could, but that her own stories were better (J.1). She had shown earlier enthusiasm for Afsāneh-e Garg, learning it from Adī while I was away in Kabul during July, as she explained, so that she would be able to tell it to me, in case Adī had to leave before I returned to Herat. Her eagerness to perform Afsāneh-e Garg, in comparison to I.33), Mār Čučeh, sheds further light on the systematic changes she made in Mār Čučeh, discussed in this chapter.

It was obvious from her remarks that she makes value judgments in the selection of her repertoire, showing strong preferences as to content and structure. Her personal aesthetic preferences were at work in her rejection of Mār Čučeh, and so I pressed her to perform the story, hoping to elicit clearer statements of those standards. Intellectual discussion of the form or content of tales was very difficult to elicit from any of my informants. Critical vocabulary is lacking, and performers do not readily articulate personal or general social standards for the performance of different types of material, standards which nonetheless operate. Mādar Zāher was among the most articulate of my informants, and even she, though possessed of conscious opinions and criteria, seldom articulated them directly. I hoped to elicit, along with the story, remarks that would explain her objections to it, without imposing my own conceptual framework on her explanation. It is unlikely that, without my demands, she would have added the story to her active repertoire. I had to press her to perform it at all.

Text C, Mādar Zāher's first performance of Mār Čučeh, was recorded on my last working day in Herat, on one of my last tapes, at my specific demand and after repeated postponements. Text D, Māhgol's first performance of the story, followed C immediately, for Māhgol was eager to demonstrate how she felt the story should be told, in contrast to her mother's version.

When I returned to Herat in February, 1976, I stayed in Mādar Zāher's household for about nine weeks. In our first recording session, I immediately requested and got from Mādar Zāher several times which had been poorly recorded before, including a story of her choice (Hussein-e Xāldār', one of the first I had heard from her and one of her favorites), a few items she had remembered which I had not previously recorded, and, at my specific request, Šīr o Palang[1], her own composition, which I had recorded the summer before. I also requested Mār Čučeh, which she was still reluctant to perform. Māhgol volunteered to perform it for me, and I recorded it from her during that first session, after a version of Little Red Riding Hood which she had learned from the children's story program of Kabul Radio. Mādar Zāher interrupted her daughter's performance of Mār Čučeh frequently, and the performance at one point became a shouting match between the girl and her mother (E.120-121). Mādar Zāher offered her version of the end of the story after Māhgol had finished, and offered to tell the story over from the beginning at another time (E.121). I recorded it from her three days later.

From all this and especially from her remarks during Māhgol's performance (E), it appears that Mādar Zāher's lack of enthusiasm for the story was due not to simple lack of interest but to definite objections to the story as she heard it from Adī. Her objections to it and her revisions

---

[1] Discussed in Chapter V, below.

of it in performance shed some light on her perception of the afsāneh as
a genre and what makes a 'good story'. This occasion of story learning
provided an excellent opportunity to examine the effect that the conscious
standards of the storyteller have in changing stories in transmission and
in creating variants. I shall try to summarize the available evidence
that, in this case, the balance of changes made by Mādar Zāher in the
story were intentional, systematic, and aimed at a definite esthetic effect. This case will, I hope, provide a concrete counter-example to the
'devolutionary' premise, as Dundes called it (1969:17), that variation in
tale transmission is the product of faulty memory or other unconscious mental processes, later 'patched up' by corrective additions.

Inadvertant changes, 'errors' if you will, do of course play a part
in the creation of variants. In Mādar Zāher's and her daughter's performances of Mār Čučeh, it is possible to separate, to some degree, intentional from inadvertant variations and omissions occurring in the normal transmission process, though the grounds for such separation are in a number of
cases inferential. Inadvertant changes are often susceptible to audience
correction, whereas intentional changes such as those Mādar Zāher makes
in Mār Čučeh are hotly defended by the storyteller. Intentional changes
also form coherent thematic and stylistic patterns, whereas accidental
changes brought on by faulty memory or an imperfect grasp of causal relations among the story's events often cause inconsistencies and/or contradictions in the internal structure of the story.

III.A: MÃR ČUČEH A and B: Adī's Story

The initial form of Mãr Čučeh is this transmission series is Text A, Adī's first performance of it in Mãdar Zãher's home. Mãr Čučeh was the ninth of ten stories Adī told, the tenth being Afsãneh-e Garg, which she first performed for Mãdar Zãher, after she had told me she had exhausted her repertoire, and I had left Herat. Mãr Čučeh was by implication not her favorite or most frequently performed story, though it did hold her interest enough to survive in a repertoire which she said was depleted by a failing memory (B.130). Adī showed no difficulty or hesitation in telling the present version.[1] Adī's second performance of Mãr Čučeh, text B, was somewhat shorter than A. The recording of B took place late at night, before a very sleepy audience who had heard the story before. Audience responses are virtually nil in text B, in contrast to the lively comments of Mãdar Zãher and others during A performance. Adī herself yawned frequently during B performance, and her descriptive detail and dialogues are less elaborated than in the first version. The narrative was nonetheless coherent, including all preliminary events, plans, etc. needed for narrative coherence. Most of the differences between A and B can be

---

[1] Several older informants, and more than one younger adult, blamed failing memory for a depleted story repertoire. Whether their powers of memory (or their repertoires) were really diminished, remains problematical. In the case of Afsãneh-e Garg (discussed in Chapter IV below), Adī may have recalled the story while she was recording for me, but avoided performing it because she was unsure of her ability to tell it. Her omission of major episodes from the performance she ultimately recorded (text H) suggests an unstable memory of the story (which she described to Mãdar Zãher as 'very long', I.332), in comparison with her stable formulation of Mãr Čučeh.

attributed to Adī's own fatigue , the lack of audience response, and her knowledge that she was speaking to an audience already familiar with the story.

The initial situation of M̄ār Čúčeh (all versions) is a familiar one in international folktales. A main character is introduced, a young boy whose social and physical existence is marginal. He is an orphan and poor;[1] he earns a living for his mother and himself by gleaning fodder for his cow (a 'little' cow, not quite a cow) from the periphery of the cultivated land. He lives between the settled world of human society and the wilderness, and in Afghan social usage, the implication of his living alone with his widowed mother is that they have no extended family, that he is marginal in his social attachment as well as his physical existence. Heroes who begin as marginal members of society (the stupid, lazy, poor, young, etc.) and make good are a commonplace in folk-tale, and audience interest is immediately focused on this boy. One expects that such a marginal or 'liminal' individual[2] would prove to be a successful mediator between his own, inadequate world and one beyond its borders, often a magical one, whose resources he alone is able to annex to supply the wants of his own situation, including wealth, women, social power, etc. With the sudden death of this boy (A.69), however, the story diverges from the 'poor boy makes good' format to one more suited to the loosely defined genre of

---

[1] Propp (1968:26,35) generalized these two circumstances as absentation (of the father), 'function I', and 'lack' (poverty), 'function VIIIa', both common features of the openings of folktales. Propp's Morphology of the Folktale has been succeeded by numerous other attempts to schematize the structure of traditional tales, e.g. Dundes (1964).

[2] On the notion of liminality and its relation to the supernatural, see, e.g., Turner (1964) or Douglas (1966).

trickster tales.

The boy's first, involuntary encounter with the supernatural[1] occurs in the border area between the sown, socialized lands and the wild,
where he makes his living, and introduces the *aufī*, a dragon-like serpent
described as a hyper-consumer (A.12-13). This creature's immediate threat
is sexual rapacity, however. He demands the boy's mother in marriage. The
boy at first 'forgets' to tell his mother (A.18). The second time he encounters the snake, the boy is convinced of the snake's clairvoyance and
vengefulness (A.20-21), and reports the snake's offer to his mother, who
instantly accepts. Thus the villain incorporates himself into human society, instead of preying on it from outside, raiding from the 'other
world'. This move is not anticipated by the audience. Mādar Zāher and
Mähgol, hearing the story, both infer that the snake threatens to remove
the boy's mother (A.31, cf. D.23), until Adī reiterates, at the end of the
wedding scene, that the snake has moved into the human household (A.31).
Mādar Zāher notes this detail.

There are several possible explanations for the unexpectedness of
this bit of detail. From the viewpoint of normal Afghan social practice,
residence after marriage is virilocal or viripatrilocal. A widow who re-
marries outside her dead husband's kin group goes to live with her new
husband and his kin, while her former husband's children remain with their
paternal kin. From the viewpoint of a child, his mother's remarriage to
an outsider threatens him with separation from his mother. The husband
comes to live with the bride's household only under exceptional circumstances, as when the woman's family has no male heir and needs an adult

[1] Propp's 'first reconnaissance by the villain' (1968:28).

male resident, who then becomes the heir of his father-in-law. Of course, the supernatural bridegroom is not expected to behave in a socially acceptable manner. His enmity for the boy has already been established (A. 16), but it seems to take a form unexpected by the audience.

From a structural point of view, the story also violates the audience's expectations, since villainy usually takes the form of theft or kidnapping, followed by rescue. More explicitly, a variant of this story reported from western Iran (Friedl, 1975:141) in cludes the human bride's rescue from the snake-husband by her son. An otherwise unrelated tale, Golmazang, which I recorded from a Heratī informant, concerns a half-human hero whose first exploit is to rescue his mother from his father, a ghoul, whom he kills. Although no such motif occurs in any of the stories in Mādar Zāher's own active repertoire, it is quite possible that she has heard stories containing this element and expected it in Mār Čučeh. Mādar Zāher's (and Māhgol's) expectations for the aufi's behavior could thus stem a) from specific expectations gained from familiarity with other story plots, b) from real fears derived from normal social practice, or c) from generic expectations of the 'normal' behavior of villains of the dragon type, who are conceived as hyper-consumers and withholders of women, water, and food.

One episode which occurs elsewhere in Mādar Zāher's active repertoire of stories, however, may suffice to explain the difficulties which Mādar Zāher and Māhgol have with the uxorilocal element in Mār Čučeh. The magic wedding, in which the supernatural spouse uses his/her powers over nature (here wind, rain) prepare the poor human spouse's wedding party, occurs in Mādar Zāher's version of Xasteh Xomār (Text G), a very popular

Afghan variant of AT425, "Search for the Lost Husband." In 13 of the 14 Heratī performances of this tale which I recorded, the supernatural bridegroom presents himself initially in the form of a snake, and residence after the marriage is virilocal, in a magical underground palace created in the dašt or uncultivated desert plain by the snake. In several versions, at the end of the wedding, the bride's relatives have been instructed to place her on a magical horse or camel which appears at their gate and to let it go without following it. They do so and the animal carries her off, in some cases changing itself into the bridegroom later. (G.45; cf. Mār Čučeh C.23, F.29-32, and D.23-25, E.25-28.) It seems that Mādar Zāher and Māhgol perceived the snake husband's magic wedding as a narrative unit, based on prior familiarity with a similar episode from a different story, irrespective of the fact that the two snakes have very different dramatic roles. In the case of Mār Čučeh, Mādar Zāher retains Adī's uxorilocal version of the magic wedding when she tells her version of Adī's story, whereas Māhgol substitutes the virilocal version she has heard from her mother.

Apparently Mādar Zāher's greater experience with storytelling and her more extensive repertoire are accompanied by a greater ability to remember and preserve in performance the minimal differences which distinguish among variants of both component episodes and whole narratives. This adept narrator can distinguish between stories or details which she perceives as similar, and retain them as separate elements in an active repertoire, while such similar items tend to coalesce in the storytelling of a less able narrator. The ability to distinguish such minimal differences is also crucial to the serial organization of repetitive or analogous elements within a single story in performance, as will be illustrated by a

comparison of Mädar Zäher's and Mähgol's performances of Mär Čučeh below.
(pp.109 ff.; Afsäneh-e Garg, J.105, furnishes an example of the adept storyteller 'sorting out' analogous episodes within a story, in performance.)

In the present case it is equally plausible that Mähgol, at a trans-
itional stage between dependent child and adult (two marriage offers had
been made for her that year, both were refused on account of her youth),
felt enough anxiety at the prospect of separation from her own family
through marriage, to make the threatened loss of the boy's mother more co-
gent to her than it was to her mother, so that personal factors also influenced her retention of the virilocal version of the motif. Whatever
the case, these multiple possibilities demonstrate the difficulty of as-
cribing the alterations a story undergoes in transmission to any single
influence or type of influence, whether psychological, socio-cultural,
or technical stylistic.

The snake proceeds to father a child by the boy's mother. The hy-
persexual nature of this union is more emphasized by Mädar Zäher, who repeatedly describes the moter as /pīrzāl/, 'an old, white-haired woman,'
(C.3 passim, C.24), than it is by Adī, who merely describes her as a widow.
Adī emphasizes the mother's disloyalty to her elder son (A.35,38,62) when
the snake decides to eat him, elaborating on the complacency the mother
showed at the marriage proposal (A.23-A.26), to stress her unnatural
qualities. (Mädar Zäher portrays the mother more equivocally in F.24-25,
where the woman resignedly agrees to marry the snake to protect her son.
This particular revision is one of a class of changes Mädar Zäher makes
in the story which reveal consistent psychological and stylistic tendencies
which will be discussed below, pp. 75 ff.).

After his birth, Mār Čučeh, the 'snake chick',[1] assumes the role

of helper and protector to the boy who has hitherto been the main charac-

ter. The human boy's fate remains the central theme of this section of

the story, but the audience, especially Mādar Zāher, shows persistent un-

certainty as to the dramatic roles of the two boys (A.35,36,39,40,49,54,

57,64). She repeatedly demands clarification as to which child is acting

or speaking. Part of the felt ambiguity of this section is due to the

fact that there is only one third person singular pronoun in Persian, $\bar{u}$,

'he, she, it', and distinctions among possible referents in speech are

usually made by vocal emphasis and by context. For a native speaker of

Persian to manifest persistent confusion, as Mādar Zāher does, however,

suggests that the shift of focus from the human boy to Mār Čučeh is unex-

pected. She requires corroboration of the vocal and contextual cues, be-

fore she can accept Mār Čučeh's assumption of the focal role in the ac-

tion. She is surprised and shocked by the elder boy's eventual death (A.

68), not at the hands of his supernatural stepfather, whose defeat she

anticipated (A.58), but at those of a second, human villain. Mādar Zāher's

ultimate rejection of the dramatic structure of Adī's story, as revealed

in her later revisions of it (C and F), is manifest as well in these early

reactions to it. Not merely the resolution of the story, which she changed

most dramatically, but the early relations and actions of the dramatis

personae violate her expectations for afsāneh.

Viewed in terms of goals and benefits, and of dramatic unity, Mār

Čučeh is paradoxical story and the personality of its main character is

---

[1] "Chick," lit. Persian jujeh.

elusive. Mār Čučeh, who displaces his brother in the central role, enforces standards of family loyalty by murdering his family. In the second
half of the story, he is no longer protecting a brother from his own family's depradations, but avenging his death at the hands of a stranger.
The net benefit to Mār Čučeh himself, however, is revenge alone. At the
end of A he departs with no improvement in his own material or social status, and the story resolves with his revenge, not with the establishment
of any new, functioning social unit (family or community) to replace the
one which has been disrupted, such as frequently occurs in folktales. In
this, Adī's tale recalls Babcock-Abrahams' statement:

> "Trickster tales generally begin with a statement of order
> followed by its dissoltuion and, thereafter, by an examina-
> tion of forms of disorder." (1975:168)

The tale of Mār Čučeh seems to go from bad to worse: a barely viable family group is destroyed by the disruptive effect of an invading supernatural.
The survivor is Mār Čučeh, whose accomplishments are entirely punitive and
destructive. The unifying theme of the two sections of the story (the
spheres of activity of the snake and the vizier) is that the subversion
and exploitation of social responsibility (exemplified by the human boy's
treatment at the hands of his mother, his foster father and his would-be
employer) are punished by a single, loyal family member.

In all his acts of deceit Mār Čučeh specializes in turning people's
antisocial plans and activities back upon themselves. Retribution by reversal of the threatened villainy characterizes Mār Čučeh's murder of his
own father. The snake is an antisocial hyperconsumer whose predatory behavior itself inverts normal categories of human behavior. He plots to

exploit his stepchild's own hunger, in order to turn him into food, and finally tries to kill and eat his stepson while the boy is gathering fuel to cook the family bread. Instead, according to Mār Čučeh's plan, the snake is consumed himself, like fuel.

Mār Čučeh's 'wise fool' guise is perfected in his dealings with the vizier, the second villain, for he achieves his first three acts of revenge (killing the vizier's only child, then his first wife, and subsequently destroying the cattle and household goods) by a feigned stupidity in his literal interpretations of the vizier's commands (A. 94,101-106,122), and by his stolid refusal to leave his place before his contract is up. A fine irony sharpens Mār Čučeh's strategy of over-literalism, since the vizier caused Mār Čučeh's brother's death by designedly over-literal interpretation of his own terms of hire ("I'll take a servant who has no belly," A. 66), counting on the boy's unquestioning loyalty to his contract in order to exploit him.

Whether (or not) one views this set of ironic reversals as a type of intellectual play with mental categories in the manner of Levi-Strauss's structuralism, or in terms of a psychological need for symmetry in retributive justice as Bettelheim suggests (1976:144), this type of ironic retribution is a common feature in folktale (cf., inter alia, the cooking of the witch in 'Hansel and Gretel' and the international motif of the villain condemned by his/her own judgment, which is present in the denouement of many Afghan tales, as elsewhere). It would be overinterpretation to ascribe the ironic quality of Mār Čučeh's acts of revenge specifically to Mār Čučeh qua trickster, or to assign his story to the rather poorly-defined genre of trickster tales on this basis. Other aspects of Mār

Čučeh's behavior, appearance and relationship to human society in Adī's story provide better bases for his assignment to this category of hero. Since it is these very aspects of Mār Čučeh's portrayal which are most changed in Mādar Zāher's retellings of Mār Čučeh, it is necessary to discuss Mār Čučeh's trickster qualities, and the relationship of his story to the trickster tale genre, in some detail.

Barbara Babcock-Abrahams in an excellent article (1975:159-160) has summarized the wide range of qualities pertaining to trickster figures in world literature:

'. . . to a greater or lesser degree, tricksters

1. exhibit an independence from and an ignoring of temporal and spatial boundaries;
2. tend to inhabit crossroads, open public places (especially the marketplace), doorways, and thresholds. In one way or another they are usually situated between the social cosmos and the other world or chaos;
3. are frequently involved in scatalogical and coprophagous episodes which may be creative, destructive, or simply amusing;
4. may, similarly, in their deeds and character, partake of the attributes of Trickster-Transformer-Culture Hero;
5. frequently exhibit some mental and/or physical abnormality, especially exaggerated sexual characteristics;
6. have an enormous libido without procreative outcome;
7. have an ability to disperse and disguise themselves and a tendency to be multiform and ambiguous, single or multiple;
8. often have a two-fold physical nature and/or a "double" and are associated with mirrors. Most noticeably, the trickster tends to be of uncertain sexual status;
9. follow the "principle of motley" in dress;
10. are often indeterminate (in physical stature) and may be portrayed as both young and old, as perpetually young or perpetually aged;
11. exhibit human/animal dualism and may appear as a human with animal characteristics or vice versa· (even in those tales where the trickster is explicitly described and referred to in personal pronouns);
12. are generally amoral and asocial - aggressive, vindictive, vain, defiant of authority, etc.;

13. despite their endless propensity to copulate, find their most abiding form of relationship with the feminine in a mother or grandmother bond;

14. in keeping with their creative/destructive dualism, tricksters tend to be ambiguously situated between life and death, and good and evil, as is summed up in the combined black and white symbolism frequently associated with them;

15. are often ascribed to roles (i.e. other than tricky behavior) in which an individual normally has privileged freedom from some of the demands of the social code;

16. in all their behavior, tend to express a concomitant breakdown of the distinction between reality and reflection.'

Although this enumeration of trickster qualities could be summarized more simply (items 5, 6, and 13 could be consolidated, as could items 8 and 10, even though not all tricksters possess all the related qualities), this list is nonetheless useful in Mār Čučeh's case. Aspects of Mār Čučeh's behavior relate to items 1,2,3,7,8,10,11,15 and 16, as will be demonstrated below. In certain regards, Mār Čučeh's portrayal is as interesting for the categories to which his behavior does not relate, as for those which are applicable.

Mār Čučeh's trickster qualities can be summarized as follows:

He exhibits preternatural mobility (#1 above) in his ability to be present at each crucial point in time and space (A.41,49,54,59-60,62,133-134), and in this recalls his father's preternatural mobility (A.20-21). Mār Čučeh's ability to hear at a distance also confounds normal spatial boundaries (A.36,39,45,50,133).

Mār Čučeh's birthplace is 'between the social cosmos and the other world' (item 2), a half-human, half-animal household, marginal in terms of social membership (lacking an extended kin group), supporting itself by gleaning the interstitial space between the sown fields and the wild desert (A.1). A striking feature of Mār Čučeh, in contrast to his human brother, is the ease with which he moves among social domains, as well as in physical space, traveling from the domestic world to the wild, then back into the most highly socialized sphere of city and bazaar, controlling the behavior of those around him in all three domains. The movement of the story's action among different social 'worlds' is modulated to reveal Mār Čučeh's growing power.

The human brother first meets the monstrous snake and is forced to do his bidding when he leaves his home and enters the borderland on the edge of the sown fields. The snake subsequently moves into and threatens the boy's domestic world as well. The snake fails to kill the boy in his first two attempts, which take place in the domestic world he has invaded, and then tries to lure his victim beyond the interstitial area, into the wild, unsocialized world from which he himself has come (A.12,37,43,50).[1] In view of this clearly marked transition from the domestic world to the wild, it is significant that the snake's first two attempts on the boy's life also show a modulation from more to less socialized domains. The first time, he tells the mother to withhold ghee from the boy. Ghee is included in the category of /ḡahteq/, cooked or processed foods served as side dishes to the staple wheat bread, and regarded by the poor as an 'extra' in the diet, whereas water, the second item withheld, is non-processed and basic. The snake's third attempt involves bread, the staple, and the gathering of wood needed to bake it, at the point where the wood first becomes a social commodity, when it is gathered. In this three-fold

---

[1] To understand the cognitive geography involved, one must know that wood-gathering in Afghanistan consists of chopping woody shrubs in the semi-arid, uncultivated desert and hill country beyond the arable lands. The boy must leave society to gather wood.

repetition, the changing physical locale and the material commodities involved modulate from more to less socialized domains.

Mār Čučeh's own power waxes with this movement. He merely averts his father's first two attempts on his brother's life, by taking his brother's place (A.41,49). As Adī points out (B.26), in the domestic social domain, Mār Čučeh's strategy exploits his father's unwillingness to kill his own son. Certain values are expressed which become increasingly important in subsequent episodes. It seems from the snake's refusal to harm his own son that blood loyalty is conceived as a natural, not a cultural phenomenon, since the monstrous snake, out of the wild, has it. The fact that the human mother does not have this loyalty to her own son indicates unequivocally that she is not only antisocial, but unnatural. Mār Čučeh's subsequent murder of his own parents is a complex act in light of the values conveyed by Adī's remark (B.26). One might interpret Mār Čučeh's murder of his parents as valuing social responsibility over natural loyalty to his nearest blood kin.

In other ways, his behavior displays a rejection of the natural, especially his asexuality (see below). Mār Čučeh's exploits from beginning to end of the story demonstrate his aptitude for the manipulation of social rules and relationships, rather than special physical powers. When the latter come into play, they remain secondary to his social machinations. In the first half of the story he repeatedly exploits people's social expectations for young children, for he conceals a preternatural perceptiveness under the guise of childish simplicity. In the first half of the story, he baldly tells his brother what his father intends to do (A.41, 49), but his warnings are not taken seriously, as a child's would not be.

He stages a child's tantrum (A.54-57) to be allowed to accompany his brother on the wood-gathering expedition, and uses childish imitations of adult behavior (the little wisp of rope, A.58), in which the older people indulge him (the little load of thorns, A.59), to conceal his real intentions.

On the snake's third murder attempt, in the wild, Mār Čučeh finally defeats and totally destroys his father (A.61), reducing him to charcoal along with the fuel his brother has gathered.

Mār Čučeh's powers have increased in the wild, and when he returns to the domestic world, he is in full control. He completes the eradication of evil within the family by killing his mother, whose 'sin' he defines as a preference for marital (sex) relations over blood relations, manifest in her willingness to feed her blood kin to her sexual partner. Paradoxically the social principle which Mār Čučeh enforces by killing his own parents is the primacy of blood kinship over contracted sexual alliances. This emphasis on kinship is perfectly consonant with Afghan social usage, in which marriage is with blood kin in the majority of cases (often between first cousins), and marriage serves as a means of reconsolidating or creating mutually advantageous blood relationships between two family groups. Ideally, individual preferences in the choice of a marriage partner are developed and expressed in the context of the needs and responsibility to priorities of the family (cf. N.32).[1]

---

[1] Urbanization has increased opportunities for unrelated individuals to meet and arrange their own marriages, but conflict between individual desires and family or communal interests in the choice of marriage partners is a perennial problem in real life (of both city and village) as well as an ancient and ever-popular topic in literary and oral tradition, from the ancient Persian Zariadres and Odatis story retold by Athenaios from the writings of Chares of Mytilene to the popular romances in current circulation, such as Najmā Šīrāzī and Sīahmuī o Jelalī.

With the second half of the story, Mār Čučeh and his brother move into the quintessentially social world of the bazaar and business contracts, and once again the human brother fails to protect himself, while Mār Čučeh demonstrates complete mastery over all situations. The human boy immediately falls prey to the vizier's verbal trickery, because he expects conformity to tacit social norms by which employers are expected to protect and support indigent hired servants during the period of their hire. In agricultural communities around Herat, labor contracted on a seasonal basis is paid in cash or kind at the end of the season or year when the employer's crops come in. Servants with no outside resources must rely on their employer for maintenance from one crop to the next. The human boy interprets the vizier's demand that he not eat figuratively (B. 52-53) to mean that he must not be greedy, but the vizier interprets this term of their contract literally and starves him to death (A.68, cf. B.54).

When Mār Čučeh comes to work for the vizier, he demonstrates his control over all situations by acts of revenge which move from the domestic center into ever more abstract social domains. His first act of revenge, killing the child, occurs in the home and exploits toilet-training, the primary element of socialization (A.76-94). His second act of revenge, also at the domestic center, exploits the authority relations between husbands and wives (A.98-107). The third act of revenge, destroying the vizier's household goods and cattle, exploits the more remote social relationship of invited guests and hosts. The visiting relationship between households allows Mār Čučeh to embarrass the vizier publicly (A.122-123). During a wedding, which bridges the boundaries between households, Mār Čučeh uses the occasion to breach the household's boundary in a destructive manner, removing the gate (A.114) from the compound wall and exposing the enclosed household to the social threat of theft. Mār Čučeh makes certain that natural chaos also encroaches on the vizier's world by promiscuously mixing all his foodstuffs and household goods together in the middle of the courtyard (A.114,A.122), converting wealth to dirt (pace Mary Douglas).[1] Mār Čučeh willfully confuses fostering and feeding with slaughter and destroys the vizier's livestock (A.113) by cutting their throats, decapitating them over their mangers.

Mār Čučeh's fourth act of revenge takes place in the border area between social units, i.e. between the vizier's own household, from which Mār Čučeh has driven him, and another, unspecified destination where he hopes to find refuge (A.132-151). In this border area two physical barriers, the irrigation ditch with the bridge and the river, provide loci for Mār Čučeh's activities. Mār Čučeh, like his father the aufi, seems to have an affinity for water (cf. A.11).

Finally, Mār Čučeh completes his vengeance on the vizier in the most intensely formal, social domain of all, in the guest room of a stranger who has taken them in in accordance with the general Afghan ethic of hospitality to strangers (A.153). Mār Čučeh uses their status as strangers to maneuver the vizier into a situation where improper social behavior is inevitable (A.154), then exposes him to their host (A.170), who has the vizier punished for violating the guest-host relationship ("Your father owes me salt," A.172). The story ends with the vizier socially impotent

---

[1] 1966:12-16, especially "Everything that can happen to a man in the way of disaster should be catalogued according to the active [organizing] principles involved in the universe of his particular culture," (p. 14).

in jail, and Mār Čučeh at liberty.

Through the shifting scenes of the story, Mār Čučeh manifests an affinity for interstitial spaces (the gate), roads (the alley where he overhears, the road on which the vizier travels) and water boundaries, as well as virtuoso ability to exploit situations in every domain from the wild to the domestic to the most abstractly social. The implicit unifying theme of the complex story is enforcement of social duties before and after their violation. Mār Čučeh does not merely mediate between "social cosmos and the other world or chaos," (above, p.57 , #2), but enforces and reasserts social rules by the judicious exploitation of chaotic and controlled behavior. Unlike other tricksters, he has a clear moral impact: he is firmly on the side of order. Yet he remains "asocial" (p.57 , #12) at the story's end, unassimilated into human society despite his enforcement of social codes.

Mār Čučeh's association with socially controlled behavior is particularly obvious with regard to the scatological content of the story. (Item #3 in Babcock-Abrahams' list, p.57 above). Coprophagy as such never occurs in the story, unless one counts the infrequent curses (A.134, cf. note 2, p. 249, and B.128) which are part of the general armamentarium of Persian obscenity and to be read as figurative expressions of aggression, just as the frequent sexual obscenities used by Mār Čučeh cannot be interpreted as explicit sexual activity. (See pp. 66 ff. below, on Mār Čučeh's sexuality.) Two kinds of controlled behavior form a counterpoint throughout the story. The most prominent is the withholding of food, first by Mār Čučeh's mother in the attempt to ambush her son and then, more radically, by the vizier. The paradigm for anti-social behavior is thus withholding food by those whose social role includes the responsibility for supplying it. The mother expects the boy to take steps to procure the food which has been withheld, thus putting himself into danger. The vizier, by contrast, does not expect his victims to take such steps. Aside from immediate miserliness, his motivation seems to be that he can make his servants leave or die before their contract is finished, so that he will not have to pay them: hence Mār Čučeh's dogged insistence that he is not leaving before his contract is up. (A.94-95,107-108,129-130,149-150. Cf. Mādar Zāher's more general, summary presentation of this point, C.72.)

In retaliation for this forced restraint with regard to food, Mār Čučeh compels the vizier's daughter, and later the vizier himself, to be excessively continent with regard to excretion. He does not permit the little girl or her father to excrete at the socially appropriate time and place and exploits their apparent violation of social rules regarding elimination in order to bring about their ruin (A.76-93,154-173).

Mār Čučeh's behavior parodies normal adult activities (wood-gathering) in the first half of the story, and in the second half he parodies adult anti-social behavior as well, specifically that of his enemy the vizier, by setting impossible standards of continence with regard to elimination, in retaliation for the vizier's setting impossible standards with regard to food consumption. The parodic aspects of trickster behavior were noted by Radin (1956). Parodic behavior, like other trickster behavior, does not always involve retribution, and may, in fact, be completely gratuitous, as in the case of the Winnebago trickster Wakdjunkaga in the texts Radin discusses. The retributive aspect gives Mār Čučeh's parodic behavior a greater specificity of reference: it is identified as the punishment for improper behavior in others, not simply a deviant or escapist fantasy.

Mār Čučeh's abilities at disguise (item #7 of Babcock-Abrahams' list) are revealed in his impersonation of the vizier's second wife (A. 143-147). It is dark, and he simply changes places with the woman while she sleeps and tricks her husband into drowning her instead of Mār Čučeh himself. In this scene, Mār Čučeh demonstrates preternatural control over his own body processes, feigning sleep but staying awake despite his earlier exertions, until his adversaries themselves fall asleep.

Mār Čučeh's sexual status (cf. pp.57-8 above, items 5,6,13) seems to be totally neutral or asexual, a quality which distinguishes him from many tricksters. Despite the phallic quality of his father (and his mother's hypersexuality), Mār Čučeh has no permanent relationships with women, either sexual or parental, nor does he engage in any casual sexual behavior. Even when he gets into bed with the vizier while impersonating his wife (A.143), the possibilities for sexual comedy, which the audience recognizes (as indicated by their laughter), remain unexploited. (Mādar Zāher later develops a sexual identity for Mār Čučeh, beginning from her revision of this scene, C.172-174). As mentioned above (p. 63), although much of the obscenity Mār Čučeh uses throughout the story is sexual, he uses the standard male cursing style common in the daily speech of the bazaar if not in polite speech, which does not imply extraordinarily hy-persexual qualities in the speaker.[1]

Regarding items 10 and 11 of the above list' (p. 57), Mār Čučeh's

---

[1] One could make a case that an opposite emphasis on the hyposexuality (i.e. passive-partner homosexuality) of the cursed is the primary implication of such expressions. The point of such cursing is not to boast of one's own powers, but to impugn the powers of the cursed.

physical indeterminacy manifests itself mostly in the paradox of the tiny child (A.34,36) who beats his monster father and other elders. He is treated as anthropomorphic, though his name suggests snake-like attributes (/mār čučeh/, 'snake chick'). Only once does he behave like a snake, when he cranes his neck out from under the bridge in order to scare the vizier's horse (A.135). His zöomorphism is not stressed, despite his parentage.[1]

Mār Čučeh's portrayal as a little child is also a key to his privileged status with regard to society (item #15, p. 58, above). In public or private contexts when young Afghan children misbehave, they are excused with statements like, 'S/he's little, and doesn't understand.' Young children (less than five or six years old) receive little or no direct training, aside from toilet training, which is very unauthoritarian, and their lack of discipline or self-control is attributed to lack of understanding and knowledge. Apart from toilet-training, discipline begins around the time when children cut their first adult teeth and are eligible to be sent to school.[2] Thus youth implies ignorance of, and exemption from, normal social constraints (cf. items 10 and 15, pp. 57-58, above).

Ironically, Mār Čučeh uses a feigned simplicity and innocence of social rules, to punish others for their knowing infractions of the social code. Mār Čučeh exploits his own supposed youth and ignorance willfully to misinterpret the vizier's commands (A.93-94,101-107,122-123), as well

---

[1] Mār Čučeh's father exhibits size indeterminacy of a more obvious kind. He is a huge snake (A.14) who nonetheless fits in a ghee jar or a water skin (A.37,43).

[2] One aspect of the Muslim concept of sin also concerns knowledge: the words, ğaflat´, ğafel , resp. 'neglect', 'neglector' refer to apostasy and sin as aspects of forgetting God and his commands, which is in the basis for all sinful behavior. Children, who have not yet learned moral behavior, are logically incapable of misbehavior.

as to circumvent his father's murder plans earlier in the story (A.54-57). The verbal misconstructions by which Mãr Čučeh revenges himself on the vizier and escapes punishment are also ironic statements on the relations between representation and reality, especially with regard to the vizier's antisocial behavior (see item 16, p.58). Just as the vizier sought to exploit his servants by over-literal interpretation of the hyperbolic statement, "I want a servant who has no belly," (A.66,A.73), Mãr Čučeh proceeds to interpret all the vizier's hyperbolic statements literally, killing his wife and child, and then in the manner of a fool-hero, goes on to feign a still greater verbal incompetence (A.98-99) by misinterpreting unambiguous verbal commands ("fasten the doors tightly," A.100). In the domain of language and meaning, Mãr Čučeh's trickery progresses from play with figurative social meaning ("I want a servant who has no belly") to play with explicit verbal meaning ("Gimme!", /Mãla jam ko/"), to outright lying ("I'll take the boots").

The vizier's hyperbolic verbal threats are not as such antisocial. Basic social competence in Persian, as in other languages, depends on the ability to deduce what is meant from what is said, on many levels. The hyperbolic threats that the vizier makes to control his wife and child when he detects disobedience, (A.94,101), are a normal verbal tactic for social control in Dari language and are not to be interpreted literally. During her performance of Mãr Čučeh, Adĩ herself (A.53) controls her small son's behavior with a hyperbolic threat to which the little boy responds with giggling obedience.

From misinterpreting commands, Mãr Čučeh goes on to misinterpret (designedly) the intent of the vizier's actions, and the pattern of revenge by ironic reversal becomes tighter. Mār Čučeh pretends to believe the wife's explanation that their flight from him is a trip to visit her parents (A.136), and that her thoughtless wish that he be present is sincere (A.136). Once Mār Čučeh has induced the vizier to drown his wife, however, he no longer dissembles his vengeful glee (A.148). In the final episode, the relations of speech to reality, and speaker to listener, are completely inverted. Mār Čučeh, the instigator, offers the vizier a plan, not in the form of a command, but as its logical opposite, a solemn promise to perform an act (A.157,159). Formerly, Mār Čučeh performed acts of devastation in response to the vizier's commands; now he initiates action. The vizier believes not the evidence of Mār Čučeh's previous actions, but his words, and is destroyed. The vizier, though he has exploited the difference between speech and reality, is finally incapable of giving primacy to reality. The cultural message is that one must distinguish what is said, from what is. The source of the vizier's exploitative power is ultimately untrustworthy and he loses his social identity and status by over-reliance on words.

The complex relations of verbal statements, objective truth and personal intent, here developed in a secular context, are also central to Muslim (and especially Shi'a) religious ethics, which permit "virtuous lying" or "dissembling in the cause of religion" (dorūğ-e bā salāh). As the most naaive Western observers note (with indignation, in many cases), standards of truthfulness in interpersonal dealings are far more complex in the Persian-speaking world than in much of the West. Full social competence, as exemplified by Mār Čučeh, requires the ability both to distinguish appearance (speech), and reality and to exploit that difference to enforce social order.

Mār Čučeh's major divergence from Babcock-Abrahams' inventory of trickster qualities (along with his total lack of libido) is his awareness of and allegiance to standards of social behavior, the firm moral ground on which he rests his choice of victims. The dominant retributive aspect of Mār Čučeh's actions separates him from tricksters like Wakdjunkaga, Coyote, or Raven, whose behavior often appears "amoral and asocial" (#16, p. 58 above). Mar Cuceh more closely resembles the Winnebago Hare, who as culture hero stands between the animal and human world as an enforcer of rules (Radin, 1956:91), or perhaps the Yoruba trickster(s) Eshu-Elegba, who by creating discord induces people to sacrifice to and worship the gods. Mar Cuceh's effect on the community is social law enforcement, and in keeping with this emphasis he rejects the natural (see p. 60 , above), and moves steadily into the social world of contracted interpersonal responsibilities. His lack of sexuality in fact is part of his rejection of the natural in favor of the social-contractual in interpersonal dealings.

Mār Čučeh's moral status, as a legitimate avenger, however, seems to be one of the "detachable" aspects of variants of this story in the wider Persian tradition. Erika Friedl (personal communication) offers a synopsis of a related story in which the trickster Gedūlak begins by killing his father and mother, goes on to trick an unjust master, but later chooses a series of victims for no apparent reason. The story ends inconsequentially with the escape of his last pair of victims.

Regarding the question of meaning, social values and social order as presented in trickster tales, it is significant that Radin came to regard

the etiological content of native American trickster tales as intrusive
(1956:167). Toelken (1969:222) raised the question of etiological statements in Navaho Coyote tales with his Navaho informant, Yellowman, and he
also concluded that etiological statements are not central to the meaning
of Coyote tales as interpreted by the Navaho.

Trickster tales, insofar as they can be considered to belong to one
genre, concern themselves not necessarily with the origin of natural and
social order, nor even with its successful enforcement, but with its arti-
culation through a series of violations. Trickster figures variously
violate, originate or enforce natural and social order, and thus elude
the Proppian categories for the functions of folktale dramatis personae,
being at times hero, villain, hero's companion, etc. Likewise the plot
structure of many trickster tales bears little resemblance to the structure of "folk tales" developed in Propp's Morphology. As yet no morphology or generically descriptive principle exists for trickster tales, despite attempts such as Babcock-Abrahams' to define trickster figures
qualitatively. Trickster tales seem to be as protean as trickster figures,
creating special problems in genre definition, but also providing striking
examples of the flexibility of folktales in transmission, as I hope to
illustrate in discussing Mādar Zāher's revisions of Mār Čučeh.

As mentioned above (p.48) the differences between Adī's two performances (texts A & B), can be ascribed largely to differences of audience familiarity, audience response and the time of day, which affected
Adī's own energy in developing the story. Her second performance shortens
certain descriptive and planning sequences (B.24, B.26; cf. A.29, A.31),
mainly by omission of repetition and interjected dialogue. The wedding

plan sequence (A.29, B.24) shortens from seven lines to five, the wedding
scene itself from fifteen lines to eight. The transition section from
the end of the snake's wedding scene to the snake's first attempt on his
stepson's life, which includes the description of Mār Čučeh's birth and
growth, contracts from nine lines to five, and so forth.

This omission of detail and dialogue does not change the basic plot
structure, but on occasion, as when the vizier gives Mār Čučeh directions
before he leaves for the wedding (directions which Mār Čučeh contradicts),
the omission of dialogue in B diminishes the ironic impact of Mār Čučeh's
later misconstruction of his orders (B.85, cf. A.110). In particular in
B, Adī omits the order, "Fasten the house door tightly," upon which Mār
Čučeh's outrageous behavior at the wedding depends for its humor. In both
A and B, Adī has Mār Čučeh repeat these instructions during the confrontation at the wedding, playing the fool to win sympathy from the guests.
An extra element of anticipation is lacking in B, however, where the order
is not given verbatim to Mār Čučeh by the vizier, in its proper place. In
speaking to an audience she knows to be familiar with the story, Adī is not
as careful to include planning and preparatory detail essential for narrative coherence. Detail she omits from the planning/preparatory sequences
nonetheless reappears in its proper place in the execution sequence which
follows, where narrative logic demands it, and in the recapitulation sequence which often follows the execution of a plan or order (B.86,B.90),
and provides a gloss on Mār Čučeh's behavior which emphasizes its ironic
relation to his orders.

Triadic repetion, in the form planning(directions, orders)/execu-
tion/recapitulation, is theoretically possible for almost any cluster of

events in a folktale, and is in fact ubiquitous in Afghan tale-telling.
Two, and often three, of these elements are present in normal narrations
of various episodes within a story. The effectiveness of such repetition
lies partly in its utility for story-learning. To an audience unfamiliar
with a story's plot, these repetition sequences provide built-in 'slots'
for rehearsal of the order of events in the story, while it is being told,
so that a listener who is learning the story hears a block of events repeated two or more times. The general importance of rehearsal in learning
process has been widely discussed (see, e.g., Bartlett, 1932; Norman, 1969).
An important point with regard to oral narrative style is that the storyteller has great flexibility, and can reduce or increase the density of
repetition, depending on audience familiarity and expressed interest.
The 'slots' remain present in the plot format, to be exploited to varying
degrees, depending on the audience. Any verbal response from the audience
seems to elicit repetition: note Adī's frequent repetitions of detail in
response to comments by Mādar Zāher (A.4,16,18,20,31,32-33,34,35,36,39,
etc.). Recapitulation in particular emphasizes and elucidates the narrative coherence, the causal and thematic relations of what has gone before,
and allows the storyteller to 'coast' while organizing the next sequence
of events in his/her own mind. Mādar Zāher, in her first performance of
Mār Čučeh, tends to slight the preparatory events, but includes full recapitulations. Each retelling of a set of events gives her an opportunity
for fuller reconstruction of unfamiliar detail. The degree to which recapitulation is elaborated may thus depend on the teller's perception of
audience's familiarity with the story, their expressed interest in the
execution sequence which is recapitulated, the storyteller's own familiar-

ity with the events of the story, or the degree to which the recapitulated events explain, motivate or prepare for other events.[1]

---

[1] The emphatic function of repetition in its various forms, its key relationship to structure and meaning, has been widely recognized in folklore studies, e.g. Hymes (1975:34), Lord (1960:220), Levi-Strauss (1958:105). Šīr o Palang (Texts L and M) provides an example of the selective use of recapitulation in particular to stress major themes (in the case of Šīr o Palang, conciliation vs. retribution as social strategies). A full consideration of this function of repetition is reserved for that discussion.

III.B: Mār Čučeh C, E and F: Mādar Zāher Revises

On first hearing, the most dramatic changes Mādar Zāher makes in
Mār Čučeh are certainly those in the conclusion. She radically changes
the end of the story by rearranging the scene at the river so that Mār
Čučeh impersonates the vizier, rather than his wife, and causes the vizier
himself to be drowned with his wife's aid (C.172, E.151-2, F.134-135).
After the vizier's death, Mār Čučeh appropriates the vizier's wife, who in
C version has been sexually compromised by spending the rest of the night
in bed with Mār Čučeh, thinking him to be her husband (C.173). In Mādar
Zāher's version, Mār Čučeh therefore acquires both sexuality (not hypersexuality but the normal human variety), which he lacks totally in Adī's
version of the story, and also a wife and a household. Mādar Zāher concludes her story with Mār Čučeh's unequivocal acquisition of full social
membership, as a husband and household head. In the light of her closing
emphasis on families, it is significant that Mādar Zāher also began the
story with an intact nuclear family, introducing the human boy's father
only to have him die, but in so doing she brackets the story with the
vision of a complete, functioning family unit, and suggests that for her,
in some sense, the story is about the need to create family units.

The ultimate socialization of some trickster figures has been noted
by Turner (1968), and a variant of the Mār Čučeh story from western Iran,
recorded by Friedl, likewise concludes with the marriage of the snake
brother (to an unspecified woman), and his settling down with his mother
and brother, who have survived the earlier episodes, as an extended family

(Friedl, personal communication). Thus, Mādar Zāher's revision of the story she heard, to accomplish the socializatioh of its main character, is a recurrent, and perhaps a reversible, phenomenon in the fortunes of this group of tales. Mār Čučeh's ultimate social incorporation, like his moral justification (the revenge theme, see p. 70, above), is detachable from the tale in transmission.

In light of the vocal objections of Mādar Zāher's children when they detected her changes in the story (C.153,182; E.120,156) and her several attempts to influence Māhgol's telling of the story (she even tries to take over her daughter's performance at the point where her own version diverges from Adī's: E.120: "You shut up, then, and I'll tell a few words of it from here"), it is impossible to regard Mādar Zāher's alteration of the story's ending as anything but fully intentional. It shows craft in the refinement of detail, as when the vizier is made the instigator of the attempted drowning, rather than his wife (E.120, E.148-50). Mādar Zāher developed this detail in performance F which succeeded the simpler C version, in which Mār Čučeh simply drowns the vizier and takes his place without any mention of retaliation for a murder plot against Mār Čučeh (C. 172-3). The process of revision here proceeds first by deletion, then by reformulation of a bit of business which brings it into greater conformity both with overall narrative coherency, and also with the original version of the story as Mādar Zāher heard it. The tendency to revert in later performances to the earlier form of certain details seems to be general, and will be discussed below with reference to Māhgol's performances as well (pp. 123,131). In this instance, Adī has made the wife the author of the murder plan (A.140, B.108) and the ironic humor of the story is furthered

by her being murdered in Mār Čučeh's place. Mādar Zāher not only preserved the woman so that she could become Mār Čučeh's wife, but also ex-
culpated her from the murder plot, first by omitting it, and in later versions by putting it in the mouth of her husband, so that ironic justice
was once more served, this time by the vizier's death.

Mādar Zāher's revisions of the story show systematic changes not
only in the causal and retributive relations of events, but also in the
delineation of character and dramatic functions. The exculpation of the
vizier's surviving wife is one of a group of changes in Mādar Zāher's portrayal of the women in Mār Čučeh, all of which contribute to an overall
change in their dramatic role, when compared with Adī's version. Adī
hints at the vizier's wives' complicity in the vizier's plan to withhold
food from his servants (B.60), but the vizier's first wife, who is killed
after her child, does not emerge as a positively evil character. Her
death, like her child's, is an act of revenge directed at the vizier. The
second wife, in Adī's version, emerges as an active adversary of Mār Čučeh.
She admits joint guilt with her husband for the death of Mār Čučeh's brother (A.131). The wife both suggests the escape plan, and points out to the
vizier that Mār Čučeh's devastating behavior is willful and planned (A.132).
Her hostile reaction to Mār Čučeh's appearance on their escape route (A.136:
"Do we have to go to the sky . . .?") is quickly followed by her lying attempt to conceal the escape plan ("We're just going - he's taking me to my
father's house . . ."). She, not the vizier, is the instigator of the plan
to drown Mār Čučeh, and Mār Čučeh's animosity at that point is directed entirely at her (A.142).

The net effect of Adī's portrayal of the vizier's wife and also of

Mār Čučeh's mother (see below) is to make the only two women active in the story into murderous, perfidious figures who earn their violent death. No woman in the story shows any affinity for the forces of social order and justice, as embodied in Mār Čučeh, and the story concludes with Mār Čučeh wifeless and family-less. Mādar Zāher, on the other hand, turns the vizier's surviving wife into a more passive individual, whose complicity in the vizier's activities is a function of wifely obedience. The vizier is made the originator of the escape plan (C.160-2, ff., E.144, F. 123) and, when it reappears, of the drowning plan as well (E.150, F.131). Although Mādar Zāher still uses the wife's slip of the tongue to reveal Mār Čučeh's presence (C.166, E.145, F.125), it is the vizier who is furious at his appearance (C.168, E.147, F.127) and the wife, silent, offers no excuse for their flight. Sexually compromised, the wife consents to Mār Čučeh's marriage proposal under duress (C.174, C.117-8, E.152-4, F. 136-9), and absolves herself of complicity in the murder of Mār Čučeh's brother (C.177, E.153, F.137) by agreeing to marry Mār Čučeh.

In the scene at the wedding, when the vizier's wife summons her husband to point out Mār Čučeh with the door tied to his back, Mādar Zāher interjects a bit of dialogue further indicative of her view of male-female relations. When summoned by his wife, the vizier in Adī's version simply comes, and in A asks, "What do you want?" (A.117). Mādar Zāher in telling this incident portrays the vizier as incensed and shamed by having to obey his wife's summons in public (C.148, F.113). The loss of face which the vizier fears hinges on the appearance that the vizier is obedient to his wife's demands.

The killing of the first wife, in all versions, has already intro-

duced the issue of wifely obedience. Mār Čučeh complains to the vizier
that the wife has not given him the tools the vizier has sent for. The
vizier tells him to punish her, and he kills her. Mādar Zāher, in version C, adds an episode which reiterates the obedience theme, in which Mār
Čučeh kills an additional wife of the vizier for alleged non-compliance
with the vizier's order to cook dinner for some guests, an order which
Mār Čučeh in fact never delivered. The vizier's anger is turned, most
unjustly, on his third, surviving wife (C.135). The vizier is thus portrayed as tyrannical toward his wives, and the wives, one and all, as innocent victims of their husband's antisocial behavior and the revenge directed against him. All these changes in the dramatic role and character
of the women culminate in Mār Čučeh's exculpation of the surviving wife,
making Mār Čučeh's reconciliation and marriage with her more plausible.

With regard to the incident which Mādar Zāher adds, in which the
wife is killed for not preparing dinner, it is noteworthy that Mādar Zāher,
while reiterating the themes of wifely obedience and victimization, at the
same time preserves and refines a second pattern of meanings present in
the story. Mār Čučeh's acts of vengeance against the vizier move progressively from the most private domestic domain (child toilet-training
and the family sleeping chamber) into progressively more social domains
(first the wedding at the house of friends, then the public road (an
interstitial space), then the final scatological incident in the guest house
of the man who is a stranger to them both. (See pp. 61-63, above). Mādar
Zāher's added material articulates this pattern further. The killing of
the second wife concerns the vizier's own status as a host, and his anger
at not being able to entertain his guests properly. This incident thus

moves the sphere of action out of the private and into the public sector of the vizier's own household, and precedes the wedding incident which moves the story further out into the public social realm, beyond the vizier's household. While reiterating the male/female themes which interest her, Mādar Zāher thus skillfully preserves the system of narrative geography with regard to other themes.

Erika Friedl (1975) has described the phenomenon of active, malign women contrasted with passive, virtuous women in the work of two Iranian storytellers, and ascribed the two narrators' different portrayals of women to the fact that one narrator was an elderly male with a poor marital situation, in whose storytelling the active malignity of women was prominent, while the other was a young, well-educated woman of high status whose personal abilities were being underutilized due to her family situation. Mār Čučeh's example corroborates the expression in folktales from this area of an ethic which equates female virtue with passivity and reciprocally connects active, authoritative women with antisocial behavior. This ethic is overtly expressed in so many ways in traditional Muslim society that its presence in folktales is hardly surprising. The fact that this dual assessment of women comes from two female narrators, and that Mādar Zāher, the woman more prone to depict women as passive victims, is of the two far more of an activist, involved in entrepreneurial and other efforts requiring initiative and decision-making on her part, suggests that the presence of one or both types of women in the work of an individual narrator may not be accounted for simply by gross data of biographical circumstance or sex. The portrayal of deviance must be measured against the degree and kind of deviance which the narrator's own behavior displays.

Mādar Zāher is a religious healer, a clairvoyant and an oral poet who at the time of this recording had recently become a recognized professional, carrying on the former two activities in the presence of women clients, not her own relatives, and free from the direct supervision of her husband (cf. N.48). Mādar Zāher's curing and divining are atypical, but socially (ie. religiously) sanctioned, and she believes these abilities would disappear if she did not keep strict purdah and otherwise protect her religious purity.[1] She has an unusually public life in which she is paid to advise non-relatives in crisis situations and life decisions, yet she portrays female virtue in this story as passive and totally non-decisive. The significant factor in her portrayal of women in this instance seems to be a distaste for portraying decisive, powerful women as bad. (See discussion of Mār Čučeh's mother, below, p. 82). She does not, however, portray women characters in Mār Čučeh who are good and decisive. Decisive women have a major role in Šīr o Palang (texts L and M), a story Mādar Zāher composed to dramatize a family dispute in which she participated. Her view of decisive women is by no means univocal. In the absence of means of personality assessment which are cross-culturally valid, it is quite dangerous to proceed inferentially, to try to extract general attitudes from single story texts, or to attribute preferences such as those revealed in these story texts to any single psychological or circumstantial factor.

Certain of Mādar Zāher's revisions of the role of women in Mār Čučeh overstep the bounds of narrative logic in order to portray women as passive sufferers. Her portrayal of Mār Čučeh's mother is particularly

---

[1] Ritual purity is a matter of universal concern for those trafficking in the supernatural. See, e.g., T.O. Beidelman, "Swazi Royal Ritual," Africa, 33 (1963), pp. 373-405.

revealing in this regard, since it makes the mother's role in the story considerably more equivocal than it is in Adī's version, while contributing further to her overall passive/sympathetic portrayal of women.

Adī firmly states Mār Čučeh's mother's guilt, both for her willingness to marry the snake (A.25, and more explicitly, B.18) and for cooperating with the snake in his attempts to eat her son (A.35,A.62,B.48). Adī attributes Mār Čučeh's mother's complicity in the murder plan specifically to her sexual loyalty to the snake (A.62). In her first performance of the story, Mādar Zāher omits any judgment on the woman's character for marrying the snake (C.21), though her complicity in the murder plan is clear (C.25). Five months later, in Mādar Zāher's second full performance of the story, the details of the marriage proposal have changed significantly. Mār Čučeh's mother appears to accept the snake in order to ward off a threat against her son's life (F.24-25), with overtly stated solicitude for the boy's welfare ("Why has all the color left your face?", F.23). In light of the mother's later complicity in the snake's plan to murder her son, this portrayal of her is somewhat inconsistent, but it underlines Mādar Zāher's general tendency to portray females as passive victims of circumstance.

As in the case of the insertion of virilocality (with its implication of bride rescue) into the theme of marriage with a monster (see pp. 50-52 , above), there are direct precedents in Mādar Zāher's own repertoire for the construction of this interesting motive for the mother's action. The story of Xasteh Xomār (Text G) is the only other story in Mādar Zāher's repertoire which includes the marriage of a woman to a snake. In it, the snake tells the father of the bride-to-be (who is the marital go-between,

as is the son in Mār Čučeh) that if one of his daughters does not agree
to the marriage, he himself will be eaten (G.15).   In this case as in the
case of the virilocality element, it seems that Mādar Zāher identifies
a complex theme (marriage to a supernatural) in the storytelling of another person and equates the handling of that theme with her own handling
of a similar event in another story, even though the structural significance of the two events is quite different.   In Mār Čučeh the snake's
proposal to the woman can be seen as a "first reconnaissance by the villain,"[1] while the wedding of the human bride to Xasteh Xomār must be seen
as part of an interdiction/violation sequence, in that the heroine contracts through her marriage an advantageous relationship with a supernatural benefactor whose terms she later violates.   In Xasteh Xomār the human
bride is portrayed as virtuously accepting the snake out of filial duty,
to protect her father.   This moral point is explicit in Mādar Zāher's handling of that wedding.

The univocal, non-developmental nature of characterization in folktales has been noted by observers as diverse as Bettelheim (1977, 'Introduction'), and Kristeva (1969).   Hendricks (1972:284) commenting on Kristeva, remarks that "in epic and folk literature psychological or character
traits obey a law of non-conjunction (or disjunction)," and Kristeva designates such figures personnages, as opposed to the caractères of novelistic
fiction, in which "the opposition of two terms (positive vs. negative) sig-
nifying character traits, is dominated by a third, resulting in an ambi-
valent synthesis."

---

[1] The term refers to an element in the structure of fictional folktales
as described by Vladimir Propp (1968: 28).

Mādar Zāher's portrayal of Mār Čučeh's mother approaches such a synthesis, insofar as her motivation undergoes a developmental change. Not damned from the start, as she was in Adī's portrayal, Mār Čučeh's mother in Mādar Zāher's telling becomes evil under the snake's influence. This novelistic tendency is visible elsewhere in Mādar Zāher's narrative (see pp. 88, ff. below), in the rationalistic flavor she adds to certain dialogues and interactions.

Hendricks' distinction between "structural motivation" and "character motivation" (1975:300) is helpful in distinguishing the type of ambiguity introduced by Mādar Zāher's rationalizing and psychologizing tendency in the formulation of dialogues, from the ambiguity which is inherent in a traditional trickster figure like Mār Čučeh, whose actions are at once "good" and "bad," as when he murders his parents to champion blood loyalty. Mār Čučeh's actions are devastating to society, but ironically appropriate. Mār Čučeh's development is simply the intensification of his personal traits and powers, displayed in his ever more radical (but consistent) reactions to an analogous series of events (the attempts on his brother's life). His basic orientation toward the social order is equivocal in Adī's story, yet static. He is an enforcer of social rules, who has no place in society himself. Other characters have equally static roles, which are univocal as well.

The development of a positive moral motive for the mother's acceptance of the snake husband in Mādar Zāher's Mār Čučeh is structurally inappropriate to her role as a disloyal parent excessively concerned with sex. It is easy for a non-native audience to miss this latter aspect of Adī's rendition of the mother's character, because it is only indicated

by her eager acceptance of the snake's proposal (A.23-26; Cf. B.18:
Right away this *bastard* mother of his said, "I'll take him. I'll take a
husband." Yeah.') The implication is that the old woman would marry
anything, even a snake. Afghan expectations for proper female behavior
require modesty and at least feigned reluctance even under normal circumstances when a woman is asked to marry. The hypersexuality of old women
is the subject of numerous oral anecdotes which I heard in Herat and elsewhere. Ideally a woman agrees to an arranged marriage which serves family
priorities, at an age appropriate for childbearing. Mādar Zāher's interpolation of a family priority (preserving her son's life) mitigates the
mother's acceptance of this marriage. The analogy to the girl's acceptance of a snake husband to save her father in <u>Xasteh Xomār</u> (Text G) is
patent.

The question remains: did Mādar Zāher supply a moral motive for the
mother's acceptance of the snake merely because she confused this instance
of marriage to a snake with the one which was already in her repertoire?
Was this fortuitous confusion, or is her alteration of the detail of motivation psychologically significant? Oral theory argues strongly for the
economic handling of thematic material: that is, given a cluster of similar events (a 'theme') occurring in more than one story, the storyteller
will tend to present the event cluster in a similar way in each story,
with regard to both details of content and word choice (Lord, 1960:
93-94). It would be a misapplication of this concept to equate thematic
continuity in oral style with mechanical substitution, however, to conclude
that a storyteller, on hearing a new story containing a theme similar to
one in his or her own repertoire, would ignore any differences and mechanically substitute the version of that theme with which she or he was already

familiar, in retelling the new story. Adept narrators in particular are sensitive to the differences in other storytellers' handlings of 'their' themes: witness Mādar Zāher's remark on the uxorilocal element in Adī's version of the magic wedding theme and her delight at Adī's description of the snake's wedding guests (A.31).

Mādar Zāher had the largest active repertoire of any woman from whom I was able to collect stories. She also engaged in the conscious manipulation of traditional materials, to the extent of inventing her own tales (see Ch. V), a creative activity to which no other storyteller in my collecting experience would admit. It is hard to imagine that Mādar Zāher was unaware of the differences between her handling of the woman's role in the supernatural wedding and Adī's, because she remarked on this human bride's attitude toward the snake's proposal (A.24), and because in this story and elsewhere she gives a great deal of attention to the mental processes of her characters (see pp. 97 ff. below).

Personal choice of the narrator, to change or elaborate detail, must be interpreted both in terms of his or her awareness of traditional options (the knowledge of many traditional tales, especially ones in which the themes in question occur), and in the light of the storyteller's personal concerns. In the presence of a tendency to reversion, whereby retellings of recently learned stories tend to revert, with subsequent performance, to detail and forms more like their original,[1] it is significant that the change in the mother's motivation appears only in Mādar Zāher's second recording of this story, when other details of her narrative are coming to resemble Adī's more rather than less. This is further evidence

---

[1] This phenomenon will be described in more detail with reference to Māhgol's performances of Mār Čučeh, pp.123, 131 below.

for the determining effect of personal choice in Mādar Zāher's alteration
of this detail.

Trying to distinguish the influence of personal concerns from that
of the prior contents of repertoire may in fact be a 'chicken or egg' en-
terprise. Personal taste or preoccupations with certain ideas generate
consistencies in an individual's repertoire from the earliest stages of
story learning onward,[1] while the recognition of familiar themes and word-
ings in new tales doubtless facilitates the oral learning of those tales.
(Complimented on the ease with which she learned a new tale, Mādar Zāher
remarked, "When you know the words of *afsāneh*, learning is easy.") With
regard to Mār Čučeh, Mādar Zāher's treatment of the mother's reasons for
marrying the snake is significant because of its internal consistency with
other changes she made in this tale, in non-related themes, such as the
exculpation of the vizier's wives. In her consistent presentation of
women as victims of circumstance, Mādar Zāher's personal attitudes shape
her repertoire in ways that cut across narrative units (episodes, as I
have called them, or 'themes' or 'motifs').

The rehabilitation of the story's women in Mādar Zāher's version
of Mār Čučeh makes Mār Čučeh's willing social integration through marriage
at the end of the story more psychologically consistent (despite internal
contradictions such as the portrayal of his mother), and also renders his
marriage dramatically possible. Perhaps it is not useful to try to decide whether Mādar Zāher was altering descriptive detail with a conscious
plan to revise the story so as to achieve a different type of resolution,

---

[1] Many collectors have remarked on the internal consistencies of repertoire as a reflection of the personal taste of the narrator. See, e.g.,
Asadowskij, 1926, or Friedl, 1975.

or whether the changes in detail are simply the consistent effect of a less conscious set of personal attitudes concerned with issues external to the story in which family membership and the role of women have a prominent place. Both influences are in evidence and work together, so that changes in detail conform in intention and effect with the major changes in plot structure which do seem to be conscious manipulations of the material which she received from Adí. Furthermore, the characterization of other persons in the story, notably Mār Čučeh himself, his brother, and the vizier, also undergoes systematic change when Mādar Zāher retells the story. These changes further illuminate Mādar Zāher's attitude toward story resolution, the way she organizes dramatic tensions in folktale plot structure, and her concept of fictional human character.

Mādar Zāher's two performances display, overall, a tendency to de-emphasize the liminal, supernatural aspects of Mār Čučeh's behavior, and thus to reduce the 'tricksterish' quality of his behavior. Starting with Mār Čučeh's first deeds in version C, we see that Mādar Zāher first omits Mār Čučeh's preposterous-sounding warning to his brother (cf. A.41, C.31), then substitutes a general, rational warning (C.37: "Tomorrow Papa's going to strike you and kill you, watch out!") In F version, she omits the verbal warning entirely (F.41), so that Mār Čučeh's behavior becomes first less rashly childish, in C, then more circumspect and cunning in the normal human sense in F. It is noteworthy that Zāher and Māhgol, the older children listening to the story, detect the changes immediately and protest (in the case of the advance warning, "He didn't say anything to him," C.38). The protest does not induce Mādar Zāher to accept correction, as she does in certain other instances (the cow-killing episode, C.153,155), or revert to Adí's form of the story.

Mādar Zāher's alteration and subsequent omission of this significant bit of dialogue must be contrasted with her tendency to interject
dialogue elsewhere. Several of her comments during Adī's first performance of the story consisted of bits of dialogue she put in the mouths of
Adī's characters (A.20,A.31,A.48,A.75). Likewise, when Mār Čučeh goes home
to kill his mother, Mādar Zāher has him start an argument before he kills
her. The verbal confrontation has no effect on dramatic structure, except
to make the boy's killing of his mother slightly less abrupt (cf. A.63:
"So just as they came in off the road, with the shovel in his hand, he
just hit his mother on the head with it, and scattered her brains," and
C.58-62, which begins with the contrived argument and ends with a second
speech by Mār Čučeh, an exegesis of the murder in which he reviles his
mother, now dead, for disloyalty to her son.) Both in forewarning his
brother and in arguing with his mother, Mār Čučeh becomes less precipitous
in his actions, and more human in strategy and emotional response.

Concerning his brother's death, Mādar Zāher's Mār Čučeh receives
no special word (though he did in Adī's version, cf. A.69, C.70-73). He
simply begins to worry when his brother does not return. Normal reconnaissance must serve him to discover the fate of his brother. Here, as
elsewhere in her handling of detail, Mādar Zāher rationalizes the way physical events such as the transfer of information happen in the story. Although the dramatic function of the incident is the same - Mār Čučeh discovers his brother's death and subsequently takes action - these changes
in mode are, once again, logically consistent with the gross changes in
tale structure and surface rationalism which culminate in the hero's social
integration. Mār Čučeh shows a normal brotherly concern which occasions
his departure from home and his search. The information he gets is imper-

sonal and objective (C.72), such as strangers in the real world would furnish, and he draws his own conclusions. Although there is nothing overtly unrealistic (much less supernatural) in the way Adī handles the theme of the transfer of information (A.69: "News came to Mār Čučeh . . ."), Mādar Zāher's treatment of the theme is much more attentive to the mechanics of Mār Čučeh's information-getting, a mundane process which reiterates Mār Čučeh's isolation ; his lack of allies or acquaintances who could give him news of his brother.

A striking example of Mādar Zāher's further rationalization of Mār Čučeh's actions occurs in the incident of the pick, when Mār Čučeh provokes a quarrel with the vizier's wife, preparatory to killing her.[1] In Adī's version, the vizier sends Mār Čučeh to fetch a pick to dig his child's grave. Mār Čučeh gets the pick, places it on his shoulder, then goes to the vizier's wife demanding an object which he refuses to name. The wife, distracted by grief, cannot discover what he wants (A.97-100). The insane logic of this scene escapes Mādar Zāher, and she cannot reproduce it, so she constructs a less bizarre strategem: Mār Čučeh hides the pick, then asks for it by name:

> He came, and said, "Mistress!"
> "What?"
> "Give me the thing. The - , the -, " (aside) No, he didn't say 'pick' when he said 'give' - he said, "Give me the shovel!"
> She said, "But the vizier just took the shovel." The mother of this - [Listener interjects: He picked it up, that one -]

---

[1] We may also see a retroactive thematic influence of this second instance of the murder of a female, in the way Mādar Zāher treats the killing of Mār Čučeh's mother. The two killings are already analogous in their manner of accomplishment (striking with a farm tool), and she extends the analogy by including a quarrel in the first murder. Recognizing similarities between two episodes, Mādar Zāher creates even more continuity in the handling of the two similar themes. See pp. 79 ff., above.

> And he picked up the pick, and hid it. And this Mār Čučeh said
> that, and he hid the pick. He said, "Mistress, give me the pick
> and shovel! The vizier says to."
>
> (C.104-107)

Once again, Mādar Zāher's children object to the change, but it reappears

in F.98, polished and told without hesitation.

In changing the strategem by which Mār Čučeh picks this quarrel,

Mādar Zāher eliminates one instance of Mār Čučeh's strategic use of verbal

incompetence, which is a part of the ongoing play on the relationship of

words to reality which runs as a thread of meaning through the whole fabric

of Adī's story. (See pp.67-69 , above, and pp. 92-94,below.) In Adī's

version, this is the first instance of Mār Čučeh feigning sheer verbal stu-

pidity. His previous plays with words have been ironically literalist, as

when he murdered the vizier's daughter by literally following the vizier's

hyperbolic orders, or when he boldly told his brother of his father's far-

fetched murder plan. Dramatically, Mār Čučeh's trickery in hiding the

pick functions equally well to motivate subsequent events (the quarrel and

the wife's death), but this change in Mār Čučeh's tactics reduces the den-

sity and economy of the story at the more abstract level of meaning, where-

in most of Mār Čučeh's acts of trickery are organized around the word /

reality relationship, which he distorts and exploits in different ways.

It seems that Mādar Zāher herself has trouble following the intricacies

of Mār Čučeh's verbal ambiguity, so she substitutes simpler types of trick-

ery.

This is not to say that Mādar Zāher is unaware of the dominant role

word play has in Mār Čučeh's story, however. In some ways she is acutely

aware of it. When she adds the incident of the second wife's death, the

killing of the woman is accomplished by Mār Čučeh's verbal evasion:

'. . . - he has a guest. He came, and he didn't say anything. He didn't say anything, and he came, this vizier, to do
some work around the house. He's not in the house, and he doesn't
know. So near afternoon prayer time, he came, and he said,
"Lòrd Vizier!"
    "What?"
    "They haven't put the pot on to cook yet."
    He said, "But didn't I tell you? Didn't I tell you to tell
them at ten o'clock?"
    "By God, they haven't put the pot on." '
                            (C.124-128)

Mār Čučeh accuses the woman of disobeying the vizier's command,

omitting to mention that he has never delivered the order. This verbal

strategem is exactly analogous to the one by which he induced the vizier

to give the order to punish the first wife, during the incident of the

pick, as Adī told it. Mār Čučeh's omission of key verbal information is

also analogous to the trick by which he provoked the vizier to order him

to kill the little girl (cf. C.80-99).

Mādar Zāher's sensitivity to word play is most clearly demonstrated

in the cow-killing episode, after the vizier goes to the wedding. She adds

a crucial word play, /Māla jam ko/, which Adī did not use, but which with

its double meaning supplies a punning excuse for Mār Čučeh's treatment of

both the vizier's cattle and his household goods. *Māl* in Farsi (western

Persian) means property of any kind. Western colloquial Persian for 'It

is my property' is /Māl-e man é/. This usage of Iranian speakers sounds

comical to Dari (eastern dialect) speakers, for whom *māl* regularly means

'livestock' only. Likewise *jam' kardan* in standard Persian means 'gather

together, consolidate,' but in colloquial Dari, with reference to live-

stock, it means 'feed, nurture'. Hence the vizier's order, /Māla jam ko/

(C.144) means <u>either</u> "feed the livestock" (colloquial Dari) <u>or</u> "gather up

all the possessions" (standard and colloquial Farsi). Herat is located in the border area between Iranian (Farsi) and Afghan (Dari) dialect areas, at the point where this pun would be most immediately comprehensible to a general audience. (Elsewhere in Afghanistan a knowledge of Farsi usage would have to come through literary channels.) Although I have no evidence from her active repertoire to prove it, I think it extremely unlikely that Mādar Zāher made up this word play on the spot. Her inclusion of it and the extra wife-killing episode in the story is the strongest evidence available for her having heard at least portions of this story from another source, although she claimed to have heard no version of Mār Čučeh before Adī's. On the basis of the word play, I would imagine the source to be a Heratī one, although I did not hear this story from any other Heratī informant. Adī is not from Herat; her community is in a Pashtu/Dari linguistic border area, and so it is not surprising that, despite the dominant role of word plays in her version of Mār Čučeh, she does not use this particular pun.

The second word play on which the wedding episode hinges, turns on the verb *bastan*, 'tie, fasten, lock,' with reference to the house gate which Mār Čučeh ties on his back, instead of locking it in its place. This word play is of a simpler nature and is used by all three narrators, but like *Māla jam ko* concerns the wrong choice among several possible meanings, a punning strategem rather than the over-literalism Mār Čučeh has hitherto exploited.

Surveying Mār Čučeh's speech behavior in Adī's story, we see the snake child going from the literal statement of real facts (the unheeded warnings) to the over-literal interpretation of hyperbolic statements (the vizier's angry commands), then to the inappropriate interpretation of statements with more than one literal meaning. Mār Čučeh's final strategic speech act in Adī's story is plain misrepresentation, the bald-faced lie he tells the vizier about cleaning the boots. This last act represents a third and more radical type of ambiguity, and the opposite of Mār Čučeh's initial truth-telling strategy (A.41). Mādar Zāher's telling of Mār Čučeh attenuates the development of this word vs. reality theme to a considerable degree: she eliminates the first and last terms, but reiterates the second, over-literalist ploy (killing the second wife at the vizer's directions) and also the third, punning strategy (*Māla jam ko*). Mādar Zāher also eliminates the most irrational of Mār Čučeh's verbal strategems, by revising the pick incident. Her Mār Čučeh displays a much narrower range of verbal strategy, particularly because she omits the first and last terms of the set, in which Mār Čučeh took the initiative in utterance, not only in interpretation.

Just as Mādar Zāher rationalizes Mār Čučeh's behavior, she also reduces its supernatural qualities. Two striking examples of this trend occur in C. Mār Čučeh no longer anticipates the vizier's escape route in a clairvoyant fashion (as in A.134), but instead waits, watches which way his victims go, and follows them (C.164-167; cf. F.124-126). Similarly, in F, when Mār Čučeh feigns sleep (F.133), he must cut his finger to stay awake, whereas in Adī's version he manifests complete self-control, staying awake without difficulty despite his previous exertions (A.139-143). Even in this detail, Mādar Zāher is at pains to rationalize Mār Čučeh's physical abilities: at F.48, Mār Čučeh's keenness of hearing is made a function of his youth: "Mār Čučeh was little, his ears were keen."

In F, Mār Čučeh puts on the vizier's clothes in order to impersonate the man (F.134), and in Mādar Zāher's appendix to E, he even imitates the vizier's way of addressing his wife (E.151), in order to carry off the

disguise. Adī's Mār Čučeh succeeds at impersonating a woman, without re-
sorting to such human precautions as disguise. As in the case of information gathering (p. 89, above), Mādar Zāher is at pains to explain the mechanics of Mār Čučeh's trickery, and in every case his strategems are mundane, his powers of perception and deceit only those of a clever human.

It can be argued that especially in the case of the disguise, but
elsewhere as well, Mādar Zāher was only striving for verisimilitude in
the portrayal of the story's events, and not intentionally undercutting
Mār Čučeh's trickster nature. I would argue that verisimilitude is what
tricksters and trickster tales conspicuously lack, and that the lack of
verisimilitude in Mār Čučeh is one source of Mādar Zāher's dissatisfaction with Adī's story. Mādar Zāher does not de-emphasize the supernatural
element in her own stories, in fact some of her own compositions (of which
more later, Ch. V) are particularly rich in supernatural content. What
she does seem to object to is the ambiguity of Mār Čučeh's *modus operandi*,
and other kinds of ambiguity as well, as can be seen from the changes she
makes in the behavior of Mār Čučeh's brother and the vizier. As Babcock-
Abrahams' summary analysis of tricksters reveals (pp. 57-8, above), ambiguity is the essential common feature of trickster figures and their exploits.

When narrating conversations and interactions between characters in
Mār Čučeh, even under rather extraordinary circumstances such as the aftermath of murders, Mādar Zāher invents dialogue which tends to rationalize
and resolve ambiguity. The first example of this is the meeting between
Mār Čučeh's elder brother and the vizier, when the boy agrees to go to work
for the vizier despite the vizier's extremely stringent terms. In version
A (A.66-68) the boy's willingness to work under these terms is not explained. He simply agrees and is starved to death. In B, Adī describes

a bit more of the boy's mental processes (B.53):

> [The boy] answered, he said [to himself] "He must just be talking," and he answered, "I don't have a stomach."

He assumes that the vizier's excessive terms are hyperbolic, rhetorical, not literal demands. The ambiguity here, as mentioned before, is that between social usage (the customary reciprocal responsibilities of master and servant) and verbal statement. The vizier's exploitation of this ambiguity backfires when, in Mār Čučeh, he gets a servant who takes all his orders literally.

Mādar Zāher's first treatment of this contractual exchange includes a flat-footed attempt by the boy to resolve the ambiguity of the vizier's terms:

> ". . . He must not have a stomach."
> He said, "How [do you mean], he shouldn't have a stomach?"
> "That he shouldn't eat."
> "I don't eat a thing."
>
> (C.65-68)

Here the vizier's meaning is made explicit, and the burden of hyperbole is shifted to the boy, who says, "I don't eat a thing," meaning "I am not greedy." F.72-74 is essentially the same exchange, in a briefer form in which the vizier volunteers a clarification of his own statement:

> '[The vizier] said, "Well, I'll take a servant who has no stomach, who doesn't eat." '

In this case, it seems that the vizier's statement needs clarification for the audience to comprehend its (literal) import. The expression, 'to have no stomach' = 'not to be greedy' is not, to my limited knowledge, idiomatic in Persian. Mādar Zāher also treats it as non-idiomatic, as a statement whose figurative meaning would not be obvious to her audience.[1] Her attempt to resolve its ambiguity, however, attenuates its force and shifts the responsibility for deception to a certain extent onto the victim. The vizier is no longer playing with the ambiguity of words in Mādar Zāher's rendition of this incident, a fact which considerably reduces the irony of Mār Čučeh's later retaliatory tactics, which Mādar Zāher also renders less verbal (see pp. 90 ff. above).

Mādar Zāher often depicts the interior mental processes of her characters in dialogue and soliloquy, which further contributes to the rational-empirical tone of interpersonal transactions in the story. A concern for everyday propriety is injected into these exchanges. At C.12, she has the human boy, faced with telling his mother about the snake's proposal, remark, "How can I ask my <u>mother</u>, 'Do you want a husband or not?'" This soliloquy is striking for its omission of any mention of the snake, especially in view of Mādar Zāher's first reaction on hearing Adī describe this exchange: "Didn't she understand that it was an *aufī*?" (A.24). The boy remarks not on the impossibility of relaying a proposal from a snake, but simply on the impropriety of his approaching his <u>mother</u> on the subject of marriage. Just as women are ordinarily expected to be shy and circumspect and to express reluctance to marry, the boy feels proper shame at the prospect of questioning his mother about her marital preferences, or acting as her go-between in sexual matters. Mādar Zāher's emphasis in this scene shifts from the horrific prospect of a monster stepfather to

---

[1] It is possible she felt obliged to elucidate the verbal expression for me, a non-native, but Adī's implication that the boy also had difficulty interpreting it, confirms for me that the expression is non-idiomatic, and therefore ambiguous, in Persian.

the mundane issue of social shame. Her inclusion of this soliloquy is
the more striking in view of Adī's explanation of the boy's failure to
deliver the message: "It went out of his mind, and he didn't tell his
mother." (A.18) One is left to speculate on the likelihood of a normal
person's forgetting such a meeting, and the psychological implications of
such 'forgetting'. Adī feels no need to explain it. Mādar Zāher, however,
finds this 'forgetting' in need of psychological explication: hence the
boy's soliloquy. Adī's omission of any speculation concerning the boy's
motivation in this instance is part of a general tolerance of arbitrariness
and ambiguity which characterizes the relations of all the characters in
her tale. People's (the boy's, the vizier's) willingness to accept ambiguity causes all their personal disasters, and moves the story through
a series of steadily more outrageous events.

In C Mādar Zāher introduces a strategic lie which the boy tells to
answer the snake:

> "Hey, Boy! Did you tell your mother?"
> "Yes."
> "What did she say? Did she say, 'I'll marry?'"
> He said, "She didn't say anything."
> "Oho! You didn't tell your mother! . . ."

The lie and the snake's instant reaction to it work well dramatically, as
they emphasize the inadequacy of the boy's ordinary human evasive strategy
(analogous to his going to another field to glean) to avoid the clairvoyant snake's demands. In adding this lie, Mādar Zāher gives the boy more
evasive resourcefulness than Adī grants him, but in this case the addition
of a psychological dimension deepens, rather than obscures, the contrast
between normal and supernatural behavior.

The first acts of revenge which Mār Čučeh perpetrates on the vizier

all involve the strategic withholding of information, as well as over-
literal interpretation of commands. Mādar Zāher's tendency to rationalize
dialogue here almost breaks the delicate web of Mār Čučeh's deceptive behavior. In making the mother address her daughter directly concerning the
child's refusal to cooperate, Mādar Zāher narrowly avoids having the mother
ask, "Why won't you pee?" which would eliminate the ellipsis upon which Mār
Čučeh's strategy depends (C.91). Mādar Zāher's tendency to rationalize dialogue so as to resolve ambiguities which are vital to the plot structure
is even more visible in the incident Mādar Zāher added, when the vizier
confronts his wife:

> This other wife is crying. This poor vizier came, and saw
> his wife. He said, "All right, you bastard! When I told him,
> that you should put on the pot, you didn't put it on, so he came
> and told me, 'By God, they didn't do what I said.'" This vizier
> said (shouting) [to Mār Čučeh] "Bastard! Go, then, I don't
> want . . ."

The logical development of the vizier's confrontation with his wife would
lead to the wife, in her own defense, replying that Mār Čučeh had never
delivered the message to put the pot on the fire. The revelation would
destroy Mār Čučeh's retaliatory strategy, which depends throughout on the
lack of rational communication among the characters, and their failure to
resolve ambiguities. Mādar Zāher takes the confrontation she has added up
to the point where the wife would defend herself, then she drops it and
picks up Adī's version of these confrontations, which involves only Mār
Čučeh and the vizier. The second wife-killing episode becomes contradic-
tory, because by its inclusion Mādar Zāher reiterates the pattern of withheld information/overliteral interpretation of commands/revenge, but her
rational empirical formulation of the confrontation scene tends to undercut
the same theme of imperfect communication. It seems likely that her ra-

tionalizing tendency operates here not at the level of conscious identification and amplification of themes (in this case, the communication theme),
but less consciously in her general concept of human interaction, its style
and consequences. Not only does she consciously reject the resolution pattern which leaves Mār Čučeh's social status undefined, but she also rejects
the ambiguity of these imperfect communicative exchanges, throughout the
story. The general ambiguity she tries to dispel is nonetheless vital to
the plot, so she stops just short of the point where further reduction of
ambiguity would have structural consequences.

The exploits of tricksters, themselves liminal characters, elucidate the terms and limits of normal human existence by their bending and
breaking of social and physical laws. Mār Čučeh in particular plays with
people's expectations in a setting of verbal ambiguity, demonstrating by
violation the exact expectations for human behavior behind the ambiguity
of statements. Mādar Zāher's impulse to resolve verbal ambiguity attenuates the style of conceptual play which is essential to Mār Čučeh as a
trickster tale.

Mādar Zāher's concern with the social meaning of events and communicative exchanges is revealed through her consistent emphasis on social
appearances. Like the boy's soliloquy (see pp. 97 ff. above), other details
of dialogue and action reveal characters' concern for social appearances
under the most unlikely circumstances. In F, after Mār Čučeh kills his
mother, the two boys give her a proper funeral, with ritual washing and a
memorial service (F.67-68), instead of bundling the body away as quickly
as possible, as they do in Adī's version of the story (A.63). To some extent Mādar Zāher's consistent treatment of death and burial, complete with
deadwashers and the memorial reading of religious texts, can be seen as

simple thematic consistency (cf. A.109 and C.139). As in the case of the virilocal element in the snake's marriage (discussed pp. 82-3, above), and the issue of Mār Čučeh's mother's culpability in marrying the snake (pp. 81 ff.), the ceremonious detail in her various treatments of themes of death and burial achieves a consistency in Mādar Zāher's narrative which is not equally appropriate to the circumstances of all the deaths. In particular, Mār Čučeh's mother's death and burial are unnatural; in Adī's version the murder and unceremonious burial are fitting retribution for the mother's own unnatural treatment of her son. Adī stresses the unceremonious disposal of the corpse (A.63), in contradistinction to normal social practice. Given a traditional audience's knowledge of the established forms for social ceremonies such as marriage and burial, divergence from the traditional pattern becomes a powerful tool for the storyteller to convey the special meaning of an occasion and direct audience attention to crucial structural elements in the story. Mādar Zāher's failure to distinguish this burial as socially abnormal complicates the issue of justified matricide with that of concern with social appearances. The special meaning of the death is thus obscured.

Mādar Zāher's concern with shame and social appearances also affects her portrayal of male-female relations. The outstanding example of this is her portrayal of the vizier's reaction to his wife's summons at the wedding (see p. 78, above). The vizier's embarrassed reaction (C.148: "Oh, what are you saying, woman, you've shamed me before the people!," cf. F. 113) stresses the power relations pertaining between Mādar Zāher's male and female characters and especially a concern with outward social expressions of these power relations.

Realism in the portrayal of everyday events and the practicalities of life is also a concern for Mādar Zāher. She tells us that the boy goes off to collect wood "for two or three days," (F.6) rather than in the afternoons, as Adī has described. While Adī describes a normal village work schedule, Mādar Zāher describes the work schedule of a person who lives in the city and has land or work in a nearby village, which is her husband's situation and the one she herself knows. Because of the difficulties of travel in such a situation, one goes out to the hinterland for several days at a time, to bring in a crop or cut wood for the household supply. She is concerned with the plausibility of the snake's ruses: at F.48, she has the snake say, "Tomorrow, no, the next day - then, you - uh - don't bake bread . . . You say, 'Dear, there wasn't any wood for me to bake bread.'" Her hesitation over the time element in the murder plan is occasioned by two factors: (a) at F.41, she has shown the boy arriving with a load of wood, so there would have had to be a supply of wood in the house, at least for the next day; and (b) at F.38, the snake has told the mother to bake bread that same day. Non-nomadic women in the Herat area do not bake bread oftener than every three or four days, some not more than once a week. Village-style bread ovens are large clay constructions that take a considerable amount of fuel to fire, and then retain heat for several hours of baking, so several days' supply of bread is baked at a time. Mādar Zāher's sense of verisimilitude in this circumstance induces her to add a time element, to avoid the implication of even such a minor failure of realism as the prospect of Mār Čučeh's mother baking bread on two consecutive days.

Mādar Zāher phrases the elder boy's solicitude for his brother in the most practical terms. When he is leaving for the city, he gives Mār Čučeh directions:

He said, "I'm going to go and find a job. You bring hay for the cow by yourself, and put it right here. Whatever stuff there is in the house, you give it to someone or other to cook for you, and eat."

Mār Čučeh replies with the same down-to-earth practicality:

"I can cook for myself, Brother, it's all right."

(F.70-71)

Even in inconsequential detail, Mādar Zāher's narrative style shows a pervasive concern for realism which is consistent with her rejection of physical indeterminacy and ambiguous action in characters. The attention she gives to the mental processes of her characters, in shaping dialogues and soliloquies, compounds the 'novelistic' effect of her attention to realism in detail.

In conclusion, it is possible to distinguish two parallel levels on which Mādar Zāher's revision of Mār Čučeh is carried out. First, there are the major structural changes, which involve the omission and/or revision of major events of the plot, and for which she had to fight in the face of her children's corrective protests. In light of these protests, her spirited defense, "Adī told it just like that! Adī told it just like that!" (E.158) protests a bit too much. The net effect of these major structural changes is to permit a final resolution in which Mār Čučeh is assimilated by marriage into a high-status place in society.

Secondly, at the level of descriptive detail and dialogue, there is a class of changes relating to

a) resolving verbal ambiguities,

b) addressing 'normal' social behavior, meaning, proprieties, etc.,

c) verisimilitude in physical causality and motivation.

All these changes in surface 'texture' or detail reinforce Mādar Zāher's major structural revisions. On all levels, the events of the story are made to resemble everyday phenomena and the behavior of real people more closely. Adding explanatory detail, Mādar Zāher moves the story's events into a more fully furnished real-world setting, at the same time that she accommodates Mār Čučeh's assimilation into that world at the structural level by rearranging the plot.

These changes in detail and structure in a single transmission event (i.e. as the story passes from Adī to Mādar Zāher) have certain implications for the study of genre and sub-genre in oral narrative. To use the Marandas' terms (Köngas-Maranda & Maranda, 1971:36), the mediation (conflict resolution) achieved in the story is intensified from level III to level IV. In Adī's story, Mār Čučeh achieves only the nullification of the initial impact, that is, he revenges his brother's death, he 'gets even' with the vizier and ends his power to do evil. In Mādar Zāher's story, there is a 'permutation of the initial impact' (level IV mediation), for in the process of getting revenge Mār Čučeh also gains permanent social membership: no longer a marginal outcast, he replaces the vizier in his own household.

In terms of resolution, trickster tales may be of level II mediation (in which the trickster/hero tries and fails to accomplish a task), or of level III or IV. Many coyote tales, such as the eye-juggler story in the Jicarilla Apache corpus (Opler, 1938:277-278) seem to be level II mediations. Other examples from that and other traditions achieve level IV, with the trickster's actions causing permanent changes in his own status and/or in cosmic order. Animal fables in many traditions concern level II (unsuccessful) mediations; folktales other than trickster tales frequently achieve levels III or IV, so on the evidence, levels of mediation are not diagnostic for distinguishing between so-called 'trickster tales' and other commonly recognized subgenres of folktale.

Though levels of mediation are non-definitive for the folklorist who seeks objective criteria for the structural distinction of genres of traditional narrative, they may be significant for the traditional narrator who sees certain levels of mediation, evaluatively, as necessary to the correct resolution of a narrative of a certain type. I have presented evidence that Mādar Zāher's objections to Adī's Mār Čučeh, which made her reluctant to perform the tale, and her subsequent revisions of its resolution and its descriptive detail are rooted in her non-acceptance of the generally liminal and ambiguous qualities of the actions of the tale's characters, especially those of Mār Čučeh himself. In particular, the revision of the conclusion implies a judgment on her part that Adī's story was not satisfactorily resolved, that a level III ending which does not resolve the social status questions inherent in this trickster tale is not proper for a well-told *afsāneh* (to use her own generic term). Although she insists that she <u>has</u> reproduced Adī's tale accurately, when her children challenge her re-formulation of the story's conclusion (E.157), her critical appraisal of Adī's tale is clear at J.1: ". . . and I know that Mār Čučeh, too, but my own *afsāneh* are better."

When pressed to perform Mār Čučeh, she judges it negatively. It seems fair to assume that the aspects of the story which she altered most consistently were those which most offended her, and they are the two aspects which identify the tale as a trickster tale: Mār Čučeh's liminal, ambiguous and somewhat amorphous supernatural qualities, and a resolution pattern which leaves the main character in an ambiguous state vis-a-vis society, a resolution which is not found in any other tale in Mādar Zāher's repertoire which she designates "afsāneh". What, then, is the meaning of this term in her usage? She shows a uniform preference for resolution patterns which include social assimilation (through marriage and/or succession to a throne) in her tales of human heroes. A minority of items in her repertoire, including certain short animal tales and some tales in which things work out badly for the human protagonists, she designates 'naql', 'narratives', rather than afsāneh, folktales. In my collecting experience, Madar Zaher's division of fictional entertainment narratives into afsāneh and naql along these lines was rather idiosyncratic. For most storytellers, afsāneh was an inclusive term for any sort of narrative recognized as fiction. Naql was reserved for historical or pseudo-historical (e.g. secular and religious legendary) narratives. In light of situations such as this, 'native' genre classifications must be tested for a consensus among the users of the terms; consensus about generic categories should not be assumed, even among adept narrators. Likewise, it should be stressed that just as there is no definitive version of a tale, there is always a range of possibilities which may bridge 'generic' categories imposed either by traditional narrators or comparative folklorists. All reformulations in transmission, even trans-generic ones, are reversible.

The transformation of the plot structure of M̄ar Čučeh in transmission from Adī to Mādar Zāher provides a case study against which to evaluate Eleasar Meletinsky's (1974a) discussion of the syntactic position of marriage in traditional narrative, which forms part of his contrastive definition of myth and folktale. He places special significance on marriages occurring as the final resolution point of stories:

> "The fabulous marriage is the last level of the syntagmatic
> chain of the subject, the most important element of semantics
> and the highest degree of axiological hierarchy; from the point
> of view of logic, it is the means of mediation and reconcilia-
> tion between contradictions [in folktale]. In primitive tales
> [=myth], marriage, as Levi-Strauss has shown, was the means of
> communication, the exchange of values, while in the fairytale
> it fulfilled quite another function . . . so the basic tests
> lead to marriage, while in the primitive tale the search for
> magical (cosmic) or ritual objects, the acquisition of guardian
> spirits (precursors of the protectors of fairytales) and tests
> of the initiation type occupied a major place, and marriage only
> played a secondary role."
>
> (1974a:55-56)

Simply put, marriage in myth is a means to ends; in folktale, it is the

end. Without espousing Meletinsky's rather simple-minded historicism, one

may examine further this very interesting observation concerning oral nar-

rative syntax. Whether marriage is an ultimate or a contributing element

in a tale is immediately obvious from its presence in the complication or

resolution phases of the narrative. Meletinsky's second major criterion

for distinguishing myth from folktale concerns the social impact of the

hero's deeds:

> [The basic difference between myth and folktale] "is that
> the first is concerned with a collective fate (the fate of
> the universe and of 'mankind') and the second with the fate
> of individuals." (1974a:67)

Meletinsky's two defining principles are of course related: marriage is

viewed as a quintessentially personal achievement in Meletinsky's scheme,

where it is not a means to an end.[1]

---

[1] Meletinsky's interpretation ignores an important component of certain
mythical texts whose evaluation is beyond the scope of the present discussion, that is, the hieros gamos or sacred marriage which is a central symbol in a number of cultic myths, notably from Mesopotamia, and
stands in a climactic, final position in the liturgy of, e.g. the Baby-
lonian New Year festival celebrating the accession of Marduk to the
divine throne.

According to either of Meletinsky's criteria, it is possible to argue that Mādar Zāher converts Mār Čučeh from a myth into a folktale. This tempting observation is invalidated, however, by the fact that Mādar Zāher would think it nonsense. As far as she is concerned, Mār Čučeh is *afsāneh*, folktale, albeit with some flaws.

Native generic distinctions aside, the utility of Meletinsky's structural definition of folktale and myth is also questionable when one observes the fluidity of the two forms in actual transmission.[1] It is probably that within this local tradition, the story which these two tellers call Mār Čučeh has gone through this 'generic' transformation numerous times, in both directions.

---

[1] I am indebted to Roger Abrahams (1969) for the idea that genre definition may be more satisfactorily achieved by ranging forms along a continuum (in his case, from participation to performance), rather than by conceiving of genres as closed and discontinuous categories. A consideration of Mār Čučeh's relation to myth could start with its comparison with the 'kingship in Heaven' theme described by Littleton (1970). Both versions of Mār Čučeh are variants of this pattern, which Littleton finds throughout Indo-European metology.

III.C: Mār Čūceh D & E:

Māhgol's Story

One can learn a great deal about the structure and techniques of
oral narrative from the problems of relatively unskilled narrators.
Often techniques of oral narrative composition not revealed in a polished
performance are made obvious by their less skilled application. In the
performances of Māhgol, Mādar Zāher's young daughter, one can observe a
narrator struggling with narrative technique in the presence of a critical audience, whose comments and criticisms also serve to illuminate the
narrative process.

Māhgol's two performances of Mār Čūčeh are full of omissions and
confusions. Her vocabulary is less extensive than that of the two adult
storytellers, and her ability to order events is shaky at times. At the
time of the recordings she was between nine and ten years old. She shared
a tendency to omit and/or alter the order of major events in the story
with the few other young storytellers I was able to record. My recording
activities did not yield material for the systematic study of children's
narrative abilities, but her performance of Mār Čūčeh was within the range
of competency I was able to observe in other storytellers aged eight to
eleven, of whom I only recorded three or four.

Māhgol's flawed and occasionally incoherent performances are interesting for what they reveal about the acquisition of storytelling technique. Some of the technical difficulties she had with organizing the
story are also visible in Mādar Zāher's first performance of it, although

in lesser degree. It seems likely that such organizational problems are inherent in the learning and organizing of new material for all storytellers, but vary in degree according to the storyteller's skill. To the extent that they result in reorganizing the story, they are important in the genesis of variants. More recording and study of transmission events is necessary to describe the general occurrence of these processes.

In addition to the insights they provide on storytelling process and the acquisition of expertise, Māhgol's performances of Mār Čučeh shed further light on Mādar Zāher's performances of the story, providing an indirect corrective and a check on Mādar Zāher's alteration of Adī's original version. Strong differences of opinion which Māhgol and Mādar Zāher voiced during their respective performances of the tale point to elements they consider to be important, both events and descriptive details. Some of Māhgol's uncertainty in the arrangement of narrative elements can be seen to derive directly from the fact that she had two different versions of the story presented as models, Adī's version and her mother's. Her own lack of assurance in organizing the narrative was exacerbated by the conflicts arising from the co-presence of two variants of the story.

To facilitate the comparison of complex processes in Māhgol's two performances and those of her mother, it will be helpful to classify the phenomena under discussion as follows:

1) verbal difficulties: problems caused by lack of technical vocabulary, confusion of tenses, etc.;

2) preliminary descriptions, 'planning' episodes, and recapitulations, their relative use and development by Māhgol and her mother;

3) analogous episodes and the syntactic ordering of 'reiterative' elements;

4) details Māhgol includes from Adī's version, which Mādar
Zāher omits or alters; and

5) elements common to Māhgol's narrative and her mother's,
which are alterations of Adī's original. These last two categories will be discussed jointly, as they are inextricably joined
in the last four performances of the tale.

All of the above phenomena are observable in text D, Māhgol's first recorded performance of Mār Čučeh. A consideration of the continuation or
reversal of these developments in Māhgol's later performance, E, will follow the discussion of text D.

1) Verbal difficulties:

At the level of vocabulary, Māhgol is somewhat inarticulate. She
has difficulty with the technical terms for tools, at D.86-93, where
shovel, adze, pick and axe all figure in her rendition of the scene in
which Mār Čučeh quarrels with the vizier's wife over a tool to dig a grave.
Adī's version of the incident involved only two picks, one of them dull
(A.97-100). Mādar Zāher altered the incident, introducing a shovel (see
pp. 90-91, above). In Māhgol's version, the proliferation of tools is random and non-functional for the purposes of the story-line. Adze, axe and
pick are all edged tools, but the first two are inappropriate for grave-
digging. Māhgol is uncertain which term to use, and includes them all in
a scatter-shot attempt to hit on the word which she could not recall at
C.107, where she interjects to correct her mother, "He picked it up, that
one --".

Māhgol is unfamiliar with the terminology of provincial bureaucracy. She knows and uses the term, 'vizier,' even insists that her mother use it (C.65: Māhgol interjects, "The <u>vizier</u> was sitting-"), but she has no term for the vizier's host in the final episode of the story, though Adī has emphasized that he is a city dignitary acting in an official capacity (A.153). More significantly, Māhgol makes an *arbāb*, a village headman, the final authority who decrees that the vizier be jailed (D.141), rather than the host himself or a *qazī* or religious judge, who would be the appropriate officials in such a case. The formality of relations between the two high-status strangers, the host and the vizier, is not emphasized in Māhgol's rendition of the incident, because she lacks an adult's familiarity with the protocol of bureaucracy. She is aware that official authority figures are involved, though she cannot come up with the correct terms, so she invokes terms with which she is familiar, 'vizier' and 'arbab'.[1]

Māhgol has some difficulties with grammar, visible when she hesitates over dialogue (D.6,14,17,22,41, et al.), especially when trying to render reported speech (e.g. D.22, " -- He -- said, 'She said, "I'll marry."'") Not surprisingly, the planning incidents in which the snake dictates dialogue in future tense to his human wife present severe difficulties for Māhgol. The problem of organizing events causes her to break off a dialogue:

> He said, "All right. Tomorrow, when he goes for the hay, you say, 'Dear --', when he goes for the hay, and he comes back, then he, he'll say, -m- 'Why didn't you do something?'" (Sighs,

---

[1] At the time of these performances, Māhgol's father was in daily negotiations with the arbāb of his home village over a land dispute. The term was heard daily in the home. See Šīr ǫ Palang discussion below, pp. 203-204.

frustrated) -- Oh. She -- she brings, she brings bread, with
water. [MZ interrupts brusquely: <u>Dry</u> bread. 'Don't put anything on to cook.' Like that. (MM and MZ laugh quietly)] OK.
"Don't you put anything on to cook." (D.29)

At D.39-40 the composition of plans and dialogue in future tense
proves too much for Māhgol, and she conflates the planning episode with
its execution, unconsciously slipping from future imperative tense to
simple past:

'Don't you bring water for him. You make something to eat with
the bread, then bring it, spread the cloth, don't bring water
for him. He'll say, 'Why didn't you bring water?: Now you say,
"I was busy. I couldn't do it, myself."' So she said (*sic*),
- m - Go, yourself, get the glass and fill it, drink.'
    She said that, and he went, and picked it up, he picked up
the glass to go and fill it, (and) his brother said - m - 'Ohhh,
Brother, my Papa's in the water jar, he'll strike you and kill
you. Give it to me to fill.'

The conflation of similar incidents which involve large amounts of verbal
repetition is a general phenomenon in Māhgol's storytelling, as will be
demonstrated below. Here the two passages fall together because she fails
to maintain the minimal difference in verb tense which distinguishes the
planning sequence from its execution.

2) <u>Preliminary descriptions, 'planning' episodes and recapitula-
tions</u>:

The last example above serves to illustrate a problem which Māhgol
shares, to an extent, with Mādar Zāher in her initial performances of <u>Mār</u>
<u>Čučeh</u>. This problem is the omission of important preliminary events or
descriptions, or planning episodes, or their collapse into the subsequent
action for which they are the preparation. Besides the truncation of the
snake's second murder plan, discussed above, there are numerous other
examples of this tendency to omit preparatory episodes. At. D.26-27,

Māhgol omits the important details of Mār Čučeh's growth to young childhood before the snake's first attempt on his brother's life:

> . . . this old woman got pregnant, and God gave her the child,
> and they called him - m - Mār Čučeh.
> He said, "When shall I eat that son of yours?"

At D.29, Māhgol omits the crucial explanatory detail for the murder plot,
which is that the human boy is unable to eat dry bread, which makes the
withholding of ghee significant (cf. A.36). Māhgol does not lose this detail completely, for it does appear at D.41, in the context of the final
murder attempt, where it is not functional. Mādar Zāher reminded her of
the detail at D.29 (see p.113 above), but she did not add the detail when
corrected. Corrective remarks from the audience are normal where relations between storyteller and audience are familiar and informal, as here
between parent and child, but despite her tolerance of these criticisms
the young narrator does not assimilate all the corrections immediately.

Having neglected to mention that Mār Čučeh has grown up sufficient-
ly to oppose the snake's first murder attempt, Māhgol also omits the important preliminary detail of Mār Čučeh's overhearing the murder plan
(D.32-33; cf. A.36). The plan is followed by its execution. Māhgol's
description of the execution of the plan is more detailed and complete
than her rendition of the snake's directions. At D.34 she includes a detail later omitted by her mother, the water glass (cf. F.41), which figures
prominently in the second murder attempt. The fact that the execution of
the first plan is more complete than the plan itself, points to the cumu-
lative mnemonic value of rehearsal. Progressive rehearsal is built into
oral narrative style, which accommodates a great deal of direction-giving,
execution of directions and subsequent recapitulation of action. Plan/

execution sequences and recapitulations of accomplished action allow for

the repeated description of each episode of thenarrative, in performance.

This aids the audience in learning new material, since they hear it more

than once, and also aids the narrator who is performing new material, by

allowing for the incremental recall and arrangement of details. Māhgol's

memory for certain details in Adī's narrative is latent at first, in her

planning episodes, but comes back to her in subsequent narration of the

same events, through execution scenes and through the later occurrence of

similar events such as the second and third murder attempts. (Sometimes

incremental recall undermines narrative conherency, however, as when a de-

tail which is distinctive to one analogous episode is transferred to another

[the mother's withholding of food, D.54-55]. This effect will be discussed

in more detail below.) The progressive reconstruction of detail is also

visible from one performance to another when a storyteller is polishing

a new story. I have designated it the 'reversion effect,' wherever it is

visible.

The detail of Mār Čučeh's overhearing the snake's plan appears in

Māhgol's version of the second murder attempt, when she describes the two

boys going out into the alley 'again' (D.39). She is manifestly unaware

that she omitted this detail in the first attempt (cf. A.36,39,49-50).

She still omits explicit mention of Mār Čučeh's eavesdropping, however.

Although Māhgol still has substantial difficulty with reported speech in

the planning sequence for the third murder attempt (D.42), at last the de-

tail of overhearing, so much emphasized by Adī, is explicitly stated. The

mnemonic utility of reiterative patterns (the succession of similar murder

attempts) is manifest as Māhgol progressively reconstructs details of the

story as she heard it from Adī.

Mãhgol's most remarkable oversight occurs at D.57-64, where she omits the murder of Mãr Čučeh's brother. The elder brother goes off to find a job, but a few lines later it is Mãr Čučeh who is working for the vizier. This crucial omission seems to be the result of a collapsing together of the two hiring scenes, that between the elder brother and the vizier, and the very similar later episode with Mãr Čučeh. The two conversations contain very close verbal parallels in Adī's telling (A.65-68, 72-74). Though similarities among incidents in a single folktale may be great (for example, the snake's three murder attempts), they are never simply identical. They are always distinguished by minimal differences (in the case of the murder attempts, by the orderly progression of locale and foods withheld), which often articulate subcategories or modulations in a unified set of meanings. When minimal differences are overlooked, similar incidents may collapse together. The mnemonic importance of minimal differences, which serve to keep analogous incidents distinct within a story, as well as their semantic value, by which they articulate series of related meanings, must not be underestimated. Meaning and memory are intimately related in the mechanics of storytelling.

A phenomenon related to retroactive interference, as described in studies on serial memory, may be at work in Mãhgol's conflation of similar incidents. Retroactive interference in memory has been described in the experimental literature[1] primarily for tasks involving the serial memorization of lists of words. When a task involves the learning of several lists of similar items in succession, parts of later lists tend to be recalled when the subject tries to reproduce lists learned earlier.

---

[1] For summaries of which see Klatzky (1975) or Norman (1969).

The learning of narrative sequences is not easily equated with the memorization of lists, however. In narrative, dramatic emphasis normally falls of the last episode in an analogous series: it 'clinches' a series of events, so its incorporation into or replacement of earlier episodes cannot be construed as a simple result of the order of memorization of the series. Emphasis may cause a climactic event to be remembered when similar events which lead up to it are not. Māhgol sometimes jumps ahead to narrate a climactic scene in a series, omitting the similar episodes leading up to the final event. A dramatic example of this appears in E, her second recording of Mār Čučeh, in which the snake's first two murder attempts conflate with the final one.

In D, Māhgol simply forgets that she has not told of the elder boy's death. Despite her mother's reminder at D.65, "He hasn't killed the brother," Māhgol makes no mention of the death or of Mār Čučeh's revenge motive farther along in the story, either. Whether they get no mention because they are not important for her, or because she takes them for granted, or simply because her nervousness in performance caused temporary memory lapse, is impossible to say, but the fact of their omission from her narrative confirms that these elements are detachable in transmission. Examples supplied by Friedl (personal communication) verify that variants lacking the death of the brother and/or the revenge motive are current in Iranian oral tradition (see p. 70 above); here we see one such variant created. Mādar Zāher's retention of the revenge motive (cf. C.177, Mār Čučeh's speech to the surviving wife) and Māhgol's subsequent reintroduction of the boy's death (E.49) illustrate the multiple possibilities for reversible variation within a few, closely related performances of a single story (see pp. 75-76 above).

In the final episode of the story, Māhgol's narration omits any detailed description of the host's treatment of the vizier and Mār Čučeh in his guesthouse. More significantly, she also omits Mār Čučeh's false promise to the vizier that he will take the boots out and clean them. At D.134, Mār Čučeh simply tells the vizier how _he_ can take them and clean them himself without being detected (cf. A.157,166). In _D_, Mār Čučeh's prior promise to take the boots out is only implied by his subsequent refusal to do so (D.135). By omitting the deceptive plan, Māhgol limits Mār Čučeh's treachery in this incident to his denunciation of the fleeing vizier to their host (D.139). Like Mādar Zāher's rendition of the pick incident, (C.106 ff.), Māhgol's simplification of this final episode eliminates the theme of word/reality relationships which was central to Mār Čučeh's strategy throughout Adī's story, and culminated in Mār Čučeh's false promise to the vizier. Given Māhgol's difficulties with verbal nuances of other kinds (see pp. 111 ff. above), it is not surprising that she loses this bit of detail, even though she preserves the final episode (D.128-142) which her mother's formulation of the story eliminated (cf. p. 120, below).

3) Syntactic ordering and analogous episodes:

The similarities among successive events in a story, although they facilitate the progressive reconstruction of detail, can also be a source of confusion for an unskilled narrator. At D.73, Mār Čučeh is preparing to take the vizier's child out to urinate, and he says, "Find the _matches_, light a lamp." While Mār Čučeh is feeling around in the dark, he finds the sack-sewing bodkin with which he later threatens the little girl. Māhgol's inclusion of matches in this nighttime incident is perfectly logical, but it is not a detail supplied by either Adī or Mādar Zāher (cf. A.80, C.81). His finding the bodkin when he pretends to look for matches is, however, analogous to his finding the matches when he pretends to look for a rope, in preparation for the wood-gathering expedition during which he burns his father (A.58, D.46). The appearance of the matches in the first incident probably suggested to Māhgol their use in this analogous incident. Moreover, there is no way to determine whether the interpolation of this bit of detail was by a process of conscious analogy, or just a fortuitous example of confusion between analogous episodes.

Other inclusions of detail are more clearly the product of analogy, but they function less well in their new contexts. When Mār Čučeh returns home to kill his mother (D.54), Māhgol has him say, "Why didn't you make anything to eat with [the bread] today?," a comment which belongs to the first murder attempt, not the third (cf. Mādar Zāher's interpolation of a quarrel at this point, C.58-61, and discussion, p.121 , below.).To punish the wife who has not started the cooking, Māhgol supplies him with a shovel out of context, with which he strikes and kills her.

Mādar Zāher in C has added a murder to Mār Čučeh's exploits which reiterates certain ideas in the story in a coherent fashion (see discussion, p. 91 above). Māhgol includes this incident which her mother added, and moves it to the initial position in Mār Čučeh's multiple revenge on the vizier (D.64-70). She also gives the vizier yet another wife. Multiple marriage is usually a rich man's prerogative in Afghanistan, due to the substantial bride-prices involved, and four wives are the maximum legal number Islamic law, so the vizier's four wives in Māhgol's story are an

appropriate indication of his status and wealth. However, Māhgol has difficulty integrating the fourth wife into the plot. The vizier has two
wives left by the time everyone arrives at the river, and Māhgol tries
to incorporate them both into the drowning plan:

> This vizier said to his wife, "When night comes, this Mār
> Čučeh - over there - one - you take one foot, and this wife can
> take one foot, and I'll take his two arms [MZ: Laughing comment
> (inaudible)] and we'll throw him in the river . . ." (D.122)

but this creates difficulties when Mār Čučeh must take the place of one

of the wives:

> . . .He went, and picked up the vizier's wife, put this - vizier's
> wife - into his own bed. He went, and lay down in the vizier's
> bed, right next to him. As the night went on, it got to be mid-
> night, and he taps the vizier's wife, like that. He says, "Get
> up, let's throw Mār Čučeh in the river." [Laughter]
>   She didn't (see), and he woke up the other wife. It was
> dark, so they didn't see. [Laughter] And he'd put on the
> vizier's clothes, too. These clothes - so he did that. This -
> this wife took one of his feet, and that wife took the other, and
> he took his two arms, and the <u>threw</u> him in the river! Then they
> went back to sleep. He threw him in the river, and they went
> back to sleep. [MZ: (They threw) the vizier!] Yes. [MM: Oh,
> OK.] They threw him in the river, then they went back to sleep.
> He, he threw another wife into the river. There's one left.
> When this wife lay down - when this youngest wife lay down, he
> threw the other wife in the river. (pauses) - Yeah. I made a
> mistake. He threw that vizier's wife in the river. He didn't
> throw the vizier. He - m - did this. He - n - when morning
> came, then he, he'd thrown both his wives in, into that stream,
> and this vizier, with the vizier, then, when morning came, he
> went on. He went, they went, like that. (D.125-127)

The problem of the surplus wife compounds Māhgol's confusion over which
version of this scene to choose as her model, her mother's version or
Adī's. She even manages to conflate the two by having the vizier <u>and</u> a
wife thrown in the river at one point, before settling on an arrangement
by which both wives are drowned and the vizier survives. In this final
configuration Māhgol's inclusion of a fourth wife is clearly non-functional

and redundant.

Māhgol's repetition of detail in non-functional positions reaches a comical extreme at D.91, where she has Mār Čučeh complain of the vizier's wife, "She doesn't pee -", an error which provokes general laughter and obviously derives from the previous murder scene, where at D.81, he complains of the vizier's little daughter, "She isn't peeing." This misstatement suggests that the reduplication of detail by analogy in parallel incidents, even though it may work quite logically, as in the case of the matches, is not a conscious, intellectual use of parallelisms, but a basic narrative technique which is applied rather mechanically, even absent-mindedly at times, by this relatively unskilled storyteller. A number of reduplications in Māhgol's narrative which are non-functional in moving the plot forward, and which lack the minimal differences needed to give meaningful structure to the repetitive pattern, suggest that reduplication as a narrative and mnemonic device is learned at a relatively early stage in the acquisition of narrative skills, while the discrimination and arrangement of minimal differences to distinguish similar incidents is learned later. This latter hypothesis is supported by Māhgol's observable tendency to conflate similar incidents such as the two boys' first encounters with the vizier.

4) Elements Māhgol retains from Adī's Mār Čučeh, which Mādar Zāher omits or alters; and

5) Elements common to Māhgol's narrative and her mother's which are alterations of Adī's original:

To some extent Mādar Zāher shares Māhgol's difficulties with the organization of new narrative material. She, too, tends to omit

preliminary details which are necessary to the working out of subsequent
events, and occasionally Māhgol retains significant details which her
mother omits, such as the water glass (see p. 59 , above). Mādar Zāher
omits the snake's directions for the magic wedding, which Māhgol includes
(D.23). At C.23 Mādar Zāher simply describes the wedding, without pre-
liminaries. This is curious in that a multiform of the magic wedding, a
complete plan/execution sequence, appears elsewhere in her repertoire
(see G.42-43 in Mādar Zāher's story Xasteh Xomār). Lack of familiarity
with the material cannot explain Mādar Zāher's omission of the planning
scene in Mār Čučeh. Her very familiarity with this common element, and/or
the presumed familiarity of the audience with it, coupled with her expressed dissatisfaction with the story as a whole, may have induced her
not to spin this episode out to its full length. It is sufficient for
present purposes to note that the truncation of episodes in a performance
does not always proceed from lack of familiarity.

When Mādar Zāher tells of the snake's first murder attempt, she
does exhibit some of the same confusion over verb tenses which confused
Māhgol's narration:

> She baked the bread and he came, then, after that, "He'll
> say, 'Ma, why didn't you make anything to go with the bread?'
> You say,'Oh, Mother's dear all right, then, today I had a lot
> of work, you go and get some ghee for yourself from the jar.'
> I'll go and get in the ghee jar, and when he comes . . ." (C.27)

Mādar Zāher retains the important detail of Mār Čučeh's overhearing, (C.26),
but in an attenuated form, not with the emphasis on distant and secret
reconnaissance which marks Adī's three repetitions of this detail (A.36,
45,50). At C.31, Mādar Zāher omits the snake child's preposterous-sounding warning to his brother. Māhgol reproduces Adī's warning exactly (D.36).

Mādar Zāher omits mention of Mār Čučeh's eavesdropping from the snake's second murder plan, and she generalizes Mār Čučeh's warning and changes its position (C.37, cf. discussion, pp. 88 ff. , above), whereas Māhgol once again reproduces Adī's form of the warning (D.40), and in the second planning episode introduces the eavesdropping, which she has omitted from the previous planning sequence. Patterns of omission which are indicative of progressive reconstruction of an imperfectly remembered story are characterized by the successively greater elaboration of analogous events in a series, such as Māhgol's storytelling reveals. Mādar Zāher's storytelling reveals other omission patterns as well, whereby details are omitted from later episodes in an analogous series, which she has included in earlier events of the series, and thus demonstrably knows. Mādar Zāher also omits details from episodes such as the magic wedding, which she can be demonstrated to know from other stories in her repertoire. The result of these omissions, at the structural level, is that new minimal differences are articulated among the analogous events in a series, and new meaning structures may emerge, such as the progressive development of Mār Čučeh's circumspect strategy with regard to his father, the pattern which emerges from Mādar Zāher's successive alterations ih the 'warning' theme.

Māhgol's selection of details from her mother's variant of Mār Čučeh, or from Adī's, often seems eclectic and random. In addition, Māhgol interpolates details of her own which her mother later adopts. Māhgol, like Adī, states simply that the human boy 'forgot' to tell his mother of the snake's first proposal, rather than elaborating on his mental process, as does Mādar Zāher (cf. A.18, C.12, D.9, E.10, but F.14, where forgetting is implied, a reversion to Adī's form). Mādar Zāher includes details of Mār Čučeh's early growth, as Adī does, but Māhgol omits them (C.24, D.26-27,

E.29). Mādar Zāher, like Adī, describes Mār Čučeh keeping watch and catching sight of his father's head inside his brother's firewood bundle (A.59, C.49), but Māhgol simply has him burn the pile, without reconnaissance (D.46-49). Both Adī and Mādar Zāher give Mār Čučeh a recapitulatory speech after he has killed his father, in which the joint guilt of mother and father is made clear (A.62, C.54-56), and Mādar Zāher in fact elaborates this recapitulation to almost twice the length of Adī's, reporting the snake's speech to his wife verbatim. By contrast, Māhgol's recapitulation is extremely short and enigmatic, although the 'slot' is present:

> He said, this one said, "Why did you do that?"
> He said, "Ohhh, I burnt Papa!" [Quiet laughter] He said, "I burnt Papa," he - m - said, "And now, I'm going to kill Ma, too."
> He said, "How do you mean, you'll kill (Ma)?"
> He said, "I'm going to kill Ma."   (D.50-53)

Mār Čučeh's justification for killing his mother comes after the fact in Mahgol's narrative (D.56).

Like her mother, Māhgol has Mār Čučeh pick a quarrel with his mother before he kills her, mitigating the abruptness of the murder as described by Adī (A.62, C.58-62, D.54-55). Māhgol's attempt to create a quarrel is analogous to previous interchanges between the elder boy and his mother but does not fit logically; the mother withholds food for no reason (see discussion, p. 89 , above). Mādar Zāher leaves vague the subject of the quarrel she invents:

> He said, - I don't know what - whether he said, "Give us water," or whether he said, "Why haven't you put this pot on the fire",

but reconstructive use of analogy is obvious in both the interchanges.

Māhgol omits her mother's pun, *Māla jam ko*, from the direction-giving scene which precedes the vizier's departure for the wedding (D.99;

cf. A.10, C.142,144), though she retains Adī's pun on *bastan*, 'tie, fasten, lock,' with reference to the gate tied to Mār Čučeh's back. She also includes the order to remain in the house and guard it, which Mādar Zāher had added at this point. This order took the place of the vizier's giving Mār Čučeh permission to come to the wedding, which was explicit in Adī's version. Omitting the permission to attend the wedding, both Mādar Zāher and Māhgol fundamentally change the nature of Mār Čučeh's disobedience to the vizier. In Adī's version, Mār Čučeh plays the fool, pretending to carry out the vizier's orders literally while being as destructive as possible. He then appeals to the wedding guests to witness how carefully he has carried out the vizier's orders (A.120). He has made all his destructive acts up to this point look like strict obedience to orders. The element of disobedience in Mār Čučeh's attendance at the wedding, in Mādar Zāher's and Māhgol's versions, undermines the irony of his perfect self-righteousness (C.151,D.108).

Māhgol corrects her mother concerning the killing of the cows, an incident which her mother seems inclined to omit (C.153), but Mādar Zāher nonetheless accepts that correction gracefully. Māhgol corrects her again at C.155, concerning the vizier's directions to Mār Čučeh:

> (whispers) He didn't either say, "I hit them," he said, "Go, let the cows out . . ."

Māhgol's correction reveals an excellent recollection of Adī's words (A.127):

> "Get up, and take your cows out to join the herd, because the herd is leaving!"

but despite her vocal objections to the dialogue Mādar Zāher substitutes at this point,

He said, "I filled the mangers, and I said, 'Eat!' and they
didn't eat, and I said - I hit them! I said, 'Eat!' So now
they're eating."   (C.157)

when Mãhgol comes to tell this incident herself, she tells it very much as

her mother did:

He said, "Go, the cows - uh - give the cows some hay, give
them some straw."

He did this - he went, he - m - he didn't give them anything,
he just pulls their tails up like this, and he yells, "Lord
Vizier! They don't eat." (giggles) "Lord Vizier, they don't eat."

He said - when he came, he saw that they had been killed,
when he lifted their muzzles, lifted their heads, he saw that
they were dead, that their heads had been cut right off. He
said, "Why did you do like that?"

He said, "But didn't you sa - you said, 'Give the cows hay,
give them straw,' so I gave them straw, but they didn't eat.
They didn't eat."   (D.111-112)

Note that Mãdar Zãher works a close analogy to the two preceding murder

scenes into this incident, through the vizier's command, "Hit them!",

once again a bit of detail which is not particularly appropriate (cf. pp.

81-82, above). Mãdar Zãher's dialogue between the vizier and Mãr Čučeh has

a rationalist tendency, whereas Adĩ did not give Mãr Čučeh any rationale

for killing the cows, nor did she make the exchange between the vizier

and Mãr Čučeh explanatory in nature. Only the vizier's anger is expressed,

and Mãr Čučeh's reciprocal anger (A.126-128).

When the vizier and his wife try to escape, Mãr Čučeh simply antici-

pates the escape route in Mãhgol's version as he does in Adĩ's. In other

respects, such as the expressed hostility of the vizier (D.119), the escape

plan and its unsuccessful execution which Mãhgol describes are much closer

to her mother's version than they are to Adĩ's (see below), up to D.122,

where Mãhgol produces the plot against Mãr Čučeh (missing in her mother's version, cf. C.171-172), but puts it in the mouth of the vizier. (In Adī's version the vizier's surviving wife instigates both the escape attempt and the drowning plot.) In Mādar Zāher's narrative as we have seen, (C.160-163, discussion p. 76 ff.), the vizier becomes the instigator of the escape plan and the murder plan is omitted. We may interpret Mādar Zāher's omission of the murder plot as an instance of the reduction of planning and preliminary episodes, as we have seen elsewhere in both Mādar Zāher's and Māhgol's first performances of this story, but in her case this particular omission contributes to a general pattern of thematically related omissions and alterations.

Māhgol's omissions seem less unified thematically. She retains the murder plot, but as her mother has done with the escape attempt, she makes the vizier the instigator of the hostility toward Mār Čučeh, a transfer of roles which coincides with her mother's overall reduction of the hostile role of women (see pp. 76 ff.) and which her mother adopts when she reintroduces the murder plan at F.131. Māhgol is also responsible for the introduction of the element of disguise in Mār Čučeh's impersonation of his victim (D.126), which Mādar Zāher adopts in E and F (E.151, F.134), even after Māhgol has dropped it from her second performance (E.123).

In the matter of the presence or absence of a murder plot against Mār Čučeh, and the passive or active roles of the vizier's wives, Māhgol compromises between her mother's version of the story and Adī's. Where compromise becomes impossible, and she must decide who will be drowned, great confusion ensues (D.126-127; see pp. 120 f.). It is Adī's formulation, with the vizier surviving, which finally wins out, and Mādar Zāher does not object, which is striking in view of her own reformulation of the ending (C.172 ff.) and her strenuous objections to Māhgol's performance six months later (E.120; see below).

The remainder of D is Māhgol's version of the episode in the guest-house, which Mādar Zāher omits from both her performances of the story. Māhgol, like Adī in A, leaves Mār Čučeh victorious over the vizier but to-tally devoid of social connections or property.

In D, Māhgol separates the incident her mother added from the se-quence of Mār Čučeh's vengeful acts against the vizier which Adī has supplied, and places her mother's incident, concerning the vizier's guests and the wife's failure to prepare food for them, first in the series. Mādar Zāher integrated this incident into Adī's series, making it fit the conceptual geography which the original series presented, which progresses from pri-vate (domestic) to public social spheres (pp.59-63, above). As Māhgol's grasp of minimal differences among similar incidents is weak, so also is her grasp of the syntactic relations among them: her ordering of the events in D, placing the incident her mother added first, destroys the sequential arrangement of social domains from most private to most public.

In E, although Māhgol omits the incident her mother added, she also changes the order of Adī's original five events, placing the invitation to the wedding and its aftermath first, then the murder of the child, then that of her mother, then that of the second wife and finally the humilia-tion and incarceration of the vizier. Although this order of events does not preserve the systematic progress through social domains shown by the older women's narratives, it has a syntactic order of its own. The losses which the vizier suffers are progressively more severe: first he loses his cattle and household goods, then his child, then his wife, the mother of the child, then his younger (and more desirable) wife, and finally his own freedom and position. With regard to the wives, "youngest last and best" is a principle of selection throughout world folktale, and particularly explicit with regard to marriage partners in Afghan tales, where the youngest potential spouse is always the most promising and desirable. On one occasion when I was the guest of a prominent village headman near Herat, my research assistant remarked, "He put you in his youngest wife's room (for the night) because he wanted to show her off." The preference of husban·s for younger wives (as well as the jealousy of elder wives) is proverbial and forms the basis of many tales and anecdotes. Although Māhgol's ordering of events seems to be in flux in these two performances, her own syntactic arrangement begins to take form in E. Adi's original thematic arrangement, which moved Mār Čučeh's exploits into ever more socialized domains, accommodated Mādar Zāher's concern with social proprieties very well (see pp. 100 ff), and she retained and even elaborated that thematic progression. Māhgol's arrangement of the episodes shows an entirely new ordering principle, which focuses on the severity of the vizier's losses rather than the social setting of Mār Čučeh's depradations.

In the resolution of her tale, Māhgol opted for Adī's construction of Mār Čučeh, rather than her mother's. In certain secondary aspects, Māhgol's version of Mār Čučeh more closely resembles her mother's than Adī's, as in the power relations expressed between the vizier and his wife (D.105), and the vizier's directions to Mār Čučeh when leaving for the wedding, which include the order to stay home and guard the house. In certain details, Māhgol's version of Mār Čučeh can be seen to influence her mother's later performance of the tale, with regard to the disguise element and the vizier's part in the murder plot.

Māhgol, like her mother, tends to put confrontation between the vizier and Mār Čučeh in the form of demands for rational explanations of Mār Čučeh's destructive acts (D.107,112). Twice, however, she omits mention of any confrontation, in the deaths of the first and last wives (D.70, 126) where by analogy with other events they might be expected to occur. In the context of confrontation and elsewhere, Māhgol and Mādar Zāher use less profanity than Adī does. Adī's profanity in A provoked some laughter and raised eyebrows. Neither Mādar Zāher nor Māhgol revile Mār Čučeh's mother in the same profane terms Adī uses (A.35). Mādar Zāher, telling of Mār Čučeh's three successive threats to the little girl, goes from "I'll fill your body full of holes" (C.81) to "I'll fill your ass with holes" (C.96). She gradually works up to using the indelicate word (cf. C.89: "If you pee, this ass of yours - body of yours, I'll fill it full of holes!") which Māhgol avoids using at all (cf. D.78,80). The cursing that ensues between the vizier and Mār Čučeh is also less vehement in Mādar Zāher's rendering, and the confrontations are further attenuated in Māhgol's story (cf. E.97-98). Although age commands respect, there is also license attached to age, particularly for older women, who are normally the primary negotiators in sexual matters (whether the licit variety - arranged marriage - or the illicit, as in folktales where they are commonly go-betweens for lovers). Older women are considered to be outspoken and are in fact permitted to be so. Both Adī's village background and her status as senior woman in this group may have affected her greater use of profanity, compared to that of the younger people.

Other details of Mādar Zāher's and Māhgol's style point to their shared concern with other social proprieties. Māhgol, like her mother, shows a greater interest in public social ceremonies and proprieties than does Adī, primarily in her choice of detail, as when she alludes to the vizier's loss of face at the wedding (D.105). Māhgol and her mother both describe the funerals of the boys' mother and the vizier's various wives (see discussion, pp. 100-1, cf. D.70-71, 98), whereas Adī has emphasized the lack of ceremony associated with these deaths (A.63,96,109). At the structural level, however, Māhgol does not preserve the story's arrangement in terms of social domains, as we have already seen (p. 128).

Māhgol's second performance of Mār Čučeh exhibits the reversion phenomenon mentioned above (pp. 114-115, 117) in many details, such as the rope which replaces a gunny sack as equipment for the wood-gathering expedition (E.37, cf. D.43). Small children among the poor in Afghan cities are sent out into the streets with sacks or buckets to scavenge bits of wood, straw and paper for use as fuel, and Māhgol thinks of this familiar sight at D.43, when she describes the boys' preparations for fuel-gathering. Like her mother and other traditional narrators (see pp.101f. above), she draws freely on her own observations of real life to describe the daily lives of folktale characters. In the second performance of the tale, she foregoes this detail with which she is familiar, and reverts to Adī's form of the incident: Mār Čučeh, in imitation of his brother, searches for a rope, the tool of adult thorn-cutters. In the study of transmission or tale-learning, this reversion phenomenon must be taken into account. The first performance of a new item of repertoire may show major and minor divergences from the 'original' upon which the storyteller is modelling his or her performance, but these divergences may disappear in subsequent performances, with the progressive reconstruction of the 'original'. To describe variation in transmission accurately, one must take into account this reversion effect, and record several performances of new repertoire, preferably on

several occasions when time and other performances have intervened between
the storyteller's learning and performing the new story for the first time.

There are numerous examples of reversion in both Māhgol's and Madar
Zaher's second performances of Mār Čučeh. At E.42, Māhgol has dropped
the argument between mother and son which Mādar Zāher added at this point,
and has made the murder abrupt as it was in Adī's original telling (cf.
A.63, C.58-62, D.54-56, and discussion, p. 89 above). Mādar Zāher follows suit at F.66, reverting to the abrupt and simple form of the murder
scene.

Māhgol remembers the episode of Mār Čučeh's brother's murder in E
which she omitted from D. Moreover, when she tells how Mār Čučeh got the
news of his brother's death, she tells it Adī's way. Delivered information (E.49: "When his brother got word"), rather than worry, prompts Mār
Čučeh's reconnaissance. Mādar Zāher's version of this sequence stressed
Mār Čučeh's internal mental processes, rather than external agency (cf.
A.69, C.72, F.75,77 and discussion, pp. 88 ff.   ).

A number of other reversions are visible throughout Māhgol's second
performance. At E.112, Māhgol describes Mār Čučeh at the bridge, craning
his neck to scare the vizier's horse just as he did in Adī's version (A.
135). By contrast, in her original D version, Māhgol made Mār Čučeh knock
on the bridge to frighten the horse.

At E.118, Māhgol once more makes the vizier's wife the instigator
of the drowning scheme, as Adī has done (cf. A.138, C.172, D.122, E.150,
F.131). By contrast, when Mādar Zāher includes the scheme again, she puts
it in the vizier's own mouth (see pp.76ff.above), as Māhgol did in her first
version (D.121). In the confusion that ensues over the drowning scene in

E̲ Māhgol later puts the plot <u>back</u> in the vizier's mouth (E.121), under her mother's direct influence, for when Māhgol asks, "Where was I?" (E. 119), Mādar Zāher supplies the catch phrase, "Where the <u>vizier</u> said to <u>her</u>" (E.120). Māhgol's tendency to reversion in this instance is complicated by her mother's direct attempts to control the structure of her story.

At. E.133 Māhgol includes Mār Čučeh's false promise to the vizier which she omitted in D̲. . The host's invitation and his recapitulation of the vizier's offenses are elaborated in E̲, with more extensive verbal parallels between the event and the recapitulation than are developed in D̲ (cf. D.128-129,139, E.128-129,137,140). The second recapitulation allows Māhgol to reconstruct Adī's version of this incident in still greater detail.

Text E̲ exhibits many of the basic confusions and coherency problems from which Māhgol's first performance also suffered. There are new problems as well: she turns the snake into a lion, but eventually (E.37) accepts her brother's correction on this point, and settles on calling the monster a 'dragon,' /aždahār/. The snake's three murder attempts have collapsed into one (E.30-38), which even omits mention of the monster father's initiating the plan to kill his stepson. Māhgol has reinstated the episode of the boy's murder by the vizier, however (E.48). The collapse of analogous incidents into each other and their rearticulation in subsequent performances, which can be observed in Māhgol's storytelling, can thus be seen to be a perpetually reversible process. We have observed that even more skilled storytellers, such as Mādar Zāher, will omit elements in one performance, only to have them reappear in subsequent performances. (This

phenomenon is also implicit in Adī's performance of <u>Afsāneh-e Garg</u>, discussed in Ch. IV, below.) Nevertheless, one cannot dismiss such omissions
as insignificant simply because they are ephemeral. Transmission consists
of a series of epemeral performance moments, of single exchanges between
storytellers and learners. The degree to which the learning of a given
story is a summary process, a compilation of several hearings, is problematical. The relative frequency of performance of any given tale (an important factor, mentioned in no study of performance that I know), must affect the degree to which one can learn it by summary process.[1] When a
story is infrequently performed, the chances are greater that ephemeral
omission or transpositions of events will be carried over in transmission,
for lack of counter-examples in subsequent performances. Different storytellers' dispositions also figure in the matter, as there are those who
are disposed to compare and integrate variants and those who are not. A
performance which is 'incomplete' in comparison to the 'original' on which
the storyteller modeled his or her narrative may occur at any time.[2]

Factors influencing completeness, besides the storytellers' familiarity with the story, include such things as audience attention and
the space of time available for the story's performance. What must be
stressed, in analyzing transmission events, is the range of choice available to the storyteller and the reversible nature of the choices he or she

---

[1] Frequent performance also tends to stabilize the performer's version
of the tale (cf. Bartlett, 1932:63), though ephemeral changes continue
to occur.

[2] The term 'original' used in this discussion, means <u>only</u> the performance(s)
of other storytellers from which the performer in question learned (or
believes he or she learned) a given story. It is not meant to imply the
existence of a 'correct' version, an 'Urform,' or anything of that
sort.

makes. 'Choice is not necessarily a conscious intellectual process, but the tradition consistently supplies alternatives and the storyteller selects among them. In E, we have a recorded instance of two storytellers defending alternative choices, both based on the same 'original' performance. Both storytellers profess themselves to be accurately reproducing the 'same story'.

In general, Māhgol's choices between her mother's version of Mār Čučeh and Adī's seem to be eclectic and random. She chooses Adī's ending, but in many ways she accepts, even extends the changes in detail which her mother used in her reformulation of the story's total structure, including such things as the reduction of profanity and confrontation, and the passive portrayal of women. Māhgol's uncertainty about how Mār Čučeh should be told, and her attempts to integrate her mother's version of the story with Adī's, are most clearly exemplified by the drowning episode in E. By the time of her second performance, she is disposed to defend the choice of Adī's ending very strongly. Awareness of alternatives and the disposition to defend a given way of telling a story do not mean that the storyteller made a conscious choice from among what s/he perceived to be alternative possibilities. Consciousness of alternatives may in fact limit the reversion effect described above, may tend to 'fix' the narrator's way of telling a story.

In Text E, there are two recorded occasions when Mādar Zāher and Māhgol, both most definitely and vocally aware of alternatives, defend the correctness of their respective versions of the story's events. This spirited defense of their different alternatives came six months after they heard the story from Adī. The first occasion for argument comes with the episode of the pick and the quarrel with the vizier's first wife, in

which Māhgol insists on Adī's version of the argument, with Mār Čučeh ir-
rationally shouting "Gimme!", while Mādar Zāher tries to interject her
construction of the event, in which Mār Čučeh hides the tool in question
and presents his demand as a rational request (E.101). Even more significantly for the overall structure of the tale, Māhgol and Mādar Zāher come
to vocal disagreement over the drowning incident. As has been noted above,
Māhgol's performance D, in which she elects Adī's version of the drowning
incident after some indecision, provoked no criticism from Mādar Zāher,
only a single clarifying comment:

> . . . He threw him in the river, and they went back to sleep.
> [MZ: (They threw) the vizier.] Yes . . .   (D.126)

When Māhgol says, a few lines later, "I made a mistake. He threw that
vizier's _wife_ in the river," (D.127), Mādar Zāher makes no protest. Six
months later, with greater distance from Adī's model performances, Mādar
Zāher repeatedly attempts to take over her daughter's performance, starting from Māhgol's first display of uncertainty over the drowning episode
(E.120-123). She finally shouts, "You're making mistakes! It was like
this -" (E.120). After Māhgol completes her performance, Mādar Zāher tells
her own version of the ending (E.144-156), starting from the point where
she makes the vizier the instigator of the escape plan:

> Now it was in my mind that when he says, the place where - this -
> yeah, these, when he said, said to his wife . . .

and ending with the repeated assertion, "Adī told it just like that! Adī
told it just like that." (E.158). This latter assertion is a direct response to Māhgol's protest, "He didn't do things like that, that -" (E.
157). Māhgol appeals to her little sister as a witness: "Šāhgol, you --"
(E.159), but her mother denies the younger girl a voice: "You don't know

it, like that - you - What do I know? Adī told it like that." (E.160)

Reassignment of actions and dramatic roles, especially with regard to the drowning episode, is facilitated by linguistic ambiguity: in Persian, the single pronoun, /ū/ serve for both 'he' and 'she,' and this ambiguity of pronominal reference allows Mādar Zāher to manipulate Mähgol's attempt to assign roles to the vizier and his wife (D.126, E.121). At several other points in the six texts, comments by the audience indicate that they find certain pronominal references ambiguous. In A text, this problem becomes extremely obvious as Mādar Zāher asks for clarifications of pronominal reference repeatedly throughout the section of the story where Mār Čučeh replaces his elder brother as the main character in the narrative (A.34,35,36,39,45,49,54,58,59,61,64,74,75). Much later (A.143), Adī volunteers a clarifying reference, "Beside - beside the vizier," to explain that Mār Čučeh has taken the wife's place in bed with the vizier, and not the reverse. This clarification was occasioned by a non-verbal cue, and exchange of questioning glances among Mādar Zāher, myself and Adī. The laughter that follows her clarification is anticipatory and expressive of ambiguous feelings: Mār Čučeh has taken a position in which he may be sexually compromised, and given the humor of profanity and scatology which dominated the story up to this point, sexual comedy of some kind was expected to ensue from Mār Čučeh's handling the vizier's wife and taking her place in his bed. That this possibility for the tale was perceived not only by me but by Mādar Zāher is borne out by her version of the tale, in which the vizier's wife is sexually compromised.

Adī pointedly resolves the ambiguity of pronominal reference in this episode because of the ambiguity of meanings which arises with Mār

Čučeh's handling the vizier's wife and taking her place in his bed. The audience becomes concerned about verbal ambiguity when the relationships among characters become ambiguous, and unresolved verbal ambiguities may also be exploited to alter such relationships in later performances. At E.118, Mähgol has made the vizier's wife the instigator of the drowning plot, but at E.120, when Mähgol has lost her place, Mädar Zäher cues her with, "Where the vizier said to her," reversing the roles. A few lines later, Mähgol says, "Mär Čučeh got up, and came, and threw this one in the river, this - " and Mädar Zäher instantly steps in to resolve the ambiguity her way, supplying "-vizier-" (E.121). Mähgol's final construction of this event (E.121) only partially succeeds at resisting her mother's influence. She makes the vizier instigate the drowning, though the wife is drowned in Mär Čučeh's place. The retributive irony of the murder is lessened, since it is not the instigator who is drowned as is the case in both Adî's and Mädar Zäher's versions.

A loosening of structure and meaning results from Mähgol's attempt to combine Mädar Zäher's version of Mär Čučeh with Adî's. Mähgol's lesser proficiency at recognizing minimal differences among events and ordering those differences so as to distinguish analogous episodes also weakens her narrative structure. Her second attempt to reconstruct the story (with her mother's help or interference) reveals two opposing processes, reformulation and reversion, which simultaneously cause diversion from and rapprochement with the 'original' tale she heard from Adî.

The same two opposing processes emerge from a comparison of Mädar Zäher's first and second recordings of Mär Čučeh, with the difference that Mädar Zäher's reformulations of the story form a consistent pattern which reduces liminality, ambiguity, irrationality and violence in the tale, and prepares the way for Mār Čučeh's final assimilation to society. By contrast, Māhgol's revisions are more eclectic, being sometimes her own innovations, sometimes her mother's, and not consistent in their thematic impact. Māhgol's eclecticism makes a detailed comparison of her narrative to those of her two models difficult to organize, but comparison serves to demonstrate the multitudinous possibilities for variation in transmission, even in such a limited consideration, which takes into account only the two most immediate influences working on this young storyteller as she shaped a single story. Other possibilities emerge, and other influences must be acknowledged, when one examines the learning process of an older, more adept storyteller, with a well developed repertoire, such as Mādar Zāher. The discussion which follows concerns Afsāneh-e Garg (Texts H, I, J), another tale which Mādar Zāher learned from Adī, and examines certain other influences, some of them extrinsic to the transmission event, which reshape tales in transmission.

The Tale of Mangy-Head

Afsāneh-e Garg supplies a second instance of Mādar Zāher learning
a tale from Adī, recording it first shortly after she learned it, and
again about six months later. The main story line of Adī's tale is unchanged in Mādar Zāher's two later versions of it. The story concerns
a poor, low-status, apparently stupid boy who encounters a wealthy, high-
status young woman, who like him is faced with an unacceptable home situation. (The girl is threatened with an unwanted marriage, the boy with
punishment, or in two versions, has already been expelled from home.) The
two meet by accident and escape together at the girl's instigation, the
boy having deceived the girl about his identity. Subsequently, she learns
that he is not the person she thought him to be; nonetheless they proceed
to another city together and set up housekeeping. Through the boy's fool-
hardy bid for favor, the king of their adopted city and his vizier become
aware that the boy possesses a wife of royal beauty. They then send the
boy off on a series of difficult errands, all but one of them involving
supernatural adversaries, in hopes that he will be killed so that the king
may take his wife.

The boy accomplishes each deed through a combination of special
help or advice, cleverness, skill, and/or trickery. In the course of the
tasks he acquires more wives, some of them supernatural, and supernatural
animal allies. Eventually, asked to perform a last, impossible task (bring
news from the world of the dead), the hero resorts to trickery against his
task-master, traps and kills his human adversaries and ascends the king's

throne.

Although Mādar Zāher's performances of Afsāneh-e Garg preserve the overall story line, major differences arise in the order and number of the boy's tasks, both between Mādar Zāher's two performances, and between Adī's recorded performance (Text H) and Mādar Zāher's performances. For the purposes of this discussion, it is important to note that Adī's recorded performance here reproduced was not the performance from which Mādar Zāher learned the story. As Mādar Zāher explains (I.330-335), she learned the story from Adī while I was absent from Herat, for the express purpose of telling it to me, in the event that Adī would have left the city before I was able to return. When I arrived in Herat, Mādar Zāher told me about the story and offered to record it immediately, even though Adī was still in the city, staying with Mādar Zāher's parents. I recorded the story from Mādar Zāher on the day of my arrival (Text I), then recorded it from Adī the next day (Text H). The two performances are presented in reverse order, Adī's standing first, in the appendix, for ease of comparison.

Mādar Zāher, telling me about the story[1], before she performed it, said, "The *garg* is like Alī Zarrīn - he goes to seven places."[2] Alī Zarrīn is a story in Mādar Zāher's active repertoire, one of the first two she told me, at our first meeting in April, 1975. It shares whole episodes, as well as general structure, with Afsāneh-e Garg. For purposes of comparison, an abridged translation of her first performance of that story will be found in text K. Mādar Zāher's comment about the two tales struck

---

[1] Unfortunately, this conversation, prior to recording I_ text, was not recorded.

[2] /be haft jā mīreh/.

me, because it seemed to indicate that she organized her knowledge of both stories schematically, in terms of a numbered list of tasks. Of the three performances of Afsāneh-e Garg, however, it is only in Mādar Zāher's first version of the tale that the main character actually performs seven tasks. In Adī's telling, he performs six, and in Mādar Zāher's later performance, (Text J), only five. From the texts alone, it would be impossible to tell whether Mādar Zāher interpolated episodes into performance I, to bring the number up to seven, or whether in fact Adī omitted portions of the story she told to Mādar Zāher, when she recorded it for me. Adī's concluding summary and her response to Mādar Zāher's corrective remarks, at the end of H, verify that the episode of the Tree of Bells, which Adī omitted from performance H, is actually part of the story as she knows it:

(H.227, Adī speaking rhetorically to the hero's dead adversaries:)
". . . you started with what was on earth, sending him to the
*div*s in their lairs, and you sent the poor guy running after the
Horse of Forty Colts with her forty *dīv* colts, and she was the
forty-first. He brought her. Lions, like that - you said,
'lions' milk, in a lion's skin, on a lion's back,' - [MZ: 'bring
it'-] - the poor guy brought it - 'because my children have the
"little fire".' [MZ: As a pretext.] As a pretext. So they
would eat him. You said, 'A *dīv* carried off my sister,' and he
brought her, too. Look at the *part* he brought on account of those
pearls. [MZ: The Tree of Bells.] The Tree of Bells and Cats'
Claws, he - he brought them, think of it . . ."

Not only does Adī accept Mādar Zāher's inclusion of the Tree of Bells episode, but she gives it a fuller name, which Mādar Zāher has abbreviated. Clearly, this episode formed part of Adī's narrative when Mādar Zāher learned it, about ten days before.

Having dispensed with the possibility of Mādar Zāher's interpolating tasks not present in Adī's Afsāneh-e Garg, we are left with the changes of omission and ordering which Mādar Zāher did effect in the story. As stated in the introduction (pp. 7-9   ), the type of structural analysis used here seeks to describe the repetitive events of folktale in terms of their distinguishing features and their interrelations, to discover whether such events are presented in a discernible order, and what part such an order plays in transmission, if it is present. The conceptual categories presented by a series of tasks such as those of Garg must first be described according to their similarities and differences. Once they have been so described, it becomes possible to see whether their distinctive features have any relationship to each other. For instance, are the tasks distinguished by the type of challenge they present to the hero? By their locale? By the type of object or person which is their goal? By the tactics he must employ to succeed? By the type of adversary? By their net effect on the hero, his immediate adversary, or on the person who set the task?

On the surface, in terms of plot structure, the significance of all the tasks is the same: each is set by the hero's undeclared enemy, and intended to do away with him. They all fail in their purpose, and each time the hero gains something by his success. If they all make one 'point,' then why the repetition? Folk narrative scholars have come from a variety of perspectives to the same basic observation, that repetition in traditional narrative marks significant structures.[1] There is the simple effect of emphasis which Olrik noted: the hero's repeated success stresses his special ability to overcome obstacles, either by good fortune or skill.

---

[1] One may contrast Olrik's literary-stylistic perspective (1965:132-33), Dell Hymes' structural one (1975:34), and Albert Lord's thematic emphasis (1965:220).

The last success, of course, is climactic and thus distinct from the others, in that it permanently resolves the hero's difficulties. It has this definitive effect, however , because in it the hero changes his tactics. If the other tasks are scrutinized for features besides their narrative effect, they are found to be similarly distinguished from each other. The most efficient way to present these differences is a synoptic diagram, listing each episode by its common and distinctive features. Each performance will be synopsized separately, in the same fashion. (Diagrams I through :V:).

Adī's story (Text H) may be divided into seven episodes, each one comprised of a problem presented to the main character, a complicating sequence in which various directions are given and carried out, and a resolution to that particular problem, which includes changes in the hero's personal status and resources (Diagram I). In all cases, the resolution of the episode involves a net gain for the hero, and these gains are always either wives, supernatural allies, or both. In all cases, these personages are female. The hero's gains look like this:

Episode 1) Human wife and household, wealth (= social power)
        2) Supernatural wife (= permanent supernatural ally)
        3) Human wife
        4) Supernatural♀animal ally (temporary) - the Horse
        5) (Supernatural?)♀animal ally (temporary) - the lion
        6) Supernatural wife (= permanent supernatural ally)

The hero's prizes are basically of only three types, combining the qualities of female sex, natural/supernatural, human/animal, and temporary/permanent ally, in different ways. The permutations of these qualities are not presented in any immediately obvious order, however. The human and *part* wives are acquired alternately, but this pattern is interrupted before its last term by the acquisition of the two animal helpers, one

DIAGRAM I

(Synopsis of Text H)

Episode

I: 1) Princess with lover engaged against her will — Problem # 1

Orphan cowherd loses calf and leaves home in fear of grandmother (♀ directions, help) — Complicating sequence

2) Princess and Garg escape together (mistake/trickery) (♀ directions, help)

2a) Princess and Garg find pearls (♀ reconnaissance, directions), Princess treats Garg's head (♀ help)

2b) Princess and Garg set up house together — Resolution

2c) Net result: gain for Garg [Physical security (home), wife #1 (Human A)]

II: 3) Garg presents pearls to king. — Problem # 2*

4) First task: fetch more pearls — Complication

4a) ♀ reconnaissance, ♀ directions, ♀ help

4b) tactic: stealth, trickery → physical destruction of ♂ supernatural adversary

4c) Net result: Gain for Garg [wife #2(Parī A) = supernatural ally] — Resolution

  Gain for king. [pearls]

III: 5) Second task: rescue king's sister — Problem #3

5a) ♀ directions, no help — Complication

5b) tactic: trickery → physical destruction of ♂ supernatural adversary

5c) Net result: gain for Garg [wife #3 (Human B)], O for king — Resolution

  [rescued sister given to Garg]

IV: 6) Third task: Horse of Forty Colts — Problem # 4

6a) ♀ directions, no help — Complication

6b) tactic: stealth, mutual help (feed and groom adversary) → improves state of ♂ animal supernatural adversary, who becomes an ally (temporary)

6c) Net result: gain for Garg [supernatural animal ally #1] — Resolution

  loss for king [killing of subjects, unable to keep Horse]

V: 7) Fourth task: Lion's milk, etc. — Problem # 5

7a) ♀ directions, no help — Complication

7b) tactic: stealth, skill, mutual help (rescue) → corrects negative state of ♀ animal (supernatural?) adversary, who becomes ally (temporary)

7c) Net result: Gain for Garg [animal ally #2] — Resolution

  Loss for king [killing of subjects, unwanted prize]

[Diagram I, continued]

Episode

VI: 8) Fifth task: Fetch laughing flowers — Problem # 6
   8a) ♀ directions, ♀ help — Complication
   8b) tactic: composite task: 1) feed animal supernaturals (ants, lions, leopards)
                               ii) stealth, theft, coercion to create negative state
                                   in supernatural ♀ adversary → compel her cooperation
   8c) Net result: gain for *Garg* [Wife #4 (*Pari* B) = supernatural ally]; 0 for king — Resolution

VII: 9) Sixth task: News from the Dead — Problem # 7
   9a) ♀ directions, ♀ help — Complication
   9b) tactic: trickery, escape with ♀ supernatural help → physical destruction
       of ♂ human adversary
   9c) Net result: gain for *Garg* [final escape, throne, established power] — Resolution
                   loss for king [final death]

*Structurally, (3) and (4) could be viewed as an episode, a cause and effect with negative results for
the hero, but since item 3 is also the indirect cause of items 4,5,6,7,8, & 9, it is a hidden term in
all the succeeding episodes, not resolved until the last. Its omnipresence is stressed by the repeated
comment of the *Garg*'s first wife: "Didn't I tell you . . ." (H.51,115,142,165).

DIAGRAM II

(Reconstructed form of Adī's <u>Afsāneh-e Garg</u>, complete version, last 4 episodes)

(Episode IV)

Episode

V: 7) Fourth task: Lion's milk, etc. (as in Diagram I)

VI: 8) Fifth task: The Tree of Bells   Problem # 6
       8a) ♀ directions, elder ♂ supernatural directions and help, ♂ supernatural   Complication
           'sibling' directions and help
       8b) tactic: composite task: i) physical challenge to ♂ supernatural → ally
                                    ii) skill, stealth, theft, physical challenge,
                                        sexual compromise of ♀ supernatural   [Resolution delayed]

       [8c) Resolution delayed]

VII: 9) Sixth task: Fetch Laughing Flowers
        9a) ♀ directions, ♀ help
        9b) tactic: composite task (see item (8b), Diagram I)
        9c) (See item (8c), Diagram I)

        8c: (resolution of fifth task), help from ♀ supernatural ally (from Episode IV)
            Net result: <u>gain for *Garg*</u> [Wife #5 = supernatural ally]
                        <u>loss for king</u> [city besieged, subjects killed]

VIII: 10) Seventh task: News from the Dead
          [As in Diagram I]

DIAGRAM III (Synopsis I)

P = Princess
K = "Kal" - bald boy cowherd, the hero

Episode

I:	1) Princess with lover is engaged against her will	Problem #1
	Orphan cowherd loses calf and is driven from home by his grandmother	Complication
	2) P & K escape together (mistake/trickery)	
	2a) P & K find pearls (♀ reconnaissance, directions), P heals K's head (♀ help)	
	2b) P & K set up house together	
	2c) Net result: gain for K [Home, Wife #1 (Human A)]	Resolution
II:	3) K offers pearls to king	Problem #2
	4) First task: fetch more pearls	
	4a) ♀ reconnaissance, directions, help	Complication
	4b) tactic: trickery + physical destruction of male supernatural adversary	
	4c) Net result: gain for K [Wife #2 (Parí A) = supernatural ally]; gain to king [pearls]	Resolution
III:	5) Second task: lions' milk, etc.	Problem #3
	5a) ♀ directions, no help	
	5b) tactic: stealth, skill, mutual help (corrects negative state of ♀ animal)	Complication
	5c) Net result: gain for K [animal ally (temporary)]; loss to king [subjects animals killed]	Resolution
IV:	6) Third task: rescue king's sister	Problem #4
	6a) ♀ directions, no help	
	6b) tactic: trickery + physical destruction of supernatural ♂ adversary	Complication
	6c) Net result: gain for K [Wife #3 (Human B)]; ♀ for king [gives sister to K]	Resolution
V:	7) Fourth task: Horse of Forty Colts	Problem #5
	7a) ♀ directions, no help	
	7b) tactic: stealth, mutual help (improves positive state of ♀ supernatural animal)	Complication
	7c) net result: gain for K [supernatural animal ally]; loss to king [subjects and animals killed]	Resolution

[Diagram III, continued]

Episode

VI: 8) Fifth task: Tree of Bells and Cats' Claws — Problem #6
    8a) ♀ directions, ♂ supernatural help and directions — Complication
    8b) tactic: composite task: i) physical challenge to ♂ supernatural → ally
                                ii) skill, stealth, theft, sexual compromise and
                                    physical challenge to ♂ supernatural

    [8c) Resolution deferred] — [Resolution deferred]

VII: 9) Sixth task: Laughing Flower — Problem #7
     9a) ♀ directions, old ♀ (human) help — Complication
     9b) tactic: composite task: i) mutual help (feed supernatural animal
                                    adversaries)
                                 ii) stealth, theft, sexual compromise/coertion
                                     of ♀ supernatural

     9c) Net result: gain for K [Wife #4 (*Part* B) = supernatural ally] — Resolution

     8c) (resolved with help from ♀ supernatural animal from Episode V) — Resolution 8c
         Net result: gain for K [Wife #5 (*Part* C) = supernatural ally]
                     loss to king [city besieged, 'sons,' officials, subjects
                     killed]

VIII: 10) Seventh task: Bring news from the world of the dead — Problem #8
      10a) ♀ directions, ♀ help (execution of task and rescue of hero) — Complication
      10b) tactic: trickery - physical destruction of ♂ human adversary
      10c) Net result: gain for K [escape, throne = absolute power]; loss to king — Final Resolution
                       [death]

DIAGRAM IV (Synopsis J)

P = Princess
K = Kal, bald boy cowherd

Episode

I: 1) Princess with lover is engaged against her will — **Problem #1**
    2) Orphan cowherd loses calf and is driven from home by his grandmother — **Complication**
       P & K escape together (mistake/trickery)
       2a) P & K find pearls, P treats K's head (♀ reconnaissance, directions, help)
       2b) P & K set up housekeeping together
       2c) Net result: gain for K [home, Wife #1 (Human A)] — **Resolution**

II: 3) K presents pearls to king — **Problem #2**
     4) First task: fetch more pearls — **Complication**
        4a) ♀ reconnaissance, directions, help
        4b) tactic: trickery → physical destruction of ♂ supernatural adversary
        4c) Net result: gain for K [Wife #2 (*Parī* A) = supernatural ally]; gain for king — **Resolution**
                                                                                        (pearls)

III: 5) Second task: fetch king's sister — **Problem #3**
        5a) ♀ directions, no help — **Complication**
        5b) tactic: trickery → physical destruction of ♂ supernatural adversary
        5c) Net result: gain for K [Wife #3 (Human B)]; O for king [gives sister to K] — **Resolution**

IV: 6) Third task: lions' milk, etc. — **Problem #4**
        6a) ♀ directions, no help — **Complication**
        6b) tactic: stealth, skill, mutual help   animal female adversary → ally
        6c) Net result: gain for K [♀ animal ally]; loss for king (threat to populace) — **Resolution**

V: 7) Fourth task: Laughing Flower — **Problem #5**
        7a) ♀ directions, old ♀ (human) help — **Complication**
        7b) tactic: stealth, theft, coercion of ♀ supernatural by sexual compromise
        7c) Net result: gain for K [Wife #4 (*Parī* B) = supernatural ally] — **Resolution**
                        O for king [unwanted flowers]

VI: 8) Fifth task: News from the world of the dead — **Problem #6**
        8a) ♀ directions, help (execution of task and rescue of hero) — **Complication**
        8b) tactic: trickery → physical destruction of ♂ human adversary
        8c) Net result: gain for K [final escape]; loss for king [final death] — **Resolution**

DIAGRAM V (Synopsis K)

AZ= Ali Zarrin, the hero

Episode

I: 1) Poor woman gives birth to forty sons at once — Problem #1
       1a) Father deserts family — Complication
       1b) Children grow up, attract notice of king
       1c) Vizier advises king that AZ will destroy him, he should be killed
       [1d] Resolution of father's disappearance and king's threat deferred] — [Resolution deferred]

II: 2) First task: Dig pool for king's garden — Problem #2
        2a) ♂ sibling help — Complication
        2b) Net result: O for AZ, gain for king [pool] — Resolution

III: 3) Second task: Horse of Forty Colts — Problem #3
        3a) elder ♂ supernatural directions, help — Complication
        3b) tactic: mutual help, force (uses whip)
        3c) Net result: gain for AZ [♀ supernatural animal ally (permanent)]; ? for king — Resolution

IV: 4) Third task: Head of White Div — Problem #4
        4a) ♀ supernatural animal advice and help — Complication
        4b) tactic: skill, physical destruction of ♂ supernatural (1 error)
        [4c] Resolution deferred] — [Resolution deferred]

V: 5) Fourth task: Tree of Forty Voices — Problem #5
        5a) directions, help from a) ♀ supernatural animal, b) elder ♂ supernatural, c) old ♀ supernatural — Complication
        5b) tactic: agility, stealth, theft, sexual compromise and physical challenge to ♀ supernatural (1 error)
        [5c] Resolution deferred] — [Resolution deferred]

     1d) AZ's father returns — Prob. #1 partly resolved
     3c) Kidnapping of AZ by White Div (tactic: persuasion) → supernatural ♂ ally — Prob. #4 resolved

[Diagram V, continued]

Episode

VI: 6) Fifth task: fetch Cat Meynaqā   Problem #6
   6a) ♂ supernatural advice (White Div)   Complication
   6b) tactic: mutual help/trickery of supernatural animal (unspec. sex) → ally
   6c) Net result: <u>gain for AZ</u> [supernatural animal ally]; ? for king   Resolution

VII: 5c [resolved with help of supernatural ♀ animal ally (Horse)]   Prob. #5 Resolved
     Net result: <u>gain for AZ</u> [supernatural spouse]

VIII: 1d) AZ kills king with ♂ supernatural advice (White Div), supernatural animal help   Problem #1
                                                 (Cat)   Finally
      Net result: <u>gain for AZ</u> (Throne - absolute power; Marriage) <u>loss for king</u>   Resolved
                                            (death)

clearly supernatural, the other less clearly so. Then the wife-winning se-

quence is concluded. That the second *parī* wife stands last in order, is

perhaps an instance of the 'law' of epic narrative which Olrik called the

"Importance of Initial and Final Position" (1965:136), although his formu-

lation of this ordering principle is not particularly helpful in the present

case, where the last personage presented is not the main character, nor

even his most important ally, although she aids him in the final episode.

Perhaps Lord's (1960:92) observation that catalogues always end with a

'capping' object or individual, is more useful. Four wives are the canoni-

cal maximum allowed in Islam, so the *parī* can be seen to complete a set.

(As will be seen, however, this principle of completion is countermanded

in Text I.) The first two wives are, respectively, the reason for the

hero's difficulties with the king and the source of his solutions. Their

initial positions are dictated by narrative significance of the most ob-

vious kind. The intervening prizes, the king's sister and the two animal

allies, have no wider role in the story, beyond being the immediate ob-

jects of quests. The order of presentation of the hero's prizes seems to

hinge on surface significance, on their subsequent role in the plot, not

on their belonging to an ordered succession of conceptual categories. No

distinct plot function besides emphasis can be assigned to the two animals

or the king's sister.

The net effects of the successful quests on the hero's undeclared

enemy, the king, are even harder to systematize, particularly since the

prizes which the boy brings him, apart from the pearls in the first epi-

sode, are only pretexts, not real *desiderata* for him (e.g. the lion's

milk, the laughing flowers). The objects of the quests do progress from desirable (the pearls) to downright dangerous for the king, but it is in the nature of the adversary in each task, and the tactics which the hero employs to achieve his goal, that a more orderly clustering of concepts may be discerned, as follows:

In episode I, the threat for both main characters originates from an older relative of the opposite sex. In the girl's case, the threat is unwanted attachment (marriage arranged by her father), whereas in the boy's it is unwanted disjunction (banishment) from his household. For both of them, the solution is flight, which is instigated and carried out by the woman.

In episodes II and III, the adversary to be defeated is a male supernatural, who is tricked, then physically destroyed.

In episodes IV and V, the adversary is a female animal who must be won over by services rendered. The supernatural horse is in a positive state of well-being, which the hero improves (grooms her). The lion, whose magical powers (if any) are not emphasized, is in a weakened and disabled state, which the hero corrects.

In episode VI, the prize is herself the adversary, a female supernatural who must be forced to cooperate by trickery, theft and sexual threat (not to return her clothes). Once coerced, however, she becomes a permanent ally of the hero. This task is composite, in that the hero must first feed some supernatural ants and other monster animals, before he can reach the Parī's country. It thus combines features of all the preceding episodes, including the first, in which the hero also uses trickery and a threat of sexual compromise to win the princess as a spouse.

In episode VII, the adversary is once again an older human, as in episode I, but is the same sex as the hero, and no kin. In this final challenge, as in the first episode, the hero is almost completely passive, letting the initiative for planning and the physical execution of the escape plan come from a female ally. Episodes I and VII can be classed together in these respects, despite basic contrasts, such as the facts that the female ally in the first episode is human, and her services to the hero are inadvertant, whereas in the seventh episode the female is supernatural and a willing ally of the hero. The old female relative in the first episode is merely left behind, while the old, male non-relative in the last episode is himself banished, to the world of the dead.

With regard to adversaries and tactics, the analogies among the episodes can be diagrammed as follows:

```
┌─1 ─────┐
│ 2 ┐    ¦
│ 3 ┘┐   ¦
│ 4 ┐│   ¦
│ 5 ┘│   ¦
│ 6 ──┘  
└─7      
```
⤴[combines features of (1), (2,3), and (4,5)]

In certain respects, (1) and (7) form a framing pair, and (6) restates and summarizes the hero's abilities as displayed in all the preceding tasks, almost in the way that a recapitulation scene would do, before his final deliverance. The qualities of the hero's adversaries and the tactics he uses to defeat them form a more orderly array, from this point of view, than his prizes in the same seven episodes, since they are clustered conceptually. At least in theory, this organization of the hero's exploits into related sets should help with memorization and recall. A permutation set has fewer features to remember than a group of unrelated items. When Mādar Zāher's performances of the tale are discussed, we will return to the question of whether these groupings function mnemonically

156

(see pp. 165 f. below.)

What are the hero's possibilities for alliance and opposition in
Adī's Afsāneh-e Garg? In the most general terms, the hero wins every female in the story to his side, except his own grandmother. He defeats
every male adversary by force combined with trickery. Animal allies (supernatural or not) are won by services rendered, and are only temporarily
helpful to the hero. Of the wives, one human (the king's sister) and one
supernatural (the first parī) are won by services rendered (bride rescue),
the other two (the king's daughter and the second parī) are won by trickery with an element of sexual compromise (bride stealing). In sum, for
the hero, the possibilities of alliance with females are comprehensive,
the possibilities of alliance with males are nil (cf. H.139: "Either you
bring them, or you lose your head . . . even if you are my brother-in-law,
now."). Not surprisingly, the hero must break with his female parent, in
order to establish alliances with female contemporaries (wives). Many
other folktales include a reconciliation or reunion between the hero and
his parent(s) after bride-winning, as part of the final resolution. The
old woman in episode IV, who helps this hero in his quest for the parī
Laughing Flower, and who 'adopts' him as a grandson (H.202), can be seen
to fulfill the reconciliatory role.

If the hero is most passive in the first and last episodes, he is
at his most independent and resourceful in the sixth episode, for his decision to steal the parī's clothes and force her to come with him is entirely his own, as is the plan by which he accomplishes the deed. His
activism in this respect is analogous to his decision to follow the stream
and find the source of the pearls in episode II. His two flashes of heroic

initiative are bracketed by his passive behavior in episodes I and VII
(when he lets his female allies rescue him) and separated by his strict
obedience to instructions in episodes III, IV and V, so that the pattern
of his tactics takes a chiastic form:

    I. passive
   II. active
  III. obedient
   IV. obedient
    V. obedient
   VI. active
  VII. passive

A few conceptual patterns are discernible in the hero's choice of
allies and tactics. What becomes of these patterns if we take into account the Tree of Bells episode, which we have deduced to have been part
of Adī's story when she told it to Mādar Zāher (p.142 , above)? Syntactically, the Tree of Bells episode is more complex, because it alone has
a delayed resolution, with another episode interpolated between its complication and resolution sequences. (Assuming, for the sake of argument,
that Mādar Zāher's narration of this incident was as close in structure
and detail to what she heard from Adī, as the other episodes in her first
performance of Afsāneh-e Garg are to Adī's recorded performance of it.)

In the Tree of Bells episode, the hero goes to the land of the
parīs, at the foot of Mount Qāf, the most distant point in his travels
(the literal 'ends of the earth'), and on the way he receives the advice
and help of two different types of male supernatural, one of whom he must
win over to his side by physically defeating him, in a wrestling match.
He sexually compromises yet another supernatural female, invading her bed-
room, taking her clothes and eating her food.[1] Instead of claiming her

---

[1] Food-sharing is a well established metaphor for sexual intercourse in
Afghan parlance as elsewhere. 'Come drink tea with me' is a form of pro-
position in certain contexts.

158

at once, he leaves the *parī* princess a written challenge, to which she
responds later by besieging the king's city with a huge army of supernaturals. Trickery and aggression, the combination which win him Laughing
Flower in episode VI of Text H, are amplified in this incident. The *parī*
is ultimately won over by the hero's display of violent aggression, when
he rides up on the Horse of Forty Colts, tearing to bits the silken carpets she has spread over the desert on the way to her tent (I.298-299).

In several ways, the Tree of Bells episode can be seen to form a
pair with the Laughing Flower episode. Both episodes are composite, in
that the hero must win over multiple intermediate adversaries (the *dīv* ants
and felines, the seven *dīv* brothers) before he can approach the real adversary, the *parī*. The adversary in the Tree of Bells episode, as in the
Laughing Flower episode, is herself the hero's eventual prize. If the
Tree of Bells episode is interpolated in the position suggested, the seven
tasks form three pairs which are analogous in the types of adversaries presented, plus a seventh, which pairs with the first episode in the ways
described above (pp. 154-155).

The Tree of Bells episode, with its unique interwoven relationship
to other episodes, invokes all the tactics the hero has used up to that
point: physical force, skill, stealth, theft, physical challenge, sexual
compromise, and finally, mutual help, in that he calls upon the Horse of
Forty Colts, whom he had earlier benefited, for aid. It also presents
some possible relations which were not used elsewhere in the story, i.e.
the friendships with male supernaturals (first the Messenger of God, an
elder male who offers 'parental' solicitude, aid and advice, then the seven
dīv brothers who become the hero's allies and foster siblings when he beats

the first one he meets in a wrestling match). If the Tree of Bells incident is interpolated in Adī's tale in a position analogous to the one it
occupies in Mādar Zāher's performance, the structure of the end of the
story is quite changed, and still more balanced (Diagram II).

The inclusion of this episode substantially completes the possible
permutations of age, sex, power (human vs. supernatural) and alliance,
which define the hero's relations to other personages in the story. Yet
there is still no positive alliance with a male human. The hero's male
allies are all supernaturals, and temporary. Even when the king becomes
his kin, through marriage, he does not become his ally (H.139). Significantly, the king alone has a human male ally, in the vizier, and his
compliance with the vizier's advice to kill the hero causes the king's
own destruction. The conclusion arrived at is that any alliance is
possible and profitable for this human male hero, except with another human male.

The question of alliance is hardly a 'hidden' theme in the story
as Adī tells it. The hero's first wife repeatedly quotes proverbs to him,
concerning the advisability of seeking one's friends among one's peers
and the danger of associating with kings (H.30,51,115). The hero, despite
these warnings, seeks an alliance which goes against conventional wisdom,
one which is defined as impossible from the start. His resulting trials
yield several unexpected alliances, but not the one he originally sought,
and he ends by holding sovereign power, without a permanent male ally. By
contrast, the king's reliance on another human male is his destruction.

If the Tree of Bells episode draws together and summarizes so many
of the story's ideas, some of which (the possibilities of male allies)

are not developed elsewhere, and the resolution of this episode stands
in the emphatic final position in the set of bride-winning tasks, how did
Adī come to omit it from her performance? Summary reviews of action,
whether they are reiterative, in the sense of a summary episode like the
'Tree of Bells,' or recapitulatory, as is the hero's speech to the parī
princess recounting how he burglarized her castle and stole her possessions, have a very important place in the final resolutions of folktales,
when the special qualities of the main character are recognized and rewarded. The 'interwoven' relation of the Tree of Bells incident with
other episodes in the story (the Horse of Forty Colts and Laughing Flower)
would also seem to attach it firmly to the structure of the tale. This
very structure, however, is anomalous in the story, and its inclusion,
with its delayed resolution, requires more 'looking ahead' than that of
the other episodes which can readily stand independently of each other.
The Tree of Bells episode alone requires that another episode be interpolated between its complication sequence and its resolution. The
writer's own experience as a novice storyteller suggests that this 'framing' structure is among the hardest to master in oral performance.

In terms of surface structure, the third parī may be considered
superfluous because she makes a fifth wife, and Muslims are only allowed
four, in theory, so that four wives are regarded as a complete 'set'.
Also only two parīs take part in the final rescue of the hero (H.224),
though the functions could readily be divided to provide roles for three
(one planner, two rescuers). Neither surface nor deep structural patterns
seem to provide a single key to Adī's omission of this particular incident from her recorded performance. "Framing" is not exemplified elsewhere in her active repertoire, as represented by the stories she was

able to tell me, whereas Mādar Zāher's Alī Zarrīn (Text K) is a tour de force of interwoven and framed structures. It is possible that Adī was not adept at this type of plot construction. It would be helpful to hear more of her performances of this story, to determine how stable its form is in her narration. It should be remembered that she volunteered to tell the story to Mādar Zāher only after I had pressed her to tell me all the stories she knew, and she had recorded what she told me was her entire repertoire. Either she did not remember the story initially, or she remembered it but did not feel secure enough in her knowledge of it to perform it in the formal, 'command performance' atmosphere which a tape recorder and a foreign guest created. In either case, the implication is that her mastery of the story was less than perfect.

I have tried to show how the episodes of Adi's Afsāneh-e Garg, taken together, present a comprehensive inventory of relationships between the hero and a set of personages whose qualities are permutations of a limited set of alternatives (person/animal, natural/supernatural, male/female, young/old). Only the first and last episodes, and perhaps the Tree of Bells episode if it is interpolated in a way analogous to the position it occupies in text I, have any prescribed position for purposes of narrative coherency. (It is perfectly conceivable that a 'tree' episode could be formulated which would not require interpolation of another episode between its complication and resolution.) Thematically, the tactics of the hero and the qualities of his adversaries present a more orderly array in Adī's version than do the benefits accruing to the hero, or the effects of his accomplishments on his ultimate adversary, the king.

Succeeding episodes in Adī's story do not present an intensification of any particular theme. The hero's accumulation of wives seems
to intensify the vizier's jealousy, but the wives themselves do not present an orderly increase in desirability or powers. Women of supernatural
beauty, power and wisdom alternate with humans, and the vizier is no less
incensed by the sight of the hero enjoying himself when he has not won a
new wife, as well (H.163). Although themes are grouped according to
similarities in Adī's story, they are not obviously progressive: the acquisition of animal allies could precede or follow the acquisition of
wives #3 and 4, without damaging plot structure. If the order of events
which Adī's story presents is not dramatically necessary, is it nevertheless mnemonically useful? Is this particular order indicative of a generative process at work in the reconstruction of stories? To explore
these questions, let us turn to Mādar Zāher's performances of Afsāneh-e
Garg. Does she retain the same order of tasks when she tells the story,
or does she alter the order? If she alters the order, either she does
not need any such thematic ordering principle as we have tried to discern
in Adī's narrative, or she is using a different principle.

A structural diagram of Mādar Zāher's first performance of Afsāneh-e
Garg (Text I) will be found in Diagram III. Episodes III through V show
a different order from Adī's story: the rescue of the king's sister, which
yields the hero his third wife (second human), is interpolated between the
two episodes which yield him animal helpers, and the two animal episodes
are reversed, thus:

Adī's version	Mādar Zāher's version
King's sister	Lions' milk
Horse of 40 Colts	King's sister
Lions' milk	Horse of 40 Colts

Mādar Zāher's ordering of these events yields an alternating pattern in the benefits accruing to the hero from each of his tasks:

Episode 1) First wife (human A)
2) Second wife (*Parī* A)
3) Animal ally (lion)
4) Third wife (human B)
5) Animal (supernatural) ally
6) Fifth wife (delayed) (*Parī* C)
7) Fourth wife (*Parī* B)

The pattern of benefits thus becomes highly symmetrical in Mādar Zāher's ordering, while the pattern of tactics and adversaries becomes an alternating one of considerable complexity:

Episode 1) tricks and compromises human female → ally
2) tricks and destroys supernatural male
3) aids female animal → ally
4) tricks and destroys supernatural male
5) aids supernatural female animal → ally
6) steals from, compromises and challenges ♀ supernatural → ally, delayed
7) steals from, compromises and challenges ♀ supernatural → ally
8) tricks and destroys male human adversary

The paired structure which Adī's tale presented is complicated by alternation in terms 2 through 5. The personages in the story constitute permutations of a set of four pairs of terms (person/animal, male/female, normal/supernatural, young/old), and these permutations may be ordered in several different ways. Adī's version sorts them according to the adversaries' qualities, Mādar Zāher's according to the allies' (wives being a permanent sort of ally). Also, Adī's ordering system sorts the adversaries into similar pairs (male supernaturals, female animals, female supernaturals), while Mādar Zāher's version distributes the allies in alternation insofar as possible, the human and *parī* wives alternating with animal allies. The alternating pattern of benefits in Mādar Zāher's story forms a near chiasm (see p. 163, and cf. p. 157, above).

By reversing the order of acquisition of the animal allies, placing the lion's milk episode before the Horse of Forty Colts, Mādar Zāher moves the incident in which the Horse is acquired as an ally as close as possible to the episode in which she reappears to help the hero, when he confronts the Daughter of Shāhg̱ol the *Parī* King (I.298ff.). Thus she places the three episodes which are interwoven adjacent to each other in the second half of the story. If Adī's 'complete' Afsāneh-e Garg is accurately recon-structed in Diagram II, then a wholly unrelated incident, that of the lion's milk, intervenes between the acquisition of the Horse and the two inter-woven episodes in which she figures as the hero's helper. This means that the 'interwoven' elements must span four episode, not three, in Adī's (re-constructed) version of the story. Nothing logically precludes this order-ing: in fact, from a certain point of view, it is quite symmetrical, in that two unattached episodes (lions' milk, Laughing Flower) are alternated with three scenes connected with each other (the Horse is acquired, the *parī* is challenged, the Horse is summoned to carry out the challenge). Mādar Zāher's version, since it spans fewer episodes, and contains only one delaying episode, may be easier to recall, but it is also less symme-trical:

<u>Adī</u> (reconstructed)

King's sister
┌── Horse
│ Lion
│ ┌ [Tree]
│ │ Laughing Flower
└─→Reappearance of
    Parī-[Tree] resolved

<u>Mādar Zāher</u>

Lion
King's sister
┌── Horse
│ ┌ Tree
│ │ Laughing Flower
└─→Reappearance of
    Parī - Tree resolved

Mādar Zāher's ordering of the hero's tasks shows one aspect which
is progressive. All the allies who start from positions of weakness are
grouped together in the first half of the story: the king's daughter,
who is powerless to refuse an unwanted marriage, the first *parī*, who is
in a living death when the hero first finds her, the lion, who is crippled and immobilized, the king's sister, who is bound and buried alive in
a cave. All the allies whom the hero wins in the following three quests
begin from positions of power in which they are potential adversaries who
must be won over (the horse, the two later *parīs*). In the last three episodes, the hero's show of force also increases progressively, in his confrontations with each of these personages, from a mere spoken order to
the Horse (I.200), to his aggressive display before the Daughter of Shāhǧol
the *Parī* King with her assembled army (I.261, 298-299). There is a progressive development both in the degree of power possessed by the females
who become the hero's allies, and the force he uses to win them over. In
this light, it is interesting that he reverts to a totally passive role
and the female allies carry the day in the last encounter with the king,
which finally yields him sovereign power.

The permutations of conceptual categories in <u>Afsāneh-e Garg</u> (and
indeed, in any folktale of reasonable complexity) lend themselves to a
variety of ordering procedures. Any one of a number of categories, such

as allies, adversaries, objects, or tactics, may be taken as the primary

feature for sorting. The ordering principle may be clustering, alternat-

ing, or progressive. Mādar Zāher's order reveals alternating and intensi-

fying patterns in the arrangement of the hero's allies and tactics, while

Adī's version reveals simple three-class sorting according to the nature

of the hero's adversaries. In both cases, the internal set of episodes is

bracketed by an initial and final episode which share thematic features.

Both versions also develop the permutations of the categories male/female,

normal/supernatural, and ally/adversary in such a way that male human al-

lies are unsuccessful or absent, while female allies, human, animal, and

supernatural, are uniformly beneficial for the hero. Although the stories

make the same 'concluding statement,' with regard to these themes, the

order in which thematic possibilities are explored has great inherent

flexibility, and several alternative ordering principles. The mnemonic

utility of one ordering principle over another, or one 'key' category over

another, remains open to question.

Mādar Zāher's second performance of <u>Afsāneh-e Garg</u> (Text <u>J</u>) is the

shortest of the three, as it omits both the episode of the Horse of Forty

Colts and that of the Tree of Bells. Compared to her first performance,

it seems thematically impoverished, both in the variety and the arrange-

ment of the conceptual categories which were identified in the two earlier

performances. The benefits accruing to the hero are arranged thus:

> Wife (human)
> Wife (*parī*)
> Wife (human)
> Animal ally (lion)
> Wife (*parī*)   [1]

---

[1] A fuller schematic analysis of the structure of <u>J</u> will be found in
Diagram IV.

The wives still alternate, human/*parī*/human/*parī*, but the omission of the two interwoven episodes precludes the development of the contrasting themes of female supernatural ally/male supernatural ally (parent/sibling), and attenuates the progressive development of power in the hero's female allies. The last *parī* wife is the only ally who starts from a position of power in this configuration. Though the same overall conceptual 'statement' is made in this story, of the desirability of female allies for the hero, and the impossibility of alliances with human males, the major theme of power is less emphasized. This is made plain in that the hero's destruction of his enemy and his escape from the fire conclude the story. His accession to the throne, though it may be implicit, (and the narrator would certainly have added it, had she been asked), is not mentioned, and thus not emphasized. This omission combined with the omission of the hero's martial confrontation with the *parī* princess and the reduction of the violence he does to the king's subjects to a mere threat (J.135-136; cf. I.150,201, H.159-160, 179), mutes the general theme of physical power and aggression considerably.

In M̄ar Čučeh as well, there are points at which Mādar Zāher seems to minimize aggressive violence, as in her initial avoidance of the cow-killing episode (C.153). If these omissions form a consistent pattern in her repertoire, however, it is not a general rejection of themes of power and aggression, for elsewhere, her main characters dispose of their enemies just as ruthlessly as any other storyteller's (vide the death of the king). Rather, they suggest that Mādar Zāher selectively rejects acts of violence by the hero which are directed at innocent bystanders, such as the cows or the king's subjects. A fuller consideration of her whole repertoire, with regard to themes of aggression and violence, would be needed to confirm this

tendency. Her tendency to emphasize social proprieties even in rather unlikely circumstances, which was noted in Mār Čučeh in connection with the
funerals of the vizier's wives (pp. 101 ff. above) is once again displayed
in Text K (Alī Zarrīn) where the hero gives the king he has just killed
and succeeded a full-scale funeral, with mourning and burial in holy
ground (K.88).

Mādar Zāher's omission of the Tree of Bells and Horse of Forty Colts
episodes from performance J can hardly be dismissed as a simple memory
failure, because close analogues to both of these episodes can be found
in one of the stories she considers her best, Alī Zarrīn (K.3-17; K.22-37,
54-70). In fact, when she comments on the complexity of Afsāneh-e Garg,[1]
she compares it directly to "the story of the Horse of Forty Colts - the
story of Alī Zarrīn" (H.227)[2] Alī Zarrīn was one of the first two stories
Mādar Zāher recorded for me, elicited by my request, "Tell me the stories
you like best." This story, recorded several months before Mādar Zāher
learned Afsāneh-e Garg, exhibits structural similarities to Garg, as well
as similarities of detail. Without going into detailed structural analysis,[3] it is sufficient to observe that the episodes of Alī Zarrīn are all
interwoven in the ways that tasks 4 through 6 are intertwined in Text I.
The Horse of Forty Colts, Alī Zarrīn's first prize, becomes the companion
and advisor on several subsequent adventures, to an extent fulfilling the
advisory role of the first parī wife in Afsāneh-e Garg. In the final confrontation with the Daughter of Shāhǧol the Parī King (K.54-70), the Horse

---

[1] She calls it 'difficult', /saxt/.

[2] The double reference designates one story only.

[3] Diagram V provides a more detailed schematic analysis of Alī Zarrīn.

has an identical role to that she plays in Garg, but she is a helper and advisor on Alī's third and fifth tasks as well.

Episode IV (the third task, fetching the White *Dīv*'s head) has a deferred resolution, like the Tree of Bells episode, in which Alī Zarrīn manages to win over the surviving *dīv*, whose 39 brothers he has killed, to his own side. Meanwhile, Alī has brought back the Tree of Forty Voices and incurred the wrath of the Daughter of Shāhǧol the *Parī* King. Before the latter episode is resolved, he is sent off on his last quest, to bring the demon Cat Meynaqā, which he accomplishes with the advice of his new ally, the White *Dīv*, and the physical help of the Horse of Forty Colts. Finally, after Alī's reconciliation and engagement with the *Parī* princess, the Cat helps him kill the king who has oppressed him, again on a suggestion of the White *Dīv*. In the end we leave him sitting happily on the throne, surrounded by his forty siblings and his supernatural helpers (K.87,92). By comparison with the order of episodes in Afsāneh-e Garg, Alī Zarrīn's episodic structure is far more intricately interwoven, the principals of one adventure becoming supporting characters in the next, and the resolution of three problems (the disappearance of Alī's father, the enmity of the White *Dīv*, the challenge to the Daughter of Shāhǧol the *Parī* King) all being delayed by the interpolation of other adventures (Diagram V).

Mādar Zāher's omission of the Tree of Bells and Horse of Forty Colts episodes from Afsāneh-e Garg J cannot be explained by any inability to handle the intricacies of alternating plot structure, nor by lack of familiarity with the episodes in question. She compared Afsāneh-e Garg directly to the story in her collection which includes both these episodes, and here, I think, is a key to how she came to leave them out of the former story. In a free-recall situation, asked to enumerate the

stories she learned from Adī, Mādar Zāher refers to <u>Afsāneh-e Garg</u> as

"the tale of the lions . . . that one with the lions' milk in a lion's

skin on a lion's back." (J.1) Clearly, she remembers this story in terms

of that one episode, which was not in her active repertoire before she

learned <u>Afsāneh-e Garg</u>.[1] Likewise, when she compares <u>Afsāneh-e Garg</u> to

other stories, she refers to <u>Alī Zarrīn</u> as "the one of the Horse of Forty

Colts" (H.227). It seems that certain individual episodes are her memory

cues for some of her stories. If she has learned an episode in the con-

text of a certain story, and uses the episode to characterize or 'key'

the story in her own mind, if she is in fact treating a certain episode

as characteristic of story 'A', it is plausible that she would reject its

association with story 'B'. Hence the two episodes which already have a

place in her repertoire, one of them at least being a 'key' episode, by

which she designates a certain story, are dropped from a new story which

contains them. Likewise, the new story is 'keyed' in her memory by a

striking episode not found elsewhere in her repertoire. Whatever her

structural perceptions of stories, it seems that Mādar Zāher recalls at

least some of her stories by way of key features, not by their overall

structure. This keying system is not perfect or comprehensive, however.

In a late recording session, she and her children recalled three or four

stories, all designated 'the story of the old thorn-picker', because they

all opened with this stock figure. Eliciting individual stories from

storytellers was in fact a persistent problem for me while collecting,

---

[1] It is, of course, perfectly possible that she had heard the episode
before, but it did not have a place in her active repertoire.

because many do not assign titles to their stories, and 'key' episodes or features are idiosyncratically chosen. Asking for the 'name' (*nām*) or 'title' (*onwān*) of a story, I would often get a synopsis of its contents, or a blank look.

With respect to certain episodes, it seems that Mādar Zāher has a tendency to 'repertoire exclusiveness,' i.e. to retaining that episode in only one of the tales in her repertoire. If this tendency were carried to its logical conclusion, it would exclude the possibility of a narrator's retaining two close variants of the same tale type in his/her repertoire at the same time. In fact, in my collecting experience, I found very few informants who were able to tell me two near variants of the same tale, which they maintained as separate entities in their active repertoire. Mādar Zāher was one of these. Though there may be a phenomenon of 'key episode exclusiveness,' it is by no means pervasive enough to dictate the overall contents of a storyteller's repertoire. In an active storytelling tradition, people hear near variants of the same tale (e.g. Xasteh Xomār, text G) all the time. They recognize similarities of both structure (Mādar Zāher: "They both go to seven places," see p.   ) and content ("This story and the story of the Horse of Forty Colts . . ." H.227). To understand variation in transmission, in such a situation, one must know how a storyteller decides 'Story A is like Story B, but is a different entity,' as against 'Story A is another way of telling Story B.' For different storytellers, the criteria for distinction are likely to be different, but the use of 'key' episodes in the recall process by an adept storyteller like Mādar Zāher suggests that a more extensive study of mnemonic cueing, on how storytellers 'key' stories for recall, might be helpful to understand the migration of episodes from story to story in transmission, and the constraints on that process.

The above discussion of 'key' episodes is not meant to suggest that similar episodes always maintain a mutually exclusive existence in folk-tale transmission, or that a storyteller hearing two similar or equivalent episodes (e.g. Adī's 'Tree of Bells and Cats' Claws' and Mādar Zāher's 'Tree of Forty Voices') always chooses one formulation and rejects the other. Examples of the hybridization or conflation of similar episodes are numerous in folktale, and in fact Adī's Afsāneh-e Garg furnishes such an example, which attracted Mādar Zāher's notice because the conjunction of narrative elements is somewhat illogical.

The major logical inconsistency in Adī's Afsāneh-e Garg (Text H) occurs during the Garg's rescue of the first *parī* (H.55-93). The *dīv* tells his captive that his life will be renewed if anyone plasters the room containing the well where the glass of his life is hidden (H.81), and in the same breath tells her how his death can be accomplished. The girl persuades him not to behead her again, so that she can spend the next day plastering the room. The *parī*'s strategem is unnecessary, since

a) the hero already knows how to revive her using a magic spell, and

b) the *dīv* has already told the girl how he can be killed.

The simplest course of narrative action would be for the boy to revive the *parī* the next morning, as he has before, and kill the *dīv* according to the girl's directions. Instead, the *parī* persuades the *dīv* to leave her alive, and spends the next day plastering the room, to no apparent purpose. Mādar Zāher, performing the story for the first time, notes this logical discrepancy:

". . . that day he didn't cut off her head, and just left her
her there, because in you don't cut off her head - he <u>could</u>
have cut off her head, anyway, because the bald boy knows the
spell . . ." (J.79)

The only result of the plastering incident is that the girl wins
the *dīv*'s confidence, but this achievement is superfluous, since the *dīv*
has already told her how to accomplish his death. In fact Adī's version
truncates a longer episode, in which the *dīv* first tells the girl a false
story because he does not trust her. In other stories in my collection,[1]
the girl is told that repairing a certain structure will increase the supernatural's power, while destroying it will weaken or kill him. The girl,
or the hero, identifies this as a false story, and the two set about re-
storing the structure in order to win the ogre's confidence. When the ogre
sees that the heroine has tried to help him, he is won over and tells her
how his death may really be accomplished. Armed with the true story, she
and the hero proceed to kill him. In this context, the girl's insistence
that the ogre leave her alive, so that she can do him a favor, also becomes logical.

Adī's story conflates two incidents which should be alternatives
to each other. Either a) the hero resuscitates or frees a girl who is
able to tell him how her captor may be killed, directly, so that freeing
the girl (reconnaissance) is a necessary prelude to the ogre's death, or
b) the ogre himself must be persuaded to free or resuscitate the girl, in
which case a deceptive story is involved. Structurally, the 'deceptive
story' version (A & B) is an elaboration of the simpler version (A) thus:

---

[1] E.g., tape XLV, <u>Qambar-e Jān Fedā</u>, a 'Faithful John' variant told by
a sixteen-year-old boy in Taw Beryān village, near Herat.

A) plan ————→ girl questions →g. wins o's ——→ ogre's ——→ ogre
   (hero/girl)   ogre   confidence   directions   killed
                                                   (true)

B) o's directions ——→ o. frees girl ——→ girl follows
      (false)   (test)   directions

In Adī's rendition of this composite incident, all the ogre's directions
are given at once, and the true are not distinguished from the false. The
error seems to be one of syntax, failing to separate the two sets of directions. The storyteller who formulated the episode in its present order, whether it was Adī or some more distant source, either made an imperfect attempt to elaborate the simple pattern, or presented an eroded
version of the composite one. It is not clear in which direction this incident was developing, as it represents an intermediate formulation between
the simple (one set of directions) and the complex (two sets of directions, one false, one true). It seems that the narrator who put this
incident into this form had heard both versions, and was either unable
or unconcerned to distinguish them.

Although Mādar Zāher notes the illogic of this conflated incident,
she does not try to correct the double resuscitation theme which attracted
her attention (J.79, I.77-91). In fact, she adds a conflation of her own,
at an earlier point in the same episode, during the hero's reconnaissance
of the dīv's fortress. She has the hero dig a tunnel under the supposedly
impregnable garden wall (I.62, J.49), then has him retreat to a pit blind
outside to watch when the dīv arrives and unlocks the garden door with a
spell. Thus she conflates two different strategies of reconnaissance,
the pit blind from Adī and the tunnel from elsewhere (possibly from the
"lion's milk" episodes which appears later in the same story: see discussion

of analogous reconstruction, with regard to Mār Čučeh, pp. 118 ff. above).

Although she retains the double resuscitation of the *parī*, in Text J, Mādar Zāher shows a tendency to omit the narrative bit which is all that remains of the deceptive story, the plastering of the wall. Her daughter Māhgol reminds her of it (J.80), and she accepts the correction. If the omission had been allowed to stand, it would have taken the episode a step closer to the simple form. The adept narrator, Mādar Zāher, retained the otiose feature which she noted (the double resuscitation), but eliminated another incident which is logically superfluous in the story's present form: the plastering. The less practiced storyteller, Māhgol, whose grasp of the order of incidents seems to be more tenuous, (cf. her Mār Čučeh), is more conservative concerning atomistic details, regardless of their contribution to narrative coherency. Narrative coherency is improved by Mādar Zāher's omission of the plastering incident, whether she intended to 'improve' it or not.[1] If her alteration of the episode is unintentional, one can view it as evidence that surface structure, the causal relations of events, influences memory for this storyteller, so that things which are superfluous to the web of cause and effect tend to be forgotten. Her less adept daughter remembers a striking detail which has lost its causal attachment, and insists that it be included. One could say that a grasp of causal (not symbolic or conceptual) structure accommodates certain kinds of revision (or certain kinds of memory lapses), even while the association of analogous events (the two reconnaissance strategies) causes the same storyteller to include other otiose elements.

---

[1] Some narrators boast that they 'improve' the stories they hear. Others insist that they change nothing, even under direct criticism (cf. Mādar Zāher, E.158).

We have seen that analogous episodes or incidents are sometimes conflated, and sometimes treated with a kind of 'exclusionist' principle, even by the same storyteller. The difference in her handling of the Tree of Bells/Horse of Forty Colts episodes, and the hero's reconnaissance strategies may have to do with the fact that the first two are distinguishing features for certain stories in her repertoire, while the last is not a particularly distinctive feature, even within its own episode. These examples have been discussed at length to try to show that the delineation and conflation of analogous episodes in storytelling are continuous, reversible processes, tied to the mnemonic techniques of storytellers in a variety of ways. Similarly, 'structure' as perceived by structural theorists supplies little more than an inventory of conceptual categories. Within a shared inventory in the single story here discussed, the ordering principles of two storytellers proceed along different lines, for reasons which remain obscure. We must look beyond the Motif Index, to the distinguishing and categorizing principles of the storytellers, to get any grasp of the flexibility of the 'motifs' in their atomistic travels through the traditional corpus. We must look beyond descriptive structuralism for the generative principles of storytelling.

V. Lion and Leopard:
Dispute to Fable

Šīr o Palang, Text L, is a very early, perhaps the first performance of a story which Mādar Zāher identifies as her own composition. This story is not the only 'original' composition in her repertoire. After initial reluctance, she performed and identified six other stories as her own compositions. Her willingness to admit to having composed stories, if not the very fact of her composing them, is unique in my collecting experience. No other storyteller I met was willing to admit 'inventing' tales in traditional style, though several said they would 'correct' or 'complete' tales they heard from others.

Mādar Zāher's performance of Saudagar Bāšī o Ney-e Pīr Mard Dīv [The Master Merchant and the Reed of the Old Man Dīv], which she recorded on June 15, 1975, was the first occasion on which she admitted to me that a story was her own composition. She initially told me she had learned this story when "very little," from an unnamed old woman in her village. I asked if this was the same old woman who had told her other tales I knew to be traditional. She answered, "No," then, "Should I tell you the truth, so there won't be any lies? It's from my own imagination [lit. 'heart']. Was it good? Or bad? Maybe you think it's bad?" Her first concern was that her own compositions would be inferior in my eyes to her traditional stories. She went on to say that two other stories she had recorded previously were her own compositions, both, like Saudagar Bāšī, lengthy, fambling adventure stories. In general, Mādar Zāher's own compositions, although they share many features with *afsāneh* which she said she had

structure than tales she learned from others. In theme and structure, the
'new' stories have some points of resemblance with the *ketābī* ['book']
romances which are themselves intriguingly absent from Mādar Zāher's
repertoire.[1] In general, Mādar Zāher's compositions concern elaborate
bride-winning and attendant adventures experienced by a human hero or
heroes. The relationships between episodes tend to be loose.

Contrary to the great literary Persian tale collections such as
Kalila va Dimna and Anvār-i Soheilī (both derived from the Indian Pancha-
tantra), or Marzubān Nāmeh, which are very rich in animal tales, neither
Mādar Zāher nor other oral storytellers from whom I collected in Afghanistan showed great interest in animal tales of the fable variety, in which
the actions of animal characters are taken as cautionary or exemplary
for human beings. Such tales, if performed at all, were usually left

---

[1] Unfortunately, a detailed comparison of Mādar Zāher's original compositions with this semi-literary genre exceeds the scope of the present
discussion. In general, I did not find women who performed *ketābī*
('book') material. In the traditional educational system, it has been
extremely unusual for a woman to achieve functional literacy, though
a certain number do attend the mosque school for a year or more between
ages 6 and 10. I met one young woman, a member of a religious family,
who was quite literate and said she performed *ketāb xānī* ('book reading') aloud for pleasure, but her religious conservatism prevented me
from taping her reading. My limited experience suggests that, in former years, literate women belonged mostly to families who had learned
religious members who educated the women at home. Religious conservatism may have inhibited these women from performance of secular 'book
reading,' even in the home. Nonliterate women, having limited opportunities to socialize outside their own families, would have had minimal contact with educated women who would be able to teach them material
from books. This does not serve to explain why nonliterate women rarely
perform 'book' material, however, since many men perform it, even men
who are illiterate. A book reader in any family would give the family's
women access to this material, as well as men. Men's access to book-
readers outside the family, plus the more leisurely, ceremonial structure of men's social gatherings, may help to explain this phenomenon.
The lengthy episodic structure of book romances calls for longer performances, or performances in installments. A full understanding of
these matters awaits further study.

until the narrator's stock of tales recounting human heroic, magical and romantic adventures was exhausted, as though animal tales were intrinsically less interesting than the more romantic adventure tales of human heroes. Certain animal stories (such as Xāleh Kamǧozak, 'Auntie Dungbeetle'), and especially chain tales, were specifically identified as stories for children.

My first request for stories from an informant was always, "Tell me the story(s) you like the best." I very seldom asked for particular items, so that the order in which a narrator performed his or her repertoire was determined, as much as possible, by the individual's own order of preference or recall. Thus the placement of animal tales at the end of the performance sequence seems to me to be significant.

Under these circumstances, Šīr o Palang was anomalous in several ways. It is an animal tale with clear moral implications for human behavior, a type of tale which is sparsely represented in my total collection and in Mādar Zāher's own repertoire. It was short (less than 10 minutes long) in comparison to traditional stories which Mādar Zāher told, which averaged half an hour in length, and even shorter in comparison to her other original compositions, several of which were over one hour in length. In her other compositions, Mādar Zāher included considerable supernatural material. This tale, except for the tacit anthropomorphism of the animal characters, is totally without supernatural content, concerned as it is with the domestic jealousies of a pair of leopards and a lioness who is the male leopard's adopted sister. At the same time, Šīr o Palang exhibits many of the structural and stylistic features discernible in traditional stories from Mādar Zāher's repertoire which have been described above.

From a stylistic point of view, Mādar Zāher's Šīr o Palang is clearly identifiable as *afsāneh*. She announces her intention to narrate in this genre by her use of the *būd, nabūd* ('there was and was not') verse formula with which she begins the story (L.1, M.17). Likewise, what Mādar Zāher called the 'words' of folktale[1] give the narrative of L and M texts the texture of traditional tales, with their repetitious phraseology and symmetrical patterns of themes, plans and recapitulations.

At the verbal level, chained phrases are frequent:

There was one - uh - leopard. A leopard . . . [L.2]
She left. Went out, and left. Went out, and left, and . . . [L.8]
. . . This lion, uh - understood. She understood . . . [L.35]
He didn't do what she wanted. So he didn't do what she wanted, and . . . [L.40]

Likewise, verbs are repeated for emphasis to indicate sustained action:

He went, searched, searched, searched, searched . . . [L.1]
. . . these two leopards were really - quarreled, quarreled, quarreled . . . [L.21]
She prowled, prowled, and found a good place . . . [L.21]
He prowled, prowled, and found a good, big lion . . . [L.31]
He went, and came to her house, and went, and came . . . [L.33]
. . . this (lion) went to a good (big) river, and washed, washed, washed . . . [L.40]

Fixed phrases for time transitions also appear, prominently Mādar Zāher's standard 'some days (time) and some while passed' (L.2,4,6,8,33, 40; M.17,24,25,27,28,55). When Mādar Zāher launches into a sustained narrative in response to questions in an interview, some of the same stylistic features appear, notably chaining (N.22,23,24,51) and fixed phrases to mark transitions, e.g. /bogzār/, 'put it (that)' (N.20,31,34,44,45). This suggests that these speech mannerisms are characteristic of narrative

---

[1] Field notes V.46, March 1, 1975.

speech in general, not only of *afsāneh*. This is not surprising in view of the fact that their main utility is to the speaker, to allow time to formulate the next statement in a continuous narrative. The needs of the listener, to rehearse and remember a story, are better served by patterns in the sequence of events, which real events may or may not show.

It is in the patterns of plans, recapitulations, and repeated themes that Šīr o Palang and traditional fictional narrative are distinguishable from narrative speech in general. Šīr o Palang offers examples of both plans and recapitulations used in the ways they are used in traditional tale plots. Recapitulations occur as L.19,25 (brief), 38 (an unused 'slot' only), 46-47 (fragmentary due to accidental erasure of tape), 56-57,63,66 (slot only), 68; and M.32 (brief), 39 (brief), 43,48 (slot only), and 61.

The utility of recapitulation for story-learning need not be argued further (see pp. 114 f. above). With ten recapitulations or 'slots' for recapitulation in a ten-minute narrative, Šīr o Palang L provides numerous opportunities for review of the story's events and the causal relations among them. Šīr o Palang M provides five slots, only two of which are expanded into extensive recapitulations, just as in L only three of the ten slots relate an extended chain of events, in such a way as to emphasize their causal relations. Most of the slots in L contain only brief references to what has gone before. Although the storyteller does not elaborate them, these repeated references suggest that she herself is frequently reviewing previous events in the process of formulating her narrative. A tendency to frequent recapitulation at this early stage of composition is readily understandable. Certain other plot elements, such as the leopard's first plan to go himself and impregnate the lioness, so that the leopardess can have her revenge (L.20, cf. M.43) are offered in <u>L</u>, but later dropped, further evidence that Mādar Zāher was still formulating the basic plot structure of <u>Šīr o Palang</u> when she recorded it for the first time.

Even though the numerous undeveloped recapitulation slots in <u>L</u> suggest frequent review of the plot by the narrator, the recapitulations are not placed at random, but at points of confrontation, where in every case a character's previous action is invoked to justify the actions or plans of the speaker. The action/reaction structure of the revenge tale and its theme of reciprocity are brought into high relief by these frequent recapitulations.

Turning to <u>M</u>, one finds only half as many recapitulation slots, with only two (M.43 and 61) developed to any length. The two long recapitulations in <u>M</u> also occur at major turning points in the action, M.43 at the point when the leopard recognizes the lioness's malevolence (despite their sibling relationship and his former kindness, which he describes in detail), and he goes off to set the revenge plan in motion. His question, "Would she come and eat my cubs?" has an implicit affirmative answer in his subsequent action. The query has a more rhetorical quality here, emphasizing the ingratitude of the lioness, than does his denial of the lioness' guilt in <u>L</u> (L.18), which causes a major quarrel with his wife (L. 21). In <u>M</u>, despite his question, the leopard goes off at once to begin his revenge (M.44; "He didn't get angry. He (just) went off . . .").

Likewise, the other full recapitulation in <u>M</u> (M.61) sets forth the moral issues of the story:

> "You and I are even. Why should you eat (mine), if I
> should(n't) eat yours? So now, you ate (mine) and I ate (yours),
> and I did a <u>good</u> thing, so (laughing as she speaks) if you're a
> <u>man</u> (sic), come and fight with me. If you're not, (then) go
> about - about your business." So then, they said, "It was <u>manly</u>

of me to eat (them), so if you're a man, come and quarrel with
me, if (not), go to your face - on your way! You came <u>first</u>
into my house, and stole and ate my children. I, who came
after - if you hadn't eaten (mine), I wouldn't have eaten yours!
For years I was sick - you were sick - I cared for you here, and
<u>fed</u> you, and for you I went and <u>stole</u> people's sheep, (and that's)
forbidden! I brought them and gave them to you so you would get
well, and <u>have</u> a bit of a mouthful of meat!

     "I mated, (and) you - I said to myself, 'The house is small,
come, let's dig a good den,' you got angry and left, and were
digging a den. So when you got angry and left, my wife had cubs,
and you came and ate her cubs. So now you've eaten, and I've
eaten, and I did a good thing. Your strength (recourse) is with
the government, so go (to them)."

The theme of reciprocity is strongly emphasized by a double recapitulation.

The lioness is left speechless (M.63) and afraid to pursue the quarrel

further. The final resolution, mediated by the leopard's angry recapitu-

lation, is a break between the lions and the leopards.

Apart from supporting detail such as the placement of reconnaissance

scenes (L.9,35 vs. M.29), the main dramatic difference between <u>L</u> and <u>M</u>

texts lies in the resolution patterns. <u>L</u> is conciliatory, emphasizing

the continuity of the family (the leopardess is given a cub to comfort her

until she can bear more children of her own), and the responsiveness of sib-

lings, even siblings as vindictive as the lioness, to appeals for help in

times of family crisis (L.68-69). The resolution of <u>M</u>, however, is schis-

matic. The lioness is punished for her vicious behavior by the loss of

her own cubs, but there is no mention of compensation or of reconciliation

between the two households. The recapitulations developed in <u>M</u> delineate

the schismatic forces at work: the leopard in the act of realizing the

lioness' ingratitude and treachery, the leopard confronting the lioness

and refusing her any compensation. In this the recapitulations in <u>Šīr o</u>

<u>Palang</u> are like those in <u>Xasteh Xomār</u> (G.50), or <u>Mār ČuČeh</u> (E.154, F.137),

which underline the moral qualities of the characters whose actions are reviewed, and justify subsequent retribution or reward.

Although all the recapitulations in L, like those in M, are located at points of confrontation between characters, and imply value judgments on actions, they do not have the conclusive quality of the two major recapitulations in M. The leopard denies his wife's indictment of the lioness, yet acts on it (L.18-21). At L.21-30, the leopard first confronts the lioness, accusing her of the murder of his children, but she denies the accusation (L.27), and he ends the exchange on a feigned conciliatory note, announcing that he is going to find his 'sister' a mate (L.29). The confrontatory recapitulation (L.25: "They're fine, I think they're in your stomach") is brief and inconclusive. When the lion forces his wife to make a full confession,[1] it is with the intention of resolving the quarrel, and he advises her not to pursue the matter further (L.50: "It would be better not to go."), but his attempt to end the conflict, like the leopard's attempt to avoid it (L.19), fails. Likewise at L.66, the leopard complains to his wife about her injury to his 'sister,' but the effect of this recapitulatory confrontation is further damage to their relations: the leopard's wife deserts him (L.67-68).

Finally, the leopard goes and reports this latest quarrel to his 'sister,' the lioness, saying that he has confronted his wife on her behalf, and that it is now her responsibility to intercede in turn on his behalf:

This leopard came and said to the lion, "All right. I

---

[1] Her speech was about 45 seconds long, and according to my recollection, quite detailed. The theft of the master copy of this tape while it was stored in Kabul forced me to rely on a defective copy, this part of which had been recorded over with extraneous material.

> quarreled with her. I got very angry. If you would, go and
> ask pardon so that my wife will come back." (L.68)

This final recapitulation has the desired conciliatory effect. All the recapitulations in L, with the exception of the first (L.19), seem to be attempts at direct negotiation to achieve reconciliation. All except the last fail to reconcile the parties, whether they are lengthy or merely brief intimations like L.25. In M, however, the two recapitulations which are developed are intended to cause schism between the characters, and in fact do so. They are thematically important justifications of hostile action. Viewed in terms of dramatic effect, recapitulations with an implied threat or defiance (L.19-20,25,46,56,63,66) are ineffectual for conciliation, though they may be effective for schism (L.19-20, M.43,61-62). Recapitulations appealing for help from a position of weakness may be effective for reconciliation (L.68: "If you would, go and ask pardon so that my wife will come back.")

The placement and development of recapitulation scenes is important in articulating the themes of a given story. As Mādar Zāher's emphasis in Šīr o Palang shifts, so does her development of recapitulatory speeches. Although folklore scholars of different theoretical schools have remarked on the importance of patterned repetition to the communicative power of oral narrative,[1] many researchers, including especially those deriving their methodology from structural linguistics (e.g. Levi-Strauss, Greimas, Mathiot), work from synopses of actual narratives from which they have edited out 'redundant' statements, so that the discussion centers on iso-

---

[1] Cf. Levi-Strauss' remark, "repetition has as its function to make the structure of the myth apparent," (in T.A. Sebeok, (1958:105), A.B. Lord (1965:220), and D. Hymes (1975:34).

morphic patterns in a skeletal chain of narrative events, what I have called 'reiterative patterns' and 'analogous episodes'. Other forms of repetition are rendered invisible by the synopsizing process. One must observe, however, that the 'redundancy' of plan/execution/recapitulation sequences, in which the same events are narrated twice or more, is at the option of the storyteller, and is a direct indicator of the causal relations between events which the storyteller feels to be particularly significant. The structural significance of recapitulation as a 'password' which ratifies ensuing action (recognition of a hero, final retribution, revenge, passage of an individual character to the next transaction, etc.) cannot be ignored. Far more than a mechanical 'stall,' the recapitulation, its placement and elaboration are indicators of thematic emphasis placed on certain causal relations, particularly revealing when different degrees of elaboration can be discerned from storyteller to storyteller, or from performance to performance.

Confrontation, as portrayed in the recapitulation scenes in Šīr o Palang, is effective for schism, but not as a technique for negotiating reconciliation. This point will be taken up again in the discussion of Text N, Mādar Zāher's dispute history, below. The recapitulations in Šīr o Palang L and M form patterns of confrontation in which the characters play out different strategies and seek opposite types of resolution: in the first text, reconciliation, in the second, permanent schism. The difference in goals relates to the time at which each version of the story was told, and the narrator's then-current views on the dispute which occasioned the story, of which more later. Here it is sufficient to observe that the degree to which certain recapitulations are elaborated, and others are not, in each story, relates to the type of resolution toward which the

narrator is working, particularly in the case of M, where the two elaborated recapitulations underscore the retributive justice which constitutes the story's resolution. The retributive justice idea is not absent
from L, for L.19, one of the more elaborated recapitulations, constitutes
the leopardess' accusation of the lioness, which prompts her reluctant
husband to seek revenge. As L progresses to its end, however, the recapitulations constitute more and more explicit appeals for conciliation. From
the point of view of internal structure, Text M focuses down to a few recapitulations which put thematic emphasis on retribution, whereas the use
of recapitulation is more diffuse in L, and tends toward conciliation.
In Šir o Palang the identity theme which is frequently prominent in traditional recapitulations (see, e.g., I.300-304, K.69) appears in both L and
M, in a more abstract form, in that the leopardess's recapitulation (L.19,
M.39) answers the question, 'Who has done this?', and at the same time reveals the true nature of the lioness to the leopard who has befriended her.

Turning to the plan and execution sequences of Šir o Palang, one
finds a symmetry of structure which is simpler and tighter than that of
any of the stories hitherto discussed. This is hardly surprising, since
the symmetries and analogies discernible among episodes in tales in general
(see discussion of Afsāneh-e Garg, pp. 143 ff. above) are here reinforced
by the theme of reciprocity in revenge which is at the core of the story.
A joint outline can be developed for the two versions of Šir o Palang
which allows for schematic comparison of their similarities and differences
(Diagram VI). The prologue and first two episodes of L and M are identical
at this level of generalization (Prologue, Plan and Execution A, Plan and
Execution B). The reasons for the lioness' departure from the leopard's

Diagram VI: Šīr o Palang Synopsis [L and M]

Prologue: 1. Leopard builds house   L.2-6;
              2. Leopard invites lioness to live with him   M.17-25
              3. Leopard takes a wife
              4. Leopard's wife gets pregnant
              5. Leopard asks lioness to leave household due to
                 space constraints

Plan A: Lioness plans revenge   L.8; M.26
Execution A: Lioness eats leopardess' cubs   L.9; M.29-33
              (successful)

Plan B: Leopard plans revenge: 1. Marry off lioness   L.20; M.43
                                 2. She will give birth
                                 3. Send wife to eat her cubs
Execution B: (as above) (successful)   L.29-40;
                                                                         M.44-57

Plan C: Lioness plans to confront leopard(ess)   L.49,51
                                                              (Consolidated with
                                                               Plan D in M, M.58 -
                                                               unsuccessful)
Execution C: (unsuccessful)   L.57-58

Plan D: Lioness plans to confront leopard   L.59
Execution D: Lioness causes separation of leopards
              (successful)   L.60-67
              Leopard confronts wife (unsuccessful)   L.66-67

Plan E: Leopard asks lioness to intercede with his wife   L.68
Execution E: Lioness makes restitution, brings leopardess   L.69-72
              back to Leopard

household, her successful revenge plan and theleopard's equally successful counter-revenge follow the same simple pattern.

In the second half of L a second dyadic structure emerges, that of
confrontation and conciliation. The lioness' first plan, to confront the
leopardess (Plan C), fails, but her second attempt, to confront the leopard
(Plan D), succeeds to the extent that he is induced to go home and confront
his wife on the lioness' behalf. (L.66). This third confrontation, like
the first, fails: the leopardess leaves home in a rage (L.68). In a second exchange with the lioness, the leopard tells her that he has taken
her part and so lost his wife, and appeals to her for help in placating
the leopardess. The lioness succeeds in carrying out this conciliation
plan (L.68-72). The alternating structure of failure/success, failure/
success interweaves with alternating strategies of confrontation and conciliation, and the final success of conciliatory behavior on the part of
both the leopard (L.68) and lioness (L.69-72) reaffirms the sibling relationship between the two animals and its effectiveness in domestic negotiations. Just as the leopard is responsive to his 'sister's' sense of injury, so she can be called upon to help redress injuries he suffers for
her sake. The three plan/execution sequences which conclude L break down
into four interactional episodes, in which the mutual dependence and influence of all three of the story's characters on each other are reconfirmed.
The alternation of unsuccessful and successful strategies, and confrontation
vs. conciliation, is neatly worked out to a resolution which affirms the
efficacy of conciliation and the mutually unsatisfactory effects of confrontation for all parties.

The structure of M is considerably simpler, and its final statement
is of the effectiveness of confrontation to cause schism in family groups.

Only the prologue and first and second plan/execution sequences remain from version L. The two confrontation scenes (C and D) are collapsed into one in which the lioness confronts the leopard(s) together, and the leopards speak with a single voice in defying her (M.58-62). The possible significance of this new solidarity between the leopard couple will be discussed below, in the context of the stories' relationships to the dispute (Text N). Text M's simplified episodic structure presents only reciprocal revenge and final schism, with no hint of reconciliation between the affinal households. The lioness' departure (M.64) may be taken as final.

The symmetry and reciprocity which are visible in Šīr o Palang in both versions are not only germane to the subject of revenge and reconciliation which is the core of the story's meaning. Analogy and symmetry among episodes are general features of traditional narrative structure in multi-episodic tales of greater complexity such as Mār Čūčeh and Afsāneh-e Garg where a limited number of themes are also being explored from a variety of angles. The episodic symmetry of Šīr o Palang is owing not only to its theme, but also to the canons of oral traditional structure. A revenge tale lends itself particularly well to construction in a series of balances, which is a basic oral technique. Although newly composed, the story partakes of the structure and style of traditional narrative.

The surface message of this animal fable is a simple moral one: vindictiveness will be punished. One animal altruistically extends hospitality to another who is disabled, and a fictive sibling relationship is created between them (L.28,66; M.22,43,46,48). Later, the leopard benefactor wishes to withdraw his hospitality because of his own family's needs, and the lioness becomes angry and vindictively seeks revenge on her

'brother's' family. The leopard makes an unsuccessful attempt to ignore
the injury (L.18, M.43), and then (in the first version only) tries to resolve the problem by direct negotiation (L.21-27), before he sets the lioness up for reciprocal vengeance (L.28, M.43,46). The vengeance, which the
leopardess exacts with her husband's help, has two different results: in
L, the lioness is punished and induced to make restitution. She gives the
leopardess a cub and persuades her to return to her husband, thus reaf-
firming the mutual responsibilities of all three characters to each other.
In M, after the lioness is punished, relations are broken off between the
two households, and the lioness is deterred from further aggressive acts
by her fear of reprisal (M.63).[1]

The 'point' of the story is a cautionary statement on sibling and
affine relations, with regard to human beings. In both L and M, the leopard's problems emphasize the primacy of the nuclear family's interests
over those of collateral relatives (his 'sister,' the lioness). In both
cases, the lioness sister is finally made to defer to the leopardess wife's
interests, specifically with regard to offspring. The moral of Šīr o Palang
combines a simple retributive theme, that vindictive acts will be repro-
cated, with a social message that, while sibling relationships imply one
set of responsibilities, the interests of the siblings' nuclear families
must and will come first.

Thematically, Šīr o Palang addresses some of the same issues as Mār

---

[1] A possible etiological conclusion, that lions and leopards are separate
species, is not stated, nor would it be of particular interest to Heratis,
for whom the real ecology of large felines is irrelevant. Though Asian
lions formerly inhabited the Caspian area and snow leopards are still to
be found in the Hindu Kush, these animal remain almost mythical to Heratis:
witness Mahgol's confusion of lions with dragons, Text E.

Čučeh and Xasteh Xomãr, i.e. the responsibilities of siblings, spouses and parents. In Šīr o Palang, parents treat their offspring's interests as primary, to the detriment of sibling relationships. In Mãr Čučeh the hero acts out of a primary loyalty to his sibling, and punishes his own parents (and patron) when they violate their responsibilities toward his brother. In Xasteh Xomãr, the main characters are made to break with siblings and parents, in order to achieve a successful marriage. The three tales, in different ways, all assert the priority of the interests of the new, nuclear generative unit and/or the younger generation, over those of the elder generation and the extended family.

Texturally, structurally, and with regard to its essential ideological preoccupations, Šīr o Palang, although an invented tale, shares many features with the traditional tales from Mãdar Zãher's repertoire that we have examined previously. Šīr o Palang makes a statement about certain familial responsibilities, and the possible consequences of their violation. What induced Mãdar Zãher to formulate this particular statement on those themes at this particular time?

Although friction had arisen between Mãdar Zãher's husband and her siblings in the past,[1] the 'sibling vs. affine' issue did not seem to be an acute problem in her immediate family at the time she offered me Šīr o Palang as a 'new story'. The original source of friction among the animals in both L and M versions of the story is a crowded common dwelling. This fact was my initial clue to the etiology of this story, for Mãdar Zãher

---

[1] Xairuddīn, Mãdar Zãher's husband, and her eldest brother Hafīz, both Peace Corps cooks, were not speaking because of a dispute over the distribution of available jobs. Several years earlier, Mãdar Zãher and her husband had stopped sharing housing with her brother on account of another dispute.

and her husband, at the time of Šīr o Palang's first performance, were involved in a very acrimonious quarrel with Xairuddīn's father's brother's son, Ğolām Nabī, which had first flared up in the form of hostilities over housing. A synopsis of events concerned in the dispute, a time line which reconstructs to the best of my knowledge the sequence of events in the spring, summer and autumn of 1975, will be found in Diagram VII. At the time of performance L, Madar Zaher was acutely worried that the dispute would erupt into violence. There was daily heated discussion about the dispute and the two parties' possible negotiation and confrontation strategies, as it progressed through the months of June, July and August, 1975, during which time Xairuddīn was making frequent overnight trips to the home village to try to resolve the matter.

The immediate object of dispute between Xairuddīn and his cousin at the time Text L was recorded was a piece of wheat land in Xairuddīn's home village which both men claimed to own.[1] Previous to this stage, however, the dispute had centered around Ğolām Nabī's residence in Xairuddīn's newly purchased house in Herat city.

Going more deeply into the reasons for the dispute, I was told that

---

[1] Xairuddīn said he had purchased the land eight years earlier from Ğolām Nabī and his now-deceased brother (N.51). Since that time he had farmed it with the help of a tenant farmer. Ğolām Nabī asserted that the land had only been mortgaged, that he had repaid the loan on time, and that this year's wheat crop therefore belonged to him. There were no written documents, and the village headman who witnessed the original transaction was mysteriously unwilling to swear to the terms agreed upon. The mortgage system in wide use in Afghanistan, called gerau, allows one to borrow an amount of cash using a piece of property as collateral (usually farm land or a house), for a set time period during which the lender has the usufruct of the property. If the loan is not repaid on time, the lender gains permanent title to the property. Under Islamic law, the taking of interest on loans is forbidden. Gerau permits money-lending for profit within this legal constraint.

FIGURE III

Kinship Chart for Xairuddīn, Ĝolām Nabī and Mādar Zāher

MZ = Mādar Zāher
X = Xairuddīn
GN = Ĝolām Nabī
T = Tīmur
Z = Zāher
H = Hanīfeh

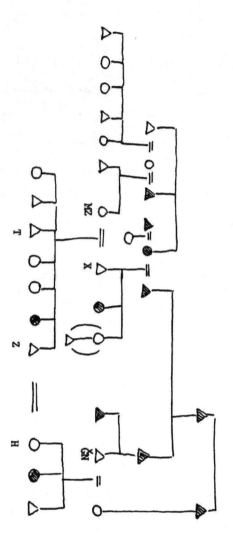

This chart is not comprehensive, in that it does not diagram the entire extended family (e.g. other offspring of Ĝolām Nabī and his deceased brother).

DIAGRAM VII: DISPUTE SYNOPSIS

1. ca. 1968   Xairuddīn buys (leases?) land from his elder first cousin,
               Golām Nabī, in their home village, and lets it to a share-
               cropper

2. 1974   Xairuddīn and Golām Nabī engage two of their children to
               marry each other.

3. 1974-75   Xairuddīn, employed in Herat City for several years, uses
               savings and borrows moeny to buy a house in the city (approx.
               cost $US 2000). (Golām Nabī is reported by X's employer to
               sold a donkey and contributed the proceeds, approx. $30, to
               help buy the house.)

4. Jan. or   Xairuddīn give living space in the new house to Golām Nabī,
   Feb. 1975   his wife, their 20-year-old son and 6-year-old daughter, who
               is engaged to Zāher, X's 14-year-old son.

5. March,   Xairuddīn finds a paying tenant (a female Peace Corps volun-
   1975   teer) and tells Golām Nabī he must leave. Golām Nabī returns
               under protest to a family-owned house in the village. Golām
               Nabī's son departs for Iran as a migrant laborer. (Hafīz, X's
               brother-in-law, later reported that G.N. had threatened to
               interfere with X's wheat harvest when he was evicted.)

7. late June, G.N. claims the winter wheat harvest, now ripe, from the land
   1975   mentioned in #1, above, refusing to let X. or his tenant har-
               vest it, and claiming that the land was only leased, not sold,
               G.N. threatens to kill his own child and himself on the land
               rather than let X. harvest it, saying he lacks other means to
               support his family. [X's interpretation: G.N. intends to de-
               lay until the wheat is spoiled, in order to hurt X.]

8. Aug. 3   MZ performs Sīr o Palang, Text L.

9. August,   Dispute taken to subgovernor's office. Additional attempts
   1975   to mediate. Hafīz, X's brother-in-law, now reports that Golām
               Nabī is basing his appeal on his age and indigency, and the
               welfare of his remaining dependent child (X's prospective
               daughter-in-law). G.N.'s son still absent in Iran.

10. Sept. '75 M. Mills absent from Herat. X's Peace Corps employer and
    to Feb.,   tenant informed me by mail in October that the dispute had
    1976   been settled by transfer of the land to G.N. 'in the name of
               his daughter'. (X's rationale: G.N. is old, unable to support
               his family, and despite his untrustworthiness, a family mem-
               ber who must be taken care of.)

11. Feb. 13,   Mādar Zāher performs Sīr o Palang (Text M and shows me a
    1976   silk handkerchief and gold pin, tokens of public engagement

given to Zāher by his fiancee's parents. MZ remarks on the inferior quality of the handkerchief.

12. Feb. 14, 1976 — In the context of a general conversation about marriages in her family (Text N) Mādar Zāher relates a summary of the dispute with Ǧolām Nabī and its relationship to the engagement of Zāher to Ǧolām Nabī's daughter and previous plans for Zāher's engagement.

13. March, 1978 — Zāher writes to M. Mills with further details on the progress of his engagement (Text O).

Xairuddīn, whose eldest son was engaged to Ğolām Nabī's daughter, had given Ğolām Nabī free living space in the house in Herat for a few months before he had the opportunity to rent the space to a female Peace Corps English teacher who arrived in Herat on a two-year assignment. When Xairuddīn told Ğolām Nabī that he had found a renter and that Ğolām Nabī would have to vacate, Ğolām Nabī at first refused to leave. He finally left, threatening reprisals, under great pressure from Xairuddīn's family. Xairuddīn and Mādar Zāher, as well as other relatives, interpreted Ğolām Nabī's claim on the farmland as a reprisal for Xairuddīn's withdrawal of hospitality (N.45-51). Xairuddīn and Mādar Zāher represented the initial offer of housing as a charitable gesture to a poor cousin, a further analogy to the events of Mādar Zāher's fable. There was no doubt that Ğolām Nabī was in an economically weak position at the time of these events. He was a man in his sixties, less able physically to earn a living by farming than he had been in the past. His adult son had gone to Iran as a migrant laborer in the early spring of 1975, and had not sent any money or word of his whereabouts back to the family, to Mādar Zāher's knowledge. Mādar Zāher's claim that Ğolām Nabī borrowed money continuously without paying it back (N.44) was one of several charges Mādar Zāher and Xairuddīn made against Ğolām Nabī and his family, another example of which was that Ğolām Nabī's son had borrowed a good man's shawl from Xairuddīn and sold it in the bazaar, saying that he had lost it.

Mādar Zāher and Xairuddīn presented a negative assessment of Ğolām Nabī's character (and that of his son) to their foreign friends, as well as mitigating circumstances to justify their withdrawal of hospitality from

Golām Nabī.[1] As in Mādar Zāher's fable, they presented their case so as
to emphasize their own moral rectitude. Nonetheless, on close examination
of Mādar Zāher's own version of the dispute history (Text N), both the
causes of the dispute and the strategies employed to settle it reveal a
reciprocity of offenses and a compromise solution in which both parties
acknowledged each other's claims.

As mentioned previously, Xairuddīn still owed a substantial amount
on the house, and this was his primary excuse for ejecting Golām Nabī in
favor of a paying tenant. Nevertheless, his original offer of free housing
to his cousin was not simply a charitable gesture. It was partly motivated
by self-interest, and partly an acknowledgement of an outstanding debt to
Golām Nabī himself, in connection with the engagement of Zāher, Xairuddīn's
eldest son, to Golām Nabī's young daughter.

Zāher was engaged to Golām Nabī's daughter Sargol, although this
match was not Xairuddīn's ideal choice (N.30), as a compromise following
a younger son's fearful reaction to early engagement (N.33). No brideprice
had as yet been paid to Golām Nabī, although a formal engagement party had
been held (N.38: another indication that Xairuddīn was reluctant to conclude the match). Given Golām Nabī's difficult economic circumstances,
he probably anticipated some financial relief from the engagement of his
daughter to his wealthier cousin's son. Instead, Xairuddīn put his surplus
capital, and all the money he could raise, into purchasing a house (N.36).
Xairuddīn offered Golām Nabī rent-free living space in his new house not
only as a humanitarian gesture which would enable the older man to seek

[1] Xairuddīn still owed about 1/4 of the purchase price of the house to
various creditors, and hoped to use rent revenues to help pay the debts.
Cf. N.46.

wage labor in the city (N.38), but also because of the brideprice he still owed Ǧolām Nabī, a fact which is acknowledged in passing in Mādar Zāher's narrative (N.38).

Furthermore, Xairuddīn needed to have the house occupied, to secure customary title to it (N.37). Although the government is pressing local officials to secure written records of sales and other private transactions (N.65-66), written contracts are still exceptional in a country with well over 80% functional illiteracy.[1] Physical possession and customary use still weigh heavily in ownership disputes (hence Xairuddīn's irate reaction to the rumor that Ǧolām Nabī was claiming title to the part of the house which he occupied[2]). Xairuddīn needed to have the house occupied so that the previous owner could not deny later that the sale had taken place. Xairuddīn was not himself in a position to move into the house, because he bought the house just before the beginning of his Peace Corps employer's out-of-country leave, when he planned to be abroad for two months. Hitherto, Xairuddīn and his family had 'lived in' at his employer's, and his presence as a guard in his employer's compound was even more neces-

---

[1] The real figure is probably in excess of 90%, although free public education has reached an increasingly larger segment of the population over that last twenty years. Vide Smith et al., 1973:135-149. The use of written contracts is not well understood by ordinary people (cf. N.64).

[2] In this connection, Xairuddīn's anxiety about Ǧolām Nabī's claim on the house was rooted in its plausibility: everyone knew that their children were engaged and a brideprice was presumably owing. His anxiety was doubtless increased by the cash value of Ǧolām Nabī's claim; 50,000 Afghanis ($1000), half the value of the house, was about twice what one might expect to pay a near relative, without power or social connections, as brideprice for a young girl of no particular accomplishments. Brideprices of 50,000 Afghanis and more were paid in Herat between wealthy families and among Turkomans or others whose young girls were already rug weavers and thus had considerable earning power.

sary during his employer's absence (N.37). Hence Xairuddīn's invitation
to Ğolām Nabī served his own interests both in securing his new house and
in helping to allay his sense of debt to his cousin.[1]

Even within the fable, there are indications that Xairuddīn, or
Mādar Zāher, felt some compunctions about their eviction of Ğolām Nabī.
The intermittent use in colloquial Heratī of ambiguous first and second
person plural verb ending, /konīm/. in Šīr o Palang L and M (L.6,19,22-23,
63; M.25,62),[2] allows the leopard to deny that he has forced the lioness
to leave his house, and assert that he intended that they should build a
larger joint household together. He never acknowledges the fact that he
has evicted his 'sister,' even though both she and his wife insist that
this was the case. The leopard thereafter treats the lioness' angry departure as an over-reaction (L.23,28,63; M.62). In the real quarrel, the
wife (Mādar Zāher), not the husband, delivered an unequivocal eviction
notice to her husband's 'sibling' (N.51). Mādar Zāher describes her own
direct role in forcing Ğolām Nabī to leave the house. The transformation
and transfer of this exchange in the story suggests that Mādar Zāher felt
her own forthright action to be less defensible than the leopard's politely

---

[1] It is unlikely that Ğolām Nabī would have agreed to rent-free housing
in lieu of cash or property as a brideprice. The most Xairuddīn could
expect from this arrangement would be reduced pressure to pay the debt,
if Ğolām Nabī succeeded in finding paying work in the city, which he
did not.

[2] -īm, the regular first person plural verb ending in literary Persian
and colloquial Farsi (Iranian), is regularly used for second and first
person plural in colloquial Herati. -am, the literary first person
singular, regularly replaces third person plural -and in Herati, while
the first person singular ending becomes -om. The use of -am for third
person plural is initially confusing for a speaker of standard Persian,
but not ambiguous within the dialect. -īm serves ambiguously for both
first and second person (polite) plural, and this ambiguity is exploited
to some degree in polite speech, to avoid the appearance of making direct inquiries or imperative statements, both of which are impolite.

ambiguous "Let's build a house" (L.6), despite the mitigating circumstances of her own family's needs.

A second significant reformulation which Mādar Zāher makes in fictionalizing the family quarrel, is her transformation of the collateral relationship to a fictive, adoptive one. Her husband and Ǧolām Nabī are real first cousins; her conversion of this relationship to a fictive one suggests that she is unwilling to acknowledge its claims on her husband's loyalty. (See pp.212, 224 below.)

The question of coresidence with Ǧolām Nabī was, for Xairuddīn, a choice between the immediate economic interests of his own household and those of collateral relatives (his cousin's economic need and the debt he owed him). Xairuddīn chose in favor of his nuclear family's immedaite interests. Despite the fact that the two households' long-term interests were tied together by the engagement of their children, Xairuddīn had no desire to cement this mutuality of interest further by giving Ǧolām Nabī part ownership of his house. If Mādar Zāher's complaints were not invented after the fact, the proximity of the indigent Ǧolām Nabī and his somewhat dishonest son was already becoming a financial burden to Xairuddīn and Mādar Zāher (N.44), in Mādar Zāher's view taking food out of her children's mouths ("Zāher went and got two oranges from the shop (on credit) -").

Both parties in the dispute, at different times, voiced their anger in terms of threats to their offspring. Mādar Zāher's complaint that she had to buy her children fruit on credit, because Ǧolām Nabī had borrowed all her spending money, was a less vehement echo of Ǧolām Nabī's threat to kill his daughter on the land which he contested with Xairuddīn (N.54). The import of his threat was that, without the use of this land which he

claimed as his own, he and his child would starve, so it would be better
for him to kill himself and his child in the face of Xairuddīn's opposition,
than to let Xairuddīn keep the land and starve slowly. His emphasis on his
own poverty constituted an accusation that Xairuddīn was exploiting his
poor relation's weakness, even to the point of jeopardizing his future
daughter-in-law's survival. The eating of offspring in Šīr o Palang is a
vivid metaphor for the actual dispute's rhetoric, in which both parties
represented their opponents' actions as threatening the well-being of
their children.

    Ǧolām Nabī's claim on the wheat field was strategically timed to
give Xairuddīn the least possible latitude for negotiation. By claiming
the land at the moment the crop was ready to harvest, Ǧolām Nabī put the
ownership of the harvest in doubt, and gave Xairuddīn no time to maneuver,
for if harvesting is delayed the overripe wheat may drop from the ears and
be lost in a matter of days. Xairuddīn's share of this harvest was a substantial portion of his family's annual bread supply, so his stake in the
harvest was considerable, apart from his contractual responsibilities to
his tenant farmer. Xairuddīn, Mādar Zāher and Mādar Zāher's brother Hafīz
all interpreted Ǧolām Nabī's tactics as those of a spoiler, who sought to
hurt his cousin's family, taking food from the children's mouths, with no
real benefit to himself, a palpable analogy to the lioness' vindictive
attack on the leopard's family.

    Mādar Zāher's rendering of her husband's defiance of Ǧolām Nabī dur-
ing the harvest (N.59: "If you're a man, come on, then . . .") echoes the
defiant speech of the leopard to the lioness at the end of M (M.16: ". . .
if you're a man, come and fight with me . . .") which was recorded the

previous day. The rhetoric rings rather oddly between two animals, when the addressee is female. In the vehemence of the moment, Mādar Zāher's artistry, by which she has cast a human dispute into animal fable, slips and anthropomorphism exceeds artistic bounds. Although impossible to confirm, it seems likely from the parallel diction of M.61 and N.59 that the rhetoric of the real confrontation, as reported to Mādar Zāher, has been carried over into the fictional confrontation.

Xairuddīn's defiance, like that of the leopard, was effective, at least to the extent that he was able to harvest the wheat (N.62-63), though Golām Nabī subsequently took his complaint to 'the government' (N.63), just as the lioness was invited to do (M.62). Taking the complaint to the local government was regarded as a last resort by the principals for several reasons, among which two are prominent: a) local officials could force an imposed settlement on the two parties, satisfactory to neither, whereas the traditional methods of arbitration were more likely to achieve a compromise resolution , and b) government officials would extract fees for service as well as bribes, before they would take action for either party, and so adjudication was likely to involve additional cash outlay for both parties (cf. N.65: ". . . then he [Xairuddīn] went, and made a complaint. So he paid out a certain amount of money, then the *qāzī* [religious magistrate] said to him, bawled out Golām Nabī . . .").[1] Hence the leopard's invitation to the lioness to go to the government is ironic not just for its anthropomorphism, but because the plaintiff may ultimately be forced to comply with government orders, against his will (N.65-66). Golām Nabī, having secured

---

[1] Given Golām Nabī's poverty, Xairuddīn's family surmised that he had a financial backer in the dispute, though I was unable to elicit more than vague accusations as to who might be involved and why.

the land and a note of agreement from Xairuddīn, was reluctant to furnish Xairuddīn with a reciprocal statement. (Once again, unfamiliarity with and distrust of written documents played a part in this transaction.) In addition, Ǧolām Nabī's reluctance to agree in writing may have stemmed from the fact that the agreement would have implied Xairuddīn's legal ownership of the land which he now transferred to Ǧolām Nabī as a brideprice for his daughter, and thus the falsity of Ǧolām Nabī's earlier claim that he owned the land. There was a certain amount of face-saving involved for Xairuddīn, who essentially forced Ǧolām Nabī to admit that the land was not his (cf. N.63, ". . . if you like this land (so much), I give it to you," and N.65). Another factor may have been that the brideprice to be paid for the girl, apparently unspecified at the time of the engagement and when Ǧolām Nabī first claimed half of Xairuddīn's house, was now established and limited by contract. Further claims on Xairuddīn for the girl's sake would be limited to gifts of clothing for the girl herself, and perhaps her school expenses, and the cost of the wedding when Zāher's family should choose to hold it.[1]

As Mādar Zāher's laughing comment suggests,

> If we do it, (i.e. the wedding), fine, we do it. If we don't do it, he'll be happy with that, coming, and coming. (laughs)" (N.69),

Xairuddīn now has power over his cousin, in that while Ǧolām Nabī cannot give his daughter to anyone else without repaying the brideprice and other expenses incurred by Xairuddīn, yet the wedding will be held at the discretion of the bridegroom's family. If they choose not to take the girl into their household for any reason, Ǧolām Nabī will be obliged to keep

---

[1] Cf. O.5.

and support her indefinitely.[1] The potential burden of supporting an extra adult woman, who could not contribute to the family's cash economy or attract a husband who would do so, was a hardship to be feared, and a threat which would deter Golām Nabī from trying to exploit his family's connection with Xairuddīn's by any further claims. Once again, like the deterrent which is introduced at the end of M (the threat of reprisals which the lioness fears: "If I go and eat the leopard's cubs, the leopard will come and eat mine," M.63), the deterrent upon which Xairuddīn and Mādar Zāher rely is their ability to strike at the well-being of Golām Nabī's own family, particularly his offspring, and through his daughter, at him.

Various aspects of the plot of Šīr o Palang relate directly or metaphorically to the events of the dispute then current in Mādar Zāher's family, as she recounted it in Text N. There are other aspects of the story, whose relation to the dispute is less clear. Xairuddīn and Golām Nabī are the primary disputants in the quarrel as Mādar Zāher reported it (Text N), yet in both versions of Šīr o Palang the females (lioness and leopardess) are the aggressors and the instigators of violence. The males' own strategies incline toward ignoring injuries, toward negotiation and conciliation unless they are forced into aggressive stands by the females (e.g. L.19-21, L.48-53, L.61, L.68, M.39-41). At one point, Mādar Zāher even praises the male lion for his desire to avoid a quarrel: "This male

---

[1] In a separate conversation, Mādar Zāher explained to me that Xairuddīn's half sister, a robust and attractive woman of about 40-45, had no children because she had only recently married. Her childhood fiancé and his family having migrated away from Herat without releasing her from her engagement, Maryām's family had consulted a mulla about their legal responsibilities to the other family. The mulla had directed them to hang her veil (čādri) on a peg on the wall, and that she would be released from her engagement when the čādri rotted and fell from the peg of its own accord. Apparently the čādri was a durable one.

lion is very intelligent, has a good brain. He stayed (behind)." (L.53)
In the final confrontation in M, however, when Mādar Zāher brings both
pairs of animals together, the leopard's voice, speaking for himself and
his mate, is anything but conciliatory, and speaks of the manliness of revenge. Two conflicting ethical standards are operative in the animal tale,
just as they are in Afghan society. In negotiations, the saving of face
and the ability to avoid conflict are praiseworthy social skills, and the
skilled negotiator is a respected figure. Yet in a society where blood
feud is still practiced (though more commonly among tribal Pashtun than
among the Heratis), a man's ability to avenge a blow to his family is also
an index of personal worth and strength. As Mādar Zāher states both in her
tale and in the dispute history, confrontation may be the honorable, 'manly'
strategy (M.61-62; N.59). Nonetheless, in the story it is the females who
instigate aggressive behavior, the males who advocate conciliation and try
to avoid confrontation. In the dispute, it was the men, Ǧolām Nabī and
Xairuddīn, who ultimately confronted each other with physical threats over
the land (N.55-60). The women are entirely in the background at this stage
of the dispute, at home listening to the news and interpretations offered
by male members of the family, expressing themselves directly only to their
husbands and near relatives, in Mādar Zāher's case to Xairuddīn and her own
brother Hafīz, who with his father (N.61) took part in holding the harvest
in trust against a settlement and in negotiating the settlement itself.

Looking back to the original confrontation when Ǧolām Nabī was expelled from the house, however, one finds women very much in the forefront
of the confrontation. Mādar Zāher and Xairuddīn are equally disturbed by
the report that Ǧolām Nabī has claimed part ownership in their house (N.45),
but Mādar Zāher prevents her husband from throwing Ǧolām Nabī out of the

house bodily:

> I said, "Don't do that . . . I'll go, I'll go to - I'll go and
> tell him, and he'll leave."

In the dispute history, the initial action of a woman (Mādar Zāher) leads
to hostilities between men, while in <u>Šīr o Palang</u> it is the leopard who
expels his own sibling, leading to hostilities between the females (see
pp.188,200 above).

The dispute does resemble the story, in that Mādar Zāher justifies
her demand, that Čolām Nabī's family leave the house, in terms which apply
quintessentially to women's interests and problems: the need for privacy
and decorum, especially in the proximity of foreigners. Gail Gentes, the
new Peace Corps teacher, provided Xairuddīn with a rare opportunity to
rent part of his house, and continue to live in the other half. She was expected to arrive in Herat at the beginning of the spring-summer school term,
when Xairuddīn's employer would also return from leave and free him to move
into his own house. Xairuddīn could only rent to a woman, because his wife
kept purdah with respect to all non-relatives, including her husband's
American employer, and the new compound was so small as to make sequestra-
tion very difficult. Peace Corps women assigned to the provinces were very
few, so a female tenant was a rare opportunity. The purdah issue was made
more compelling by Mādar Zāher's newly acquired status as a professional
diviner and religious healer (amulet maker), which made it necessary for
women clients to visit her at home (N.48). Mādar Zāher felt that her special powers were directly dependent on her maintaining strict religious
purity, including strict purdah. She was certainly accurate in saying that
her women clients would be reluctant to visit her in the home of a foreign
male, where she had hitherto resided, and her fear of government disapproval

and/or interference was justified (N.48). Thus the sources of Xairuddin's new income, and of his immediate need for new living space, were both female. The metaphorical connection between his situation and the leopard's good fortune in finding a wife seems clear.

Although Mādar Zāher, by her actions and arguments, forces Golām Nabī to leave, she avoids direct confrontation over the issue of house ownership which has aroused her (and her husband's) anger, and confines her argument to external considerations such as the possibility of renting part of the house, and her own new professional needs, as grounds for her action. She does not express her anger (and fear) at Golām Nabī's alleged claim on the house, which was the immediate instigation of the confrontation (N.45). This circumstance is quite accurately reflected in the leopard's argument, "We need more room," and the lioness' interpretation, "They don't like me." (L.7). The blame for taking offense is transferred to the lioness, but behind Mādar Zāher's impersonal arguments for the eviction of Golām Nabī lie a strong personal animus and apprehension stemming from Xairuddin's real debt to Golam Nabī, the unpaid brideprice.[1]

Mādar Zāher's report of the dispute in Text N also leaves unexplained her reasons for casting the main aggressor in the fable, the

---

[1] If Golām Nabī hoped to consolidate a claim on Xairuddin's house as brideprice, as Xairuddin feared (N.44: "And he went before the qāẓī and said, 'He's given half this house as brideprice for my daughter,'"), and failed, it seems clear that Golām Nabī's subsequent claim on the wheatfield was intended to force Xairuddin to settle on the brideprice, not merely as a spoiler's tactic to hurt him by ruining the harvest. Golām Nabī's arguments were ambiguous from the beginning. Although Golām Nabī claimed the land as his own, he also argued that his own poverty made it impossible for him to live without it (N.54). Ultimately, he forced Xairuddin to give him the land as brideprice, which was probably his original intention. The claim to title to the land was an extreme measure to force Xairuddin to negotiate, which Golām Nabī's claim on the house while he lived in it failed to do. The fable puts a purely destructive interpretation on the disgruntled relatives' tactics.

husband's foster sibling, as a female. Her report of the actual quarrel puts Golām Nabī in the aggressor's role. In comparing history and fable, this assignment of gender is the chief obstacle to a simple correlation of human and animal characters. Golām Nabī's wife plays no discernible role in Mādar Zāher's report of the quarrel, except as the immediate recipient of Mādar Zāher's eviction notice (N.46). Earlier, she had advocated the engagement of the children as well (N.32), but the invitation to come to the house was extended by Xairuddīn directly to Golām Nabī, on his own initiative (N.38).

Not only does Mādar Zāher make the primary aggressor in the fable female, but she imputes the lioness' resentment partly to female jealousy (M.24: ". . . she was female, she got a little angry") at having to share the house with the leopard's new wife, even before she is asked to leave. Why, then, does Mādar Zāher make the protagonist's 'sibling' female, and relegate her spouse to a subsidiary, background role? My inquiries at the time of the dispute did not yield precise information as to Golām Nabī's wife's kinship relations with the rest of the family. Recent inquiry has yielded additional information about both her blood relationship to Xairuddīn and her role in the marriage negotiations (Text O). She is not a near relative of the family (O.2). Zāher's portrayal makes her out to be a classic mother-in-law, unpleasant, insatiably demanding, and the main source of continuing friction between the families (O.4: "Golām Nabī and his children are silent. His wife is not silent.") Although she does not figure prominently in Mādar Zāher's version of the original quarrel, Zāher's later interpretation of her character suggests that she has played an aggressive role behind the scenes, and Mādar Zāher's fictional emphasis on female aggression may in fact be accurate.

Ǧolām Nabī, like the lioness, was forced out of his adopted household by female priorities close to the economic interests of his male
relative. The confrontation by which he was forced to leave the house was
carried out by women. Just as women are primary negotiators for family
alliances contracted through marriage, so they are primary in confrontations which may lead to family schism. I believe this is the case because
there is equal potential for losing face, if the first foray (marital or
schismatic) does not have its desired results. Turning back to the earlier incident which Mādar Zāher describes, in which an older girl was considered as a potential bride for Zāher, but ultimately rejected on the advice of family and friends (N.21-24), one sees that even when the engagement may have been conceived originally by the father(s), (N.21: ". . .
Zāher's father said, 'I'll give her to Zāher,") it is the mothers who carry
out primary negotiations:

> ". . . for ten days, this woman was in my house for a visit. Her
> husband came after her, to take her (home). Her husband came after
> her, and took her, then. And we didn't go after her, or follow up
> what was said, or say anything . . ." (N.24)

Women carry out the first round of negotiations concerning an engagement so that, as in this case, if the arrangement falls through, it can be
ignored as "women's talk," and neither family need treat it as a serious
defeat or loss of face. Similarly, in the later case where a difference
threatens to cause family schism, it is the women who undertake the first
aggressive moves. If these confrontation tactics prove inconclusive, the
incident can be treated as a 'women's quarrel' without great loss of face,
and the men may or may not step in either to negotiate or to confront each
other in other ways. If Mādar Zāher's attempt to eject Ǧolām Nabī had succeeded without repercussions, it would have been the lowest-risk tactic for

achieving that goal, for the men could have treated the incident as a case of quarreling women who made coresidence impossible, too trivial a cause for male/male hostilities. The party that loses, like the rejected suit-or's party, has the option of treating the incident as unimportant. If the losers are confident or desperate enough to try new tactics, they may, like Ğolām Nabī, shift the terms of the argument to new, male ground. In Šīr o Palang as in the real-life dispute, males may work behind the scenes in female-female confrontations (as when the leopard gets his 'sister' married off, then sends his wife to exact her revenge), and in so doing can absolve themselves of direct responsibility for these hostilities, in future negotiations (L.33, M.56).

Male and female members of couples, by dividing aggressive and con-ciliatory strategies between them, can provide themselves with various fall-back plans in the management of family disputes. The lack of solidarity between the leopard and his wife in Text L, which threatens family unity at two points (L.21, L.67-68), in fact enables the leopard to behave in a conciliatory manner toward the lioness, and ultimately to preserve both the affinal and collateral family ties. By contrast, the lepard and his wife in M are never close to schism, work harmoniously to avenge themselves on the lioness (M.43), and in the final confrontation, speak with one voice in defying the lioness (M.61). Affinal solidarity never falters, but the result is a breaking of collateral bonds.

What relationship do these two configurations have to the actual dispute and its settlement? Version L was formulated in late July or early August, 1975, when the quarrel between Xairuddīn and Ğolām Nabī was at its bitterest, when Xairuddīn had harvested his crop by force and Ğolām Nabī

was soon to take his grievance to the local governor for arbitration.
Version L portrays a great deal of divisiveness in the nuclear families
of both the disputants. The leopard detaches himself from his wife's desire for revenge,(L.33: ". . . the sin will be yours, not mine,") and the
lion advises his wife to drop her quarrel (L.50). Nonetheless, the final
resolution is a compromise in which both halves of the family acknowledge
each other's grievances, and their mutual responsibility for preserving
family harmony. It seems fair to read this as a projective formulation
of what Mādar Zāher hopes will happen in the resolution of the real dispute, at this stage.

Mādar Zāher's portrayal of schism between the leopards is not only
tactically interesting, but also seems to reflect certain facts about her
and her husband's views on the subject of Zāher's engagement to Ğolām Nabī's
daughter. Mādar Zāher did not advocate Zāher's engagement to Ğolām Nabī's
daughter (N.29). Nevertheless, when the girl's engagement to her younger
son Tīmur became unworkable, she acknowledged that Xairuddīn might still
want to honor his cousin's wish for an alliance (N.33: "If you're going to
take Ğolām Nabī's daughter in Zāher's name, do it . . ."), in the same
breath that she suggests the possibility of calling off the alliance ("If
you don't do it, that's all right . . . "). It is clear that she originally favored a proposed alliance between Zāher and the daughter of a prosperous ex-village chief who was not a relative (N.32: 'I said, "Let it be
like this till they grow up, if this other guy says he wants our son, we'll
give him . . .") She dissociates herself from Xairuddīn's ultimate decision
to engage Ğolām Nabī's daughter to Zāher, their eldest son (N.34: "Put it,
Margaret dear, he sent for him . . ."). A lack of solidarity between Mādar

Zāher and her husband concerning this alliance underlies all later interaction with Ǧolām Nabī. The absence of women at the formal engagement
party (N.35) may be another indication of Mādar Zāher's disinclination to
celebrate the event. It is difficult to tell how deeply Mādar Zāher and
her husband were divided over the engagement, and to what degree Mādar
Zāher's loyalty to her husband prevented her from criticizing him openly
to outsiders such as myself. Some division did, however, arise, with
Xairuddīn giving decisive weight to the reinforcement of his collateral
ties through marriage, while Mādar Zāher's expressed preferences were for
an alliance outside the family, to a prosperous and influential non-relative. At a midpoint in the dispute, Mādar Zāher constructed her fable in
which both collateral and affinal quarrels were resolved by conciliatory
behavior.

When I returned to Herat after a five-month absence in the early
spring of 1976, the dispute had been settled and the engagement reconfirmed
by the transfer of the contested property from Xairuddīn to Ǧolām Nabī.
The conciliation reconfirmed the collateral ties between Xairuddīn and
Ǧolām Nabī. Now, however, Mādar Zāher's formulation of her fable's ending was not conciliatory, but schismatic. Her fiction now projected a
permanent break between the two families. She interpreted the actual
transfer of the land as a humanitarian gesture on her husband's part.
Both she and her husband, when challenged about their compliance with Ǧolām
Nabī's demands, replied to the effect that 'Ǧolam Nabī is an old man, he's
unable to take care of himself, and he's damaged his reputation in the village of lying about the land. It was the least we could do.' I myself
raised a question as to whether Ǧolām Nabī might continue to take advantage

of the engagement, to extort more property or money from Xairuddīn. Mādar Zāher replied, smiling, that they now had the power to work a hardship on Golām Nabī, if they chose to delay the wedding. She reiterated this point at N.69 (see discussion, pp. 204-5, above). M, with its schismatic ending, expresses a good deal of residual bitterness on the part of Mādar Zāher concerning the actual outcome of the dispute. Her remarks about the possibility of delaying the marriage also suggest that the bitterness between the two families could resurface with further hostilities in the future.

Paradoxically, M depicts a solidarity between the leopard husband and wife which was absent in L, and which probably does reflect a new solidarity prevailing between Xairuddīn and Mādar Zāher, at least where Golām Nabī is concerned. In conversation, Xairuddīn and Mādar Zāher both portrayed themselves as sacrificing land that was rightfully theirs to restore family harmony, not as absolving themselves of a debt they owed. It is only by close reading of Mādar Zāher's version of the dispute that one discovers what Golām Nabī's real moral claim must have been, in the issue of the unpaid brideprice. Mādar Zāher portrays her husband as a wronged party who acted in a spirit of self-sacrifice (N.63), and who then had to force Golām Nabī to do his part in ratifying the agreement (N.65-66). This suggests a solidarity of opinion between Mādar Zāher and Xairuddīn in the latter stages of the dispute, which was absent in the negotiation for the engagement. In M, Mādar Zāher's projection of the dispute into fiction likewise portrays a new solidarity between the leopard and his wife, in their assessment of their adversary's character and their determination to thwart her. Xairuddīn's anger at Golām Nabī during the dispute (N.45,59) vindicated Mādar Zāher's earlier reservations about the engagement. Meanwhile, by the time

she recorded M, the real dispute's potential for mutually destructive revenge and irreparable schism was safely past, leaving her free to work out
a fanciful scenario in which revenge is fully realized and final.

Like Afsāneh-e Garg, Šīr o Palang provides an example of a story
which is of a certain complexity when it first appears in Mādar Zāher's
repertoire, but which is eroded and shortened by the omission of significant content over a six-month period following her first performance of it.
Šīr o Palang in particular has a complex relationship to real events in
Mādar Zāher's own life, which she reinterpreted between her first and second formulations of the tale. The fable is a working out of Mādar Zāher's
own feelings and beliefs about a certain real situation, her fears and her
hopes, and the process of 'forgetting' or revising such a tale is affected
in complex ways by her continual experiences. In the case of Afsāneh-e
Garg, the question of the simplification of that narrative through the
omission of certain episodes is complicated by the presence in Mādar Zāher's
prior repertoire of stories of equal or greater complexity, which furthermore include the very episodes she has omitted from the newly acquired
story. It is possible that her prior knowledge of 'key' episodes is what
caused her to omit them from the story she learned later. Taken together,
Šīr o Palang, Afsāneh-e Garg and Mār Čučeh, by the internal changes which
they undergo between single performances, graphically illustrate the flexibility of oral narrative in performance and transmission. When these
changes are viewed from the perspective of external circumstances such as
prior repertoire and the occasions of composition or performance, the
reasons for change are seen to be even more varied than the changes themselves, and to an extent enigmatic. Even these three dramatically different instances of change in transmission cannot be taken as setting the

range for possible variation, or a range of possible causes for variation. The limits of the foregoing study will be taken up in the chapter which follows.

VI. Conclusion

In chapter I (p. 6) the question was posed, "Is the variation observable in normal transmission significant at the structural level, or
is it merely the substitution of structurally equivalent objects, personages, and events into a single narrative ⁻framework?" The answer arrived at in succeeding chapters, that variation is indeed structural,
implies a criticism of both Proppian and diffusionist approaches to traditional narrative form. A further question was posed as well, namely,
"What does the structuralist concept of 'meaning' have to do with the
changes that arise in transmission?" My analysis of three tales revealed
changes in the orderly juxtaposition of conceptual categories indicative
of basic differences in emphasis and in final resolutions on the part of
three narrators.

In the case of Mār Čučeh, the changes Mādar Zāher made in the story
she heard from Adī are clearly structural, as they affect the final resolution of themes ('mediation' of conceptual categories, in structuralist
parlance), with particular reference to the main character's integration
into human society. One may ask, "Is Mādar Zāher's revision process as
exemplified in Mār Čučeh 'normal transmission'?" Yes, for the configuration of ideas which she derived is present elsewhere in Persian oral
tradition, on the evidence of Friedl's (1975, 1977) examples. Also, there
is potential even in Adī's storytelling for the domestication of Mār
Čučeh, as when, at the end of B (B.128), she has Mār Čučeh carry off the
vizier's remaining possessions to his own house.

Not only does Mädar Zäher rearrange the events of M̄ār Čučeh so as
to achieve a different final resolution of relations between the natural
and the supernatural, but she alters surface (descriptive) detail throughout the tale. As Barre Toelken (1969:222) observed with regard to Navaho trickster tales, diction can be as important to meaning as structure or
even more so. Structural and semiotic approaches to narrative factor out
diction, 'texture', which is regarded as superficial to meaning, which latter
is said to be mediated at the structural level. Toelken has shown this
assumption to be inappropriate in the Navaho case. The case of M̄ār Čučeh
illustrates the interrelated nature of structure and texture in Mädar
Zäher's storytelling, and this argument could probably be extended to traditional storytelling in general in Persian. There is no reason to regard
harmony of structure and diction to be a literary invention. The effects
of Mädar Zäher's changes in structure and texture in M̄ār Čučeh are univocal, substantially reduce the arbitrary, ambiguous and violent elements
in the story, and combine to normalize the main character's relations with
the everyday world.

Even with an unchanged resolution pattern, the arrangement of episodes
within a single tale shows great flexibility among traditional narrators.
In the different versions of Afsāneh-e Garg different ordering principles
govern each storyteller's arrangement of episodes. Although this group of
episodes is a set of permutations on a very limited set of ideas, the permutations can be arranged in several different ways for (or because of) different narrative emphases. The order of events in a story is determined
by the storytellers' choice of distinguishing features to treat as primary
(e.g. types of adversary or types of quest object), and also by their disposition toward chiasm or clustering of similar items. Meaning emerges

from a series of events through the emphatic power of repetition, and through variation on a few simple themes. Each storyteller's mnemonic patterns are tailored by his or her choice of meanings. Semantic emphases change from narrator to narrator, which in turn changes the order of presentation of the analogous events within the tale.

If it is accepted that Mār Čučeh and Garg exhibit structural changes in transmission, and that structural change is normal in the traditional transmission process, this line of argument leads to the issues of structure, genre, and 'the story'. To what extent can one change the relationship among a story's parts, without making the whole into a different entity? The proverbial, "This is my father's axe. My father gave it a new handle, and I gave it a new head," is apt to describe variation from the Proppian and diffusionist points of view, but in Mār Čučeh at least, we have, "This is my father's axe, and I put a new shovel blade on it." Yet the storyteller represents it as "the same story". Generic distinctions based on structure (e.g. Maranda & Köngas-Maranda, 1971, and Meletinsky, 1974a) must be set against actual narratives asserted by tradition-bearers to be 'the same'.

Certain elements or episodes within the tale seem to be perceived as equivalent by traditional narrators. Two discussed above are the magic wedding, as it appears in Mār Čučeh and Xasteh Xomār, and the 'Tree of Bells/Tree of Forty Voices' incident in Garg and Alī Zarrīn. In the case of the magic wedding, the marriage proposals in the two stories have different structural roles: in Mār Čučeh, the snake's proposal is the villain's first foray against the main character; in Xasteh Xomār it is a test of filial loyalty, which the heroine passes by accepting the snake, and for

which she is rewarded. Mādar Zāher casts the mother's acceptance of the
snake in Mār Čučeh as an act of self-sacrifice, and in so doing conflates
the two structural uses of the theme of supernatural courtship. The extreme consistency of detail between Adī's version of the magic wedding
(A.29-31) and the one which was already part of Mādar Zāher's active repertoire (G.42-44) obscures for Mādar Zāher the different structural uses to
which the episode is put.

In the case of the 'Tree of Forty Voices/Tree of Bells and Cats' Claws'
episode, the former variant is a key episode in Mādar Zāher's tale, Alī
Zarrīn (Text K), while the latter appears in Adī's version of Afsāneh-e
Garg (texts H-J), in a very analogous position. Adī and Mādar Zāher each
omit the Tree episode from one performance of Garg (texts H and J). In
Adī's case, it is hard to determine exactly why she does so, though there
are indications that the tale is not one that she knows well (pp.
above). In Mādar Zāher's case, the omission is even more puzzling, in
the light of her demonstrated knowledge of an extremely similar variant of
the incident in a favorite tale of her own (K.22-37,54-70). The two episodes are even analogous in the way they 'intertwine' structurally with
other episodes in a chain of quests, and Mādar Zāher demonstrates her
skill at narrating intertwining plots in Alī Zarrīn and elsewhere. The
fact that she uses the 'Tree of Forty Voices' episode to designate Alī
Zarrīn (H.227) suggests an exclusionist principle at work in the designation of stories by key episodes, whereby an episode used to 'cue' one
story in the narrator's memory will be dropped from another story (see
p.   above). This hypothesis is complicated by the fact that Mādar
Zāher's active repertoire, prior to her learning Garg, already included
a Tree episode in yet a third story (Kākol Zarrīn o Māh-Pīšnī, 'Golden

Locks and Moon-Brow', Cassette # F3A). This tale, however, is <u>not</u> a
bride-winning, but a variant of the 'calumniated wife' story, in which
the twin children of the calumniated and imprisoned wife, who were stolen
from their mother and exposed at birth, perform several tasks (including
fetching a branch from the Tree of Forty Voices) before they return to
their father's court and exonerate their mother. The Tree episode in
<u>Kākol Zarrīn</u> is distinguished from that in <u>Alī Zarrīn</u> and <u>Garg</u> in that it
is not involved in bride-winning, and also not 'intertwined', but stands
alone as a quest which the hero simply accomplishes, one of a series of
separate tasks. It does not contain the delayed resolution and recapitu-
lation/apotheosis of the hero which climax the Tree episode (and the bride-
winning sequence) in both <u>Alī Zarrīn</u> and <u>Garg</u>. I infer from this that the
object, the Tree, is not the feature which makes this episode distinctive
to <u>Alī Zarrīn</u> in Mādar Zāher's memory, but rather it is the syntactic position of the task, as an intertwined adventure whose delayed resolution
caps the hero's adventures in the other world. That is, the simple quest
for the Tree branch in <u>Kākol Zarrīn</u> does not have the same <u>significance</u>
as the intertwined, climactic, bride-winning Tree episode in <u>Alī Zarrīn</u>
and <u>Garg</u>, because it does not occupy the same syntactical position, and
so it is not the 'same'. Being syntactically distinct, it is not affected
by the exclusionist tendency which causes Mādar Zāher to drop the Tree episode from <u>Garg</u>.[1]   Although Mādar Zāher remarks on <u>Garg</u>'s structural similarities with <u>Alī Zarrīn</u> (H.128 and pp. 141 f.above), she shows little tendency to preserve them in later performance (Text <u>J</u>).

---

[1]Whether this omission is temporary or permanent is of considerable interest:
more performances of the tale by Mādar Zāher must be recorded to establish
whether her omission of the incident is ephemeral.

Stroytellers' identification of tales and episodes as similar proceeds on both structural and contentual grounds, and 'key' episodes also
seem to be distinguished in part by their syntactic position. If two episodes are extremely similar in content and syntactic position in two different stories, and one is the 'key' or 'cue' to its story in the mind of
the narrator, there may be a tendency to omit its analogue from the other
story. This exclusionist tendency needs to be identified in the learning
process of other narrators, as well as corroborated in other work by Mãdar
Zãher. What I have said about it here is largely inferential and based on
too few observations. In order to establish the general significance (if
any) of such a process, it is necessary to have the entire active repertoire of a storyteller at hand, and then go on to observe that storyteller
as s/he learns new stories. This is an imposing set of requirements, but
the study of transmission is inevitably bound up with the study of repertoire. The processes of selection at work in transmission need to be understood extrinsically, in the context of the selections a narrator has previously made from the rich body of tradition, as well as intrinsically, in
terms of the individual circumstances of the immediate transmission event.

The circumstances of performance have received illuminating study in
recent years (Hymes, 1975 and Bauman, 1975 are exemplary in this area).
A major flaw was inherent in the collecting process which yielded my texts,
in that normal context would not be approximated in the presence of a
foreign folklorist and a tape recorder. Particularly with regard to male
informants, my presence must be regarded as a potentially distorting ano-
maly in the performance situation. The distorting effect of my presence

is also difficult to estimate or factor out. Certain features of my collection, especially the predominance of *afsāneh* (fictional folktales) and book
romances among my recordings, now seem to me to be artifacts of the peculiar
performance situation created by my recording activities. I tried to make
my request for stories as undirected as possible ("Tell me the things you
like the best"), yet this very undirectedness was itself a direction: a
request for entertainment, not for didactic tales. Baghban (n.d.:10) divides
traditional Herati tale-telling into two sub-genres, on the basis of length
and context of performance:

> According to length, stories fall into shorter ones that usually
> do not exceed three or four minutes, and into longer ones that reach half
> an hour or more of recording. The shorter and the longer stories begin
> and end differently and are told at different times and different places.
> Different kinds of raconteurs present different kinds of stories. The
> mullah, the old men and other people in a position to give advice or
> teach a lesson use the shorter type. Shepherds, illiterate farmers, black-
> smiths, etc. will usually tell the longer type. The stories are told for
> different purposes, have different characters, different thoughts, and
> different audiences.

The longer tales are primarily entertaining fantasies, while

> The shorter stories are similar to Aesop's Fables and can be part
> of any talk . . . Like proverbs, they are part of one's everyday life and
> are used giving a lesson, offering advice or making others laugh. The
> wiser the man, the more of these stories he knows.

> (Baghban, n.d.:10-11)

The /bud,nabud/ distancing formulas (described above, pp. 11-14   )
introduce the longer type of tale, while a simple "It is said" (/mīgah/)
introduces the shorter, didactic or commentary tale. Short, didactic tales
and fables address specific people's acts or current events, constitute
cautionary or exemplary statements just as proverbs do, and thus are brought
forth by appropriate occasions in the course of daily affairs. It is not
surprising that they did not come first to mind for my informants, when

I asked them to tell tales outside of any didactic context.

In light of this traditional contextual distinction between story genres, Mādar Zāher's fabrication of the fable-like Šīr o Palang in connection with a family dispute which disturbed her greatly is clearly appropriate. The retribution theme is cautionary and aimed at relatives of her husband whom she views as exploitative. Within her didactic framework, several social issues are present as well as the moral one: these include the choice between confrontation and conciliation in real interpersonal dealings, and Mādar Zāher's casting the female spouses as the aggressors, which dramatizes real features of inter-family negotiating strategy in her society. By making the culprit female and a _fictive_ relative of the main character, Mādar Zāher may also be blaming the 'outsider' for family conflict. Zāher's comments on his mother-in-law (text O) confirm that Mādar Zāher's family's hostility to Ğolām Nabī's family eventually focused on Ğolām Nabī's wife, who is a comparatively distant relative.[1]

In context as well as form, Mādar Zāher's composition, Šīr o Palang, fits traditional generic rules. Yet Mādar Zāher's distinction between _afsāneh_ and _naql_ (see p.105 ff.) is somewhat idiosyncratic, in that she excludes from the category of _afsāneh_ certain long, non-didactic entertainment tales, apparently because they do not have comedic endings. Mādar Zāher's idea of genre may not exactly match her use of traditional forms in

---

[1] Power relationships between wife-givers and wife-takers, which have material expression in the payment of brideprices (a sore issue on this particular occasion) also figure in Mādar Zāher's metaphorical formulation of the family's dispute, for the leopard furnishes his 'sister' with a bridegroom, exactly as Xairuddīn intends to do for his cousin's daughter, and in so doing acquire power over her. This aspect of the fable's metaphorical relation to the dispute deserves more detailed study than space permits.

context. To understand native performance categories (individual and collective), one must take into account both the realities of performance, and the intellectual distinctions made by individuals,.insofar as they are articulated.

The foregoing chapters provide a limited set of observations on a very small sample of oral narrative events. They have some illustrative value, providing examples of some of the changes that occur in the narrative structure of a single tale in oral performance and transmission. The tenor of my argument has been the fluidity of oral narrative structure, the multiplicity of forces which shape it in performance, and the interrelatedness of structure and diction. I have isolated a few details from the stories presented, to discuss some aspects of the transmission process, but others remain unexamined and there is no hope that such a discussion could ever be comprehensive.

There is much more to be learned about the artistry of the storytellers whose work has been presented here, and that of traditional storytellers in general, from material already in my collection. In particular, constraints of space and time prevent a complete discussion of Mādar Zāher's new compositions, for to shed light on her construction of adventure tales, one must refer to the style and structure of popular prose literary romances, as well as that of oral *afsāneh*, and the basic stylistic study of the former genre still waits to be done. At the outset of my field work, I hoped to address the complex relationship of oral and literary traditions in Afghan Persian language. The present study of oral transmission between two illiterate storytellers was intended as a prologue, a reference point from which to assess Mādar Zāher's appropriations from literary style and structure in her lengthy, improvised adventure tales.

Not surprisingly, the problem of oral and literary connections in Persian, even in the work of a single storyteller, outgrew the dimensions of a reasonable doctoral thesis. Some ground work still needs to be done, to support such a comparative study. To my knowledge, except for my as-yet unanalyzed recordings, no one has tried to record or analyze the performance of popular literary romances, or how they enter and nourish the oral tradition, and how oral tradition nurtures them. Studies of Persian popular romances (e.g. Hanaway, 1970, or Rypka, 1968:162 ff.) have addressed certain features of content and story pattern in single manuscripts, from the viewpoint of the literary historian, and in general have treated romances as fixed documents. Such studies inform the folklorist about the genre as a series of literary documents, but do little to explain the process of composition of these documents, or their relations with their analogues which live a distinct but connected life in oral tradition. At this stage, as is the case with medieval European romances, one would wish to know whether the compositional processes of romance in oral and literary tradition are separate, or to some degre joint, shared or hybridized.[1] In Persian, the process is still alive and available for study, whereas the medieval European phenomenon can be reconstructed only by conjecture.

My collecting experience and that of others confirms the fact that new romances are still being composed orally in Persian in western Afghanistan. A well-known example of a romance composed in a courtly literary

---

[1] Haymes (1973) provides an extensive bibliography of studies on medieval oral and literary tradition , primarily concerned with narrative forms in European literatures, up to five years ago.

milieu is the nineteenth century Qajār romance, <u>Amīr Arsalān</u>, composed by

Mohammed 'Alī, Naqīb al-Mamālek (d.1891). Recently appearing romances in

Afghanistan include the oral tale of <u>Siāhmuī o Jelalī</u>, originating in the

mountainous region east of Herat, which has been discussed in a brief study

by Māyel Heravi entitled <u>Siāhmuī</u>, <u>Lītān</u>, <u>Maryam</u> (Kabul: Govt. Press Book

Publishing Institute,1346/1968, pp.1-12). There is sufficient information

available for an informed comparison of oral and literary romances in Per-

sian, and it is to be hoped that this study will be undertaken soon, before

radio, television, cinema and popular novels with their increasing access-

ibility and radically different narrative formats drive out the more de-

manding performance genre of the oral romance.[1]

Even within the scope of the present discussion, certain basic ques-

tions remain unanswered. Foremost among them is that of the effect of the

storyteller's conscious intentions in shaping a story. My interpretation

of Mādar Zāher's revision of <u>Mār Čučeh</u> argues that the changes she made in

that tale, while they were well within the normal range of variation for

the genre, were also not random, but systematic in their effect on narra-

tive structure. In the field, I stopped short of direct confrontation,

and abstained from asking Mādar Zāher whether she planned these changes

consciously. Likewise with regard to <u>Šīr o Palang</u>, I neglected to ask the

basic question about intentionality: I never asked Mādar Zāher whether she

intended the story as a comment on the feud.

---

[1] The influence of traditional Persian narrative forms on the 'modern'
novels now appearing in popular editions in Iran and Afghanistan is a
topic for yet another detailed study.

I did not present Mādar Zāher with the questions of intentionality
which her creative storytelling inspires, because of a perhaps over-
conservative desire not to interfere with what might be unconscious creative processes, by rendering the artist self-conscious. Her hesitancy to
admit that she composed stories at all made me reluctant to confront her
on the subject of change and improvisation. I hoped that longer observation of Mādar Zāher performing and composing stories for her normal audience, her children and other relatives, might give me insights into the
creative process, and help me to distinguish unconscious from conscious
mechanisms of composition. I hoped that by letting Mādar Zāher supply her
own terms for what she does, I might come to understand her notion of the
creative process. Very few hints were forthcoming, however: of direct
discussion of story structure, there was very little, only a few comments
such as her observations that knowing the 'words' of *afsāneh* makes it
easy to learn new tales (Field Notes V:46, March 1, 1976), or her remark
when she discovered that she had confused details from two analogous episodes in Afsāneh-e Garg, "No, God of Repentence! That's from another
layer." (J.105: emphasis mine).

Perhaps a more aggressive field strategy would have yielded further
information along these lines, but in my experience, the general eagerness
of my Herati informants to please me, coupled with their mystification at
my interest in folktales, led them to agree with me at every turn, and to
tell me what they thought I wanted to hear. Even my attitude of utter
stupidity and naiveté (real in some cases, feigned in others) did not protect against the leading question. I was very reluctant to present any
terms or distinctions of any kind, for fear of polite agreement.

One distinction which I waited in vain to hear articulated in any

way was one which is basic to western notions of intentionality: that is,
the distinction between conscious and unconscious intent. In performance,
narrators would discover (or be reminded) that they had left something
out (as is Mādar Zāher's case at J.105, cited above), and immediately correct themselves: one may assume that their first formulation of the item
was unintentional, or if you will, unconscious. In this case, Mādar Zāher's
standard expression when she discovers an omission, "Oh, God of Repentence!"
(/xodā-ye tobeh/), which may be found here and there in her stories (G.93,
J.105), is telling: 'forgetting' is a matter for repentence, a sort of
venal sin.

On other occasions, narrators will flatly deny, in the face of criticism, that they have made any changes in their tale (e.g. Mādar Zāher regarding Mār Čučeh: "Adī told it just like that"). Storytellers boast of
their ability to reproduce stories exactly as they hear them: whatever the
reality of oral transmission, the ideal among my Herati informants was
accurate reproduction. Does a protest like Mādar Zāher's mean she does
not know she has changed the story, or is she defending the legitimacy of
her reformulation in the only terms which the traditional standard provides? It is possible (I think probable) that the distinction of conscious
and unconscious mental processes is artificial in regard to the intentionality of an artist like Mādar Zāher. Other spontaneous verbal compositions
of hers (elegiac poetry, speaking in tongues in the course of divination)
are intentional and purposive, but only in a limited sense premeditated
compositions. It might be more useful to view intentionality as a range
of possiblities, with varying degrees of conscious premeditation observable in different aspects of performance or composition. In any case, I
would still stress the importance of trying to understand the storyteller's

230

creative activity on his or her own terms, not to impose categories and distinctions which are not part of the storyteller's own intellectual equipment or experience. This is particularly important when dealing with an activity which is to some extent deviant, as is Mādar Zāher's invention of stories. Recognizing implicit categories takes longer than imposing one's own, however. I am convinced that further work with Mādar Zāher on this and other aspects of her verbal artistry would yield more information about her own understanding of the creative process in folk-tale and other verbal forms, and I hope to be able to undertake that study at a future date. Meanwhile, the butterfly remains unpinned.

APPENDIX

.Folktales and Related Texts

Orthography and Abbreviations

Used in the Texts

1. Names of participants in the performance are abbreviated as follows:

> X = Xairuddīn, Mādar Zāher's husband
> M = Māhgol, Mādar Zāher's 9-year-old daughter
> MM = Margaret Mills
> MZ = Mādar Zāher
> Z = Zāher, her oldest son, 14

2. In each text, the narrator's speech is unbracketed and unmarked by initials. Remarks by everyone except the narrator are enclosed in square brackets and preceded by the speaker's initials.

3. Material enclosed in parentheses includes descriptions of gestures and tones of voice, explanatory comments, and occasional phrases supplied by the translator for clarity.

4. Underlining is used to indicate the speaker's louder or higher-pitched utterance, the speaker's emphasis.

5. Where a distinction is made between literary and colloquial Persian words, the literary words are in italics, the colloquial are phonetically spelled and enclosed in slash marks (/   /).

6. lit. = literary Persian

7. met. = metaphor(ically)

8. Letter values indicated by superscripts are as follows:

> ā = 'aw' as in 'awning'
> ī = 'ee' as in 'sheen'
> č = 'ch' as in 'chart'
> ğ = a glottal fricative, a little rougher than a French 'r', = غ
> š = 'sh' as in 'sheen'

> Also, q = a more explosive, voiced sound, like Arabic ق , not Iranian
> ق and غ , which are identical
> x = 'ch' as in German 'nach', = خ

Title: Mār Čučeh [The Snake Chick]
Narrator: Adī
Recorded: 25 June 1975
Tape # CCLXVII - CCLXIX

A.1   . . . There was a - a mother with one son. This poor woman,
her husband was dead, and she had one little boy, and a little
cow. [MZ: She has a cow?] Yeah. This cow, this boy, then,
mornings he goes out to the gullies, and gets a little firewood,
a little fodder, and afternoons after he's had his bread and tea
and water, he picks up his sacks again, and goes out around the
cultivated fields to gather hay for the cow. And he's an orphan.
She was a widow woman. Had just one son. She -- had one cow too.
A calf. So he was going and cutting and cutting hay around the
fields, and, Mādar Zāher, then, some days and some while passed
like this, with him cutting hay like this and bringing it to the
calf.

A.2   This one day when he was cutting hay like that, around the
cultivated lands, all at once he noticed a *fīīš, fīš, fīš*. --
[MZ: Oh! Mama!] OK. It was a *fīš, fīš*.

A.3   This boy turned his head this way and that. He said, "Oh,
God, what a hissing! Is it an aufī,[1] or what is it?"

A.4   Now when it got close, now he sees that there, it's an auf-
a thing. It's an aufī. [MZ: Ohh! Mama!] Yeah. It's an aufī.
So this aufī stopped right there, and he called to the boy, "Hey,
Boy, what are you doing?"

A.5   "Nothing. I'm cutting hay. I have a little cow. I'm taking
it to that cow of mine."

A.6   "All right..do you have a mother?"

A.7   "Yeah."

A.8   "Do you have a father, too?"

A.9   "No."

---

[1] /Aufī/: Lit. Persian /af'ī/, a viper. See description below in text.

A.10   "All right. Deliver my respects to your mother. Tell her, 'If you want to marry, take me." [MZ: Xxxxx! (gasp of disapproval) Didn't he know that this was an aufī? This boy of hers? Or did he know?]

A.11   Well, how could he not know? He knew very well it was an aufī. [MM: What's an aufī?] [MZ: An aufī is a thing like this, it lives in water,[1] and they're no longer found, but they used to be in the old days, and there is something like --]

A.12   They are found in the mountains -- [MZ: (quickly) They're in the mountains. So when they get close to a person, they go like this -- 'xxxxx' (Noisy sucking in of air) -- when it's inhaled --]

A.13   It gulps him, eats - [MZ: But it doesn't jump. Once it's inhaled like that, he's inside its stomach. That's an aufī. That's an aufī.]

A.14   Yeah. OK. [Zaher: Is it like a fish, that thing?] [MZ: I don't know about that.] Like a snake! (impatiently) A snake that gets big and powerful, gets to be an aufī. [MZ: Like when a snake gets big, Margaret?] [MM: Yeah.] [MZ: A snake. Some snakes that get big, that they bring with a truck.[2] That gets to be an aufī.]

A.15   OK, then. That's an aufī. So this time, when he said, "All right, I'll tell her," out of fear for his life, the poor kid, he said, "I'll say it." He doesn't eat, this, this (inaudible phrase) doesn't eat, that evening. This once from fear for his life he says, "All right, I'll say that. To my mother."

A.16   He filled up his sacks with hay, quick, quick, and put them on his back, and he says, "Oh, Boy! Tell her, don't forget, or else anywhere you -- next time, in the hay, I'll strike you, I'll eat you." [MZ: Mmmm!] He said that to the boy. [MZ: He's become an enemy for him.] Yeah.

A.17   He said, "All right."

A.18   He came and loaded up, and it went out of his mind and he didn't tell his mother. [MZ: Oh! My God!] It went out of his mind, and he didn't tell his mother.

A.19   The next day he picked up his sack again, and as he was coming towards the hay, all at once it came into his mind. He said, "Oh!

---

[1] *daryā:* Properly a large lake or gulf. Also used for large rivers.

[2] Large constrictors, brought from India, are displayed at local markets and fairs by snake handlers, who sell snake oil and other traditional medicines said to be prepared from snake products.

God! Didn't that aufī tell me that!?" And finally - (replying to inaudible question by MZ) - no - finally he said, "Oh, on your shit, I won't go to, to that part, I'll go there, to those other lands."

A.20   There! So he came along peacefully, going this other way, and was cutting hay again, and so on, and again all at once he heard a fĩs, fĩs, fĩs. The aufī came, again. He said, "Hey, Boy! Did you say it? Did you give your mother my greetings? What was her answer? Whatever lands you go to, [MZ: 'I'll be there.'] - I'll be standing there with you. [MZ: I'll find you.] I'll find you. If you don't tell her this time, by God, if the wind of the world touches your face, it's certain that I'll eat you, I'll go (there)."

A.21   So this boy, without any way out, he said, "By God! I didn't even go to those places today, because I thought he would see me. I came here. I left my own land. And here he came after me, like this. He came."

A.22   So today when he came home, he told his mother.

A.23   His mother said, "That's fine. Tomorrow wish him 'Peace be on you,' and say, 'She'll marry, she'll take a husband, my mother.'"

[END OF TAPE]

TAPE # CCLXVIII:

A.24   Listen to that. [MZ: Didn't she understand that it was an aufī?]

A.25   She under<u>stood</u>! He <u>said</u>, just like that, "It's an aufī."

A.26   She said, "That's fine." No - then - "I'll do it. I'll take him, I'll take this aufī."

A.27   So this night turned to morning, and in the morning he took his sack to go, and went for the hay, and dear Sister, here came the aufī again, and said, "Hey Boy, what did your mother say? Did you tell her?"

A.28   He said, "Yeah. She said, 'I'll take him.'"

A.29   He said, "That's fine, then. Now I - for these three days, you wait for me. Once - on that day, then, there'll come a wind first. It'll sweep out your rooms, and your courtyard, clean, clean. After that it will rain, and sprinkle them. Then after that clouds will come, and when red and green and all different colors of clouds come, you'll know that I've come, and brought these clothes for your mother." [MZ: Laughs] Watch this. This aufī tells the boy.

A.30   He says, "All right."

A.31   So these two, three days passed, then he saw, there came a
wind and a rain. The boy's heart quaked. He said, "He's coming."
[MZ: 'He's taking away my mother.'] Yeah. This poor kid, then,
after that the rain came and after it the clouds, all different
colors, and an hour passed. He saw that all the creepies and
crawlies, snakes and scorpions and all those kinds, were coming
with himself in front and them following behind. [MZ & others:
(Sounds of incredulity, laughter)] They came in the house and
they said, "This is our wedding, now." [General laughter] So
he came and peacefully made his party there with them, and made
the meeting and so forth - gave the thread and needle for her[1]
and bound the contract and did this and that. After that, then,
they took off the woman's clothes and put on these, and in their
own way they made the accounting and the books. And after that
he excused all the others. [MZ: Excused them.] Mm. And he himself stayed. [MZ: He himself stayed.] He himself stayed, and
took his place right there.

A.32   So this boy is doing the same job and occupation. He goes in
the morning, and comes at supper-time. He brings that - hay.
This - God willed it - this mother of his, from this, from this
snake she got a belly. [MZ to MM: She got a baby, from this
aufī.]

A.33   This - so it went that nine months and nine days passed, and
his mother gave birth. She had a little boy. She had a little
boy, had her child, like that.

A.34   This one day, this boy had gotten to be a nice little thing,
and - [MZ: This aufī's child.] Yeah. He got to be like
Azīzollah[2] and one day this, this aufī turned to the boy's mother
and he said, "When can I eat that boy of yours?" [MZ: Oh! God!]

A.35   Yes. [MZ: Viiiii!] Viii! 'May he eat death! You bastard,
what do you want with my boy?' Yeah. But this bastard bitch
mother picked it up and said, "Any day, you can eat him." [MZ:
Which boy? The big one?] The big one. [MZ: Oh! Mother!]

---

[1] A symbolic exchange in traditional wedding ceremonies: the groom's
people give a thread and needle in exchange for the woman they are
taking. The 'meeting' serves the function of formal witnessing, in
the absence of written contracts as well as in their presence, legal-
izing the marriage. The parody here is obvious to all the listeners.
Dressing the bride in new clothes provided by the groom is also basic
to the ceremony.

[2] Her own 3-4 year old son, who was present.

A.36   OK, then. Watch this. This boy has a peculiarity, that he can't eat plain, dry bread. This big boy. These two, then, in the alley, the two brothers had gone, out in the alley. So then this, this snake speaks to the mother. And way off, this once, this boy that - this little, bitty green kid that the snake had gotten on her, from way off in the alley he heard what his father was asking and what he said. [MZ: This little boy.] This little boy.

A.37   He said, "I -- Tomorrow when your boy comes, don't cook anything to eat with the bread," he said to his mother, "Bring plain, dry bread and put it in front of him, and put a glass of water in front of him. I'll go and get inside the ghee jar." This, this snake says that. "I'll go and get in the ghee jar - you go, and make yourself busy with some chore." He says to his wife, "You go and make yourself busy with some chore, bring the cloth, with the dry bread, and the water glass for him, and then I'll go and get inside the jar, and he'll call out, 'Ma, how can I eat dry bread? If you didn't make anything to go with the bread, what did you bring me to eat with it?' She[1] (sic) says this, 'Go, dear,[2] my hands are were full, I didn't make it, I was busy, my hands are full. I couldn't - can't pour it.' She said, 'There, take the - cup, go and get ghee from the jar for yourself. Eat the cupful.' When he puts his hand into the jar, I'll strike him and kill him."

A.38   She said, "That's fine." This mother is a bastard, she said, "That's fine."

A.39   This father - [MZ: The little boy heard.] This little boy is playing there in the alley, where his brother took him, to pass the time. So he heard. This boy heard, and when the next day came, the boy went for the hay and came back, the bread was cooked and she brought the bread to the boy with the cloth and the water glass and put them down in front of him, and then she went and pretended to make herself busy at something. He called out, "Ma, didn't you make me anything for the bread, now that you brought me the cloth?"

A.40   She said, "No, Mother's dear, I was busy, my hands were full, and I didn't get to it, to make something. So take the cup, and go and get some ghee for yourself from the jar. If there's nothing to eat with the bread for one day, it's not judgement day, dear!" [MZ: Where's this little boy?]

---

[1] Adi forgets that the snake is dictating this speech to his wife.

[2] Lit. 'Ma': Adults routinely address younger people with the kin term used by that individual toward themselves, the mother calls her son 'Ma,' to show affection.

A.41   This little boy is right there, too. He got up, too. He
got up, and got the cup, and turned to go to the jar. <u>Right</u> then
the big - the little boy came in from outside, and said, "Brother,
Brother," he said, "Give me the cup so I can bring the ghee for
you. My Papa's in the jar, and he'll strike you and kill you."
[General laughter. MZ: This is a very good story!]

A.42   Yeah. Yeah. He took the cup out of his hand, and went, and
brought the ghee, and put it in front of his brother. He ate.
When he'd eaten and filled his little stomach, the two went back
out in the alley.

A.43   Then the aufī came out of the - out of the jar. He said,
"Curse the father of that son of yours, there, now - it happened
this way today, it didn't work out. So tomorrow you make something to go with the bread, but don't bring water. I'll get inside the water skin. Don't fill the water glass, and make yourself busy at something again. After he's eaten the bread, 'My
throat is blocked,' he'll say, 'I want water. Papa,'[1] she said,[2]
'Mother's dear, my hands are full, get up, get your own water.'
When he has come to fill the glass from the mouth of the water
skin, when he puts his hand inside the mouth of the water skin,
I'll strike him and kill him."

A.44   She said, "That's fine."

A.45   Once again, far off, that boy, that boy that she'd gotten from
him, -- and they called him 'Mār Čučeh' - [MZ: Mār Čučeh.] Yeah.
Mār Čučeh. So now, it's way off, Mār Čučeh heard. [MZ: He heard.]
[Laughter] Yeah. Yeah, he heard, again.

A.46   After he heard, then, the next day when the boy came from the
hay and she made something to go with the bread and some greens,
and she brought the bowls and put them in front of him, she didn't
bring water.

A.47   When she didn't bring water, he said, "Ma, it's two days now,
what death have you taken up?[3] Yesterday you made nothing to eat
with the bread, [MZ: Laughs] and today again you don't bring me
any water."

---

[1] A slip - see note 2, p. 237.

[2] Another slip - see note 1, p. 237.

[3] Roughly, "What's the problem? What kind of foolishness is this? Why
are you falling down on the job?" - hence laughter at the son nagging
the mother.

A.48   She said, "Mother's dear, what can I do? In - my hands are full, you get up and fill the glass for yourself. There are a hundred chores to having children, and a hundred commands. Can't you get up, for your own stomach's sake, and serve your own stomach?" [MZ: 'Go get the water.'] Yeah. "Go get the water, yourself, and drink it."

A.49   Finally he got up. As he picked up the glass, right then his brother got up and came. [MZ: Mâr Čučeh.] He said, "Brother, Brother, give me the glass, I'll fill it. Papa's in the water skin, he'll strike you and kill you." [General laughter] He took the little glass out of his hand, went and filled it with water, and brought it back to him. So he ate, and filled his stomach again, and again they went out in the alley. [Continuous laughter. MZ giggles quietly for some time . . .]

A.50   He said, "That bastard son of yours, he must be behind the door, he heard us. Now, tomorrow, don't you make bread dough. Don't make dough, don't make it, you say, when he picks up his sack, to go get that - hay, you say, 'Mother's dear, there's no more baked bread, and besides, there's not a sliver of wood for me to heat the oven. I'm not even making any dough. What can I cook it with? You take your little rope and come, take it and go, and bring me a little handful of wood, bring a load and come.' I'll go that way, and quietly get into the load, then I'll strike him and kill him." [MZ: 'I'll get in the load'?] Yeah. This Mâr Čučeh, way off, alone, he heard. [Laughter.] [MZ: He's going to rescue his brother.]

A.51   (Adī pauses, sipping tea) When the next day came, he picked up his sack and his saw (sic) to go for the hay, and his mother said that. She put away the sack and said, "Dear, that hay dried out in front of the cow last night," - [MZ: The cow - (inaudible)] - "Go, bring a handful of wood, to bake a piece or two of bread with, or else today, until evening, it's today you'll be hungry." [MZ, sipping tea: What a bastard that aufī is!]

A.52   (Adī refuses tea) That's enough for me. I'm not drinking any more. I don't drink a lot of tea in the evening - it gets to be a nuisance.

A.53   All at once, then, he took it up, again, this boy. As he was tying his rope - (Aside to child, who reaches for microphone) Are you thirsty? May you not see health! What do you want with me, then? If you get inside that radio, what will you do then? She'll carry you off to her country, and what can I do? Inside the radio - [MM, laughing: People are always like that. In their own place -] -- She says, "I'll let your mother back out of the radio."[1] There,

---

[1] Threats are a standard way of controlling children's behavior. The 'radio' is the tape recorder.

you hear? [Azīzollah, giggling: Yeah.] <u>Don't</u> you go tell
Mesterī!1 Because you know he'll fight with me, and say, "You go
there and tell tales, and sing songs, and -- what-all." [Laughter]

A.54   So all at once, Sister, when he was tying up his rope, and
picking up his shovel, this boy <u>throws</u> himself to earth and heaven -
[MZ: This little one.] This little one. [MZ: Mār Čučeh.] - "Heyyy,
help!" He pulls a tantrum, "I'm going with my brother!"

A.55   "Dear, you're little and silly, where are <u>you</u> going?"

A.56   "No. As God is One, I'm going, going with my brother."

A.57   Finally she said, "Dear, (Inaudible phrase), take him, lose
(sight of) him, then, take him with you!" His mother said it.

A.58   And he quietly searched around, and around and fou - "I'm
finding myself a rope," - searched around, and found a little wisp
of rope for himself, and he picked up the matches, and put them in
his pocket. [MZ: This little one.] This little one. [MZ: Laughs]
(Adī laughs) [MZ: He sets fire to his father.] Huh? [MZ: He
sets fire to his father.] Yeah. Now you watch this. So he came,
then.

A.59   They chopped thorn, and chopped, and the boy tied up his load,
fixed it, and tied up a little bit like that for him. When he came
to his load like that, just when he was going to put it on his back,
just right then he saw his father's neck showing. He said, "Pa -
Brother, Brother, put down your load, your load has come loose."
Yeah, this - [MZ: little one -] Mār Čučeh says it. To his brother.
"Brother, Brother, put down your load. Your load has come loose."
[General laughter] - "Your load has come loose, Brother, you'll
have trouble later, if you go along that way, you'll have to put
it down here and there. Don't move yet."

A.60   As he was going like this with his load, the snake stretched
out his neck toward his head, - [MZ: To strike it -] - to strike
it, and this boy's eyes were on the job to the rear, he hadn't moved
his own load, this little one was that clever. Here, he's watching,
listeni -- that, "That father of mine has come, and he's gotten
into the load, hidden." So when he lifted the load like that, he
saw his father's neck showing. He said, "Brother, Brother, your
lo - don't load it on your back, your load's come loose! You'll
have to put it down here and there, and you'll have trouble. Don't
move it yet, untie it again, and tie it over."

A.61   This boy bent down, then he stood up and was leaning over to
untie it, while he on this side silently struck the matches to the

---

1 Mesterī is her oldest son, in his late twenties, married to MZ's sister
and 'modern'.

thorns. [MZ: The little brother.] This little brother. What a
sight! Gurr-o, gurr-o, gurrr!!¹ He's claaaping, and "Haaay,
Brother, I burnt Papa! Haaay, Brother, I burnt Papa!" [General
Laughter]² All this laughter and delight, and this boy was clapping that his own papa burnt and turned into charcoal. He made
this snake of his into charcoal.

A.62   He said "Fuck Mama's Papa!³ [General Laughter] All the
guilt is with that bastard Ma! By God, if the wind of the world
touches her face⁴ -- [Laughter] -- You look here, if I hadn't been
there, that very day Papa would have struck you and killed you,
when he was inside the ghee jar. And her own husband - that
bastard preferred her husband to you, Brother. [MM; Oh, yeah!]
She was ready for you to die, but not for her husband. Fine! To
the point that she was going to make a new-grown young man into
provisions for her husband! My God, if I get their little fathers
into my mouth!" [Laughter]

A.63   So just as they came in off the road, with the shovel in his
hand, he just hit his mother on the head with it, and scattered
her brains. [General Laughter] He took her right away and put her
in a shroud and buried her, dug her grave and got rid of her. And
he'd burnt him right there.

A.64   He said, "Brother," this big brother said, "You've done all
this to help me, dear Brother," he said, "Brother, you stay here
and take care of the cow, and I'll go and become a hired servant."
[MZ: The big one spoke.] - the big one spoke. "I'll become a
servant, Brother, now, I'll make the effort, and bring things, so
you can eat." [MZ: He was little, anyway.] This little one, "Until you get big, too. Because while you were this small, you saved
me from three spots, saved me from destruction."

A.65   He stayed there, and he went, like to - where shall I say?
[MZ:A city or a village, like that.] Like, like those village
places that are around a city, like to Goryān, or like in this direction, more this way, he went, and became a servant. There was
a company sitting there with this one person, and he called out
there, "Oh, Brothers! Won't you take a servant?"

---

¹ Imitates sound of roaring flames.

² Ironic humor hinges on the common insult, "Your father was burned," an
extreme form of execution, to Muslims implying a heinous social crime.

³ An extremely foul insult, further ironic used by a child toward his own
mother.

⁴ I.e., 'Wherever she is' - an unfinished threat. (cf. A.20).

A.66   There was one, a vizier, sitting there. He said, "I'll take a servant who has no belly. Who doesn't eat."

A.67   This boy said, "I don't eat."

A.68   He came and became his servant. He became a servant and in the evening he didn't give him food, and the next day he didn't give him food, and the day after that he didn't give him food, and the day after that this little one died of hunger.[1] [MZ (shocked): Bu!] Oh, yeah! That boy died. [MZ: Oh! God!]

A.69   This boy died, and the news came to Mār Čučeh, "Come, because your brother was with this one called 'vizier', and he had become a servant and for two or three days he didn't give him food, and the boy - your brother - is dead of hunger."

A.70   He said, "Weyyy, I'll fuck your Pa! Am I to be alive in the world, to let you kill my brother like that?"

A.71   So he closed and locked the house doors, and dear Sister, he left his cow with a neighbor, and shut up the house and yard, and set his foot on the road.

A.72   He came, and again that company was sitting there, and the bastard vizier was sitting there. He came and called out, "Oh, Company, won't you take a servant?"

A.73   And again, the vizier took it up, and said, "I'll take a servant who doesn't have a stomach."

A.74   He said, "Brother, I have absolutely no stomach!" [MZ: This Mār Čučeh said it.] Mār Čučeh said it. He knew that "This guy - this is the one who owes me blood. I'll fuck your Pa! You watch, what I do to you."

A.75   So, dear Sister, he came, and at supper-time prayer, he brings the cows and stock in and feeds them, and from there he watches and watches, and comes into the house looking for something, and grabs a piece or two of bread and hides them under his arm, and goes out in the alley and eats out there. [MZ: This Mār Čučeh.] (Coughs) This Mār Čučeh. And it began to appear, then, they said, [MZ: 'He doesn't eat' - ?] - He doesn't give him bread, or anything, yeah. No, so then - then he says, "He doesn't eat. No. Not he."

---

[1] Servants and sharecroppers are hired for an agricultural year, servants only receiving board and lodging until the crops come in, when they receive an annual wage. The boy has interpreted the vizier's terms figuratively and rationally, to mean that he should not be excessively greedy. The vizier's behavior is incredibly miserly; master and servant contract almost a familial set of responsibilities, in village custom.

A.76   So it's a month, twenty days and he's with them, there, and mornings the bread, like that -- [MZ: He stole it and ate it, and ate it in the evening, too.] Yeah. Just like that. Then one evening came, one evening - this vizier had two wives. Two wives, and besides, like those tall beds of yours (to MM), you people sleep on platforms, and it's winter, too, and he put covers on a cot and he's asleep on the cot with his wives, and this one is asleep inside the house. This vizier has one little girl, too, from one of his wives. It's night, and this little girl needed to pee. This girl needs to pee, and she says, "Ma, I need to go."

A.77   She said, "Mār Čučeh."

A.78   "Huh?"

A.79   She said, "Get up, and take this little girl outside, she says she has to go."

A.80   He answered, "All right, let her get up, while I open the door."

A.81   (Whispers) He felt around, and felt around with his hands, and found the sack-mending bodkin. [Audience giggles] He found the bodkin, a bodkin - ? [MM: Yeah, yes, I understand.] Do I make it clear to you? [MM: Oh, yes.] He found this bodkin, and he took the girl in his arms, and took her outside. He said, "By God, if you pee --(giggles) -- you see this bodkin? -- I'll fill your ass full of holes." [General laughter] (Adī laughs de- lightedly) [MZ: What a story! (Laughing)]

A.82   This poor gi - (Chokes with laughter) - she said, "I don't have to go, take me back to my mother. I'm going to my Ma!"

A.83   He brought her back, and gave her to her mother, and he went back and lay down, and this little girl still has to go. After he lay down, again - this little girl starts to whine and whimper, "Ma, I have to go! Ma, I have to -"

A.84   She said, "Mār Čučeh, take her and let her squat so she can pee. You must not have set her down so she could pee!"

A.85   "What am I supposed to do? I put her down, but she didn't go, and she said, 'Take me back to my Ma!' So I brought her - now what am I supposed to do?"

A.86   So he took her again, and put her down, and again he got out the bodkin, and said, "By God! If you pee, I'll fill your ass full of holes with this bodkin!" [Gentle laughter]

A.87   This poor kid says again, "Take me back to my Ma, to Ma! I don't have to go!" So he took her back, and in a minute she's whining and whimpering, "I have to go!"

A.88   He said, the vizier said, "You bastard! Curse your son-of-a-bitch father![1] Why don't you put her down, so she'll pee?"

A.89   He said, "What am I supposed to do with her? Curse your own father! Your daughter - she doesn't pee!" [General laughter] He said, "Now what? Hah?"

A.90   He said, "You stay there for a while so the little girl can pee."

A.91   "But I - wasn't she squatting? What am I doing?"

A.92   He took her. He took her, and showed the little girl the bodkin again. And again she doesn't pee. He said, "Lord Vizier! What should I do? She doesn't pee, the little bastard child of a dog!"

[BREAK IN RECORDING][2]

A.93   . . . (he) didn't want (   ). So he lifted the little girl up, and threw her down, and with one - with one gasp her breath left her. He said, "Lord Vizier! There, she died!"

A.94   "Curses on your father! You bastard! What if I did tell you, 'Lift her up to your head and throw her to the ground' - did you kill her? Leave, you bastard! You're not working for me! Get out!"

A.95   "Bastard yourself! I came to you for one year. And I should leave now?" Like that - "By God, if you can turn me out - Don't you do it! - (stutters) I'll tie God's whole body on you!"[3] [General laughter]

A.96   He came down and said, "Let's go, let's go, and dig the grave tonight, - if people find out, they'll say 'His daughter was fine. What did he do to her?'"

A.97   He went off to the graveyard with Mār Čučeh. There's one pick in his hand, - in his hand. He brought him along, and the pick, and he's digging the grave, but the pick was too dull. He sent him, and said, "Go, Mār Čučeh, bring the other pick, that's sharp,

---

[1] Quite strong and inflammatory cursing.

[2] Omits vizier's instructions to Mār Čučeh to pick up the girl and drop her - scare tactics are regularly used to control children - often violent threats like, "Your father will hit you with a stick!" or "We'll let the dogs eat you!" See note 1, p. 239.

[3] I.e. 'I'll give you more trouble than you dreamed possible'.

and be quick."

A.98   Now he comes for the pick, and the mother of the girl is sitting over her daughter, with her co-wife, and they're crying over the girl. He came and found the pick for himself, and it's on his shoulder. This pick is on his shoulder, and he says - standing over the two women, he says, "Gimme!" And he says, "Gimme!"

A.99   These two women say, "God's wrath on your eyes, <u>what</u> are we to give you? Doesn't it have a name, that, that you could tell us, 'Give me so-and-so'? And you say, 'Gimme!' And you say, 'Gimme!' How do <u>we</u> know what to give you?"

A.100   And he has the pick in his hand. And then he went out in the alley, (imitates shouting) "Heyyy, Lord Vizier, they won't give it. What should I do with these wives of yours?" [Laughter] Now watch this. Because he's going to kill another one. "Heyyy, Lord Vizier, these bastard wives of yours won't answer. What should I do? I've walked all around and I can't see it."

A.101   He said, "Take a rock to (their) head" - (chokes with laughter) - and the pick was in his <u>hand</u>. And he came with the pick and he <u>hit</u>! Right in the middle of her head. So she fell, too. And there's still seven years' revenge to take. That's two.

A.102   "You bastard, would you kill my brother? If you hadn't killed him --" He came. He came, and said, "Lord Vizier?"

A.103   "Yes?"

A.104   "Dig two graves." [MZ laughs]

A.105   "What did you do, you bastard?"

A.106   "Vihhhh! Didn't you say, 'Pick up a rock and hit her on the ear!'? I hit her - what else was I supposed to do?"

A.107   "Curses on your father, if I told you! And you hit my wife, killed her? Go, you bastard, get out of my service, I don't want you! You've put me in the midst of the field of destruction[1]!"

A.108   "Curse your father, yourself! I came to you for one year, and I should leave <u>now</u>? By God, if you put me out one step!" Yeah [MZ: God! What a story!]

A.109   Dear Sister, that all went before, and this same night - however much the bad fortune, he dug two graves, and he brought the mother and daughter and put them under, and praised God, and now one husband and wife were left.

---

[1] /Mašerat/ - unverified translation from context.

A.110   And one time, after some time had passed, there was a wedding there. There was a wedding, and they came and told the vizier and his wife (to come). They told them, and they went to the wedding. He turned to Mār Čučeh, and said, "Do you understand? Fasten the house doors tightly. When you go to sleep here in the house, when your cows have come, all of them - gather them all up and tie their feet, then you can leave the house, then get up, and come to the wedding."

A.111   "Oh, rest assured. By God, if I move from my spot!"

A.112   "Good."

A.113   Supper-time prayer came, and these - the cows came, and he filled the mangers with straw, and he drew a little knife, and if there were ten cows, [laughter] or twenty, he slaughtered them all. [General laughter] He slaughtered all of them, and he put a mouthful in each of their muzzles, in the straw. [Zāher: Now, I've heard - Now you watch this!

A.114   So this day, he comes, then, and comes into the house. And all the household goods there were, barley, wheat, all! He scattered them in the middle of the courtyard. [General laughter] (Adī laughs and coughs) He scattered it all in the middle of the compound, and then he took down the door, and fastened it, tight! To his own back! [MZ: All those things that were valuable. Yeah. He tied it to his own back, and where (did he go)? "Oh, Lord of the Lands!"[1] Off he went to the wedding. [Laughter] With this door tied to his back!

A.115   So he came, by God, and the men were gathered, and he came right into the gathering, like that. And just then the vizier's wife was going like this -- (imitating stealthy peeking around) -- The vizier's wife was going like this -- like this -- [Laughter] -- looking around like this, with her hand like this (in front of her face). All at once she said, (whispering), "Oh, little girl -- isn't that Mār Čučeh standing in the crowd with the door tied to his back?" She said, "Oh, little girl, oh, little girl, come here, to me." The girl came, and she said, "Auntie's darling, bless you, go and see where the vizier is sitting with the men. Tell him 'Your wife says to come here for a minute.'"

A.116   The little girl went, and found the vizier there, and said, "Your wife needs you and says, 'Come.'"

A.117   He, he came and said, "What do you want?" [MM interrupts recording to check batteries] [MZ: Please go on.] This -- when he came, he said, "What do you want?"

---

[1] An invocation of Hazrat 'Alī, for starting journeys.

A.118   She said, "Vīh! Father of So-and-so,[1] isn't that Mār Čučeh
standing in the crowd? He has the door tied to his back!" [MZ
laughs]

A.119   "Let it not be so!"

A.120   "By God, if you look there -- you go and look!"

A.121   Now when he went out among the men, he looks, and sees, "By
God, she's right!" (Voice rising) He starts hitting him, (Adī
shouts), "Bastard, your father was cursed! What have you got the
door tied to your back for?"

A.122   "Vih!? Oh, oh, creatures of God, you listen well! Listen well!
My back is paralyzed! He told me, 'Fasten the door tightly,' how
can anyone fasten it more tightly than this?" [Laughter] [Zāher:
He'd taken the door off its hinges?] Yeah. He'd taken it off its
hinges, and put it on his back, and went there. And all the stuff,
all the goods and household stuff, bedding, everything, together,
he took it all and threw it in the middle of the compound. And he
left the door of the compound open, and the house door, he took the
house door, tight on his back -- [MZ: He'd taken off the door!]
Yeah. Sure. He tied it from all four directions onto his back,
and came to this thing. And he slaughtered all the cows there.
And he, dear sister, said, "Oh, oh, people!--" 'There are lots of
people at the wedding -- "Do you see it his way, or mine?" And Mār
Čučeh says, "Look, here, tighter than this -- He turned to me and
said, 'Fasten the door tightly!' Is there any bastard who can
fasten it tighter? Hah? My shoulders are lame! It's that tight,
on my back -- could anybody tie it tighter?"

A.123   By now is there anyone who isn't laughing? What are they doing, then? Now when he'd said -- [Voice outside in courtyard interrupts her] Now when he said that, he says to his wife, "Get up,
we're going! By God, if he's left us any livelihood!"

A.124   Now when he comes into the compound, and lights a lamp, he sees
that everything from inside the house, all the household goods,
barley, wheat, flour, all there was in the house, bedding, all, is
dumped together in the middle of the courtyard. In the courtyard.
OK, so that very night, this poor guy gathered them all up that
same night, and took everything back in the house, and put the
door back.

A.125   Morning came. Morning came, and then it got to be noon. "Mār
Čučeh! Mār Čučeh!"

---

[1] Adults are normally called 'parent of so-and-so' if they have a living
child. For a vizier, this would be a familiar honorific used by family
and close friends of equal status to himself, but outsiders would call
him 'Vizier Saheb', 'Lord Vizier' or 'Mr. Vizier.'

A.126   "Huh?"

A.127   "Get up, and take your cows out to join the herd, because the herd is leaving!"[1]

A.128   Now he goes out and takes the cows' tails, and tries to lift them, but "Lord Vizier! What should I do? These bastard cows of yours won't get up, won't go! What am I supposed to do?"[2] And he'd slaughtered them himself! [laughter]

A.129   The vizier came. Now when he looked, and "Pu!" - took them by the ears, with a "How come they won't get --" now when he takes their ears, their heads come up in his hand! "Oh, you bastard son of a bitch! You've left us with four walls and a hearth! Go! Get out, I don't need you, you son of a bitch!"

A.130   "Son of a bitch, bastard yourself! I should go now? I came to you for a year as your servant! When my year is up, I'll go! I came to you for a year -- now I go? I shamed my father and mother to take such a position! What a servant that other little servant was! There, now!" He said, "Yeah." He said, "That little servant of yours was a servant, and, and, and -- it's tomorrow's blood, you brought blame[3] on your own neck, you killed him, you didn't give him food, and you killed him. He was a good servant of yours. And I go out, wandering and begging this way and that, and feed myself, and come back, and now you want me to leave? Your tyranny over me will pass - I go and stand by the house door, and eat a bit of bread, then I come in and do your work, and now I'm leaving?" Yeah. He told him.

A.131   Well, Sister dear, he gave (the cows) away as alms, and thanked God, said, "Oh, God, it was put on our foreheads, both husband and wife, that 'We would come to this.' Yes. We played the trick in the first place."

A.132   So after that a few days passed quietly. One day, one evening, he went out to play with the boys. This Mār Čučeh. He went out, and he's playing in the alley. (To Zāher:) Are you asleep, Zāher? [Zāher, sleepily: No.] He'd gone out to play, and just then, this wife of his, to her hu- spoke up, and said to her husband, "Curses

---

[1] Village or city people often cooperate to hire a communal cowherd, who takes the cows to fallow lands and brings them back daily.

[2] At the end of winter, stock, especially cows and donkeys which have been kept on very limited fodder, are often too weak to rise by themselves to go out to graze. Nazīf Shahrānī described going out to the stable to push and haul them into a standing position so they could walk. (Personal communication, March, 1977.)

[3] /malmaša/ : Unverifiable translation inferred from context.

on his father, now. . ."

[END OF TAPE]

TAPE # CCLXIX:

". . . he'll never let you alone of his own free will, this
bastard! Look, he killed my co-wife there, and my co-wife's daughter there. He did that to our cows here. Today or tomorrow,
(see) if he doesn't kill either me or you! Now that monster's gone
out to play, and we won't see a sign of him, he'll play till midnight. There. OK, you go quietly and lock the house door, and
take your stuff to the neighbor's, now, and lock up the house, and
get on the horse without a sound or a sign, and go somewhere else,
and hide for ten or twenty nights, get lost. Surely he'll leave,
and we'll lose track of him. He'll let us alone."

A.133 He's heard, way away. This Mār Čučeh. He's way off, and he
heard. And as he left there quietly, dear Sister that we consider
you,[1] this husband and wife, quick, quick, - they took their goods
and went, like, to Mādar Zāher's house with them, and (asked), "Can
these stay here safely for four or five days? And if our servant
comes and asks, 'Where did they go, and what happened to them?'
say, 'I don't have any idea.' Because he's poured dust on our
heads, from one door to the other, and surely he'll leave and get
lost." They took away their things, and locked up their door, dear
Sister that we consider you, this husband and wife mounted the
horse. Ha! Go, for you aren't going yet!

A.134 The other went, and got on the their road, down in a ditch.
Down in the ditch, under a bridge. He hid there. This, this Mār
Čučeh. "I shit in your Papa's little mouth,[2] where are you going
to run to, to get away from me?" [General laughter] He went and
got down in a ditch, under a bridge, like that.

A.135 And so the sounds of their voices came, that they're about to
get up, up on the bridge, and he streeetches out his head, like

---

[1] Expostulatory formula. The masculine form also exists, and was used
toward MM by male informants: 'Dear Brother that I (we) consider you'.
Adī's faulty Persian grammar distorts this, lit. 'dear Sister that you
have'.

[2] This is a woman's curse, in contrast to the masculine-style ones she
uses elsewhere. Male Afghans hearing this tape registered surprise at
her use of male cursing styles - logical in the mouths of male characters, as this curse is not.

this. (Demonstrates, stretching and peering) The horses <u>rears</u>, jumps back. And they hit the horse and hit it, and when he wants to get near the bridge again, he does the same thing with his head. And this horse <u>rears</u>, up to the sky, and comes down to earth. And he jumps back, and right then the wife says, "To dust with it![1] If only Mār Čučeh were here. Now he would go in front of the car - wha - the horse, with you. Whatever it was, he'd go down in the ditch and see, what death[2] it was, that makes the horse shy." [Laughter] They're just talking to themselves - and right then he says, "Lord Vizier! What did you say?" [Laughter]

A.136   (In an undertone) She said, "Wǐǐ! (claps once) Curse his father! God's truth" - [Laughter] - "Do we have to go to the sky, for him to leave us alone?" - this wife of his, - says, (aloud) "It's nothing. Just wondering about this ditch, and 'What death is in it?' We're just going - he's taking me to my father's house. He was just saying, 'It's better to go at night than during the day, the air is cool,' and then we got here, and no matter what he does, the horse won't cross the bridge. How do we know - what's down in the ditch, there?"

A.137   Now he says, "Stay here, and I'll go down, I'll look." He got down, and looked that direction, and said, "Lord Vizier, there's nothing."

A.138   "Good, go in front then, so he'll go."

A.139   They came, came, came, came, until it was morning. They came to the bank of a river. The bank of a river. Then they stopped right there. He said, "Let's stop right here and have a little sleep." When the husband and wife spread their bedding, this Mār Čučeh went off some distance and lay down. He started to snore, as if 'I'm asleep, already'.

A.140   This husband and wife - the wife spoke up quietly, and said, "Well, you came here on horseback. You haven't gotten tired. He <u>has</u> been tired out, and now that he's put his head down, he'll be fast asleep. When he falls asleep, let's the two of us take him and throw him in the river!" [Laughter]

A.141   Her husband said, "Good."

A.142   And way, away, Mār Čučeh heard him. He said, "I fuck your Pa! You just watch what - what I do with you!" [MZ laughs] And there he is, peacefully snoring.

---

[1] Indicates mild annoyance.

[2] 'Troublesome thing,' 'nuisance'.

A.143   The husband and wife, when they put their heads down, went sound asleep. Went to sleep. And this other isn't asleep at all, Mār Čučeh. Sooooftly he sneaks up, and he picks up the woman from beside him. He took her and put her in his own place. This Mār Čučeh. This one wife of the vizier, the only one left. [Laughter] He picked her up like that, from beside him, soooooftly, and she herself didn't know it. He picked her up softly, and brought her and put her in his own place, and went back himself, right away, and lay down there. Beside -- beside the vizier. [Laughter] And right then - he said (to himself) 'If only the woman doesn't wake up!' And he saw that the woman didn't even know, she's sound asleep. And he, too.

A.144   (Adī whispers) He says, "Lord Vizier! Lord Vizier!"

A.145   "Huh?"

A.146   "Get up, that monster Mār Čučeh is asleep!" [Laughter]

A.147   And his eyes were all full of sleep, and he didn't look to see that it's Mār Čučeh, himself. He said, "Let's go, that monster Mār Čučeh is asleep, let's go throw him in the river! Come on!" [Laughter] (Adī laughs).

A.148   So here he comes and one took the two feet and the other took the two hands, and kersplash! threw her right in the river. All of a sudden, he starts clapping, "Hayyy, the vizier threw his wife in the river!" (Adī laughing and clapping) "Hayyy, the vizier threw his wife in the river!" [General laughter]

A.149   "Curses on your father! [Laughter throughout] Curses on your offspring! From two wives, you've made me wifeless! Bastard, go, get out! I don't want you!"

A.150   "Bastard yourself! I came to you for a year, and now I should leave? I fuck your father, if I'll leave!"

A.151   This poor guy at this point is pouring dust on his head, saying, "Oh, God! What do I do now? Which way can I go? Where shall I go, this far from home?" Yeah. [Outside, male voice from court-yard interrupts. Māhgol, to outside: What is it?] [Pause]

A.152   Now Mādar, dear, from here - finally, this poor guy, he picked up his two hands and struck himself in the face, (and set out) for another city. Along with the other. He was with him.

A.153   He came, came, came, and came to a city. The officials saw him, and said, "Friends! This is our responsibility." So one of the officials invited him for the night, and took him to his place. He took him home and gave him - they ate food and drank, and so they were sitting there together, and talking back and forth.

Half the night passed. Half the night passed, and he himself[1] went outside quietly and peed, and came back and lay down quietly to sleep.

A.154   When he lay down, the vizier hadn't peed, or anything. This guy got up to leave, to go to his own room to sleep, and as he left the room, all at once Mār Čučeh (says), "Ho, Uncle! Lock the room door from the outside! or else tomorrow morning, if something is missing, you'll say, 'These people took it.'" Watch this. This guy, this guy hadn't gone out, hadn't peed or anything. And when they'd put their heads down, it was the middle of the night, and the vizier is taken short. He's tossing and turning, and he can't go to sleep.

A.155   "Lord Vizier! Where does it hurt you? Lord Vizier! Where does it hurt you?"

A.156   "You bastard! Curse your father! If the guy hadn't locked the door, or anything, had just gone away, a Muslim could have gone to sleep! 'Hooey, Uncle, Uncle, lock your door!' Now I'm taken short, and where can I pee?"

A.157   "Oh! Look around, here - feel around. Aren't there some shoes or something left around? Pee in them. I'll go early in the morning myself and wash them!" Yeah.

A.158   "You bastard, you! By God, if you'd take them! You're just going to disgrace me here, in front of these officials. You're going to shame me!"

A.159   "No, by God's Truth! I'll take a binding oath."

A.160   Now he felt around, felt around, and found there's some tall boots left there. [Laughter] He said, "There, there's some boots. Should I shit in them?"

A.161   "Yeah. I tell you, I'll wash them in the morning." He promises with a binding oath, "I'll wash them," and in his own heart he's saying, "Enshāllāh!" [2]

A.162   This one, this one quietly fills the boots with shit! [General laughter] This vizier. [Zāher: Did they belong to the vizier?] No, no! They belonged to the guy, to the host! To the vizier? He was peacefully shitting in these boots, Mādar Zāher -- (Chokes with laughter) -- He shat in these boots, and the boots were full, and he put them there in the corner.

A.163   Morning came, and the man came early, and opened the door, and he said, "Mār Čučeh! Mār Čučeh, get up now, take these out and

---

[1] Mār Čučeh. Equally ambiguous in Persian.

[2] 'If God wills' : ironic

wash them! (undertone) I'm going now, to wash for prayers. You go, too, take these and wash them in that stream. Then bring them back where they belong."

A.164   He said, (shouting) "I fuck your father! I, carry them, wash them?! You do the shitting --- and I pollute my hands?" He says, "By God, by God if I'll touch them! You did the shitting, and I should carry them, pollute my hands, wash them, and then the guy pulls them out from under my arm-you'll say, 'He stole them'! Whoever did the shitting can take them and wash them!"

A.165   "You bastard, you promised yourself with a binding oath, that you'd take them out! To dust with it, even if I'd been uncomfortable all night long, even if I wouldn't have slept, would I have done this?"

A.166   "Wiiii! There's your overcoat around you! Put them under your *postīn*1 carefully and carry them. While you wa--, wash for prayer, clean them, and put them back under your coat and bring them and put them back -- what's there to say?" Watch this. (Adī clap once) [General anticipatory giggling. Laughter continuous throughout following passage]

A.167   Now, (Adī laughs) dear Sister, this poor guy had no choice. He said, "God did it! Oh, Lord!" He picked them up in his hands and put them under his coat, and went! toward the stream.

A.168   This one came outside right away, and said, "Hey, Uncle! Hey, Uncle!" -- to the host, he's calling. "Hey, Uncle! Come here, look me over, so you won't say tomorrow, 'He stole something-or-other of mine, took it.'"

A.169   So this guy came, and looked him over, this way and that, and said, "What kind of a person is this?"

A.170   Finally he said, "That person looks like he's got something, he's going so fast. That friend of mine." [Laughter] Watch, now. How he gets into this disaster, now - (chokes with laughter) - he said, "That, that friend of mine, it looks like he stole something. Oh, Uncle! What did he do that for? Look how he's running! You (better) go!"

A.171   He, dear Sister, when he was looking him over - (chokes with laughter) - he was looking him over, and poor guy, until he was about to pull back his coat, and the guy's hand went right into the shit, and his beard - and the shit went kersplash! all over

---

1 A warm sheepskin coat. Good ones are expensive. A servant probably wouldn't have one.

their faces and hands. This guy's whole beard and face were covered
with shit,[1] and his hands, covered with shit. [Horrified laughter]
Go! Then, on his head - on your head may it rain flowers! - on
this poor vizier's head it's punching and hitting! (Claps) Ha!
Hit, for you don't hit enough!

A.172   "Your father owes me salt[2], and now you're taking my boots, to
hide your own shit?"

A.173   They dragged him through the middle of the bazaar, dear Sister
that we hold you for, they slapped him and took him right to jail!
"This, this --- All right! (shouting) I saw him and for pity - it's
the responsibility of an official - I took him in for the night,
and I honored this bastard, and made him my guest for the evening,
it's obvious he's an official, and he owes me salt, and he shits
in my boots and he's taking them off secretly to get rid of them!"
So he went, hit! For you don't hit enough! And they took him and
locked him up.

A.174   And as God granted him his object, may God grant the people of
the Prophet theirs[3]! Yeah! That's how the story was! That's how
Mār Čučeh was. And this from my mother's sister - I had this aunt
who was lame, lame in her legs. That's where the story's from.
She got it. Yeh. That's how Mār Čučeh was. Look, how many animals he killed in payment for his brother. He killed three people,
and he took (the man) himself and got him locked up. Then he let
him alone. Yeah. That's how the story was. He killed his own
mother there. Killed his father here. In payment for his brother.
Yeah. That's how. That was Mār Čučeh.

---

[1] A figurative expression for self-disgrace, commonly used, is "He ate
shit" or "He got shit on his beard". Literal self-pollution so extreme
is horrifyingly comical to an Afghan audience.

[2] I.e. "You owe me a debt of hospitality".

[3] Standard ending formula.

Title: Mār Čučeh [The Snake Chick]
Narrator: Adī
Recorded: 6 Aug. 1975
Cassette # E3B - E4A

B.1   There was, there was a - a woman - a widow woman. This widow
had one son. She had one son, and this boy, he had a cow. He had
a cow, and this boy would go, from morning to morning, and after
he'd eaten his bread and water for lunch, he'd take up his sacks,
and he goes and cuts hay in the fields, and brings it for his little cow. And his mother is staying like that with this one son.
She was a widow. This boy's father died.

B.2   Then it was God's will, one day the boy was cutting hay like
that, and all at once he saw a snake was going fīš, fīš, fīš. He
came, and came up to the boy, and said, "Hey, Boy!"

B.3   "What?"

B.4   "What are you doing?"

B.5   "Oh . . . I'm cutting a little hay."

B.6   "What have you got?"

B.7   "I have a cow."

B.8   "Do you have a father and mother?"

B.9   "I have no father, but I have a mother."

B.10   "That's good. Give my greetings" - this snake said - "Give
my greetings to your mother, (that) if she wants a husband, I'll
marry her." To this boy. Yeah, this snake said it. Then he said,
"Hey, Boy! You tell your mother. If you don't tell her, I'll
strike you and kill you."

B.11   He said, "All right." He came (home), and that day it went
out of the boy's head, and he didn't tell his mother. The next
morning as he came along, coming along the road to cut hay, all of
a sudden he thought, "Oh, didn't that snake tell me? He'll be
waiting for me." Finally he said, "Go on, to these - I won't go
to those fields, I'll go to some others."

B.12   So he went to these fields, and he's cutting hay like that,
and suddenly this snake came again. To these lands, too. And

he shouted, "Hey, Boy! Did you tell her?"

B.13   "No, I forgot. I didn't tell her."

B.14   "Today you tell her, or always - wherever you go, I'll be following you. Today - if you don't bring me word by tomorrow, I'll
strike you and kill you right away. You say, 'I won't go to these
fields, I'll go to others, and he won't come.' Any place you go,
I'll come." This snake told him that.

B.15   This boy, when he came, that day, he turned to his mother and
said, "Mother?"

B.16   "What?"

B.17   "Yesterday when I went, there was this snake, and he said, 'Deliver my respects to your mother; if she wants a husband, I'll marry
her.' But I didn't tell you yesterday. (Yawns) Today I went to
different fields, too, and he came again, and said, 'I'll strike
you and kill you, if you don't say it.' What do you say?"

B.18   Right away this bastard mother of his said, "I'll take him,
I'll take a husband." Yeah.

B.19   The next morning, the snake asked him, "Did you say it?"

B.20   "Yeah."

B.21   "What did she say?"

B.22   "She said, 'I'll take him.'"

B.23   "Good."

B.24   He turned to this boy and he said, "Any day that there comes a
wind first, and blows in your house and sweeps all the floors, and
after that a little bit of cloud, that rains, and settles the dust,
and after that clouds come, red, yellow, and this, and that happens,
you will know that I've come and I'm bringing these clothes for your
mother."

B.25   He said, "All right."

B.26   A few - two or three days passed, and then came a wind, and a
cloud and a rain, and then after that those clouds, all different
kinds, all different colors. And then, after a while, he saw that
all kinds of snakes, and all kinds of sc- , of scorpions, and all
their babies and young - he had sent them all before him, and he
came. The house was filled. Her, her - they gave the thread and
needle for her. They brought these, these clothes for her. And
then he excused them. These others. And the snake stayed there
with her. After he'd been there for a while, this boy's mother got

pregnant from the snake. She got a baby. Yeah. She got a baby. She gave birth. And so this baby got like my Azĩzollah, my son, about that big. This one day, they had gone, gone out to play in the alley, these two brothers, they went to play, and just then this snake, this snake turned to the mother, and said, "When can I strike your son, and eat him, and do all that?" He said, "Tomorrow, I'll get in the ghee jar, and don't you make anything for your son to eat with his bread, just bring the cloth with the bread, and a glass of water, and put it in front of him. - He can't eat dry bread. - You go, and make yourself busy at something. He'll call to you, 'Ma, look, why didn't you make anything to go with the bread? Can I eat dry bread?' You say, 'Mother's dear, my hands were full. I didn't get to it. Now you take the cup and go get ghee for yourself from the jar, and eat it with your bread.' When he puts his hand into the ghee jar, I'll strike him and kill him." The snake said that to the mother. About the first son. You know, the one who belonged to this woman? The one who goes after the hay! About - about that boy. The boy that he just had, himself - he's not talking about his own son. He's talking about that boy of his wife's.

B.27   This, this Mãr Čučeh was playing by himself, way off in the alley, and he heard it. What his father said.

B.28   The next day came and he got in the ghee jar, and when the boy had brought his hay and come in for lunch, all tired and worn out, when his mother brought the cloth and the bread, and put the water glass in front of him, she went off (yawns) and got busy with something else. When she'd gotten herself busy, he said, "Eh, Ma!"

B.29   "Huh?"

B.30   "Why didn't you make anything to go with the bread? Can I eat dry bread?"

B.31   "Mother's Dear, if I - if there isn't something for one day, it's not resurrection day. I - I was busy, and I didn't get to it. You do it, go take this - the, the cup, and go to the ghee jar and get some for yourself. Bring it and eat it."

B.32   This boy washed his hands and he washed the cup, and got up to go to the jar, when this - all at once this Mãr Čučeh, the boy who came from the snake, all at once he said - they named him Mãr Čučeh. All of a sudden he spoke up, "Brother, Brother, give it to me, I'll get the ghee for you. Papa's in the jar, and he'll strike you and kill you!"

B.33   He took the cup out of his hand and went and filled it and brought it and gave it to him. The boy ate, and then they two went back out to play.

B.34 He said, "There! That Early Death[1] of yours, right there, he must have heard it. Now tomorrow I'll get into the water skin. This time you make something to eat with the bread, and bring it to your son, but don't fill the water glass, don't bring that, so that he'll go get water for himself to drink. When he brings it to fill it, I'll strike him and kill him."

B.35 Once again, way off, Mār Čučeh heard. Yeah.

B.36 The next day came, and she made something to eat with the bread, and brought it, and spread the cloth before him. And she didn't fill the water glass, and didn't bring it. He said, "Ma, give me some water, my - my throat is blocked."

B.37 She said, "Dear, my hands are full. You get up - can't you fill the glass for yourself? Get up and fill it."

B.38 He got up, and when he picked up the glass to go to the skin, all at once Mār Čučeh said, "Brother, Brother, no! Give it to me, I'll fill the glass. Papa's in the water skin, and he'll strike you and kill you!"

B.39 So he took the glass out of his hand, and took it and filled it, and brought it back to him.

B.40 He spoke up and said, "This one, he's doing this. Now tomorrow, now, don't you make any bread dough. Say, 'Until - ' tell your son, 'Until you bring some wood, I won't make any - any dough. When you bring wood, - then I'll make bread. Now there's none of that wood, and I can't make bread without it. For one day don't go after hay for the cow, go and bring wood.' Tell your son that. Then I'll go to those lands, there, and I'll get in the load, and I'll strike him and kill him." This, this snake to his mother. And way off, alone, Mār Čučeh heard.

B.41 Next morning, the boy - his mother, that morning, said, "Mother's dear, this - a - today, don't go bring the hay. Go get me a bit of wood, because there's no thornbush left, and what can I make bread with? Until you bring some wood, by God, even if ten days go by, I (can't) make dough or bake bread."

B.42 He went and got his little rope, and his shovel, and went off to do that. To go for the wood. This Mār Čučeh throws himself to earth and heaven, saying "I'm going with you, too! Hooey-" He's hollering and yelling, "I'm going, too."

B.43 Finally he said, "Brother, you're a little one, you can't bring wood."

---

[1] /javān margī/ - an epithet for particularly troublesome children, who take years off their parents' lives.

B.44   He said, "No, I can, too."

B.45   So finally his mother said, "To dust with it! Let him go, may disaster dog his tracks! Go!"

B.46   He silently picked up a box of matches, and put them in his pocket. This Măr Čučeh. And he picked up a little piece of string, too, and went off with his brother.

B.47   So he was gathering wood and gathering, and he tied up his load, and he was about to put it on his back, and all at once he saw his father's head (whispers) <u>stretching</u> out, and he was going to bite the boy's neck. He said, "Brother, Brother, Brother! Put your load down right here, your load's come loose! Untie it, and tie it over again." Now watch. He took it off his back, and put it down, and he said - he took the rope off his shoulders, and he said, "Tie up that side. You don't know how. I'll fix it. I'll tie it." This ignorant kid, this little one, said that. From this side, he said, "you tie up that side -" and he struck a bunch of matches under the load. <u>Gŭ</u>, <u>gŭ</u>, <u>gŭr</u> it burned, and he burnt that snake. That father of his.

B.48   He said, "Do you see, if I hadn't been there, yesterday, and the day before, when you went to the jar to get the ghee, he would have struck you and killed you. That bastard mother of yours, he tells her and she doesn't say, 'What do you want with my son?' or anything like that. She says, 'You can suit yourself.'" He said, "All the blame belongs to Mo - Ma." He tells his brother. And when he came, came from, from that, from that - Lord! (tiredly) - When he came from that wood, and his mother was sitting right there, just like - he lifted up his shovel like that, and hit his mother on the head, and he killed his mother, too.

B.49   Then his brother said, "You're the little brother. You did all these good deeds, and saved me from being killed. You stay here now, and I'll go and become a servant, and work, and bring (things) for you to eat." His brother said that.

B.50   He said, "OK."

B.51   So off he went, and went to another country. There he saw a big company sitting. He said, "Oh, Brothers, won't you take a servant? I'm looking for work."

B.52   There was one, this vizier. This vizier was sitting there. He said, "I'll take a servant who has no stomach." Watch this! A person with no stomach? "You - I'll take a servant who has no stomach - "

B.53   He answered, he said (to himself) "He must just be talking (that way)," and he answered, "I don't have a stomach." This boy.

B.54   He took him as a servant and took him to his house. And in the evening he didn't give him any food. And it got to be the next day, and he didn't give him any food. The next day, and no food. This boy just died of hunger, there. There! He died of hunger! (Claps once)

B.55   Then the news came to that Mār Čučeh, "Come, because your brother - there was this one called 'vizier', who hired him," they said, "And he didn't given him any food, and your brother died."

B.56   He fastened the doors of his house up tight. He said, "Weeyy, I'll fuck your Pa, you vizier!" And he picked up and came there.

B.57   He came, and there was the same group sitting in front of the serai, and he said, "Oh, Brother, won't you take a servant?"

B.58   And he saw that this vizier answered again, "I'll take a servant who has no stomach."

B.59   He said, "I don't have a stomach." He knew, then, "This one - this one killed my brother." He said, "I don't have a stomach."

B.60   So he came along. And he watches, and watches - and he has two wives, this guy - and he watches and watches till he goes out of the house. Then he goes in, takes two pieces of bread, and puts them under his shirt, under his arm, and goes out in the alley, and eats peacefully.

B.61   And it gets near three months, four months, that pass, and he was with him. And one evening, he has one little daughter, and she needed to go out and void. She had to go void, and he said - the vizier called out, "Do this, Mār Č- -Mār Čučeh-" [MM interrupts to check tape recorder batteries.] . . . A daughter, then, one evening, he had this daughter, and she spoke up, and said she had to go void. She had to go void, and the vizier yelled, and said, "Mār Čučeh, Mār Čučeh, get up and take the little girl to pee."

B.62   He said, "All right."

B.63   He got up, and felt around, felt around with his hands, like that, and found a big bodkin. He found the bodkin, and kept it in his hand. He went and picked up the little girl, and carried her, and took her out in the courtyard. When she squatted down to pee, he said, "By God, if you pee, you see this bodkin - (just see) if I don't fill your ass full of holes!" He says that to the little girl.

B.64   And out of fear she said, "Take me back to my mother. Take me, I don't have to pee, take me back to my mother!"

B.65   He brought her back, and took her back to bed, and this little girl - still has to pee, and she says, "Ma, I have to pee," she's crying. So he called him again, and he took her again. Again he showed her the bodkin, "If you pee, by God -- your ass full of holes --"

B.66   So he brought her back again, and the third time that he took her, he said, "Lord Vizier, what shall I do? She doesn't pee, this girl of yours." Watch this!

B.67   He said, "Lift a big rock up over your head, and (hit her) on her heart -" And all this, right after these words, he says, "He killed my brother, - I fuck your Pa, and I'll do that!" As soon as it was out of his mouth, he lifted her up, and threw her to the ground. Her breath left her. This little girl died. He said, "Lord Vizier, there, your daughter died." (Aside to her son) Azīz?

B.68   He went. Now, he said, "You bastard! Even if I said to do that to my daughter - what I said, to throw her to the ground from over your head, did you really lift her up to your head and throw her down? Go! Bastard, leave my service!"

B.69   "I fuck your father if I'll leave! I came to you for one year, and I should leave now!? And lose my wages?" Yeah.

B.70   This same night, he said, "Pick up the pick, let's go dig the grave." He went with him, that night. And this pick, this pick was dull. They couldn't dig the grave, and he said, "Go, bring the other pick from the house."

B.71   He came with the pick in his hand. And he's standing over the two women, and he says, "Gimme!" And he says, "Gimme!" And he's holding the pick in his hand.

B.72   These wives said, "The wrath of God on you, may disaster stalk you, this, this - doesn't it have a name, that you could say, 'Give this thing to me'?"

B.73   And he says, "No. No, you just gimme it. Gimme it." Finally he went outside, and said, "Lord Vizier, these bastard wives of yours won't give it to me. What should I do?"

B.74   He said, "Take a rock and hit her on the head."

B.75   And his pick is in his hand. He hit! Right on the wife's head. And the little woman died too. He brought the pick, and he said, "Lord Vizier -"

B.76   "What?" Watch this. How this, this - Mār Čučeh gave it to him.

B.77   He said, "Lord Vizier, you'd better dig two graves. Your wife, too -"

B.78   "You bastard! What did you do?"

B.79   "Didn't you say yourself, 'Take a rock and hit her on the head'? I hit her, and she's dead."

B.80   "Bastard, go, curses on your father, go, leave my service!"

B.81   "Curse your father, yourself! I came to you for one year, and now I leave your service? By God, if you put me out!"

B.82   "Bastard, you killed my daughter, you killed my wife, tomorrow you'll kill my other wife, and wreck me and ruin me this way!?" Yeah.

B.83   These few days passed, and they put them under, he put his wife and daughter under. After some days had passed, there's this place, some distance off, on the other side of Herat, there was a wedding, and they gave him word. When they'd gotten word and they were going, to the wedding, he said, "Mār Čučeh!"

B.84   "What?"

B.85   "Don't leave the house alone, in case a thief comes, and takes all our stock and things. You go to sleep right here by the door, and when the stock has come, the cows have come, you tie them all up." (Yawns)

B.86   "All right." He filled the mangers with straw. The cows, those four or five cows of theirs came, and he slaughtered all four, five. He puts their heads down, in the mangers. He came into the house. All, everything there was in the house, he took it all and threw it in the middle of the courtyard. Then he took off the door, and tied it tight to his own back, and where? Off to the wedding!

B.87   Now he went, and stood, there in the middle - in the middle of the crowd of men. And the door tied to his back.

B.88   All at once, the vizier's wife was sitting there, all at once - she's looking at the crowd[1] -- (very low whisper) -- she took her hand like this (gestures), and said, "Weyyyy, isn't that Mār Čučeh with the door tied to his back? Standing right there with the men?" She called this one little girl about the size of Azīz, a little kid, and said, "Hey, Little One. Go, call the vizier and tell him, 'Your wife says to come here.'"

B.89   She came and called, and the vizier came and when he'd come, she said, "Isn't that Mār Čučeh? Look at him, with the door tied to his back. The thieves must have come and carried off everything

---

[1] From behind a partition separating the women's area from the men's.

you had - and here you were sitting at this - at this wedding without a worry. And we came and now he's come. Vīh! Mār Čučeh!"

B.90   This vizier started to hit him and push him around. And he
says, "Huh? Oh, People! You, host of the wedding! Stop the
drums! All right. He told me 'Fasten the house door tightly.'
Now you look at my shoulders - the door has bent them down. Who
could tie it tighter to his back than I have? I tied it to my
back! And he's still complaining, and cursing and beating me!?
He says, 'Why did you do that to the door?' My shoulders are lame!
Who could make it tighter than I have?"

B.91   So the man and woman went out, following him, putting him in
front, and they came and lit the lights, and he sees that everything, whatever they had was all together in the middle of the
courtyard. All night until morning they dragged and carried it all
back into the house.

B.92   Morning came. The sun came up, and "Mār Čučeh!"

B.93   "What?"

B.94   "Go, let your cows loose, so they aren't left behind the herd.
It's going already."

B.95   He takes the cows by the ears. And he's killed them, already!
"Lord Vizier, they won't get up, no matter how much I hit them.
What should I do?"

B.96   Now the vizier comes. And when he takes them by the ears, he
looks behind, and "Vih!" The heads come up in his hand.

B.97   "Ayy, curses on your father!! Go, you bastard! Go, get out!
You've reduced me to two rooms and a hearth!"

B.98   "Curses on your own father! I, go now?! I came to you for a
year!"

B.99   "Bastard! You'll finish me off to the very floor, before your
year is up! My -- already you've killed my wife there, and you
killed my daughter there, and here you've done this to my cattle,
and you scattered all my possessions in the middle of the courtyard. Aren't you going to leave me a livelihood?"

B.100   In his heart he says, "I'll fuck your Pa. You'd kill my
brother - if you hadn't killed him -" (Yawns)

B.101   For these few days, a little while, the man and wife were
feeling trapped at his hands, and finally she spoke up, and said
to her husband, - He went out to play in the alley, it's evening
and he's playing, and she says, "Lord Vizier, that monster bastard's
gone out to play. Now you lock up the house, tightly. Take your

things to the neighbor's house, and fasten the house doors tightly, and get on a horse without making a sound, and go! Hide yourself for a few nights, surely he'll leave, and after that he'll get lost, and let us alone."

B.102   He says, "Good."

B.103   These two ran inside the house quickly and dragged things, like to Mādar Zāher's house, and locked their door tightly, and the man and wife got on their horse, and oh! Go, for you aren't going!

B.104   Way off, Mār Čučeh heard. And before they left their house, he's come along on their road and gotten down in a ditch, hidden, below a bridge. Now, the horse comes along, about to get up on the bridge, to go over it, and he puts his head out from under the bridge like this. (Craning neck) The horse shies, and jumps back. No matter how much they hit him, no matter what he does, no matter what, the horse won't go. Finally the wife spoke up, "If only Mār Čučeh were here, he could lead the horse for you."

B.105   All at once -- [END OF CASSETTE, with short gap in recording]

CASSETTE E4A:

B.106   So then, he did that. When he went from there, then, this, this Mār Čučeh went ahead, and the man and wife behind. Ha! Go, for you aren't going! They came, came, came, came! It's beside a big river. They - the vizier said, "Let's sleep here, then."

B.107   They put their heads down, and the wife and husband went far away, and stretched out. Mār Čučeh lay down here.

B.108   She[1] turned to him,[1] as they were lying down, and she said, "Lord Vizier, now you came mounted, and you're not tired. He came all that way on foot, and he's tired, now when he puts his head down, he'll fall sound asleep. Then you get up quietly and throw him in the river! (Rising pitch) You'll be free of trouble, then we can turn around and go back."

B.109   This Mār Čučeh, way off by himself, he heard. He said, "VĪĪ, I'll fuck your Pa! Just watch, if he doesn't throw you in the river!"

B.110   So the husband and wife put their heads down quietly, and fell sound asleep. And he came and sooooftly lifted this woman up from beside him. He took her and put her in his own place. Then he came and quietly lay down. A while later, he said, (whispers)"Lord Vizier, Lord Vizier, get up, because that monster Mār Čučeh is asleep. Let's throw him in the river."

---

[1] Ambiguous in Persian. The two pronouns are interchangeable.

B.111 (Speaking voice) So he came, all sleep - all sleepy-eyed, and lifted her up. Mār Čučeh took her feet and her husband took her hands, <u>kersplash!</u> into the river! All at once he started clapping, and clapping, and cheering, and the blame is on his hands, that "Hayy, the Lord Vizier threw his wife in the --(giggles) -- threw his wife in the river! Hayy, the Lord Vizier threw his wife in the ---"

B.112 "Oh, you bastard, curse your father! Didn't I say you would finish me off to the floor, you bastard? Go, go, then, let me alone, now that you've killed both my wives, and done that to my animals, and things, go, get out!"

B.113 "I fuck your father, I came to you for a year! I, go <u>now</u>?"

B.114 "You bastard, now, now - why stay with me? What could a servant do for me now? Hah? I'm finished!"

B.115 Finally morning came, and he came, came, came, to another city. And there was an official there, who recognized the vizier and took him in for the evening, to his own house, and (yawning) made him his guest, and like until now, late in the evening, he's an official, and he has a party for you, until this time of the night they're partying and laughing. And time passes, and Mār Čučeh, having gone out to the outhouse and voided, and come back, lay down to sleep. And the vizier and the other guy are still up, talking. And the vizier didn't go outside. And he hasn't gone out when this other one finally - and he said, "You - this - " - This guy is going off to go to sleep, and all at once he calls to the guy, "Oh, Uncle! Lock the door from the outside!" Mār Čučeh says it, "Lock the door from the outside, or else tomorrow, if something or other gets lost, you'll say, 'They took it - this servant of his.' No. (Lock) the door."

B.116 And he hadn't gone to the outhouse to pee, the vizier. And when the night was about half gone, he needed to void. He fidgets and turns over on his back and on his face, and he can't go to sleep. And the door is locked from the outside. "Oh, Lord, can I pee in a corner of this guy's house? What shall I do?"

B.117 All at once this Mār Čučeh called out, "Lord Vizier, Lord Vizier, how you're fidgeting! Where do you hurt?" Watch this!

B.118 He says, "I don't hurt anywhere, I need to void, and you told the guy, 'Lock the door,' and he's locked it tightly from out there, now am I supposed to shit in some corner of his house? What shall I do?"

B.119 "Look around, feel around in the room, isn't there something? You can void in that. Tomorrow <u>early</u> I'll take it and wash it."

B.120 "Oh, you bastard, you won't wash it, or anything, you'll just shame me here, you. Just like you killed my two wives, and put my quilt on my back."[1]

B.121   "Oh, no! I'll take a binding oath that I won't do that."

B.122   So, Margaret dear, this, then - he felt around right there and found that some tall boots had been left there. He shat them full. Filled them with shit, shat in them. He set them there. In the morning early, this guy came and opened the door, and he - he said (whispers) "Mār Čučeh! Mār Čučeh! Get up, then, take these and wash them, and bring them and put them back."

B.123   He said - he said, "I fuck your Papa! You did the shitting, am I supposed to pollute my hands? By God, if they'll be washed at my hands! You have a long coat, your coat is on your back, nice and long, so you just put them under your coat and take them! You just go out like that, and wash for prayer, and wash them there, and put them back under your coat and come."

B.124   He said, "All right."

B.125   So, dear Sister, he, he quietly takes himself off from the house, and all at once he called out to the master of the house, "Hey, Uncle, come here! Look me over, under my pants-band[2] and all around, so that tomorrow you won't say, 'He stole something.'"

B.126   This guy came, and looked him over, and saw that there was nothing. And he said, "You see him, how fast he's going? He stole something!" Pointing out the vizier. This guy started running, and when he pulled it back - the corner of the thing - this guy got entirely covered with the shit. Ha! Hit, for you don't hit this vizier (enough)! And he took him off, and locked him up.

B.127   And so he did in the wife and kid that way, and ruined all his stock and possessions right there, and took him, too, and got him for stealing - so as God gave him his object, (may He give) the object of the people of Mohammed the Prophet! [MM, laughing: Thank you!]

B.128   That's how Mār Čučeh was! (Claps once) For the sake of one brother, look how many people he killed! Yeah. [MM: Yes, yes.] All of them. [MM: His own mother and father -] Yeah! [- and two wives and a daughter, and the vizier -] And these cows, and he took him, himself, and got him caught for stealing, and came back and gathered up all the possessions he left behind, and took them.

---

[1] I.e. 'made me into a vagabond'.

[2] Afghan equivalent of a pants pocket, the tight drawstring is used to hold small objects.

To his own house. "I'll fuck your father, you – You'd kill my brother? There, now, I'm putting my shit right here and you can eat it."[1] Look how he killed his wife and child, too, like that.

B.129   [MM: Who did you hear this from?]

B.130   I learned this from that aunt of mine. I had an aunt. She was lame, poor thing. She got the $\bar{a}te\check{s}ak$, and her legs were lame.[2] She never had any husband! She died a virgin, passed away. She was a virgin, and she died. She told me this. When we were children – [MM: You were little?] We were little. Yeah! We were little. She told me it, this very one. I knew so <u>many</u> stories! I knew <u>so</u> many, and when my father used to go somewhere, that he would hear (something), he would come back and tell them to us, and my aunt like that . . . He had an aunt with a husband, he was a mullah[3] and <u>he</u> knew <u>so</u> many stories! And he knew so much poetry[4], that – In those days, there was no such thing as these tapes, there were gramophones. [MM: Yes?] They would take re--, re--, records. And this husband of my aunt, there was this other person, who was a great poet, a real singer, and he was a mullah, too, and a singer (of poetry), and he knew lots of these stories. And these, they invited them to Kabul several times. [MM: To make the –] Yeah, to record them. They would sing, and they would record them. And then that husband of my aunt's died. And that other person died, too. And he told a lot of stories while I was there, but now my thinking has gotten – like that. Of those literary, of those – of those stories. Of– [MZ, hoarse with sleep and impatient: If a person learns a story when he's small, Adĭ, it <u>doesn't</u> go out of his mind, for –] But Mādar – so many, I knew, by God, if it isn't true, Mādar Zāher, by your head and by my death[5], and you-don't I have an oath on your salt? Now, if I have to think it out this way, bit by bit, really, from the day this sickness came on my head, the root of my soul is divided in pieces. Nothing! There's nothing in place! How do I know, what kind of a death[6] it is? Yeah. It's like that. –– One time –– [END OF TOPIC]

---

[1] A highly ungrammatical phrase – translation conjectural.

[2] Lit. 'the little fire' – perhaps polio, although in Herati this designates an inflammatory skin disease.

[3] I.e. was somewhat educated, or literate.

[4] $\check{g}azal$ – lyric poetry in monorhyme.

[5] 'As you may live and I may die' – the discussion was quite heated.

[6] Bad thing, misfortune.

Title: Mār Čučeh [The Snake Chick]
Narrator: Mādar Zāher
Recorded: 11 Sept. 1975
Cassette # E75A - E75B

C.1   [MM: Please go ahead. What will you tell about?]

C.2   The story of Mār Čučeh. [MM: Mār Čučeh.] Yeah. The story
of Mār Čučeh. [MM: Please. The one you learned from Adī?] Yes.
From Adī.

C.3   There was this old man, and an old woman. [Māhgol: Nooo -
it was an old woman and a boy.] Shut up! Oh, her husband died,
and so she and her son were left, like that. There was and
there was, there is no one better than God, there were an old
man and an old woman. This old man and old woman had one son;
after some days and some while passed, this poor old man died.
The old woman and this boy remained.

C.4   They remained, and some days passed. This little boy had a
cow, and he would bring hay for his little cow, and feed it. His
mother would milk it, and they would sell the milk, or the butter,
and they made their living. They lived.

C.5   After some days this little boy went to the plain to cut hay,
and as he went, he noticed a fīš, fīš, fīš like a pressure cooker.
Just like that. This boy said, looking this way and that way, he
saw there was something, like a snake, but big, like a (   ).[1]
It came near, coming toward him, and this boy can't run or cry out.
There's no one out on this plain. Then he said, "Hey, Boy, what
are you doing here?"

C.6   "I have a little cow, and I'm cutting hay for it."

C.7   "Whom else do you have?"

C.8   "I have an old mother."

C.9   "Will your old mother take a husband?"

C.10   "How do I know?"

C.11   "All right. Go today. Tell her. If she'll marry, come

---

[1] /jowā/ - untraceable.

tomorrow and bring me word."

C.12   This poor boy said "All right." He tied up his load of hay, and put it on his back, brought it home, and gave it to the cow and the cow ate, but to his mother, nothing. He said, "How can I ask my mother, 'Do you want a husband, or not?'"

C.13   The next morning ca- oh, yeah. It escaped his mind, then. [MM: Oh.] As he came, that morning as he came, when he got close to that plain, the thought came back to the boy. He said, "To dust with it! I won't go to these fallow lands, I'll go to those other fallow lands, that other direction."

C.14   So he went in another direction, and he heard a fīš, fīš. As soon as this boy heard that fīš, fīš sound, his color fled and his body started shaking, and when he looked, he saw that aufī standing there. He said, "Hey, Boy! Did you tell your mother?"

C.15   "Yes."

C.16   "What did she say? Did she say, 'I'll marry'?"

C.17   He said, "She didn't say anything."

C.18   "Oho! You didn't tell your mother! You'd better realize that anywhere you go on land, to heaven, or on earth, I'll find you. You tell your mother. If she'll marry, you bring me word right away!"

C.19   He said to him, "All right. By my eyes."

C.20   He gathered his hay, and the next day, this poor kid went. He said to his mother, "Ma, there's this sort of a person,[1] asking, 'Will you marry?'"

C.21   She said, "Yes, dear, I'll marry."

C.22   He came. He came, and saw the snake in the midst of the plain. He said, "My mother says, 'I'll marry.'"

C.23   The day came and clouds came and a wind came up and swept all the ground. And after that, settling the dust, a sprinkling of rain came, and it settled the dust. After that snakes came and aufīs came and snakes came and aufīs came, and all these things came, and their house was filled. These clothes came down, and this, this old woman put them on. That was his wedding, then.

C.24   Some - after he married her, some days, some while passed, and this old woman got pregnant. She got pregnant, God gave this child, and they called him Mār Čučeh. They called him Mār Čučeh, and some

---

[1] Implying that the boy described the aufī in detail.

days passed, and this Mār Čučeh got a little bigger, and he spoke, this aufi, he said to this - he said to this old woman, "This b- this boy of yours - when can I eat him?"

C.25   She said, "Any time you want, eat him. Suit yourself."

C.26   He said, "Good." That was that, and this Mār Čučeh heard it, and he said, "Tomorrow, don't you - " cooking bread - no - oh! "Bake the bread. But don't make anything to eat with it." This boy was such that in his whole life, in his whole life, he didn't - he'd never eaten plain dry bread. There was yogurt sauce or there was egg broth or there was soup or there was rice, something like that, and he never ate dry bread. He said, "Don't cook anything."

C.27   She baked the bread and he came, then, after that, "He'll say, 'Ma, why didn't you make anything to go with the bread?' You say, 'Oh, Mother's dear, all right, then, today I had a lot of work, you go and get some ghee for yourself from the jar.' I'll go and get in the ghee jar, and when he comes to get ghee, I'll strike him and kill him."

C.28   She said, "That's fine."

C.29   She came, and brought the bread to him, and he said, "Ma, is it possible to eat this dry bread?" She brought the water glass, too, and set it down. Then this, "Why didn't you make anything to go with the bread?"

C.30   "Oh, dear, every day, every day, something to go with the bread, and I'm not short of work. I was busy with work. Go on, get some ghee for yourself."

C.31   And this Mār Čučeh said - the boy picked up the cup to go and get ghee from the jar. Mār Čučeh said, "Aeyyy, Brother, give it to me so I can get it for you!"

C.32   "Get it, then!"

C.33   When he went, and put the cup into the jar, he saw the little boy, and he filled it and brought it back. Nothing, then. This little boy ate. After he ate, they went, out to the plains. They went out to the plains, and afterwards he came out of the jar of ghee. He spoke up, "Hey, old woman!"

C.34   "What?"

C.35   "Did you see that? What this Mār Čučeh did? He went and pulled a trick." He said, "Tomorrow, you make something to eat with the bread, prepare everything, but don't fill the water glass or bring it. I'll go get in the water jar." - And this Mār Čučeh had come back early, and he heard that, too. He went, and he said, "Brother! Brother!"

C.36   "Soul of your brother!"[1]

C.37   "Tomorrow Papa's going to strike you and kill you, watch out!"

C.38   "All right." [Zāher: He didn't say anything to him.] [Māhgol: He's right.] Shut up already! You both shut up, already. [MM giggles]

C.39   Now, after that happened, the next day came, and she brought him bread and something to eat with it, but she didn't bring any water. And this aufī has gone and gotten into the water jar. He'd gone, and the boy said, "Ma, why don't you bring any water?"

C.40   "Mama's dear, go yourself, and get your water, you're a youngster."

C.41   When he got up to fill the glass from the jar, this Mār Čučeh said, "Aeyyy, Brother! Give it to me, so I can bring water for you." He took the glass, and took it and filled it, and brought it back and gave it to him. He drank. [Zāher: (Inaudible comment] I'll say that, but later. He ate, and when he'd eaten, then, he left.

C.42   He came out, and he said, "All right, what am I to do? Tomorrow I'll go, I'll go to the plains. You tell him, 'Dear, there's no wood, today. There's not a bit of wood. You go, then, and bring a load of thorns, or brush, or something. No bread - there's no wood for me to bake bread with.' I'll go, and when he's tying up his load, I'll go inside it. I'll strike him and kill him." This time this little boy heard, (too). This Mār Čučeh.

C.43   When the next day came, when he was about to go after the wood (sic), this Mār Čučeh spoke up - this mother of his said, "Mother's dear, there's not a bit of wood today, and we're all hungry. You'll have to bring a bit of wood."

C.44   "Good, Ma, by my eyes, I'll go and bring it."

C.45   Mār Čučeh started crying. Mār Čučeh started crying, saying, "I'm going too!"

C.46   She said, "Don't you go, Mama's dear!"

C.47   "No, I'm going!" And he's screaming and throwing himself to earth and heaven, "No! I'm going!"

C.48   The boy's mother said, "What can I do now?" And she said, "Even if he goes to destruction[2], give him a little piece of rope,

---

[1] Idiomatic affectionate response.

[2] /lahad/ - unverified translation from context.

and take him, too."

C.49   He came. He came, and they gathered wood, and gathered, and gathered, and this little boy tied up a <u>biiig</u> load for himself, and the aufi went and got inside the load. Now he tied up Mär Čučeh's load and put it on his back, and he said - then he went to pick up his own. And this Mär Čučeh, this talk is still in his ear. Standing there, he's waiting for an ambush. Just as the boy was about to put the load on his back, he saw his father's head showing in the middle of the load. [Zäher: This Mär Čučeh saw?] This little boy saw it, Mär Čučeh saw it. You're making a liar of me. He said, "Aeyyy, there, Brother! Put down your load, it's come loose. Tie it up again, or it'll fall down along the way."

C.50   "He said, "It's all right, like this."

C.51   "It's not! Put it down!" And when he put it down, this little boy, this <u>very</u> moment Mär Čučeh, standing behind the load, put down his load - and he'd taken the matches. Quietly, without his brother or mother (knowing). And he struck these matches underneath the load. Then this load burns, just going <u>jaul</u>, <u>jaul</u>!

C.52   He said - and he's clapping - "Aeyyy, Brother, I burnt Papa! I burnt Papa! I burnt Papa!"

C.53   "How do you mean, you burnt Papa?"

C.54   "I just burnt him, like that. Yesterday he said to Ma, 'When tomorrow comes, you tell your son - don't make bread - tell him, "There's no wood, for me to bake with. Go get some wood." Then I'll go, and get in his load.' I heard. I took the matches in the morning and put them in my pocket, and I came along. He was going to - he went into the load, in order to strike you and kill you. Now, I'll fuck Ma's little father - that father of mine - all this - Now that I've burnt Papa, I'll fuck Mama's Pa, I'm going to kill her, too."

C.55   "How can you kill Ma?"

C.56   "By God, don't <u>you</u> kill her! If she cared about you, or me - if she'd cared about you - to go - when he wanted to go hide in the ghee jar and strike you and kill you, I went and brought the ghee. He went into the water jar, and was going to eat you, and I brought the water. And to her - she said, 'Go get wood,' and he went and got inside the load in order to eat you, her <u>husband</u> was going to eat you. I burnt him. I'm going to kill her, too."

C.57   "All right," he said.

C.58   So they got up, and they came back to the house, and he said, "Ma?"

C.59   "What?"

C.60   He said - I don't know what - whether he said, "Give us water,"
or whether he said, "Why haven't you put this pot on the fire?"

C.61   She said, "Dear, you went, and came back, and there wasn't any
wood, where was I to get it?"

C.62   He said, "Aeyy, I fuck you father's little corpse! There wasn't
wood? Sure there wasn't wood!" And he picked up the shovel, and
just like that when he raised it up, (MZ laughs) he hit his mother
on the crown of the head, and she gave one screech, and she fell
down dead. He said, "Now do you want to deliver my brother to your
husband's jaws? So he can eat him?" He killed her. When he'd
killed her, Margaret, then he said, "Brother, now, then, God has
given us our object."

C.63   This big boy said, "Now, then, you take care of this little
cow, and I'll go and get a job. You did (me) so much kindness. And
you're little, besides. So you take care of the cow, and this milk,
or yogurt, whoever wants it, give it to them, and they'll give you
bread, so you can live peacefully here. I'm going."

C.64   This big boy left that city and went to another city, and said,
"Doesn't anyone want a servant?"

C.65   One person said, "I'll take a servant who has no stomach."
[Māhgol interjects: The vizier was sitting.] He was a vizier.
"He must not have a stomach."

C.66   He said, "How (do you mean) he shouldn't have a stomach?"

C.67   "That he shouldn't eat."

C.68   "I don't eat a thing."

C.69   He hired him as a servant. He hired him as a servant, and
took him. When he took him there, then, this poor little guy,
that day he didn't give him food, and he worked, and the next day
he worked, and he gave him no food, and the day after he worked,
and he gave him no food, and so he died. This brother of Mār Čučeh
died.

C.70   He died, and this Mār Čučeh, some days and some while passed,
(and) he said, "My brother hasn't come. Whatever it was, (something) has happened."

C.71   He came. He has information that in this city, there's this
person, who takes servants, and so he came. He came there, and he
said, "What is there, in this city?"

C.72   They said, "Nothing, Brother, (it's) like this, in this city,

there's this vizier, and whoever the person, he takes him as a
servant, and he doesn't give him any food, and the poor people die."

C.73   So he, this poor kid, he said, "All right."

C.74   He went and sat in the middle of the bazaar, and this vizier
came. When the vizier came, he said, "Who'll become a servant,
who doesn't have a stomach?"

C.75   This Mär Čučeh said, "I don't have any stomach at all. I'll
be a servant."

C.76   He said, "Good." He took him as a servant, and took him (home).
When he'd taken him, then, this day, they didn't give him any food,
then, and as soon as the wife and child turn their eyes away, he
goes and takes a piece of bread or two out of the bread box, and he
goes out and eats in the alley. And he drinks water, and nothing
else, he brings it secretly. The next day he did the same, and
the next day the same. So some days and some while passed, and
he didn't die. And the vizier is happy, because he has no stomach.

C.77   And what did he do after that? He did like this - he said,
"What shall I do to him?"

C.78   Evening came. Yeah. Evening came, and this vizier's little
girl said, "I have to pee." And he was the servant. So the wife
called and said, "Mär Čučeh!"

C.79   "What?"

C.80   "Come here, take this child, so she can pee."

C.81   He came and took her. When he took her, he said, "Eh! See
this bodkin? By God, you - I'll fill your body with holes if you
pee!"

C.82   This little girl was little, and she was afraid, so she voided.
(sic)[1]

C.83   He brought her back. After he brought her back, she started
crying again, "Ma, I have to pee!"

C.84   So now the vizier called, "Mär Čučeh!"

C.85   "What?"

---

[1] A slip of the tongue. MZ omits negative prefix.

C.86   "Death![1] Why don't you take her so she can pee?"

C.87   He said, "King - " 'he said, "Lord Vizier, I just took her! She doesn't pee."

C.88   He said, "Come and take her!"

C.89   He took her, and he said, "If you pee, this ass of yours, body of yours, I'll <u>fill</u> it full of holes! . . . (laughter) - You see this bodkin?"

C.90   She didn't pee. When she didn't pee, after that, he brought her back. This little girl, when she sees her mother again, she's crying, "Ma, I have to pee!"

C.91   "May you see no good fortune,[1] dear! You just said, 'I won't pee'! Măr Čučeh!"

C.92   "What?"

C.93   "Curses on your father, why don't you put her down so she'll pee?"

C.94   "By your death, she doesn't, she doesn't pee, what am I supposed to do!?"

C.95   She brought her, and said, "Take her, take her out so she'll pee."

C.96   He brought her. He said to her, "If you pee, you - I'll fill your ass with holes!"

C.97   This little girl doesn't pee. He shouted, "Lord Vizier, she doesn't pee!"

C.98   He said, "Throw her to the ground so her breath will leave her!"

C.99   So he lifted the girl up over his head and <u>threw</u> her to the ground, and the child died. He said, "Lord Vizier, there, she's dead."

C.100   "Eh, bastard, how did you kill my daughter?"

C.101   "All right. You're the bastard, yourself, you said, 'Lift her up over your head, throw her to the ground,' so I threw her. She fell."

C.102   So after that, the vizier said, "What can I do? Let's go,

---

[1] A very mild oath.

we'll dig her grave tonight, so that no one will know what became of her."

C.103   He got himself up and picked up the shovel, and they went to a shrine to dig the grave. He said, "This can't be dug." It can't be dug. He said, "Go, get the thing - get the pick from the house."

C.104   He came, and said, "Mistress!"

C.105   "What?"

C.106   "Give me the thing. The -, the -," (aside) No, he didn't say 'pick', when he said 'give' - he said, "Give me the shovel!"

C.107   She said, "But the vizier just took the shovel." The mother of this - [Māhgol interjects: He picked it up, that one.] And he picked up the pick, and hid it. And this Mār Čučeh said that, and he hid the pick. He said, "Mistress, give me the pick and shovel! The vizier says to."

C.108   She said - they were crying, both. He has three wives. All these three wives of his are shedding tears and crying.

C.109   And he got up on top of the roof. He said, "Eh, Lord Vizier, hey! These bastards won't give me the pick!"

C.110   He said, "Hit them! Right on the head. (Laughing) Get the pick from them and bring it."

C.111   He came, and raised this thing, and hit the wife on the head, and the wife died. She dropped.

C.112   He went, and said, "Lord Vizier."

C.113   "Yes?"

C.114   (Laughing) "Dig two graves!"

C.115   "Why?"

C.116   "All right, you said, 'Hit!' and I hit her on the head, and she's dead."

C.117   "Eh, bastard, how could you kill the daughter, and the mother, too?"

C.118   "All right, bastard, yourself, I say, 'Gimme the pick, and the shovel, gimme!' She says, 'It's not here.' OK, you said, - I called out, 'Hey, Lord Vizier, I keep saying "Gimme," and she doesn't.' You said, 'Hit her! Right on her brain so she'll give it.' And I hit her, right on the brain, and she died."

C.119   He dug two graves and they buried his wife and daughter that night, and put them in the earth. When he'd buried them - (to Māhgol) - You tell some, tell a little now. [Māhgol, whispering: . . . I don't know . . .] From the place where he buried the mother and daughter. Then he started something else. [Silence]

C.120   Yeah, then, he, when he buried the mother and daughter, he stayed, then. He stayed, after that. And some days and some while passed, and the vizier said, "Mār Čučeh?"

C.121   "What?"

C.122   "Go, tell them at home that the vizier has guests tonight."

C.123   [Māhgol: It was a wedding] No, this wedding was the other wife - ohh . . . (she remembers and agrees) [MM to Māhgol: When your mother gets finished, you tell the story from the beginning . . .] Good. [MM to Māhgol: Is that all right?]

C.124   Oh, this - if - he has a guest. He came, and he didn't say anything. He didn't say anything, and he came, this vizier, to do some work around the house. He's not in the house, and he doesn't know. So near afternoon prayer time, he came, and he said "Lord Vizier!"

C.125   "What?"

C.126   "They haven't put the pot on to cook yet."

C.127   He said, "But didn't I tell you? Didn't I tell you to tell them at ten o'clock?"

C.128   "By God, they haven't put the pot on."

C.129   He said, "Go, those bastards, curse their fathers, why haven't they put on the pot?"

C.130   He was doing like that, so he could get his brother's blood (back), now. He came, and he hit! He killed the middle wife. The youngest wife was left. He said, - he went, said, "Lord Vizier!"

C.131   "What?"

C.132   "There, I hit her, and she's a corpse, (laughingly), she fell there."

C.133   "How could she fall?"

C.134   "How do I know? She fell, and passed out, there."

C.135   This other wife is crying. This poor vizier came, and saw his wife. He said, "All right, you bastard! When I told him,

that you should put on the pot, you didn't put it on, so he came, and told me, 'By God, they didn't do what I said.'" This vizier said, (shouting), "Bastard! Go, then. I don't want --"
[END OF TAPE]

E75B:

C.136 "Ah, Mār Čučeh! I fuck your father! Go, get out!"

C.137 He said, "I fuck your little father, you made me your servant for a year, and I'm not going till my year is out."

C.138 "He said, "What can I do? What dust I've put on my own head! How can I put him out?" He said, "He killed my daughter, he killed my wife, now he killed this wife, what can I do?"

C.139 This poor wife of his, they brought the dead-washers, and they washed her, and put her in the ground, and they had a service for her, and it passed.

C.140 After that, some days, some while passed, and there was a wedding. There was a wedding. He said, "Mār Čučeh."

C.141 "What?"

C.142 He said, "You stay right here in the compound, and watch over the house, we're going to the wedding. Fasten this gate tightly, now. So some thief or other won't come in."

C.143 "All right."

C.144 When he'd left, this vizier left, and everything there was - paddy and - he'd said, "Māla jam ko,"[1] he told him, "Māla jam ko."

C.145 Now he did something different, Mār Čučeh. All the paddy that they had, all the rice, and the wheat, he took it all and poured it out together in the middle of the courtyard. He brought all his possessions[2] out into the midst of the courtyard. He brought them all out of the rooms. And he took down that door, and tied it on his own back. Off he went to the wedding.

C.146 (Laughingly) He went, went to the wedding, and this wife of

---

[1] Key word play. In Herati, this means either 'Feed the livestock' or 'Gather the possessions'.

[2] /māl/ - In Iranian Persian, 'property', in Afghan Persian, 'livestock', in Herati dialect the alternate meanings are distinguished by context.

the vizier is using her eyes, and she sees Mār Čučeh, with the door tied to his back, standing in the midst of the crowd. She called, and said to a child, "You tell the Lord Vizier, tell him (laughingly) to come here."

C.147   This one said to them, "The Lord Vizier, the Right-hand Vizier of the King, which is he, please?"

C.148   He came. He said, "Ah, what are you saying, woman? You've shamed me before the people! Why did you call me?"

C.149   She said, "Well, you look, whether Mār Čučeh isn't in the midst - (Stammers, laughing) - in the midst - of all this."

C.150   "Va!" So he looked at Mār Čučeh, and he saw the door fastened to his back. "Oh, my God!" He came, and said, (in an undertone), "Why did you do like this? (rising to a shout) Bastard, why did you do like this?!"

C.151   "You're a bastard yourself, didn't you say, 'Fasten the door tightly'? All right, I fastened it tightly, to my back, and I came."

C.152   After this, the poor vizier said, "Come on, because I'm going. What has he done?"

C.153   They came back, and they saw all the wheat, and paddy, and ghee, everything scattered in the middle of the courtyard. And the cows, and livestock, he let them all out of the compound. (laughingly) They all went off on their own business. Everything there - [Māhgol, whispering: He killed the cows.] There, he - all the carpets, and rugs and dishes and bedclothes and trunks, every bit of it was dumped in the middle of the courtyard. And the heads off the cows. [Māhgol whispers, inaudibly] Yeah. What did he do with their muzzles? [Māhgol, whispering: . . . in the mangers . . .] He put them down in the mangers? [Māhgol: Yeah.] He put them down in the mangers, and he filled the mangers.

C.154   He came, and said, "All right, why did you do that to the cows?"

C.155   He said, "I filled the mangers, and I said, 'Eat!' and they didn't eat, and I said, - I hit them! I said, 'Eat!' So now they're eating." [Māhgol, whispering: He didn't either say, 'I hit them.' He said, 'Go, let the cows out . . .' (inaudible whisper) . . you aren't saying . . .?] (MZ interrupts Māhgol) He did so do it, they weren't - he didn't do that, anyway.

C.156   "These clothes - these bedclothes, why did you bring these out?"

C.157   He said, "You said, 'Gather up all the possessions!'[1] So I
gathered them! You said 'gather them', and I gathered them, I put
them all in one place. I found a little in this part of the house
and a little in that part of the house, and I gathered them all
up."

C.158   He said, "Bastard, leave us alone, go, about your own business, I don't want you for a servant, I don't want you!"

C.159   "Bastard yourself, by God - you took me for a servant for two
(sic) years - if I move one step!"

C.160   He didn't leave. When evening came, the vizier thought and
thought, and said, "Wife?"

C.161   "What?"

C.162   "Come, let's run away from him. All these goods and property,
let's leave them to him. He'll kill you and me as well!"

C.163   She said, "Good!"

C.164   He said, "Nothing, (now). When the night is well along, get
up, and we'll go without a sound. He'll stay here. We'll have to
let this house go, and and leave."

C.165   This Mār Čučeh overheard, right then. He's heard, this eve-
and he's still awake. This king - this vizier got up, and all the
money that he had, the cash, like gold and coins, he took it, put
it in a saddlebag. And he got out two horses. He left with his
wife. And Mār Čučeh was awake, and he left. They go, and he goes
along behind them. So he went, and he went, went, went, and he saw
that in front of them there's a river.

C.166   The wife said, "All right, with this river in front, how are
you going to get these horses to cross? Now if Mār Čučeh were here,
you could give the bridles to Mār Čučeh, and he could go in front.
If the water carried (someone) away, it would carry him. Then we
could turn back."

C.167   All at once Mār Čučeh said, he said to them in front, "Mistress, what did you say? Here I am, I'm right here."

C.168   The vizier said, "Oh, curse your father, you were asleep!"

C.169   He said, "Eh, Lord Vizier, when the house door made a noise,
I heard it, and I said, 'I'd better go, so the wolves and lions
and leopards won't eat the Lord Vizier. He's been so kind to me.'
So I came with you."

---

[1] /Māla jam ko/.

C.170   He said, "Well, then, (so it) was."

C.171   So they went and they went and they went and they went, and
they passed this river and they went to another place, and they
went, and they got sleepy. They said, "Come, let's sleep."

C.172   He said, "All right." And he went to sleep. He - asleep -
they're sleeping peacefully there, then, this wife and husband
are sleeping. Mār Čučeh is awake. When he saw that they were
sound asleep, he went and picked up the vizier. First he went
and looked, and looked, and saw a place that was nice and deep,
with plenty of water. Like for a water-wheel.[1] So he picked up
the vizier, carefully, gently, and it's right there - he brought
him and threw him in this water-wheel pool. It took him, then,
it was a big river. He killed him, he went, the water took him.

C.173   After that, he came and laid down his head. Next to his
wife. When he'd put down his head, then, he - fell asleep, then.
Didn't say anything. He didn't say anything, then the vizier's
wife woke up. The vizier's wife woke up, she'd gotten thirsty,
she got up and drank, and when she looked she said, "Vīh! (claps
once) But where's the vizier? This is Mār Čučeh!" She said, "Oh,
God! The poor vizier was right, look! This Mār Čučeh did what
he wanted."[2]

C.174   She didn't say any more, she was compelled, after all, she
couldn't say anything.

C.175   When he got up he got up, this Mār Čučeh, he said, (harshly),
"Do you understand?"

C.176   His mistress said, "No."

C.177   He said, "All right. By God, I fuck the vizier's mother's
little father! My own brother - two times, three times, I compen-
sated him for being killed. He starved him to death. I still had
business with him, (shouting) I don't have any quarrel with you,
if you want to marry me, marry me. If you don't want to, I'll
kill you, too."

C.178   She said, "All right, I'll marry you."

C.179   After that he went back to the vizier's house with the vizier's
wife, and for seven days and nights they hit the stick with the

---

[1] A wheel-type water bucket system is used to raise water from low-level
irrigation ditches to fields above water-level. A pool may be ex-
cavated for it.

[2] A euphemism for sexual contact. She is compromised, in any case.

drum, and the drum with the stick, and

C.180   They gave the Hindus raw food and the Muslims cooked,

C.181   And I didn't get one little burnt scrap from the bottom of
the pot.[1]

C.182   (Claps once) He married the vizier's wife. [Māhgol: There
was a mistake at the very end, too. He, mmm - for - a guest, too -
(she stutters)] (MZ replies harshly) All right, then! I got to
here, now if you want to, you tell it! (forcefully) Or else I'll
tell another story. [Māhgol: No, I'll tell it.] [MM: No, first -
if Māhgol - would you tell it from the beginning, (indistinctly) -
I understand, if there's time, if we don't - what it is,--] That's
fine. You tell it.

---

[1] Standard wedding feast formula, used often at the end of a tale. The
last two lines rhyme.

Title: Mãr Čučeh [The Snake Chick]
Narrator: Mãhgol
Recorded: 11 Sept. 1975 (Follows performance of Text C immediately)
Cassette # E75B - E76A

D.1   This, there was, there was not, there were an old woman and an old man. They - [MZ: They had a son.] They had one son. Some time and some while passed, this - m - old man died. The boy and the old woman remained. They had one cow. They - m - had a cow. This, this boy went for hay in the morning - and came back at noon, the(n) -- after he'd eaten lunch, he'd go back to his hay. [MZ: (whispers inaudibly)] [MM: Shut up, then! So she can talk now -] So some time and some while passed, he - m - went, like that, every day, every day, he would go for hay.

D.2   So - every day, every day, he would go for hay. Then this day, and one night, that he - (uncertainly) - it was one morning when he went for hay, he saw, it was this - thing. This loud hissing. When he looked, he saw there's this thing, this aufī. He sat down there silently, and went on cutting hay.

D.3   This - when - it came, it stopped, and called to him, "Hey, Boy, what are you doing?"

D.4   "Nothing, it's nothing to do with you, I'm cutting hay and carrying it. I have a cow, and I take it to my cow."

D.5   He said, "OK." He said, "Do you have anyone else?"

D.6   He said, - m - "I have a mother."

D.7   He said, "Good, I - today, when you go, ask your mother. 'Do you want a husband? Will you marry?'" (muffles laughter) "'Will you marry?'" (giggling) [MM: Speak!] "'Will you marry?'"

D.8   He said, "All right."

D.9   He tied up his load of thorns (sic) and went home, and it went out of his head. When it went out of his head, he went. In the morning, when he was going, as he came, it came back to him. As he sat down there, he said, "Since I haven't told her, if I stay here, now, he'll come, too, and he'll eat me. I'd better go to that other land."

D.10   He went to that other land, then, all at once this sound, this great hissing. When he looked, he saw that the aufī is standing there again. He called to him, "Oh, Boy! Did you tell your mother?"

D.11   He said, "Yes."

D.12   "What did she say?"

D.13   He said, this one said, "She didn't say anything. She didn't say anything."

D.14   He said, "All right, you're lying. Now if you don't tell her tomorrow, - now - wherever you go, I'll eat you."

D.15   He said, "All right."

D.16   He tied up his load of hay, and he went, and told his mother.

D.17   His mother said, "Good. Go tell him that - 'She'll -' that' She said, "I'll marry,"'"

D.18   He said, "All right."

D.19   When morning came, he went, to the hay, and he saw, the aufi was coming. He stopped, and said, "Hey, Boy, did you tell (her)?"

D.20   He said, "Yes, I told her."

D.21   "What did she say? What did - she say?"

D.22   He - said, "She said, 'I'll marry.'"

D.23   He said, "Good. Tomorrow, then - after three days. After three days, now, a wind will come. First a wind will come, then it will be swept, the floor of the courtyard will be swept all clean, then a little sprinkling, little sprinklings of rain will come, then the courtyard floor will be sprinkled (to settle the dust). Then a rain wind will come, and clouds will come, red, and black, and green, all kinds. And this bundle of clothes will fall, then - your mother must put them on, and you will know that I have come. I'll take away your mother. That will be your mother's wedding."

D.24   He said, "Good."

D.25   This day passed, and the next, and the next [MZ: Speak up!] (louder) Then the day after that came, clouds - m - green and red and black clouds, all kinds came, and the clothes came down. After the clothes fell, the mother put them on, and all their courtyard got full of snakes and scorpions and all kinds of things. This aufi came to the gate. The aufi came to the gate, then, he came, then, he came, and there, he took the mother, and the boy, on his back, and he went, then. He went, to his own place. He went to his own house, came to his own house.

D.26   This - m - some time, some while passed, and he - said, "I-" - she got pregnant, this old woman got pregnant, and God gave her the child, and they called him - m - Mār Čučeh.

D.27   He said, "When shall I eat that son of yours?"

D.28   She said, "Any time you want to, eat him."

D.29   He said, "All right. Tomorrow, when he goes for the hay, you say, 'Dear - ' when he goes for the hay, and he comes back, then he, he'll say, - m - 'Why didn't you do something?' (sighs, frustrated) - Oh. She - she brings she brings bread, with water.]MZ, interrupting brusquely: Dry bread. 'Don't put anything on to cook.' Like that. (MM and MZ laugh - muted)] OK. "Don't you put anything on to cook."

D.30   She said, "All right."

D.31   "I'll go and get in the ghee jar. Then, when he says, 'Why didn't you fix anything to eat with the bread?', you say, 'Go, then, get some ghee out of the - jar - for yourself, -ah- I was busy today.'"

D.32   She said, "All right."

D.33   The next day came, and in the morning he went after the hay, and when he'd gone for the hay, she did that. She said, - m - she didn't cook anything.

D.34   When he came back, she spread the cloth, and put down the dry bread, and filled the water glass and brought it, and set it in front of him. She left, and got busy doing something. She went, and swept the house - she was sweeping. And he said to his mother, "Ma, why this - why didn't you cook anything today?"

D.35   She said, "To - today I was busy, and so what, if there's nothing to eat with the bread for one day? Go, take the glass, g- , - f-, -from the ghee jar - take this, get a cup of ghee for yourself."

D.36   He said - he went, and got the glass, and this Mār Čučeh said, "Brother, gi-- Ohhh, Brother, give it to me! I'll go get the ghee for you. My Papa's in the jar, and he'll strike you and kill you!"

D.37   He said - he gave it to him, and said, "All right, get it- bring the ghee, then."

D.38   He filled it with ghee, and brought it for him.. And he put it in front of him, and he - ate, then.

D.39   When the next morning came, he went out in the alley again, -
the - these two. [MZ: (Inaudible whisper)] These, these two went,
out to the alley, they went out to the alley, and he did (some)
thing. This Mār Čučeh - this father of Mār Čučeh, said, "All
right. Today - yesterday he did like that, now today - tomorrow -,
today he did like that, now what shall I do tomorrow?" He said,
"All right, tomorrow," he said, "I'll do something. This, -th-
just this, then, I'll go and get in the water jar. Don't you bring
water for him. You make something to eat with the bread, then
bring it, spread, the cloth, don't bring water for him. He'll say,
'Why didn't you bring water?' Now you say, 'I was busy. I couldn't
do it, myself.'" So she said (sic)," - m - Go, yourself, get the
glass and fill it, drink."

D.40   She said that, and he went, and picked it up, he picked up the
glass to go and fill it, (and) his brother said - m - "Ohhh, Brother,
my Papa's in the water jar, he'll strike you and kill you. Give it
to me to fill."

D.41   He took it from him and filled it, brought it and put it in
front of him. He ate. He ate - m - , he - when he'd eaten, then,
again this day he came out of the jar, out of the water jar. He
said, "Uh - today, uh - that he did like this," the aufī said, "Now
that he did this again today, Mār Čučeh, tomorrow, now, I'll do
something. This, say to him, now, 'I'm going - Go - uh - do this.
This - hay - uh - bring this, bring firewood, because today, I -
we don't have any wood, we're all hungry. Tomor- today, I want to
cook fresh bread for you, because you don't like dry bread.' He'll
say, 'All right.'"

D.42   Now, this Mār Čučeh heard, too. This Mār Čučeh heard, (and)
he didn't tell his brother anything. When the next morning came,
this - uh - mother of his said, - oh - "Dear," she said, "Darling,
go, now, for the hay - for the wood, - don't go for the hay, today,
go for the ha- the stuff. For the wood. Because we don't have any -
any bread. And there's no wood, either, for me to bake bread.
Bring wood so that I can bake you warm bread. You don't eat dry
bread, either." (Pauses while others whisper.)

D.43   He said, "All right." [MM, over whispering: Please go on.]
He said, "All right." He went, and did - this - . When the next
morning came, - m - she, - g - gave him a gunny sack, took it to
him, and this Mār Čučeh started to holler,[1] "I'm going too, I'm
going too, I'm going too!"

D.44   He said, "All right, - uh - Ma, I'll take him, too."

D.45   She said, "All right, go."

---

[1] /taju/ - unverified translation.

D.46   He, this da- did this. He went, and put the match box in his bag, and went. And he took a rope for himself, (and) they went, -uh - to the, to the thorn. They were chopping thorn, chopping thorn, chopping thorn, (and) when there were <u>lots</u>, this Mā - this - this same, boy - boy, - the brother - brother, - this big boy. This big one bound up his load first, with <u>lots</u>, (and) for him a little - he bound up a little bit for him. When he put it on his own - put it on Mār Čučeh's back, and was about to put his load on his own back, his brother said, "Ohhhh, Brother, put it down, your load has come loose!"

D.47   He said, "No, it hasn't."

D.48   He said, "Put it down, it's come loose. If you go farther, it'll fall."

D.49   So he put it down, and all at once he struck a match under it, and it caught fire.

D.50   He said, this one said, "Why did you do that?"

D.51   He said, "Ohhh, I burnt Papa!" [quiet laughter] He said, "I burnt Papa," he - m - said, "And now, I'm going to kill Ma, too."

D.52   He said, "How do you mean, you'll kill (Ma)?"

D.53   He said, "I'm going to kill Ma."

D.54   So, when they went, they went, these, he did this, picked up this thing, this shovel. She went, for the - brought bread for them. She hadn't made anything to eat with the bread this day. He said, "Why didn't you make anything to eat with it today?" M - Mār Čučeh spoke.

D.55   She said, "I was busy today. And if there's nothing to eat with the bread for one day, what of it?"

D.56   He said - all at once he hit her right on the head with the shovel, and said, "You won't make anything for the bread any more, you whose husband - - m - you give your son into your husband's mouth, for him to eat!" So he killed her, too. He killed her, too.

D.57   This one said to the - the big brother said to his little brother, "All right, I'm going to find a job. You did me so much kindness, I'm going to find a job, become a servant, you (stay) right here, - all - milk this cow, - uh - do this, just milk her morning and evening, and give it to people, and they'll give you bread and things."

D.58   He said, "All right."

D.59   This other one went, called out, this boy - uh - "Do you want a servant?"

D.60   This one said, "Yeah. I want a servant who - " this vizier was sitting, - m - said, "I want a servant who - m - will be stomachless. He mustn't have any stomach at all."

D.61   He said, "I don't have a stomach. I don't eat a thing."

D.62   He said, "All right."

D.63   He - m - took him to his house, this one, some days, and some while passed, this - m - , _every_ day, _every_ day, _every_ day he goes for hay, and brings it for the cows. He, he had twenty cows. He had twenty cows. He had twenty cows, this one, and he took the cows every day, and also put one or two pieces of bread under his arm, and he would go. He would go, and pasture the cows.

D.64   He, this one day, he brought the cows, then, this vizier had - had guest(s). He had guests, and said to - m - him, "Mār Čučeh," he said, "Go, tell them at the house, 'Put on something to cook, put on something to cook, because the vizier has guests this evening.'"

D.65   He said, "All right." He - he did this. This Ma - he went to the house, but didn't say a _thing_ to them. He didn't say a thing, and then - [MZ interrupts in undertone: He hasn't killed the brother.] He went to the gate. So he went to the gate, and was playing. The vizier came, said, "Did you tell them?"

D.66   "Yes."

D.67   So, when he'd gone, he came back to the gate, and saw that they hand't put anything on to cook. [MZ: You made a mistake here, Māhgol. First he killed his daughter.] No, it isn't. Oh yeah. [MM: Tell it - whatever it - is - tell it.] He - m - did this. They said, - then - he went. He looked, saw that - that they hadn't put anything on to cook, they - he went to the house, and to the - at the gate, he told the vizier, "Lord Vizier, they haven't put anything on to cook."

D.68   He said, "Go, hit - Pick up that shovel, go, _hit_ them! Right on the head!"

D.69   So he went, picked up the shovel, and hit this one on the head.

[END OF TAPE]

E76A:

D.70   He picked up the shovel, hit her right on the head, and she died. He, he - m - told all these people, he made the funeral and the service, took her, and buried her.

D.71   He buried her, then, some days, some while passed, then, evening came, this evening, they went to sleep. After they went to sleep, the daughter of this - Mār Ču - this - Čeh is still awake. He was

awake. He hadn't gone to sleep. He was awake, (and) this little
girl started to cry, "Ma, I have to pee."

D.72   She said, to this Mār Čučeh, "Mār Čučeh! Get up! Take her out
so she can pee."

D.73   He said, "Find the matches, light a lamp." He was feeling around,
feeling around, like this, (and) he found a bodkin. He found the
bodkin - [Nabī, MZ's 14-year-old cousin, interrupts: I know two or
three stories, ---] [MM: That's good. Be quiet, now, and tell them
later. (To Māhgol) Please go on.] He found it, picked her up, and
took her out to pee, and he said, "If you pee, here's this bodkin,
I'll stick you full of holes with this bodkin." (Māhgol suppresses
a laugh.)

D.74   Then she - uh - shut up. He took her back. To her mother. This
girl lay down again. She started to cry again, "I have to pee!"

D.75   She said, "Mār Cucèh! May you see no good! Take her, so she
can pee!"

D.76   He said, "See no good, yourself! She - doesn't pee."

D.77   She said, "Take her! Let her pee."

D.78   He took her, and again there he showed her the bodkin, and said,
"If you pee - [MZ aside to kids in audience: Go quickly, quickly,
both of you, go see -] - I'll fill you all full of holes with this
bodkin." [Laughter, including MM and MZ] "I'll make lots of holes!"

D.79   She shut up again, he took her back and she started to cry
again. She started to cry again, and the vizier said, "Mār Čučeh!
May you see no good! Take her, so that she can pee, ah —"

D.80   He took her, and said, again, - showed her the bodkin, and said,
"If you pee, I'll punch you full of holes." [Suppressed laughter]

D.81   So then to her - he said, he said this same thing. She started
crying, this girl. This Mār Čučeh said, he called out, "Lord Vizier!
She isn't peeing."

D.82   He said, "Pick her up, drop her! From above your head. Pick
her up and drop her on the ground, so she dies!" [Laughter]

D.83   He picked her up, threw her on the ground, and she died, this
one. He said, "There, Lord Vizier, she died."

D.84   He said, "Oh, you bastard! I said, her - I said that, then - m -
you believed it!?! You threw her on the ground?!"

D.85   He said, "Curse your father, yourself, you're a bastard, yourself! You, you said yourself, 'Go, pick her up, throw her from above
your head onto the ground so she dies!'"

D.86   He didn't say any more, this - m - they picked up the shovel, and the adze (sic), they picked them up, carried them, and dug a grave for her - it couldn't be dug, this grave. He said to this Mār Čučeh, "Go, get the pick from the house, and bring it."

D.87   He picked up the pick, first the pick - ah - the thing - oh - got the pick and the axe and put them on his shoulder. He came up to them and stood over them. And he said, "Gimme!"

D.88   She said, "Ah, may you see no good! What should I give you?"

D.89   He said, "Gimme! Gimme!"

D.90   She said, "What am I to give?"

D.91   He went up on the roof, and called, "Lord Vizier! She doesn't pee - She won't give it to me!" Mm - [MZ and MM laugh at error.] [MM: About the grave -] Yeah. "This - eh - She won't give it. The pick."

D.92   He said, "All right, hit her! Pick up the adze and hit her on the head, break her head. Let her die." [MZ laughs]

D.93   He picked it up, and hit her on the head with the pick, and she died. And he - they - then, he came - two wives died. These two wives, then - oh! She's crying, and this Mār Čučeh, after he went, he said, "Lord Vizier, dig two graves!"

D.94   He said, "Why two graves?"

D.95   He said, "Didn't you say, 'Pick up and hit her, so she dies'?" [MZ and MM laugh.]

D.96   (Māhgol laughs) So - he said, "Eh bastard! I said it. Did you believe it, then?"

D.97   He said, "Bastard yourself! Bastard yourself, you said - you said yourself, -um - 'Hit her so she dies!'"

D.98   So he, so they dug two grave, and they came, and the two of them, washed them, and they took his daughter, too, and they buried them, and so, then, two, four, five days, six days passed, and there was this wedding.

D.99   There was a wedding, and he - the vizier said to him, "Mār Čučeh, fasten the house door tightly, and sweep out the whole house, and pick everything up, then, do this, sit down in the house and look after it."

D.100   He said, "All right, by my eyes!"

D.101   He - when they went off to the wedding, they went to the wedding, he did this. This Mār Čučeh, with the door <u>tight</u>! <u>All</u> this, this millet and everything that he had, he scattered it in the midst of the courtyard, and these house doors, he took out the two house doors, and tied them <u>tight</u>! To his own back. [Laughter] He'd tied them on so tight, that his shoulders couldn't move. [MZ and MM laugh] He went off to - went into the house with the wedding, and stood there. He stood there, (and) this wife of the vizier was watching, like this, doing like this, watching, and she said, - there, to this little girl who was standing in the house, she said, "Oh, Daughter, go, tell the vizier of the right hand, tell him to come, tell him, 'Your wife needs you for something.'"

D.102   She went, and called out, "Where is the vizier of the right hand?"

D.103   He said, "What do you want?"

D.104   She said, -uh - "Your wife is calling you."

D.105   He went, and said, "What do you want? You've shamed me in front of these people!"

D.106   She said, "But isn't that Mār Čučeh?"

D.107   He said, "How do I know?" When he looked, he saw that it was Mār Čučeh. He went, and slapped him twice, and said, "Why are you doing this, you bastard?"

D.108   He said, "Bastard yourself, you said, 'Fasten the house door tightly, sweep out the house, and sit there.' There, I fastened it tightly, now. You can see I fastened it tightly, I fastened it so tightly, oh people, look how my shoulders - (giggles) [MZ:'- are lamed -'] They're lamed. [MZ: "There, he says, 'Fasten the doors -'"] " 'There,' he says, 'Fasten the doors - '"

D.109   So he said - then he said, "I'd better go," and he took his wife and he sa- , he went, and when he saw that, when he saw that, <u>every-thing</u>, everything in the middle of his courtyard, barley and millet and rice and <u>everything</u> there was, he'd scattered it in the middle of his courtyard - [MZ: Jars of ghee were upside down - MM: Yeah.] - scattered it, and these - he'd killed these cows, too, and he'd put their muzzles - (giggles) - he'd put them down in the hay. He'd <u>filled</u> the mangers with straw, and put their muzzles down into it. [Background whispering] They - did this, when they came, the vizier and his wi- his two wives came, he saw that this - uh - everything is scattered in the middle of the courtyard and the millet and every-thing are scattered, and he didn't say anything.

D.110   He said, "Go, the cows - uh - give the cows some hay, give them some straw."

D.111   He did this - he went, he —m— he didn't give them anything, he

just <u>pulls</u> their tails up like this, and he yells, "Lord Vizier!
They don't eat. (giggles) Lord Vizier, they don't eat."

D.112   He said, - when he came, he saw that they had been killed, when
he lifted their muzzles, lifted their heads, he saw that they were
dead, that their heads had been cut right off. He said, "Why did
you do like <u>that</u>?"

D.113   He said, "But didn't you sa- you said, 'Give the cows hay, give
them straw,' so I gave them straw, but they didn't eat. They didn't
eat."

    He said, "All right." He didn't say anything. He cleaned up
his courtyard, then, as it got to be evening, he cleaned it, cleaned
it all up - he cleaned it - he cleaned it and he said to his wife,
that evening when they'd gone to bed, he said to his wife - to his
wives, said to his wives - uh - "Now, we've got to escape from this
Mār Čučeh! From this - we've got to escape from this Mār Čučeh, or
in the end he'll kill us, too. He'll cast us into destruction!"

D.114   They said, "All right."

D.115   That night he did it. He got two horses and -uh- the - uh -
whatever gold and silver and coins that he had, he put in saddlebags, and loaded them on the horses. He loaded them on the horses,
then, and then, they mounted, the two wives on one horse, and this
man - this vizier on one horse, -m- - he mounted.

D.116   This Mār Čučeh was awake. He heard. He went on ahead of them,
and he hid under a bridge. He hid, under a bridge, and he - then he
saw them coming, the two horses coming. From underneath the bridge
he's going like this. He hits the bridge. He hits it. The horses
stopped. No - they - they're looking at the bridge, and watching it
like that, and they won't go, they're standing.

D.117   (She) said, "Now if that Mār Čučeh were here, he could take
them across."

D.118   These -m- horses had stopped, and Mār Čučeh came <u>quietly</u> out
from under the bridge, and he called out, "What did you say? Mistress!"

D.119   He said - this vizier said, "<u>Death</u> to 'What did you say, Mistress'! [laughter] You were <u>asleep</u>, in the house!"

D.120   He said, "Lord Vizier! [MZ: Inaudible comment] I heard the
sound of the gate, so I got up. I said, 'What if - you've gone, what
if -m- what if something, a leopard or something meets you, it might
eat you!'"

D.121   He said, "All right. Now that you've come, that's all, then."
He put him - the vizier mounted him on his own horse, and they went,

to the edge of a river, and when they came to the river, at the si-, on the banks of the river, they lay down to sleep. They lay down, and went to sleep.

D.122   This vizier said to his wife, "When night comes, this Mār Čučeh - over there - one - you take one foot, and this wife can take one foot, and I'll take his two arms [MZ: Laughing comment (inaudible)] and we'll throw him in the river. Into the river."

D.123   She said, "All right."

D.124   This Mār Čučeh heard. This Mār Čučeh heard. This Mār Čučeh heard, and he didn't go to sleep. He said, "He's tired, besides."

D.125   He didn't fall asleep, but they did. They fell asleep, and he went, this Mār Čučeh. He went, and picked up the vizier's wife, put this - vizier's wife - into his own bed. He went, and lay down in the vizier's bed, right next to him. As the night went on, it got to be midnight, and he taps the vizier's wife, like that. He says, "Get up, let's throw Mār Čučeh in the river." [Laughter]

D.126   She didn't (see), and he woke up the other wife. It was dark, so they didn't see. [laughter] And he'd put on the vizier's clothes, too. These clothes - so he did that. This - this wife took one of his feet, and that wife took the other, and he took his two arms, and they threw him in the river! Then they went back to sleep. He threw him in the river, and they went back to sleep. [MZ: (They threw) the vizier!] Yes. [MM: Oh, OK.] They threw him in the river. There's one left. When this wife lay down - when this youngest wife lay down, he threw the other wife in the river. (pause) [MM: Oh. All right.]

D.127   This - wife - (in undertone) - Yeah . . . I made a mistake. He threw that vizier's wife in the river. He didn't throw the vizier. He -m- did this. He -n- when morning came, then he, he'd thrown both his wives in, into that stream, and his vizier, with the vizier, then, when morning came, he went on. He went, they went, like that.

D.128   He went and he went, he went and he went, like that, then, and they knocked on the door of a serai, and they said, "We don't have any place to go, we just came, like this, hunting. Give us a place here!" This Mār Čučeh said that.

D.129   He said, "All right, by my eyes.[1]" He took them, took them and unlocked the door of his own room, and took them home.

D.130   This - one said, Mār Čučeh said, "Oh, Brother, lock your door, so if - if something of yours is missing, you won't blame us."

---

[1] Polite oath: "Of course, certainly, I promise".

D.131   He said, "All right." He locked the door of his house, and
when night came, the vizier needed to pee. (giggling)

D.132   The vizier needed to pee, and he taps this Mār Čučeh, and taps
him. This Mār Čučeh woke up, and said, "What is it, Lord Vizier?"

D.133   He said, "Death to 'Lord Vizier'! You said, 'Lock the house
door', and now the guy has gone to sleep. What shall I do? Now
I need to pee."

D.134   He said, "A handker - uh, do this. Look around. Aren't there
some shoes - (giggles) - or something? Pee in them. When morning
comes, put them under a coat - put them under your coat, and take
them out by that river, [laughter] where you were, it's close, and
when you're out there, wash out the boots, and wash for prayer, too,
come, and put them back under your coat flap, and bring them.
[MZ and MM laugh].

D.135   When morning came - he peed in them. When morning came, -m-
he did this one thing. This Mār Čučeh said - m - like this, like
this, (quietly) he tapped him, and Mār Č-, Mār Čučeh said, "I won't
take them!"

D.136   He said, (resignedly), "All right." He peed in them, and when
morning came, he tapped Mār Čučeh, and said, "Mār Čučeh! Get up,
now! Take these boots!"

D.137   He said, "I curse you father! [MZ: Laughs] You did the peeing,
and I'm supposed to carry your shit?" [General laughter] [MZ: Inaudible comment]

D.138   He - m - said, (Softly, pathetically) "Now what am I going to
do? What a disaster . . ." [MZ: Laughs] He went, and wrapped his
coat around himself, and put the boots (laughs) under his coat flap.
His coat - all his clothes got full of it. They got full of it, and
he went out, then, and he's going fast, this vizier.

D.139   This Mār Čučeh, when the guy came, he said, "Now, Brother! I
didn't take anything, but you see that guy, how fast he's going, he
stole something from your house." [General laughter. Inaudible
comments. MZ: The boots -]

D.140   He ra- this one went, running, like that, this guy went, he
went, and he said, "What did you take from my house?" Just like that.
Like that - he went like that with his hands, he wanted to grab his
wrists, and his hands went right into the boots. It went splash!
All over his body, and on th- on their faces, they were all covered -
[General laughter] - all covered.

D.141   He washed himself, and the vizier - he took the vizier by the
hand, and he said, "You just sit like that!" He took him to prison,

and he told the - the headman[1], he said to the headman, "You see him? Look. I - last night he knocked on the door of my serai, and he said, 'I came here hunting, can you give me room in your house?' I said 'All right.' And now he's stolen my boots, and he peed in them, and stole them, and -he came."

D.142   He said, "We'll have to lock him up." They locked him up. And they say he went, this Mār Čučeh, and (as God) gave him his object (mumbles) . . . and the community of Islam. . . .

D.143   [MM: May you see good fortune! That was good.]

D.144   (Mähgol to Qamarī, a young girl neighbor who is listening) Come on, I've told it, now you . . .

---

[1] Lit. "Village head-man," *arbāb*.

Title: Mār Čučeh [The Snake Chick]
Narrator: Māhgol
Recofded: 13 Feb. '76
Cassette # F1B-F2A

E.1   There was, there was not, there was an old woman with a son, and they had this one cow. This boy would go, mornings, and come back evenings, and he would bring hay or something.

E.2   One day he had gone, like that, and it was almost lunchtime, and he, he saw this dust, he saw it was a li- lion, a lion. He, he sat quietly, and cut the hay.

E.3   When he'd come, he stopped, this, this lion stopped, and said, "Hey, Boy, what are you doing?"

E.4   He said, "Nothing, I have one cow, so I'm taking this hay to my cow."

E.5   He said, "Don't you have a mother and father?"

E.6   He said, "I have a mother, I don't have (a father)."

E.7   He said, "OK. Today when you go, ask your mother, 'Will you marry?'"

E.8   He said, "All right."

E.9   He said, "If you don't say it, I'll eat you."

E.10   He said, "All right." So it got to be dinner time, but when he went, he forgot it. He forgot to say it.

E.11   Then the next morning when he went, he was cutting this stuff, and all at once he saw the dust. As he was watching, (it was him) again, and he said, "Now he's going to eat me. I didn't say anything."

E.12   Now when he came, he stopped, and said, "Hey, Boy, did you tell your mother?"

E.13   He shut up, shut up, didn't say a thing.

E.14   He said, "All right, if you don't tell her tomorrow, I'll eat you. Wherever you go, I'll find you, and eat you."

E.15   He said, "I'll tell her."

E.16   So he went, and when morning came, he told his mother, he said,
"Mama, Mama!"

E.17   "Soul of your Mama!"

E.18   He said, "There's this lion who says, he said to me, 'Ask your
mother, "Will you marry?"'"

E.19   She said, "Yes, Dear, tell him, 'She'll marry.'"

E.20   He said, "OK." This boy, then, he got angry, in his mind.

E.21   In the morning when he went, this lion came, sto- uh- this
lion loo- , this boy looked, like that, saw that it was this lion.
So he came, this lion stopped, and said, "Hey, Boy, did you tell
your mother?"

E.22   He said, "Yes."

E.23   "What did she say?"

E.24   "She said, 'I'll take him, yes.'"

E.25   He said, "All right. Now tomorrow, - a -, -a-, a wind will
come, and - then - aprinkle of water, and sweep your courtyard,
then a bundle of clothes will fall, now, you put them on your mother.
Then, for your mother - this thing will come, a cow - a horse, a
horse will come (laughs), then, it will stop, and whinny, then you
put your mother on this - put her on this horse."

E.26   He said, "All right."

E.27   When the next day came, he saw that - this boy was bringing
water, and a wind came, and then a sprinkle of water, and this bundle
of clothes fell, and so many snakes came, and snakes came, so many
came - what can I say? Their whole house got full of snakes. Then
a bundle of clothes fell, and he put them on her, they put them on
her, these things.

E.28   Then this - this thing came, too. This horse came, and whinnied
at the gate. He took her, took his mother and put her on the horse,
then, and hit it, and the horse went, then. He went, and took her
to his own house. He took the boy, too. He took him to his own
house, like that, they were like that, this old woman and the boy -
and this old woman had a baby.

E.29   She had a baby, and they called him Mārčučeh. They called him
Mār Čučeh, and this, this cow was there, too, they brought the cow,
then, this cow -- In the morning he would go, this boy, and bring
her hay.

E.30   Then this one day it happened - every morning, - then, she said to the boy (sic), "Dear, Dear!"

E.31   "Soul of your mother!"[1]

E.32   She said, "Today don't bring hay, bring some of that - [Zāher: brush] - brush, bring some of that stuff, thorn."

E.33   He said, "OK."

E.34   This, this boy started crying, "I'm going, too!"

E.35   He started crying, and he, he- - m - said, "All right. Let it be, I'll take him, too."

E.36   She said, "Take him!"

E.37   So he took him, too, and as they were going, to the plains, he did something there -uh - he was cutting, cut thorn, and cut thorn, and he, he tied - tied it in that thing of his, tied up the rope, and tied up his thorns, and then this, this - for (this) (load) and Mār Čučeh's, they tied up a little with a rope. He put it on his back, and he put his own thorns on his own back, and as he lifted them. All at once this thing - [Zāher: Snake?] No, this lion . . . he came. The lion, as he lifted it, put it on his back, in the thorns - [Zāher: It was a snake, a dragon, it was like that . . . (inaudible)] The dragon, this - got into - got into this thing. The thorns. This, all at once this Mār Čučeh said, "Put it down, put it down, Brother, your load has come loose."

E.38   He said, "All right, just let me put it down. As I go along, it will all spill."

E.39   So when he put it down, all at once he struck a match under these thorns, and the thorns burnt up. Then he said, "Now, let's kill Ma, now this Ma, like this, - look, this very day, she was going to feed you to this dragon."

E.40   He said, "All right." He said, "How will you kill her?"

E.41   He said, "I'll pick up the shovel, this one, as we go into the house, and I'll hit her on the head, and then she'll die."

E.42   He went to the house, and said - he spoke, just like that. He lifted it up, hit with the shovel, and split her, split her head.

E.43   He said, "Now, then, you and I, I'll go, and do some kind of work, and bring things, and you stay right here."

---

[1] See note 2, p.237. She has addressed her son as "Mama," and Māhgol adds the standard response - here an inversion, and garbled.

E.44   He said, "All right."

E.45   He went, this older brother went, and - did this. He went, to this place, and said, "I want a servant." (<u>sic</u>)

E.46   This vizier said, "Yes." Yeah, he said, "I want a servant who hasn't any stomach. Who hasn't any stomach."

E.47   He said, "I haven't any stomach at all."

E.48   He said, "Good, come."

E.49   So he took him, he did this. He would go in the morning like that, and pasture the cows, then he'd come back at dinner, he'd go in the morning, and bring them back at dinner. He got so, this boy, this boy died of hunger. He died of hunger, and then, his brother got word. When his brother got word, Mär Čučeh came, then, Mär Čučeh -- This vizier came, came to this - beside the road. Now when this vizier came, he said, (sneezes), this Mär Čučeh said, "Don't you want a serv- "

[END OF TAPE]

<u>F2A</u>:

This Mär Čučeh said, "Do you want a servant?"

E.50   This vizier said, "Yes, I want a servant who hasn't any stomach."

E.51   He said, "I haven't any stomach at all."

E.52   He said, "Good. Come."

E.53   He went with him. He said, "Take these cows out in the morning, and bring them at dinner time." So mornings when he would go, he would put a couple of pieces of bread under his shirt front, and would go out to the plains, and take the cows. He'd eat them. When he came again at dinner time, he'd put two pieces of bread under his shirt, and would eat.

E.54   Then one day there was a wedding, and they sent word to the vizier and his wife.[1] Three- he had three wives, this vizier. So this evening, he said, this vizier said, "Mär Čučeh, this - these rooms - you fasten the doors to these rooms tight, now. I'm going to the wedding. Take the cows, too, and give - give them hay."

---

[1] I.e. invited them.

E.55   He said, "OK." He went, the cows – after they left, this Mār Čučeh fastened the gate this way, and all these cows – [Zaher: He said, "Fasten it tightly"–] OK! He killed all these cows – [Zaher, in background: <u>Tightly</u> –] He cut off their heads like that, and put their muzzles down in the straw. So then, it didn't look like they'd been killed.

E.56   He went, and fastened the doors tightly to his own back. He went to the – to the house, the house with the wedding, and stood there. All at once this vizier's wife looked, like that, and saw, –m–, she called that girl, and said, "Oh, little girl, come here."

E.57   She said, "What do you want?"

E.58   She said, "Go,·tell the vizier, 'Come!'"

E.59   So she went, and shouted, "Lord Vizier!"

E.60   He said, "What? What do you want/"

E.61   She said, – m – "They're calling you."

E.62   He said, "Who was it, calling?"

E.63   She said, "Your wife."

E.64   So he (laughs) – he went, and said, "What do you want? You've shamed me, in front of the people."

E.65   She said, "Isn't that Mār Čučeh?"

E.66   He said, "How should I know? Let me take a look." He said, "Yes, it <u>is</u> Mār Čučeh." He said that, (and was) hitting him on the head like that, and saying "Why this? I told you, 'Fasten the house doors'!" He said, "You took them and tied them on your back!"

E.67   He said, "Well, didn't you tell me, the way I fastened them on my back?"[1] He said, he said, "Hey, people, look! My shoulders are completely paralyzed! (laughs) Tighter than I – how, I <u>fastened</u> them!"

E.68   He said that, and he, he cursed him, and he went back to the house with his two wives. [Zāher: Inaudible comment] He got up with his wives, then, and went home . . . And all this stuff, everything there was, he'd scattered in the courtyard.

E.69   When he came, now, he saw, every, everything there was, millet

---

[1] This is garbled and ungrammatical – lit. "Didn't you say yourself, you fastened them on my back?"

and barley and wheat, everything there was, was scattered in the courtyard. He said to this Mǎr Čučeh, "Why did you do like this?"

E.70   He said, "Well, didn't you say yourself, 'Clean up the rooms, and fasten the doors'? Now these shoulders of mine, look, I'm lame," he was saying.

E.71   He said, "Go, you bastard! I don't want you, go!"

E.72   He said, "Bastard yourself. You took me for a year, and I - until my year is up, I'm not going."

E.73   So then, he didn't say anything to him. He gathered up everything there was - [Recording interrupted by lunch][1]

E.74   So the vizier and his wife came, and looked in the house, and now they saw that the millet and barley and wheat, everything there - rice, everything there was, was scattered around the courtyard. He said to him, the vizier said to this - m - this Mǎr Čučeh, "Why did you do like this?"

E.75   He said, "Didn't you say, 'Sweep out the house clean, the rooms - uh - sweep them, clean . . . and fasten the doors tightly?'"

E.76   Yeah, he said, "Go, you bastard, I don't want you."

E.77   That one, he said, this, this, this Mǎr Čučeh said, "You - you took me on for one year, and I, until my year is up, I'm not going."

E.78   So he didn't say anytying more, he just gathered up, cleaned up the courtyard with his wife, then, when, when he said to Mǎr Čučeh, "Go, to the cows -" [MM interrupts to move a coughing child away from microphone] - he said, "Go give the cows some hay."

E.79   He went to the cows, and he said, "The co- Lord Vizier! Whatever I do, they don't eat."

E.80   He said, "<u>Hit</u> them, so they'll eat."

E.81   He said, "Uh, they don't eat."

E.82   When the vizier came, and lifted up their heads, he saw that they all, they'd been killed! He said, "Why have they been killed?"

E.83   He said, this Mǎr Čučeh said, "Didn't you say yourself, 'Give them hay'? They -" [Zǎher: inaudible comment]

---

[1] MZ, who had been in the adjacent kitchen, cooking lunch, joined the audience only for the second half of Mǎhgol's performance.

E.84   He didn't say any more, then, when evening came, that evening, he wasn't asleep. This, this daughter of the vizier started
crying, - m - she said, "I have to pee." [MZ: His daughter said
it.] Yes. So she said, "I have to pee."

E.85   Now this wife of the vizier said to this, this Mār Čučeh,
"Mār Čučeh, Mār Čučeh, get up! Uh - take her out to pee, so she can
pee."

E.86   So he said, -uh-, he spoke up, and said, "Light the lamp!" As
he was feeling around, and feeling around, he found the bodkin. So
he found the bodkin, found it, and he said, uh - he lit the lamp,
"Yeah, I lit it."

E.87   She said, "Good, pick her up and carry her out, so she can
pee."

E.88   So he picked her up and took her, and he said, "If you pee -
(giggles)" [MZ: Oh, Girl, don't laugh -] " - lots of holes -
(giggles)" [MM:' If you pee', what? MZ: 'If you pee, I'll punch
holes in your bottom with this bodkin.'] (Māhgol laughing and
coughing) [MZ: He scared her.] [MM to Māhgol: Tell it, Tell it
right.]

E.89   So she said, "I won't, I'm going back to my Ma." So she didn't
pee, and he took her, uh - when she'd lay down, she started crying
again, this girl, "I have to pee, Ma!"

E.90   She said, "Mār Čučeh! Go on, take her, so she can pee, and
bring her back."

E.91   He said, "She doesn't pee, what am I to do?"

E.92   She said, "Take her."

E.93   So he, he took her, then this - and again, he said, "If you
pee, I'll fill your bottom (giggles) full of holes with this bod-
kin-" (giggles) So then, he yelled, "Lord Vizier, she doesn't pee!"

E.94   He said, "Lift her up over your head, and throw her to the
ground! " [MZ: No, he said, "Throw her! To the ground," then there
comes a big screech -] He said, "Throw her! On the ground."

E.95   He lifted her up over his head, and threw her to the ground.
She died. He said, "There, Lord Vizier, I threw her to the ground."

E.96   He said, "Oh, you bastard, did I say that seriously? And you
believed it?" [MZ: 'I was lying about that.'] "I was lying about
that."[1]

---

[1] I.e. "I didn't mean it."

E.97 He said, "OK, you said it, how do I know if -" [MZ interrupts:
he said, "Bastard yourself! Bastard yourself!"] Finally he said,
"Bastard yourself." [MZ: 'You said yourself, "Throw her to the
ground."']

E.98 So he, he said, "All right - ", he didn't say anything more,
he just said, "The pick, go, get the pick," - her, they washed her
and put her in a casket, then, (and) he said, "Go, get the pick,
we're going," just that evening, this vizier to Mār Čučeh: "Let's
go dig the thing, the grave."

E.99 He said, "Fine."

E.100 He got the pick and they went, and they dug a little, and dug,
then he said to Mār Čučeh, "Go get the axe (sic), too, because we
can't dig it with this, by itself."

E.101 So he went, and came to the house, and he said, "Gimme!" He
picked up the thing, the axe, [MZ interrupts: He took it, and hid
it, fr - (inaudible)] (Māhgol speaking simultaneously with MZ) He
picked up the axe. [MZ: He took it, and hid it! Both - (inaudible)] The axe was in his he- , in his hand. He said, "Gimme!"
[MZ: He'd hidden it, he'd hidden the axe, and he came, and said to
the wife, um -] "Gimme!" [MZ: 'Give me the axe and the shovel!']
(Māhgol shouts) He didn't say it like that! He said, "Gimme!"
He said, "Gimme!"

E.102 She said, "What should I give you, then?"

E.103 He said, he's still saying, "Gimme!" [MZ or MM: Yeah.] He
yelled, "Lord Vizier, she won't give it!" [MZ: He got up, got up
on the (roof).] Yeah. "Lord Vizier, they won't give it."

E.104 He said, "So pick up a rock and hit her on the head, so she
died (sic)."

E.105 So he picked up a rock, like that, and hit her - [MZ interrupts: He hit her with his axe, then.] OK. He hit her on the
head, and she died. He yelled, "Lord Vizier, there, I hit her."
[MZ: 'Dig two graves!'] "Dig two graves!" (laughter)

E.106 He said, "Oh, you bastard! Did I say that seriously!? I was
lying about that! I was lying about that, and you believed it!?"

E.107 He, again, he said, "Dig two graves." He took that thing,
took that axe, and they dug two graves there. They dug two graves,
and they came and they took this, this mother and this daughter and
buried them.

E.108 They buried them, that evening, then, that evening, he said to
his wife, this vizier, (in undertone), "Let's do something, so that
(mumbles) ---" (to MZ) What? [MZ: Speak clearly!] (louder) "Keep

yourself awake, so then, when this Mār Čučeh falls asleep, now,
we'll get up and run, quick, and go, go someplace so this Mār Čučeh
will let us go."

E.109   She said, "All right."

E.110   Now Mār Čučeh, like this, Mār Čučeh wasn't asleep. So he, like,
Mār Čučeh, they - when they fell asleep, this Mār Čučeh started running, and went, on a bridge, under a bridge, and hid himself."

E.111   So they, they came, then - uh - the horse, they got two horses,
and this stuff - supplies for the road (giggles) - so, they did
this, got some stuff for themselves, then, and they came.

E.112   They came, and came, and when they got to the bridge, like that,
like that, his he -- Mār Čučeh stuck out his head [MZ: He didn't
(do that) with his head! The horse reared!] No, finally he saw,
then the horse reared. And whatever they do, he won't go. So this -
this, wife of the vizier said, "Now if Mār Čučeh were only here, he
would get us across here." [MZ: (interrupts) "You've been so dumb,
you haven't even brought Mār Čučeh!" (MZ laughs)].

E.113   So all at once Mār Čučeh came out from under the bridge, and
said, "What did you say, Mistress?" [MZ laughs]

E.114   He said, "Eh, Mār Čučeh, where did you come from?" [MZ: "Death
to 'Mistress'! Curses on your father, everywhere we go, you're upon
us! (Inaudible phrase)!]

E.115   So he said, said to him, "I was in the house! I came so that
some wolf or jackal wouldn't eat you."

E.116   He said, "All right, come on up." -- He said, "All right," he
didn't say anything (more), so he was running, running, running like
that behind the horse, to the banks of a river, there, then they dismounted.

E.117   They said, "Let's get down, right here."

E.118   So when they dismounted there, they, right there, they went to
sleep, then, this Mār Čučeh was - this, this wife of the vizier said,
(in undertone) "This Mār Čučeh, then, he's been running and running
like that, now, here, we - when he falls asleep tonight, now . . ."
[MZ: Speak clearly] (louder) - "let's take him, let's take him, and
throw him in the river."

E.119   He said, "All right."

E.120   A little while passed, and this Mār Čučeh got up, and took this,
this vizier, took the vizier by the arms, to - oh, there was his wife
[MZ: You be quiet, then, and I'll tell a couple of words of it from
here . . .] (Māhgol speaks louder) This one took his wife, he picked

up this wife of his, [MZ: I'll tell it.] he picked up his wife, and
threw her in the river, and went and lay down next to the vizier.
[MZ: Oh, to dust with you!¹ It isn't _like_ that!] Look, finally,
here, then, then, the vizier, there, at the party - [MZ: Shut up!]
- doesn't he go there? [MZ: No! It's all (inaudible) . . .] (Māhgol,
angry:) Oh, I don't want that! [MZ, heatedly: Wait a minute, till
I tell a couple of words! You're making mistakes! It was like
this -] [Zāher: Didn't I say -] [MZ: Now right here when the
vizier said-] (Māhgol) _I_ say - [MZ: -said, said to his wife, "Wife?"
She said, "Yeah?" "Since he won't let us alone, and we'll be -"]
(Māhgol:) I _told_ it, already. [MM to MZ: Shut up -] [MZ: "He'll
kill us! When he falls asleep -"] [MM, laughing, exasperated:
Wait! This was Māhgol's. If Māhgol makes mistakes, all right, it's
her business, anyway!] [MZ: Should _she_ tell it?] [MM: Let her tell
it!] [MZ (mildly): Fine. Let her tell it.] [MM to MZ: People
know that you know about it, you understand?] (Māhgol laughs) This
-- [MM: Fine. You tell it. You tell it.] (giggles) I - where was
I? [MZ: Where the vizier said to her -]

E.121   All right, So the vizier said to her, "Now when he, he (inaudible) - he, now, he, when he falls asleep, we, let's stay awake like
this, and throw him in the river. So, when a little while passed,
this, this Mār Čučeh got up. [MZ: Mār Čučeh didn't go to sleep -]
He didn't go to sleep, this Mār Čučeh got up, and came, and threw
this one in the river. This - [MZ, faintly: - vizier -] - vizier.
He threw the vizier in the river, then he went to the vizier, and
lay down (sic) Snickering by audience (Angrily, to them) _What's
it to you!_ [MZ to MM: I'll tell it to you again later. (to
Māhgol) Tell it.] Then he went, there, and lay down next to the
vizier. (pauses) [MZ: Tell it, then.] (laughs) Beside this -
(laughs) [MZ: Next to Mār Čučeh! Death!] He . . . OK. When this
morning came, and he got up, this - was it the vizier? Ohhh - [MZ:
It was the vizier.] [Zāher: He threw the vizier into the river.]
[General laughter, Māhgol and audience] No, no, no, now, this, this
vizier said to his wife, "Let's throw him in the river."

E.122   She said, "All right." That wife of his said "All right."

E.123   When he fell asleep, after a little while had passed, this Mār
Čučeh got up, and threw the vizier's wife into the river, and came
and lay down next to the vizier. He came and lay down next to the
vizier, and when morning came, he went like this (under tone) "Lord
Vizier, Lord Vizier, get up!"

E.124   So he, wh- when he got up, he said, "Death! Where have you
been?"

E.125   He said, "I was right here." [MZ: "I was, all along!"]
[laughter] [MM: "I was what?"]

---

¹ Mild oath for expressing impatience.

E.126   He said, "Death! Where have you been?"

E.127   He said, "I was right here."

E.128   So he came, they came, like that, came, and knocked on the door of a serai, and said, "We're travellers like this, so - " (Affirmatively, to smiles of MZ and Zäher) Yes! "So, we came, tonight, to this place, give us a space!"

E.129   This Mär Čučeh said, "Oh," he said, "Oh, Brother, hey, fasten the door of your serai - fasten the door of (this) room of yours! Because if something or other, if something or other is missing from your house, you'll blame us."

E.130   So he fastened the room door, and this time when night came, this vizier woke Mär Čučeh up - uh - he said, "Mär Čučeh, Mär Čučeh, get up! You said, Fasten the door, now what am I to do? I need to void!"

E.131   He said, "Death to 'Mär Čučeh'! Go find something, some shoes or something, in them - " (giggles)

E.132   He said, "How will I wash them, then, who'll take them out?"

E.133   He said, "I'll take them! Go on!"

E.134   So he went, and found the high boots, felt around and found the boots, and shat in these boots. (giggles)

E.135   So morning came, and he said, "Mär Čučeh, Mär Čučeh, get up, now, take these, run."

E.136   He said, "Oh - I - "You shat - I should take it out for you? Your shit - ! (giggles) So he said, he said, "Put it under your coat, on your shoulders (sic), go put it behind your coat," he said, "Go on - "

E.137   He opened the door, then, there, he opened, opened it, then. He put the boots under his coat, put an old coat on his shoulders, and went. Running, then, he flees like that. All at once Mär Čučeh said, "Oh, Brother, hey! Didn't that one take something or other - (Garbled, giggling and laughing) [MZ Laughs] (inaudible comment) -- he ran like that.

E.138   So this one says, "What did you steal?"

E.139   He said, "Nothing!"

E.140   So then he put his hand right in that -- (Collapses giggling) [MZ Laughs] And it got all over him - He took this, this vizier - (aside to Zäher) - What's it to you? This vizier - he went, and made a complaint about this vizier and so, he said, he went, (with) this complaint to the - he complained, he said, "So it was - these ones came to my door and knocked, and they said, 'We're travellers, like this, we don't have a house, give us a place in your house for one night.' N - Now, last night they slept here, and this - guy of his said, 'This - ' - the one guy said, 'Now, lock your house door so if something is missing from your house, you won't blame me.' So I locked the house door, and morning came, and this, this guy who said, 'Lock your house door', he said, 'Oh, hey, now, Brother, didn't that one steal something from you"', and he was running along, so I came, and all at once when I did like this with my hands, <u>all</u> this stuff (laughs) got all over me."

E.141   So they locked this, this vizier up, and then this Mār Čučeh came back, all the property from the house, all his property, he took it all for himself, then.

E.142   It's over,

My cover

Fell in the river!¹ Haa! (laughs)

E.143   [Šāhgol, her younger sister mimicking: It's over,

My cover

Fell in the river!]

E.144   [MZ: Now it was in my mind that when he says, the place where - this - yeah, these, when he said, said to his wife, "Come on, let's run away and escape him -- ?!] [MM: Yeah?] [MZ: It's right then, they fled, when they go, when they go, and they were talking (Louder, over Šāhgol's and other kids' talk) when they were talking, he himself heard, this side and that. After he heard, he went ahead, and they did that -- he hid under the bridge. (Into microphone) When he hid there, he came. After he came, his head in front of the horse, something - he stretched his head out in front of his horse, and showed it. When he showed it, the horse reared. The horse -] [Zāher: Inaudible voice over] The horse - when the horse reared, that time, it wouldn't cross over. However much he hit the horse, it wouldn't cross over it.

E.145   This wife of his said to him, "All right. You tell that Mār Čučeh, 'This way,' and 'That way,' now if that Mār Čučeh were here, he could take this horse across this bridge. He could get down in this ditch and take a look, (and see) what it is. If it's a wolf, or a leopard, or a lion, or something or other."

E.146   He said, just then he spoke up, he said, when, boo! When the wife spoke like that, he said, "Mistress dear, what do you want? Here I am, right here!"

---

¹ Nonsense ending formula, free translation.

E.147   The vizier said, "Death to 'What do you want, I'm right here'!
hah! Curses on your father!" So there was that, and they said, "To
dust with it, anyway, now that he's come, let's go!"

E.148   He went with them. They were mounted, and they (sic) on foot.
They went, went, went, went to the bank of a river, and got down.
After they got down there, now, put it that the husband and wife
lay down, and went to sleep. This, this vizier quietly said to
his wife, "Wife?"

E.149   "What?"

E.150   He said, "He's following us around in order to kill us. Let's
you and I not go to sleep now, let's you and I not go to sleep, and
when he's gone to sleep, let's take him and throw him in the river."
[MM interrupts to move a coughing child away from the microphone]
"Let's you and I not go to sleep, let's stay awake, when he's
asleep, let's pick him up, and throw him in, throw him in the
river."

E.151   Let's put it that this Mär Čučeh heard. After he heard, he
didn't go to sleep. He didn't go to sleep. [Näder: Water!] Put
it that when the night was well along, this husband and wife went
peacefully to sleep. When they were asleep, they (sic) came, and
picked up the vizier. He picked up the vizier, and took him, and
put him in his own bed. He came, and lay down by the wife. This –
he put on the vizier's clothes, the clothes were in the saddlebag
on the horse, and he put on a nice suit. He did just like that:
(to) the woman – "Get up!" He knew her name, too. He called her
name, "Get up, woman, get up, now! Get up, because Mär Čučeh is
asleep." (Laughs) Heh! His wife got up fast. He said, "Get on
up, so we can throw him in! So we can throw Mär Čučeh in the river!"

E.152   He went like that and one took his two feet and one took his
two arms, (dissolves in laughter) -- then he threw the vizier in the
river! With his own wife! The wife, who didn't know! He, this Mär
Čučeh said, who's (looking like) the vizier – he'd disguised his
voice, besides. Just as he threw the vizier in, he went like this,
he said, "Heyyy, Mistress! How I've killed the master!" (Laughing)
She in affliction -- he says -- "Hey, Mistress, how I've killed the
master!"

E.153   This wife of his says, "Now look what you've seen! This – now
I, poor vizier! I was right. What black dust I'm making![1] Is my
fate any better than the vizier's?!"

E.154   He came, and said, "Mistress, this vizier didn't give this
brother of mine any bread, and he killed him, like that. So I

---

[1] ("for my head") – i.e. 'How I've brought grief on my own head!'

killed his wife, and I killed his daughter, and I killed him, too. Nowww, -- if you'll marry me, I don't have any quarrel with you."

E.155   She said, "All right, I'll marry you."

E.156   So they swore an oath, and came back together, to the vizier's place, and he settled down there, and took the wife. So he killed the vizier, his other wife and daughter, and did the rest, like that.

E.157   (Māhgol interjects) Look, look, now. He didn't do things like that, that --

E.158   [MZ: Adī told it just like that! Adī told it just like that.]

E.159   (Māhgol) (Inaudible . . . .) Šāhgol, you --

E.160   [MZ: You don't know it, like that, you - What do I know? Adī told it like that.]

E.161   [MM to Šāhgol: Do you know it?]

E.162   [MZ, laughing: You go ahead! OK, what time is it now, Margaret dear?]

E.163   [MM: It's 10:30.] [Subject turned to another story]

Title: Mār Čučeh [The Snake Chick]
Narrator: Mǎdar Zāher
Recorded: 16 Feb. 1976
Cassette # F5B

F.1   There was and there was, a . . . a person. This person, some
days, some while passed, this poor person died. His wife remained with
one son. -Shall I tell this story of Mār Čučeh, then, now --?   MM:
Mār Čučeh, yeah.   There were this old woman and this boy. The old
woman, then, she was old and this little boy was small. They had
one little cow.

F.2   She said, "Dear, Dear-"

F.3   He said, "Soul of your dear -"[1]

F.4   She said, "What can I do, now, your dear father has died, now
you have to bring the water and hay for your little cow."

F.5   He said, "All right. I'll bring it."

F.6   So days, he would take his rope, and for three days or so he
would go and bring hay for the cow, then for another three days he'd
go, and at noon he'd bring firewood from here or there. So his
mother could bake bread and things.

F.7   It was some days, some while that passed after that, and the
little boy was going to the plains, when he noticed that behind
him there was a fīs, fīs. When he turned his head, he saw that it
was a snake, and it was going fīs, fīs like an aufī and hissing,
and coming through the hay.

F.8   It said, "Hey, Boy, where are you going?"

F.9   He said, "What do you want from me? I have a little cow, and
I'm going to cut hay."

F.10   He said, "Whom else do you have?"

F.11   He said, "I have an old mother."

---

[1] The same inversion as noted fn.1,p. 298 and fn.2,p.237 . She addresses
her son affectionately as 'Mama' and he responds with the fixed phrase,
'Soul of your mother'.

F.12   He said, "OK. Now go and ask your mother, 'Won't you marry?'"

F.13   He said, "All right, by my eyes."

F.14   This little boy tied up his load of hay, quick, quick, and he came back to his house. He came back that day, and the next day came. He went out to go to the hay, he came, came, and he remembered, along the road. He said, "To dust with it, I won't go to this part of the road, I'll go to another place. So he won't - meet me." He thought that he wouldn't be there, in the other direction. So after that, he went, left this one area, and went to that other area.

F.15   He was in the hay, cutting, when all at once this fĭs, fĭs sound came to his ears. "By God, what's this? After my body? All at once he saw it was this same aufi, making that loud fĭs noise, again.

F.16   He said, "Hey, Boy!"

F.17   "What?"

F.18   "Did you tell your mother?"

F.19   He said, "No, I forgot."

F.20   He said, "It's this way - you think that if you leave here, and go to some other place, I won't see you. Any place you go, I'll see you, and I'll come and eat you. So it's this way - now tomorrow, I order you to bring me word whether your mother will marry me or not."

F.21   This little boy came and tied up his hay and shouldered it, and "Oh, Thou God!'[1] Off he went, to the house. And his mother saw that the color had left his face, and she said, "Dear?"

F.22   "What?"

F.23   "Why has all the color left your face?"

F.24   He said, "It's nothing, only there's an aufi out on the plain, and yesterday he met me, so today I left that area, and went to another place, but again I noticed a fĭs, fĭs behind me. He said, 'It's this way, you tell your mother that if she wants to marry, fine, she can take me; if she doesn't take me, then I'll eat you.'"

F.25   She said, "I'll do it, Dear, to dust with it! I'll marry."

F.26   This little boy, when the next day came, he went, all grief-stricken, and he saw that the aufi was waiting for him, hissing. He said, "Did you tell your mother?"

---

[1] "Yā Allāh!" 'Muslim invocation for starting demanding tasks, especially physically demanding ones.

F.27   "Yeah."

F.28   "All right, then. Now, tomorrow, a wind will come and sweep your courtyard and rooftop and all, and after the sweeping a little water will sprinkle down, and then a bundle of clothes will fall from the air, for your mother to put on, and then a lot of guests will come for you."

F.29   He said, "All right." He came back, then. He said, "Ma, he said, like this, he said, 'Now, a wind will come tomorrow, and sweep out all this house and courtyard, and after that a sprinkling of water, and after the sprinkling, then a bundle of clothes will fall, for your mother to put on.'"

F.30   She said, "That's fine."

F.31   That evening this boy and his mother went to sleep, and when morning came, this wind came up and every feather and straw that was in the house, the wind took them all, and when it was swept, the sprinkling of water came. After that a bundle of clothes fell, and this old woman took up the costly fabrics and washed her head and hair, clean, clean, and put on the things and arranged her hair and pinned it, and then he came, and snakes came and aufīs came and snakes came and aufīs came, and these - their rooms got <u>full</u> of these things! After that, that one aufī that they saw, <u>way</u> back amidst the others, said, "There, now, I'm your husband."

F.32   She said, "OK." These others were excused, and that one aufī alone stayed there.

F.33   Some days, some while passed after this, and this old woman got pregnant. The old woman got pregnant from this aufī. The nine months and nine days passed, and God gave. God gave, and the aufī named him Mār Čučeh.

F.34   This Mār Čučeh, then, is doing well, and understands a little bit of speech, and has gotten bigger, when this aufī spoke up, - and this little boy wasn't there, because he'd go off after hay for a few days, for his cow, then he'd go off after wood for a few days, for his mother. He spoke up, this dragon, and said, "Old woman?"

F.35   She said, "What?"

F.36   He said, "Now when am I going to eat that boy of yours?"

F.37   She said "Any day you eat him, eat him." This Mār Čučeh heard.

F.38   He said, "Any day I can eat him, I will, then. So today you - don't make anything to eat with the bread. Don't make anything to eat with the bread, and I'll go and get in the ghee skin. Then you bake bread. When he comes, put dry bread in front of him." -- This boy had never eaten plain dry bread in his life. There had to be either yogurt sauce or broth or buttermilk or yogurt or fresh milk, whatever there was, there was. I would eat (it). (sic) -- "Then he'll say, 'Mother dear, why did you bring me dry bread? Didn't you make anything?' You say, 'Dear, my hands were full, go get a little ghee for yourself, and put that on your bread, and eat it. The bread is warm!' Then he'll come to get the ghee, and then I'll strike him and kill him." This Mār Čučeh heard, right away.

F.39   After he'd heard, he went and said to his brother, "Brother! Brother!"

F.40   "Soul of your brother!"

F.41   Actually, he didn't say anything. He didn't say anything, and this little boy came from the stuff. Came from the - firewood. He came from the firewood, this boy put down his load and came, and set it down, and his mother brought the bread. She'd baked warm bread, and she brought it.

F.42   He said, "Ma, didn't you make anything to eat with the bread? I don't want dry bread."

F.43   She said, "Ah, Dear, day in, day out, something to go with the bread, it becomes (   ).[1] Go get yourself a little ghee, and eat it with your bread."

F.44   So this boy took the cup to go and get the ghee from the jar, when Mār Čučeh said, "Nooo, Brother, don't you go! I'll go, and bring you the ghee."

F.45   He let him go, and he took the cup from him, and went and put it into the ghee jar, and filled it, and brought it. And his father saw it was Mār Čučeh, so he didn't strike him. He brought it, and put it in front of his brother, and his brother ate, and left.

F.46   When his brother had gone, the aufī came out of the ghee jar, and said, "Did you see what your boy did?"

E.47   She said, "What could I do?"

E.48   He said, "Nothing now, tomorrow, no, the next day - then, you, uh - don't bake bread. To - he'll come back, hungry. He'll say, 'Ma, bring some bread!' You say, 'Dear, there wasn't any wood for me to bake bread. Go after some wood.' Then when he goes to the plain, after the wood, I'll go and get into his load. The moment he puts the load on his back, I'll strike him and kill him." Put it that it's early, and later, Mār Čučeh was little, his ears were

---

[1] /ma'asal/: untraceable word. Sense seems to be a complaint about cooking each day.

keen, and he heard. When he heard that talk, again he didn't say a _thing_.

F.49   The next day, nothing, and when the day after that came, this old woman didn't make bread, or even dough. This Mār Čučeh (sic) came, hungry, and put down his load of hay, and gave hay to the cow, and came, and said, "Ma?"

F.50   She said, "What?"

F.51   "Bring me a little bread."

F.52   "Mother's dear, if you had brought wood, I would have brought a little bread. Now that you've filled the cow's stomach, we're still hungry, and there's no wood!"

F.53   He said, "All right, I'll go for your wood. Make the dough, then."

F.54   This old woman went and made dough, and this little boy took up a rope, to go for the wood, and Mār Čučeh screeched, "I'm going, I'm going!"

F.55   He said, "Ma, what should I do? He's following me!" This Mār Čučeh.

F.56   She said, "Death, if he goes, dust, if he goes, let him go!" This Mār Čučeh went.

F.57   As this Mār Čučeh was going, he'd put the matches in his pocket, and silently took them with him. He went. This boy chopped thorns and chopped thorns, and picked brush, and this Mār Čučeh, and lots - he tied up a little, bitty load for Mār Čučeh and a great big load for himself, and as he was about to put his bundle on his back, all at once Mār Čučeh saw that his father's head was inside a layer of the load. He said, "Brother, put it down! Your load has come loose. It'll fall! It'll (come loose)[1] put it down, put it down, put it down! So you can tie it up yourself!"

F.58   He said, "No, Brother, it hasn't come loose."

F.59   "No, it has, too! Put it down!"

F.60   When the little boy put it down, as he'd told him to, as soon as he'd put it down, he went and struck a match underneath the load, and the thorns in the load caught fire all at once. He said, "Brother, get back!" And as the thorns caught fire, he started clapping, (claps) "Brother, how I burnt Papa, burnt him, burnt him!"

---

[1] Inferential translation of /rodok mišeh/.

F.61   "What do you mean, burnt him!?"

F.62   He said, "Nothing, only - that day when I brought you ghee, Papa was inside the ghee jar. He was going to strike you and kill you. Then yesterday Ma - he said to Ma, 'Now tomorrow, don't you bake bread, and when he comes back hungry, you say, "There's no wood." Then you say, "I'll make dough, you go to the plain after some wood," and when he goes, I'll get in the load, and then I'll strike him.' So I killed Papa, and I fuck the dear father of this Ma's Mama, I'm going to go kill Ma."

F.63   He said, "How are you going to kill your own mother?"

F.64   "No, Brother, she cared more for you than for her husband (sic).[1] She preferred the snake, preferred the dragon, I'm going to kill her."

F.65   He said, "All right. It's your choice."

F.66   So the two came, one in front and the other behind, they came and this old woman, I don't know what Mār Čučeh said, or what the big boy said, or what the old woman said, that Mār Čučeh lifted up his pick and hit! Hit this old woman one clip on the (top) of her head. She dropped, and died, went! About her own business.

F.67   So there was this big boy and he brought the dead-washer, and they washed her, and put her in a shroud, and took her and buried her. Then this Mār Čučeh remained and this big boy.

F.68   Some days, some while passed after this, and after they'd held the service for his mother, then this boy said, "Mār Čučeh."

F.69   "What?"

F.70   He said, "I'm going to go and find a job. You bring hay for the cow by yourself, and put it right here. Whatever stuff there is in the house, you give it to someone or other to cook for you, and eat."

F.71   "I can cook for myself, Brother, it's all right."

F.72   He left. This little boy came to this city, to another city for work, and a vizier came, and hired him. He said, "Well, I'll take a servant, I'll take a servant who has no stomach, who doesn't eat."

F.73   And the little boy said, "I don't eat."

---

[1] A clear slip of the tongue - the opposite is meant.

F.74   He took him. He took him, and he hadn't eaten even a taste of food, and the next day he didn't eat, and the day after he didn't eat, but he worked for him, and it was four or five days, then, and he died of hunger. He died of hunger, and it was like this, that this vizier, whenever he took a servant, he wouldn't give him any food, and he would die.

F.75   (So then) Mār Čučeh, his brother didn't come, and he said, "Huh? I'd better go after my brother, and see." This track, that track, tracking here, and tracking there, and tracking here, he came, and he found those cities, and he came to that city, and he said, "I'm going for a servant. Doesn't anyone want a servant?"

F.76   This vizier came, from somewhere. The vizier came, and he said, "I'll take a servant who doesn't have a stomach."

F.77   He said, [Nāder: Water! Water!] "I don't have a stomach. And I'll go as a servant."

F.78   A while before, he'd asked questions here and there, and people said, "Yes, he had just such a servant, but when he takes servants, he doesn't feed them, he says, 'I'll take a servant who doesn't have a stomach,' - so he died of hunger -- they all die."

F.79   So put it that he hired Mār Čučeh, and Mār Čučeh came, and every time he gets hungry, he takes half a piece of bread and puts it under the edge of his (shirt)[1] and runs off, and goes into the alley, or out in the fields, and eats. He passed this day and the next and the one after, and so on like that.

F.80   So let that go, and listen to this, one night, it happened, this daughter of the vizier started crying, "I have to pee," and she got up.

F.81   He called out, this vizier, and said, "Mār Čučeh!"

F.82   "What?"

F.83   "Come here, take her out, so she can pee."

F.84   He said, "All right."

F.85   And he picked up the bodkin, and put it in his pocket, and he went and took the girl, and put her down. He said, "If you pee, I'm going to stick your rear full of holes with this bodkin!" [Her children laugh] This little kid was simple, and she got scared, and she didn't pee, and he picked her up and brought her in. He picked her up, and brought her, and went back to his own bed.

---

[1] Inferential translation.

F.86   Again this kid got up, "Ma, I have to pee."

F.87   They called out, "Măr Čučeh, come and take her!"

F.88   He brought her (sic), and took her, and put her down, and said,
"If you pee, I'll stick your rear full of holes with this bodkin!"

F.89   This little girl got frightened, and she didn't pee. He took
her back to the house. He said, "Well, she doesn't pee. So I
brought her back, anyway."

F.90   It was just a short while later, she said, "Mama, I have to pee."

F.91   He said, this king - vizier said, "Death to 'I have to pee'!
Come here, Măr Čučeh, take the bastard out so she'll pee!"

F.92   He brought her, picked her up, and took her. He said, "If you
pee, I'll stick your bottom full of holes!" This little girl is
sobbing and crying, and he said, "Lord King (sic), what - Lord
Vizier, what should I do? She doesn't pee."

F.93   "Throw the little bastard to the ground!"

F.94   He picked her up, and raised this girl up over his head, and
threw her on the ground! She let out one shriek, and died. He
said, "There, I threw her."

F.95   "Death, you 'threw'! You bastard, if I said, 'Throw her, throw
her to the ground!' I meant 'Scare her', and you raised her up over
your head and threw her to the ground, and you killed my daughter!"

F.96   Her mother started weeping and crying justice and injustice,
and finally he got up and they picked up the girl and brought her
into the house - she'd died, anyway, (inaudible phrase).

F.97   He said, "Let's go and dig a grave tonight, so that people
won't see, or in the morning they'll say, 'What happened to the poor
vizier's daughter? Did the servant kill her?'" He went with Măr
Čučeh. This shrine was near, and he went to dig a grave there.
They had taken the shovel, but they hadn't taken the pick. He said,
"Go, get the pick from the house, too."

F.98   He came, and picked up the pick and hit it, and then came and
stood over this wife of his - um - he has two wives - and he said,
"Give me the pick, then." [Măhgol: He didn't say 'Give me the
pick,' he said, 'Gimme.'] He said, "Gimme!", then, "Give me the
pick." These poor women got up and searched here and there. Then
again, "Gimme it! Gimme it!"

F.99   She said, "May you burn, may you fall to pieces! What am I to
give you? The name -- (garbled) -- if I (sic) could name it, no
matter how much I look, I can't find it, what, what did you come
for?"

Vizier."

F.112   This child yelled to him, "Lord Vizier, come, they want you."

F.113   The vizier came and he said, "Don't you have any shame? That you go and tell someone, 'Go call the Lord Vizier'!"

F.114   She said, "Oh, look, look at Mär Čučeh," she said, to him, "He was keeping the ⋮. gate, he had all the things, and now look, the gate is tied to his back."

F.115   This poor vizier went, and said, "Bastard, why did you do like this?"

F.116   "Bastard yourself, you said to me, 'Take (sic) the gates tightly, and gather all the things.' I gathered, I gathered all your things, and I fastened the gate on my back so the thieves wouldn't take it. Then I came."

F.117   He came, hitting and talking and running, and came to his house. When the governor came, all the paddy and wheat and beans and rice, are all heaped in the middle of the courtyard, and the jars of ghee are upside down, and everything is heaped in bits and pieces. He went to the cowshed, and saw that the cows were all beheaded, and their muzzles down in the straw. He came out, and said, "For God's sake, you bastard, Mär Čučeh, (with sobbing and head-shaking) go, go, go, go, I don't want you, don't want you, don't want you!"

F.118   "Bastard yourself, I'm with you for a year -- you hired me for a year, by God, I won't move a step till my year is up."

F.119   This vizier said, "What can I do?"

F.120   He took his gate, and he cleaned up all those things and took them out, and poured them in sacks, and they shook out all their things and carried them into the house. The beheaded cows they took out, and any Muslim who wanted, took some, and those who didn't didn't. The dogs ate them.

F.121   Some months, some while passed after that, and there was an evening, this vizier said to his wife, "Wife?"

F.122   She said, "Yeah?"

F.123   He said, "This - he won't go, come, let's run away from him. Because whatever happens, today or tomorrow, he's poured dust on our heads, and he'll kill me, and he'll kill you, too, and (our heads . . . in the dust) (garbled)

F.124   It's early, and after that this Mär Čučeh heard. He was awake, and he heard. This, this night passed, and the next night passed, and the vizier got up, and there were two horses, and he saddled and bridled them and filled two saddlebags with jewels and coins and plenty of valuables and put suits of clothes in them, and he took two guns, and he went out. This Mār Čučeh had gone out before he did and hidden, then, in the alley. Put it that even as they got on the road, as they came out, this Mār Čučeh was watching for a sight of them, this way and that, to see, "Where are they going?"

F.125   He, - they came near a stream, where there was a bridge, Mār Čučeh got himself ahead in the dark and went, and hid under the bridge. After he hid under the bridge, when the vizier's horse came along, he raised his head, and the horse got frightened. The horse got frightened and reared, and he won't pass the bridge. So his wife spoke up, and said, "Now, if we had brought Mār Čučeh, Lord Vizier, he would have led this horse across here, but now however much you hit him, he won't go."

F.126   Just then he stuck his head out of the ditch, and said "Mistress dear, what do you want? Here I am, right here!"

F.127   This king (sic) said, "Death to 'Mistress'! Dust to 'Mistress'! Lumps to "Mistress'! You bastard, where were you, that now you're right here?!"

F.128   He said, "Oh, I - I - , I came. The moment when you fastened the gate, I found out, I saw that the vizier wasn't there. I said, 'I hope a wolf or a jackal doesn't eat them on the road - I'd better go with them.'" Watch, now.

F.129   Let that be, and take up this, with this vizier and his wife on horseback, they go in front, and he goes behind the horses. They went and they went and they went, and they went to the bank of a river, and there they got down. Put it that they got down there, and this vizier said to his wife, "Wife?"

F.130   "Yeah?"

F.131   The night was well along -- he said, "This Mār Čučeh is all tired and worn out, now when he goes to sleep, when the night gets along, you take his two arms, and I'll take his two legs, and we'll throw him in this river."

F.132   This wife of his said, "All right."

F.133   After that Mār Čučeh took his little finger and cut it a little bit with his knife and after that, he doesn't fall asleep. He's awake, under his covers.

F.134   Put it that this husband and wife fell peacefully, peacefully to sleep, and they're _breathing_, deeply, like sleepers. Mār Čučeh got up, and opened their saddlebag and put on the vizier's clothes,

put on one of his suits. Then after that he quietly went, and
picked up the vizier, and brought him, and put him in his own bed.
And covered him up with the quilt. After that he went and put his
things (sic) under the vizier's wife's covers, then he did like this
to the vizier's wife, tapped her, and said, "Mistress! Mistress!
(sic)[1] Get up now! Let's throw Mār Čučeh in the river!"

F.135   The vizier's wife got up like that, in a hurry, with her head
full of sleep. After she got up, they came, and they uncovered him,
it was dark, and she didn't see, his wife. One took his hands and
the other took his feet, and they threw him in the middle of the
river. After they threw him in the river, he said, "Heyyy, Mistress!
How I killed the master!"

F.136   And after that, this wife of his said, "Oh, my God! How he's
oppressed me! What shall I do?"

F.137   He said, "Mistressssss, I won't do a thing to you, I won't kill
you. Come, marry me. I had this vow, because he brought my brother
and made him a servant and he killed him with starvation. I killed
his daughter, and I killed his wife, and I killed him. He took one
person's blood from me, and I took three. Now, if you marry me, I
have nothing against you, and if you don't marry me, I'll kill you,
too."

F.138   "I'll mar -- I'll marry you."

F.139   That's all. They took an oath there. The two took an oath
there, and he came, peacefully, to the vizier's house, and he married
the vizier's wife with a Muslim ceremony, and for seven days and
nights they hit the wood on the drum, and the drum on the wood.
They gave the Hindus raw food, and the Muslims cooked, and we didn't
get a burned bit off the bottom of the pot. He let the cows go,
there, and married the vizier's wife. There, that's how the story
of Mār Čučeh was. [MM (laughs): Thank you!] Poor, dear Adī!

---

[1] Honorific indicates woman has higher status than the speaker. The vizier
would not use this title for his wife.

Title: Xasteh Xomār [Proper Name of a Character: See Note #1, p. G-2.]
Narrator: Mādar Zāher
Recorded: 14 April 1975
Tape #CLVII-CLVIII

G.1   Some things that bear fruit,
              (Some that) bear none,
              Cypress and poplar,
              Pomegranate and quince,
              Pistachio and pomegranate.[1]
              The mouse did the carding.
              The mother mouse the spinning.
              The louse did the tailoring,
              The tick the dyeing.
              We went to the house of Mulla Abbās,
              There we ate bread and *mās*,[2]
              He put us over there,
              With a felt rug on top of a cotton mat.
              We suffered with the cold.
              We fell asleep in the evening,
              Morning came, we mounted our donkey in the morning,
              With our water jar behind.
              The wall fell down and out water jar broke.
              The cow gave birth, a female calf.
              Her bowl broke and her *mās* spilled.
              Lord, Lord (   )[3]

G.2   Spring comes and much rain falls, and the trees turn green,
and put out blossoms, and they bloom, pomegranate and quince and
pistachio and almond, and -- mulberry and apple and apricot, everything blooms! And we slaves,[4] we people of Afghanistan, when they're
ripe we eat them and enjoy them.

G.3   There was, and there was - there was no one better than God -
there was a clan of nomads, herdsmen. Did you hear? Or not?

---

[1] /mūšleh/: conjectural translation. See notes to I.1, p. 377.

[2] /māst/ 'yogurt'.

[3] This is an example of a *'Būd, nabūd'*, a nonsense verse used to invoke the
fantasy world of *afsāneh* at the story's outset. The last phrase is inaudible.

[4] /bandeh/: figurative, not a political statement!

[MM: We heard!] This nomad herdsman - is this the story of Hussein-e
Xāldār? Or Xasteh Xomār? [M[1]: Xasteh Xomār! MM: Xasteh Xomār.
Or it's up to you -] But you've written it down - [MM: It doesn't
matter - I'll write it over.] No -- I'll tell it. I'll tell
Xasteh Xomār.

G.4   There was and there was, there was an old man. OK? He was
an old thorn-gatherer. This old thorn-gatherer would go and cut
thorns and would take his thorns and sell them, and would bring
things for himself and his little daughters to eat.

G.5   One day came, some days and a while passed, and he was cutting
his load of thorns and tying it to pick it up, when he saw a flat
stone, there. When he lifted up the flat stone, he saw a storeroom
full of wheat there.

G.6   He said - then he picked up his load of thorns - he didn't
throw it away! He put it on his back and took it and put it down
in his own house. He said, "Wife!"

G.7   "What?"

G.8   "Come, God has given!"

G.9   "What has God given?"

G.10   "God has given a storeroom full of wheat."

G.11   "Good."

G.12   Then he went and got donkeys and sacks from these Muslims, and
found some people, two or three workers, and he came and loaded up
that little room full of wheat, and carried it off. From about morning when he started, it was close to supper time prayer when he
finished and he went after a broom, to sweep out the last of it. -
OK, it was enough, like that, if you'd just taken it all, and hadn't
swept the floor, too. So you wouldn't have seen all those troubles!
- He was greedy, though, he came and took the broom, to go sweep it
out, and when he came back, he saw a snake lying on top of the storehouse, curled up.

G.13   Then he said, "For whom have you carried off this storehouse
full of wheat? It was mine."

G.14   He said, "This storehouse of wheat - I have an old wife, and
three daughters, and I've been cutting thorns. Today I came and
cut a little load of thorns, and I saw a flat stone, and I said,

---

[1] MM indicates the author, M indicates Māhgol, the nine-year-old daughter
of the storyteller.

I'll take that flat stone home, it'll be useful.' - We don't have anything else - 'When my kids wash their feet, they can stand on the stone.' Then I saw there was a storeroom full of wheat. I went and got sacks and donkeys, and loaded it up, and I brought this little broom to sweep it out."

G.15   He said, "All right, now, if you give me one of your daughters, fine, but if you don't, I'll eat you." This snake told him that. And the snake's name was Xasteh Xomār.[1] [MM: Xasteh Xomār.] Xasteh Xomār - "I'll eat you."

G.16   He said, "That's all right, I'll give one."

G.17   He came back to the house and sat down sadly. [M: No, he said to him -] Shut up! He came to the house and sat down sadly, and said - his eldest daughter came and said, "Papa! Papa!"

G.18   "Soul of your Papa!"

G.19   "Why are you so sad, now that God has given to us?"

G.20   "Oh, darling, don't ask!"

G.21   "No, by God, you must tell!"

G.22   "Well, I went and there was a snake lying on top of the store-house. He said, 'You must give me one of your daughters and if you don't, I'll eat you!'"

G.23   "Oh, to death if he eats you! To dust (with it) if he eats you![2] What's one old wom- one old man, an old fart, if that's all he'll eat? I'm young - am I supposed to go and marry that snake, so he won't eat you, my father? What if he does? To dust, if he eats you! I should wreck my life?"

G.24   Put it that the middle daughter came along. The middle daughter came along and said, "Papa! Papa!"

G.25   "Soul of your Papa!"

G.26   "Why are you sad?"

G.27   "Don't ask, darling."

---

[1] complex pun on /mār/, 'snake', /xasteh xormā/, 'date seed', and/or /xasteh/, 'weary', and /xomār/, 'languid (glance)', the latter two terms used frequently in classical Persian poetry to describe the gaze of the idealized lover. I am indebted to Shahla Haeri and Aminollah Azhar for these suggestions.

[2] mild oaths: 'So what?' 'to Hell with it!'

G.28   "Oh, Papa! By God, you must tell - now that God has given to us, what are you sad?"

G.29   He said, "Well, then, when I went back to sweep out the store-room, there was a snake in it. He said, 'To whom did you take the wheat?' I said, 'I have three daughters,' and he said, 'All right, out of these three daughters, if you give me one, good, if you don't, I'll eat you.'"

G.30   She said, "Eh, to death if he eats you! Dust, if he eats you! Should my heart be sad if he eats you? Should I be grieved if he eats you? Should I go marry a <u>snake</u>? He'll eat <u>me</u>! You've seen your life, it's gone by, you've gotten old, let him eat you, to dust with it, forget it!¹"

G.31   So then the poor old man sat there sadly. His little daughter came along. His little daughter came and said, "Papa! Papa!"

G.32   "Soul of your Papa!"

G.33   "Why are you so sad, now that God has given us this storehouse of wheat? If we eat for the rest of our lives, it's enough for us!"

G.34   "Oh, darling, don't ask!"

G.35   "No, by God, you must tell!"

G.36   "Go away, you crop-haired heathen!² And you worse than the rest!"

G.37   "Papa, if you tell me, 'Die!', I'll die, if you tell me, 'Come to life', I'll come to life, but you must tell me. Tell me."

G.38   "All right, there was this snake in the storehouse, when I took the broom there to sweep it, and he said, 'If you give me one of your daughters, I won't eat you. If you don't, I'll eat you.'"

G.39   She said, "Eh, Papa, to death if he eats me! To dust if he eats me! I'll accept that snake." This little sister spoke. She said, "It must be that God has given me this snake as my lot. I'll marry this snake."

G.40   He said, "Good." This old man, overjoyed, he came, and that Xasteh Xomār who was a snake - he <u>wasn't</u> a snake! He'd put a snake skin over himself, but he was a *parīzād*.³ He'd said, "You bring me

---

¹ /gom konīm/, lit. 'lose it'.

² women's hair is cut off as a sign of disgrace.

³ /parīzād/ or /parī/, a good supernatural, cognate to English 'fairy'.

word, if your daughter accepts me, you bring me word, and if not, if she says 'No', you come so I can eat you, then. Even if you sit at home, I'll come and eat you."

G.41   The old man came, overjoyed, and said, "My little daughter accepts you."

G.42   "All right, when tomorrow comes, there'll come a wind, and your house and courtyard will all be swept out at once. After that some little drops of rain will fall, and settle the dust. After the dust settles, a suit of clothes will fall down. Wash your little girl's hair well, and put the clothes on her, and after that a camel will come, and bellow at the gate. Put the girl on it, and go - slap it, (let it go) off toward the west[1]. So it will go that way."

G.43   He said, "All right."

G.44   The next morning came, and those clouds came and the wind came up, and didn't leave a thorn or a straw in his house. It was swept, then the raindrops came and the dust was settled, and a suit of clothes fell out of the air. When it fell, they took it - they'd washed her hair clean, and they put the clothes on her, and all at once they heard the bellow of a camel --- No, God of repentence,[2] -- Oh, yes - (first) they saw that snakes came,[3] and out of fear this poor guy doesn't say anything. All the rooms got full of snakes. Then after that they saw a camel come to the gate, and it bellowed and bellowed, and when the old man went out, he saw a camel, white as milk. So he put a little shawl over his daughter's face and mounted her on the camel, and smacked it a good one and said, "Go! Off toward the west!" The camel went.

G.45   The camel went off as far as, say, from here to the Mālān bridge,[4] where there was nobody, just desert and empty land, and he set the girl down. He rolled over, and he was a young man so beautiful his own sister would fall in love with him, seeing him from behind! That's what a fine young man he was! And he put her on his shoulders and came to that same place where the stone and the storehouse were. He lifted the stone and went and she saw, wow! There's a whole house here, with carpets of silk spread all over and piles and piles of meat, and so much ghee that it couldn't be gathered

---

[1] /qiblah zamīn/ 'the land of the qiblah (Mecca)', to the west relative to Afghanistan.

[2] an expression of regret for forgetfulness.

[3] The snake's wedding party: invitees to weddings serve as witnesses on behalf of each family.

[4] Perhaps three miles.

together, and rice like that, and sweets, and tea, and there were dresses like that, and pearls and jewels and gold, and good things like that.

G.46   This - then this Xasteh Xomār is the girl's bridegroom, -- Xasteh Xomār was a *parī*, not a *dīv* or a *bārzangī*[1] or a snake, but he'd pulled on a snake skin over his body, so no human would know what he was. (They'd) think he was a snake.

G.47   So he said, "Do you know what this is all about?"

G.48   "No."

G.49   "I'm no snake, I'm a person. Though I'm of humankind[2], I have this snake skin on my body. All this house and wealth, all this is yo(urs) - I'm a person and of humankind, but I wear this snake skin during the day."

G.50   She said - this girl said, "These two sisters of mine, the older and the younger, when my father brought the wheat, they were very happy about the wheat and the storehouse. My poor father came, and sat down sadly. When he sat down, my older sister said, 'Papa! Papa!' and he said, 'Soul of your Papa!' She said, 'Why are you so sad, now that God has given to us?' He said, 'Darling, don't ask!' She said, 'Why?' He said, 'When I went back to sweep out the storehouse, there was a snake curled up in the room. He said, "To whom did you take this wheat?" I said, "I have three daughters, and I'm just a thorn-cutter, I don't have a thing. I took it to eat with them." Then he said, "If you give me one of your daughters, good. If not, I'll eat you."' She said, 'Eh, to death if he eats you! To dust if he eats you, one old thing, an old man! Should I go and marry a snake? Wreck my life?' So then, when she said that, like that, she left. It was left to my middle sister. When my middle sister came, she said, 'Papa! Papa!' He said, 'Soul of your father!' 'Why are you sad like this?' He said this - 'Don't ask, darling! You're worse than she is!' She said, 'No, by God, you must tell!' He said, "All right, this wheat, that God gave and I brought, when I took the broom and a sack back to sweep it out, all at once I saw a snake in the storehouse. The snake said, "To whom did you take this wheat?" I said, "I have an old wife and three little daughters, I took it for them." He said, "If you give me one of those daughters of yours, fine and good, but if you don't, I'll eat you."' My sister:

---

[1] /dīv/ a malevolent supernatural, often monstrous and associated with bride-stealing in folktale; /bārzangī/: "like a *dīv* only bigger, worse" according to MZ.

[2] MZ sees *parī* as sexually compatible with humans, but not with *dīv*, as she explains in another story in my collection. Here she considers *parī* to be human - not a generally shared idea.

said, 'To death if he eats you, to dust if he eats you. Should it wound my soul if he eats you? You're old, you've consumed your life, anyway, so if you die, to dust with it, if a snake eats you! Should I go and marry a snake, so he can eat me?' My sister spoke like that to him. It was left to me. It was left to me, and I went, and my father said, 'Go! You crophaired heathen! You're worse than they are! Look what they did, and they're older and wiser, and look what they said to me. How should you give me an answer?' I said, 'No, you have to tell me.' When he told me that, I said, 'Eh, Papa dear! It's better that he should eat me, than eat you. God made this snake my fate. I'll marry this snake.'"

G.51   Xasteh Xomār got very happy with this girl, and she found love in his heart. And this girl - just think, this Xasteh Xomār has a face that shines, and eyes like cups, and great beauty, a fine countenance.

G.52   Put it, then, that they were living here, and after some days and a while, these sisters of hers - he said, "Oh, wife, this house, this gold, this wealth, all this, everything is yours. If you want to eat, if you want to use it, anything you want to, do," - when he would go out in the morning to hunt, Xasteh Xomār he would give her a ring. He said, "When you get hungry, or you want something, give this ring a twist and say, 'By the truth of the excellent Prophet Solomon, I ask that such-and-such will come to me.'" And it would come and appear in front of her and she'd eat.

G.53   So she was here, and these two crop-haired heathen sisters of hers, one day they said, "Papa, Papa!"

G.54   "Soul of your Papa!"

G.55   "You gave that sister of ours to a snake. We'll go and get news of her."[1]

G.56   He said, "Oh, darling! That snake ate her, he killed her, or whatever. Where will you go?"

G.57   "No, we're going."

G.58   Their mother said "No," too.

G.59   They said, "No, we're going."

G.60   These two got up and went to the city, and bought two cooked sheeps' heads. And each sister wrapped one up in her carrying cloth, saying, "We'll take our sister a present, a nice, wholesome

---

[1] A few days or weeks after her wedding a new bride will normally receive a visit from her relatives, who may then take her home to visit her own family.

cooked head."   (MZ laughs)[1]

G.61   They came. Their father had showed them the way, already.
They came and came and came and came, and they found that plain.
They came, came, came, came, came, came, came, and it got to be
past afternoon prayer time, anyway, stage by stage, and all at once
they found that flat stone. They knocked on the stone, and then
their sister came. She said, "Who is it?"

G.62   "It's I."

G.63   "Who is it, here?"

G.64   "We've come as guests."[2]

G.65   When she raised the stone, she saw it was her two sisters, and
she said, "Lofd! What's that on your heads?"

G.66   They said, "We brought you cooked heads, dear Sister."

G.67   She said, "Take them and throw them away."

G.68   They took these heads off, waay away, and dug a hole and threw
them in it, and covered it up again, and came back.

G.69   She took them to the hamām right away, and washed her sisters'
heads and bodies clean, and she took those fine clothes that she
had in the house and put one suit on each, and golden bracelets on
her wrists and necklaces at her throat and golden rings and hair
ornaments on her head, and the other just the same, so that "When
Xasteh Xomār comes, he won't laugh in his beard at us."

G.70   The rooms and everything were in her keeping, anyway.

G.71   Supper prayer time came and Xasteh Xomār returned, and he said,
"You're talking - who is it?"

G.72   "I have guests."

G.73   "Who are your guests?"

G.74   "My sisters."

---

[1] Cooked heads and trotters, sold by vendors on the street in many cities,
are regarded as poor people's food, although others will admit, laughingly, that they like them.

[2] When knocking on a private door, people do not ordinarily give their
names, but state their business and/or are recognized by voice.

G.75   "That's fine, then, that your sisters have come."

G.76   That evening, they sat down to talk and they were talking and telling their news, and their hearts' secrets, and later, they went to sleep. It got to be morning and they got up. This - eldest sister of hers was a rascal, and in the morning she said, "Sister, Sister!"

G.77   "Soul of your sister!"

G.78   "You're with this snake, now - how can you sleep with him? What do you do? Aren't you afraid? He's a snake!"

G.79   "Eh, Sister! He's no snake."

G.80   "How do you mean, he's no snake? Of course he's a snake!"

G.81   "All right, tonight when we're going to sleep, you come and peek around the door, and see what kind of thing he is! Then after that, say 'He's a snake.'"

G.82   That evening when the husband and wife were going to sleep, these two sisters went and looked through a hole in the door, and they saw the room was on fire from his beauty!

G.83   She said, "Ehhh!? That sister of mine, so at ease and well cared for! Come, let's burn his snake skin! Why should he cover himself with a snake skin? This - this boy mustn't cover himself with a snake skin!"

G.84   After that, this eldest sister - she was a rascal, the elder one - morning came and she said, "Sister, Sister!"

G.85   "Soul of your sister!"

G.86   "By God, we looked, last night, and he's quite a thing! But Sister, why does he cover himself with that skin? Come, let's burn his skin, so that he won't put it on."

G.87   She said, "This - what would it burn in, that a person could burn it? OK, let him put it on - let him wear it. As soon as he comes, he takes it off, anyway, he doesn't wear the skin when he's with me. When he goes out to hunt, he (puts it on.)"

G.88   She said, "No, he shouldn't put it on at all." This older sister of hers said that.

G.89   Put it, dear, kind friends, that she said, "What shall I do?"

G.90   "Nothing, only, tonight, when you're going to sleep, laughing and talking, and joking, all at once say, 'How can your (snake) skin be burned?' He'll tell, then. Then after that, we'll burn it."

G.91   She said, "All right." She was her sister, anyway - if she hit one side of her face, it would hurt, and if she hit the other side, it would hurt, too. On this side, there was her husband. He was her husband, and she was at ease and well cared for, and this husband had a fine countenance, he was beautiful, and she had everything she wanted - and on this side, there was her sister, and she was fond of her sister, too.

G.92   When the evening came, and they were laughing and talking and telling their secrets, and joking, all at once she brought it up and said, "How does your snake skin burn?" "How does your snake skin burn?"

G.93   He said, "Oh, foolish human! Whoever said this to you, said it out of enmity. Without this skin, I can't be with you. My snake skin -" first, oh, God of repentence, I forgot! - First, he hit her with his hand, when she said, "How does your snake skin burn?", he took and hit her on the cheek, like that, so that her head spun around backward. Yeah, well, he got mad then! He said, 'Now, if she burns my skin, now, I won't be with her, then, these sisters- she'll be in trouble, then!' Of course, he was a *parī* and it was <u>clear</u> to him. He swung his hand and hit her, and her head spun around backwards. After that, his heart burned. Xasteh Xomār's heart burned. So he gently slapped her face back the other way, and it went back where it belonged,[1] and his heart burned, and his tears poured down. He was very fond of her. He said, "Oh, foolish human! Whoever said that to you, said it out of enmity. If someone burns my snake skin, I won't be here any more. My skin burns in onion and garlic skins." He told her, anyway.

G.94   He told her, and morning came. When morning came, these two sisters said - they saw their sister's face looking like it had been hit, and her cheek swollen like that. She said, "Sister, sister!"

G.95   "Soul of your sister!"

G.96   "Did you ask?"

G.97   "Yes, I asked."

G.98   "What did he say?"

G.99   "Nothing, only - first he hit my face, so my head spun around. After that he shed tears, then I understood, he gently hit me so my face went right again, then he said, 'Oh, foolish

---

[1] This incident is a commonplace, and occurs most often when the female captives of *dīv* question their captor/lovers, in order to learn a means of escape.

human, whoever said this to you, said it out of enmity for you. My skin burns in onion skins and garlic skins. You have your choice. If you burn it, I won't be with you any more.'"

G.100   "Ehh, Sister, let's burn it - where will he go? He was ly-ing - if we burn his skin, where will he go?" She didn't realize that if they burned the skin, he would take flight like a dove and go. Ye-es. He was a *parī*. She didn't understand, she was a human, foolish and simple.

G.101   After that, they gathered up onion and garlic skins, and they threw them in the bread oven, and the bread oven got hot, as red as a copper coin. When it got red, all at once - they went and got the skin from the room. When she'd gone and brought the skin and given it to her sister, and she was about to throw it in the oven, he came down out of the air, in the middle of everything. This Xasteh Xomār suddenly stood there, like something that goes up and comes right back down. When he came down, he said, "Oh, human! Hold back your hand! Oh, human, hold back your hand!" She threw it in the oven! [Interrupted by MZ's husband speaking off microphone.]

G.102   She threw it - threw it in the oven, threw the skin. It burnt. It burnt, the skin, and he went on his way. He went on his way, and the girl was left there, then. He told her that these things and property - Xasteh Xomār went, then, he disap-peared - after he went, then, these carpets and jewels and gold and this food and clothing - not a bit was left in the house! Nothing - he left - like an ant going into its hole, and nothing remained. He left, and it was finished. The three sisters were left there.

G.103   These three sisters were left, and the one suit of clothes that the girl was wearing, Xasteh Xomār's wife, that was valuable - only it remained. She took off those clothes and sold them. Said-as he was flying up, to go, he said, "Human, hold back your hand," and she held back, and he said, "Oh, foolish human, you'll remem-ber these days! If you come, head toward the west. Take seven iron walking sticks and seven pairs of steel shoes, and maybe, stage by stage, you'll come to me, but there, my mother's a *dīv*, my father's a *dīv*, my aunt's a *dīv*, her daughter's a *dīv*, and they'll eat you. It would be better if you didn't come. But if you come, head toward the west." He told her that, and he went. And when he went, all the valuable goods disappeared.

G.104   She sold those clothes, and she had seven iron walking sticks made and seven pairs of iron shoes. Then she took a packsack, and put seven plain homespun suits of clothes in it, and put it on her back. And this ring is on her finger. And she went, then, head-ing west. She went by night, she went by day, she went by night, she went by day, she went by night, she went by day, and one pair of shoes fell off, and one stick broke. And she'd brought seven

sticks! So she put on another pair of shoes, and took another
stick, and stage by stage, she went on, night and day, night and
day, and nights she would sleep in mosques, or out in the dry
desert. Another pair of shoes got worn out and full of holes, and
she threw them away, and she hit them with the stick and it broke,
and she threw it away. Why should I give you a headache? Six
pairs of shoes and six walking sticks were finished, and the
seventh was in her hand, and she's still heading west. After
that, from far away, she saw a herd of camels appearing. They
were herding camels there. She went and when they got close,
she asked, "Whose is this herd of camels?"

G.105   He said, "This herd of camels
                    Belongs to Xasteh Xomār,
                    To the brideprice of Bibī Negār."[1]

This man who was herding the camels said,

                    "This herd of camels
                    Belongs to Xasteh Xomār,
                    To the brideprice of Bibī Negār.

That is, 'Xasteh Xomār has given this herd of camels as brideprice
to Bibī Negār.'

G.106   After she left the camels, she came, came, came, came, and
she saw a herd of cows. She came up to the cowherd. She said,
"Whose is this herd of cows?"

G.107   "It belongs to Xasteh Xomār,
                        To the brideprice of Bibī Negār."

G.108   So she came. She came, came, came, came, came, and she saw
a herd of sheep, ewes and lambs. She said, "Whose is this herd
of sheep?"

G.109   He said, "It belongs to Xasteh Xomār,
                    To the brideprice of Bibī Negār."

G.110   She said, "What sort is this Xasteh Xomār?
                     And what is the 'brideprice of Bibī Negār'?
                     Where is their place and their house?"

G.111   He said, "Wayyy - if you go - can you see that herd of goats?
If you go past those goats, you see those trees that look black?
Those trees are in front of the house of Xasteh Xomār."

G.112   She came and came and came, and arrived at the herd of goats,

---

[1] The name /Bibī Negār/ means 'Lady Beauty' or 'Lady Idol'. MZ sometimes uses the phrase, /mar-e Bibī Negār/, 'brideprice of Bibī Negār',
as though it were the character's name. See below, G.114, G.216.

and said, "Whose is this herd of goats?"

G.113   He said, "It belongs to Xasteh Xomār,
                To the brideprice of Bibī Negār."

G.114   She said, "Where is the place of Xasteh Xomār, and the 'brideprice of Bibī Negār'?"

G.115   He said, "Wa-ayy, off, by those trees that look black - it's
there, beside a stream of water. The door - the gate is there."

G.116   She came and came and came and came, and she came to the trees
and the stream. Right there by the door, she leaned her back
against the wall and sat down. After she'd sat down, Xasteh
Xomār's servant girl came out to fill a pitcher in the stream, for
him to wash for prayers. So he could wash for prayers.

G.117   Then she said, "My little mother, my little sister, give me
one little drop of that water to drink, for I'm so tired and weary,
that if I bend down to the stream, my back will break!"

G.118   She said, "Drink death! Drink dust! I'm taking this water
for my master to wash for prayers," - this servant girl said that.

G.119   She said, "Oh, Lord, just as you carry it -" and that ring of
Xasteh Xomār's was on her finger - "by the truth of the excellent
Prophet Solomon, I ask that this water may turn to blood!"

G.120   When she took it and poured it over his hands, he saw that it
was blood. He didn't say anything, Xasteh Xomār - he knew it was
a sign of her.

G.121   So this girl came back. He - he didn't say, "What is this
blood?"

G.122   This girl emptied it out, and came back to the stream and put
it in the water and filled it.

G.123   When she filled it, she said, "Oh, dear mother! Dear lamb!
Give me a little drop to drink, for if I bend over to drink, my
back will break, I'm so tired!"

G.124   She said, "Drink death! Drink dust! Drink lumps! My master
is washing for prayer, should I give you to drink, so he can wash
in your leftovers?"

G.125   She said, "Oh, Lord, just as you carry that water, by the
truth of the excellent Prophet Solomon, I ask that this water be
pus!"

G.126   When she brought it and poured it, it was pus. He said, "Why
was it blood when you brought it the first time, and now, again,
it's pus that you brought?" By now he understood it all, and he

said, "Oh, Lord God! What faith this human had, to come! Now what do I do?"

G.127   She said, "There, now, master, there's a traveler sitting at the gate, who says, 'Give me a drop to drink.' I don't give it, and that time it turned to blood, and now it's turned to pus."

G.128   He said, "You go and draw water in the pitcher from the stream for the traveler to drink, then bring me the remains for me to wash. It's all right." Xasteh Xomār said it.

G.129   This girl came and filled the pitcher and she said, "Give me a drop to drink."

G.130   She said, "Drink death! Drink dust! Take it and drink, then, and be satisfied."

G.131   And she - who didn't want water, anyway - it was an excuse - when she took the pitcher, the other one looked away, and she dropped her ring into the pitcher. She gave it back to the girl, and out of fear she didn't pour it out, she took it in.

G.132   When she took it in, Xasteh Xomār took the pitcher from her and said, "Leave, then, you're dismissed." He dismissed her, and when he'd dismissed her, he poured out the water and washed, and at the very last, the ring fell out with a clatter, his own ring. He said, "Lord God, a faithful human, she's kept faith, and come!"

G.133   He came out, then. He came out fast! He came and saw her sitting by the door, and said, "Didn't I say that you'd be sorry? Now what will I do with you? My mother's a dīv, father's a dīv, my aunt's a dīv, her daughter's a dīv, and if my mother doesn't eat you, her sister will, and if she doesn't, her daughter will."

G.134   She said, "Whatever you do, I've come, now."

G.135   He put her on the ground, and he sang over her, and sang, and sang, and sang, and sang, and sang, and sang, and sang, and by dear God's will she became a needle. He picked up the needle and stuck it in his coat and went back in the house.

G.136   When he went back in the house, Xasteh Xomār's mother said,

"Pah! Pah! A human smell!
If a horse comes, it casts its shoe,
If a bird comes, it casts its plume,
What is a human being doing here?"

G.137   He said, "Eh, Mother! You think it's a human. I - with humans- I am always going among the humans, and their smell is on me."

G.138   She said, "No, darling! You were always with humans, didn't I know? There's a human on you, somewhere!"

G.139   "No, there isn't!"

G.140   "Yes, there is a human. Xasteh Xomār, you've a human on you!"

G.141   "Mother, there is no human! I go around among humans, I'm always among them, and their smell is on me."

G.142   She said, "Darling, I'm a $d\bar{\imath}v$! I can tell by the human smell, that there's a human on you somewhere!"

G.143   He said, "Well, Mother, it's nothing, only tomorrow is my wedding night, and I've brought a servant girl for your sister's daughter."[1]

G.144   She said, "Good, bring her out."

G.145   He said, "No! You swear, now, and then I'll bring her out."

G.146   She said, "By the idol on the left-hand side, Xasteh Xomār, I swear I won't eat her -"

G.147   He said, "No."

G.148   She said, "By the idol on the right-hand side, I swear I won't eat her -"

G.149   "No, I won't bring her out. You'll eat her."

G.150   "I swear by my mother's milk,[2], darling, Xasteh Xomār, my dear, bring her out! I won't eat her."

G.151   After that, he took the needle out of his collar and put it down there, and sang over it, and the same girl as before, it turned into that girl.

G.152   So then, after that, his mother didn't say any more. She got an idea, though, saying, "All right, now that I've sworn this to my son, I'll send her to my sister's house. My sister hasn't sworn, and she'll eat her."

---

[1] Xasteh Xomār is engaged to marry his cousin.

[2] Hafizullah Baghban in his translation of this story (Dorson, 1975, p. 237, note 16) explains that /haykal/, lit. 'statue, image' is the worship object of evil supernaturals, and that 'Left-hand haykal is the ogres' real worship object, so promise is kept when sworn by it; an ogre's swearing by the right-hand haykal is not reliable.' Several of my informants treat only swearing by the mother's milk as binding to supernaturals.

G.153   Morning came, and that evening was to be Xasteh Xomār's wedding with Bibī Negār. She said, to the girl, "Go and sweep the <u>whole</u> castle and sprinkle water to settle the dust. Go first and sweep."

G.154   The girl went and got a broom and started sweeping, but by noon she hadn't even finished one of the roof platforms. Xasteh Xomār came and said, "What are you doing?"

G.155   "Nothing, she told me 'Go and sweep the castle, for tonight is Xasteh Xomār's wedding. And after that, sprinkle it with water.'"

G.156   He said, "Very well, even if you swept from now till tomorrow, could you finish even <u>one</u> roof platform? Didn't I tell you you'd be sorry?" He said, "Throw away the broom." She threw it away and he said, "By the truth of the excellent Prophet Solomon, I ask for a little gust of wind, so that not a straw or a twig or a bit of dust will be left on the roof or in the castle."

G.157   By the will of God such a wind came up that not a twig or a straw remained. The wind took them. She went and said, "Peace be with you."

G.158   (His mother) said, "And peace be with you.
                    Were it not for your wish of 'peace',
                    You would be a raw mouthful for me.
Did you sweep?"

G.159   "Yes, I swept."

G.160   "This was your master's deed, not yours. Go and sprinkle the water."

G.161   So she went and got water from the stream, and she was sprinkling it to settle the dust. She was sprinkling it, and Xasteh Xomār came along - he's always in hiding, to see what she does - he says, "What are you doing?"

G.162   She said, "Nothing, she told me to sprinkle water."

G.163   Xasteh Xomār said, "All right, didn't I tell you you'd be sorry? If you sprinkle water for the next two or three days from now, will you finish it? Go, put away your bucket." She went and put it away, and he said, "By the truth of the excellent Prophet Solomon, I ask for a cloud to come and rain a few drops on this land, to settle all the dust at once."

G.164   The cloud came and rained its few drops, and the land was all sprinkled, and then the girl went and said, "Peace be with you, I've settled the dust."

G.165   "This was your master's deed, not yours." His mother, she knows. She said, "Take this black mat,[1] and wash it white in the stream, and bring it, for tonight is Xasteh Xomār's wedding."

G.166   She took the mat down to the stream, but no matter how she rubbed it and wrung it and scrubbed it, it wouldn't turn white. Xasteh Xomār came out and said, "What are you doing?"

G.167   She said, "Nothing. She told me to take this black mat and wash it white."

G.168   He said, "Does a black cloth turn white? How can it turn white? If you wash it in this stream for ten years, till it all wears to pieces, would the threads of it turn white?"

G.169   She said, "What should I do, then?"

G.170   "Get up out of that stream, and bring the mat."

G.171   She brought it and he said, "By the truth of the excellent Prophet Solomon, I ask that this mat may turn as white as milk - white!" By the will of God, when he recited the Great Name,[2] the mat turned as white as milk. She took it back.

G.172   "Did you make it white?"

G.173   "Yes."

G.174   "This was your master's deed, not yours. Take it back, and make it black again."

G.175   Xasteh Xomār hadn't even gone back up to the castle, and at the bottom of the stairs, by the door, he saw her bringing the mat back. He said, "What did she say?"

G.176   "She said, 'Take it back and turn it black again.'"

G.177   He came out, and sat on the doorstep and said, "By the truth of the excellent Prophet Solomon I ask that this mat be blacker than before!" It turned black.

---

[1] /palās/, properly any sort of coarsely woven cloth. Often used in Herati to describe a heavy woven cotton which is used as an inexpensive floor covering.

[2] In Muslim tradition Solomon controlled the dīv and understood the language of birds, and was a white magician who knew the greatest Name of God. Xasteh Xomār's magic is all of the white variety, and he prays, Muslim style, while his mother, a dīv, is evil, and an idol-worshipper. Parī and dīv divide the supernatural world into good and bad halves.

G.178   After it turned black, she took it back to that *bārzangī*. She said, "Did you turn it black?"

G.179   "Yes."

G.180   "This was your master's deed, not yours. Now go, and bring the comb and the scissors and the mirror from my sister's house. Tonight is Xasteh Xomār's wedding." She's sending her there, because she's <u>sworn</u>, already, and she'd said to her, "If you don't make this black mat white, I'll eat you."

G.181   She made it white, so she said, "Go, make it black again. If you don't make it black, I'll eat you." And she made it black again.

G.182   She said, "Go get the comb and mirror and scissors from my sister's house, because tonight is young Xasteh Xomār's wedding."

G.183   She said, "All right. By what road do I go?"

G.184   "Just go, and bring them, by any road you choose."

G.185   She went out, and Xasteh Xomār was by the door and said, "Where are you going?"

G.186   She said, "It's nothing, only she told me 'Go to my sister's house and bring the comb and mirror and scissors, for tonight is Xasteh Xomār's wedding.'"

G.187   He said, "All right, now, as you go -" -eh-, oh - "As you go, there's a spring of blood. You say, 'My, my, my! What a fine spring of red syrup! If only you had time, you could sit and drink half a bowl of it!' When you get a little farther on, ther's a spring of pus. You say, 'My, my, my! What a fine spring of yellow ghee! If only you had time to sit and eat a little of it, and dress your hair with it!' After that you'll come to a bent tree. You say, 'My, my, my! What a lovely, straight mulberry tree! If only you were free to sit in its shade and let the cool breeze touch your body!' Then, as you go, there's this - a camel, and a dog. There are bones in front of the camel, and straw in front of the dog. Take the straw and put it in front of the camel, and put the bones in front of the dog. After that you'll come to a ruined cook shed.[1] You say, 'My, my, my! What a nice, well-built cook shed. Here I am, sweating. If only I had time, I'd sit in its shade.' You go by, then, and you'll arrive at the house. You say 'Salām.' When you say 'Salām', she'll say

G.188   'Were it not for your wish of "peace",

---

[1] /mādbax/, a cooking enclosure with a hearth, partly or wholly detached from a building to which it belongs.

You would be a raw mouthful for me.'

G.189 You say, 'Your sister has sent me for the scissors and mirror and comb.' She'll go into the next room to sharpen her teeth. There's a niche above the door, and the mirror and scissors and comb are on it. Take them and run, then."

G.190 "All right."

G.191 She went, and as she went she arrived at the spring of blood. She said, "My, my! What a fine spring of-! - what was it? (MM: -syrup-?) -"What fine red syrup!" - this - that we people of Afghanistan make, this syrup from mulberries - well, now it's not made very much, but in the old times they made a lot of it, now they make it less. She said, "My, my, my! What a fine spring of red syrup! If only you had time, you could drink half a bowl of it," and she went past.

G.192 She went past, and she went and went and went and went, and arrived at the spring of pus. When she arrived at the spring of pus, she said, "My, my, my! What a fine spring of yellow ghee! If only you had time, you could scoop some up in your hand to eat, and dress your hair and oil your feet!" She went past.

G.193 After she went past, she saw a bent shade tree. She said, "My, my, my! What a fine, straight, shady tree! If only I had time, I'd sit in its shade and enjoy the cool breeze." She went past.

G.194 After she passed, she came and saw a camel and a dog tied up. There were bones in front of the camel, and straw in front of the dog. A dog can't eat straw - he eats bones, not straw, and the camel eats straw, not bones - he's an animal (sic). So she took the bones and put them in front of the dog, and put the straw in front of the camel, and she went, and she saw the broken-down cook shed, and she said, "My, my! What a fine, well-built cook shed. If only I had time, I could go and sit in its shade!" Then she went, and said, "Peace be with you!"

G.195 She said, "Were it not for your wish of 'peace',
    You'd be a raw mouthful for me!"

G.196 She said, "Tonight is the wedding of Xasteh Xomār and Bibī Negār. I came after the scissors and mirror and comb."

G.197 "Good, you sit right here while I go in the next room and find them."

G.198 "Fine, you go, then."

G.199 After she went into the other room, she heard, xarrīt-tā, xarrīt-tā, xarrīt-tā, xarrīt-tā, she's whetting her teeth, and she's going to come out and eat her. So she carefully reached up

above the door and got the mirror and comb and scissors, all three.
She had two feet, and she borrowed two more, and she ran!

G.200   She said, "Ruined cook shed, get her!"

G.201   "Why should I get her? Why should I get her? You say 'ruined',
she said, 'well-made.'"

G.202   "Dog, get her!"

G.203   "Why should I get her? You gave me straw, she gave me bones."

G.204   "Camel, get her!"

G.205   "Why should I get her? You gave me hunger, gave me bones. She
gave me straw."

G.206   "Crooked tree, get her!"

G.207   "Why should I get her? You said 'crooked', she said 'straight',
and 'fine', and 'shady'."

G.208   "Spring of pus, get her!"

G.209   "Why should I get her? You said 'pus', she said 'yellow
ghee.'"

G.210   "Spring of blood, get her!"

G.211   "Why should I get her? You said, 'blood', she said 'red
syrup'. I won't get her."

G.212   So she ran, and got away. She went and said, "Peace be with
you!"

G.213   "Did you bring them?"

G.214   "Yes."

G.215   "This was your master's deed, not yours." Xasteh Xomār's
mother said that. She said "All right." So she brought them, then.
She brought them, and it got to be supper prayer time, and her sister came, and it's Xasteh Xomār's wedding, this evening. This girl's
fingers - this girl who was Xasteh Xomār's wife from before - they
took her fingers and tied cotton around all ten of them, and greased
them with ghee. Then they lit the ends of them with matches. Yes.
They lit them, and when they'd lit them, they said, "You go in front
of Xasteh Xomār and Bibī Negār, with their water jar on your head,
and light their way."

G.216   So she went in front of them, and she sang,

"Xasteh Xomār, my little thumbs are burning!
Bibi Negar's brideprice[1], my heart and soul are burning!

"Xasteh Xomār, my little thumbs are burning!
Bibi Negār's brideprice, my little heart and soul are burning!

"Xasteh Xomār, my little thumbs are burning!
Bibī Negār's brideprice, my heart and soul are burning!"

G.217   He said, Xasteh Xomār said, "Mama! That's enough, now! Let's put out the flames. There's light enough."

G.218   She said "Eh, darling! Tonight is the wedding of Xasteh Xomār and dear Bibī Negār. Let them burn, let there be light for you to see in front of your feet."

G.219   She sang,

"Xasteh Xomār, my little thumbs are burning!
Bibī Negār's brideprice, my heart and soul are burning!

"Ay, Xasteh Xomār, my little thumbs are burning!
Bibī Negār's brideprice, my heart and soul are burning!

"Xasteh Xomār, my little thumbs are burning!
Bibī Negār's brideprice, my heart and soul are burning!"

G.220   So she sang these two little verses, and her hands burnt, her fingers, and they were half burnt down, then.

G.221   Xasteh Xomār said, "By God, I swear to God, this human was faithful, and my mother, who was a *dīv*, and my aunt, they burnt her hands like that, by God, if I don't roast her daughter in oil before this night turns to morning!" He said that in his heart, then.

G.222   So then when this was finished, he said – it was time to lay out their beds. When it got to be time to lay out the beds, Xasteh Xomār said, "Mama!"

G.223   "What?"

G.224   "Put this servant girl's bed right inside the door, for tonight is our wedding, and we may want water, or my cousin may want to go outside, and she mustn't be afraid."

G.225   She said, "Eh, darling! I'll come and give you water! Your aunt will come and give you water! She shouldn't sleep by the door- it's not necessary."

---

[1] See note 1, page 332.

G.226   "Mama -"

G.227   "Yes?"

G.228   "Am I your child?"

G.229   "Yes."

G.230   "Did you swear to me?"

G.231   "Yes."

G.232   "All right. Do as I say, and put the bed right by the door."

G.233   "Tonight is your wedding, and tonight in this room, you'll be kissing, and playing, and fooling around, and she should be by the door? A human?"

G.234   He said, "That doesn't matter."

G.235   He kept saying this, so she said, "To dust with it! I'll put it there, and once we've put it by the door, and Xasteh Xomār has fallen asleep, I'll tell my sister to go and eat her."

G.236   [X, MZ's husband: How much is left?] There's just a little left, just a couple of words.

G.237   "She'll eat her, my sister."

G.238   So then - these were $d\bar{\imath}v$ and $b\bar{a}rzang\bar{\imath}$, and they sleep the sleep of forty.[1] When they'd put their heads down to sleep, Xasteh Xomār, - and his cousin fell asleep, too - he's awake, and he got up, He got up and got a great, biig cooking pot with ring handles, that would hold twenty or thirty man[2] of water or oil. A big pot like that. He dumped out all the cans and got it ready, brought the pot and all the cooking fat there was in his mother's house, he brought it all and threw it in the pot. And he split the wood and poured a little petrol over it and struck a match and lit it. The wood burned and the fat melted and got so hot that dough would burn in it right away, if you threw it in. After that - that cousin of his was sleeping the sleep of forty, and he just picked her up in a lump and carried her and threw her in the pot of fat. She got cooked. When she was cooked, he took her and set her in the corner of the room, and put a shawl over her head.

G.239   Then he fastened the door from behind, from inside the room,

---

[1] Forty times as deep and long as human sleep.

[2] a *man* in Herat equals about 8-9 lb.

and he - God knows how, he was a *pari* - he got out of the room, and he took the girl, and a glass of water - a pottery water bottle, and a handful of needles, and a lump of salt. Then they left. They left, and went and went and went and went and went and went and went and went.

G.240   Let that be and listen to this, that morning came. Morning came, and his mother and aunt woke up. The mother said, "I don't know why Xasteh Xomār - they haven't gotten up for prayers yet."

G.241   Her sister said, "Eh, sister! Last night was their wedding night. OK, what do you want with them?"

G.242   The sun got higher, and Xasteh Xomār didn't get up, and she said, "Sister, sister!"

G.243   "Soul of your sister!"

G.244   "He's not up."

G.245   "Eh, sister, don't bother them! Let them sleep!"

G.246   Noon came, and afternoon, and she said, "Sister!"

G.247   "What?"

G.248   "By God, this seems strange to me. By now Xasteh Xomār would have performed the two mealtime prayers!"

G.249   "Sister, it was his <u>wedding</u>! They didn't go to sleep last night."

G.250   She said, "No." So Xasteh Xomār's mother came and banged on the door with both her feet, and the door br - oh - she came to the door - God of repentence - and said, "Xasteh Xomār, dear, Xasteh Xomār, dear, get up, now!" She saw there was no talking, no sound, nothing. She saw someone sitting in the corner of the room, with a shawl on her head. She said, "Bibī Negār, Bibī Negār, come and open the door!"

G.251   She didn't come.

G.252   She thought, "Whaa? She's sitting, and I'm saying, 'Open the door'?" Again she spoke, "Bibī Negār, Bibī Negār, auntie's darling, don't tease, come, open the door!"

G.253   She didn't come.

G.254   After that she hit the door a good one, she was a *bārzangī*, a *dīv*, and the door broke in two, and she went into the room. When she lifted the shawl, she saw she was hunk of roasted, burnt charcoal, like a loaf of bread that burns, in the corner of the room. She said to her sister, "Sister, sister!"

G.255   "Soul of your sister!"

G.256   "Did you see how this human has gotten her way?"

G.257   "What has she done?"

G.258   "There, look at what she's done!"

G.259   "All right, sister, when you catch up with them, you eat Xasteh Xomār. When I catch up, I'll eat this human, because I[1] swore an oath."

G.260   "No, I swore an oath. When I catch up, I'll eat my own son. When you catch up, you eat the girl."

G.261   "All right."

G.262   They went. They went, and they came like a cloud or a dark wind, or a jet plane, they're coming - they're *dīv*. All at once Xasteh Xomār looked back and he saw them coming like two bullets. He said, "Human, didn't I tell you not to burn my snake skin? See what times you've brought on my head!"

G.263   They were almost catching up with them, and he said, "Oh, God, now what shall I do?" He threw the needles behind him and said, "By the truth of the excellent Prophet Solomon, I ask for a plain without head or foot, covered with needles, so that the needles will go in the bottoms of their feet and come out the tops, and they won't be able to come."

G.264   These two came to the needles and when they put their feet down on them, they went in the bottoms of their feet and out the tops, and they came!

G.265   They came, and they got close, they took out the needles, got rid of them, and came.

G.266   "Didn't I tell you not to burn my skin? Now do you see what times you've brought on my head?" He threw the lump of salt, and said, "By the truth of the excellent Prophet Solomon, I ask that as the needles cut them, this shall cripple them and tear them to pieces!"

G.267   Their feet were crippled and torn to pieces, and they're coming. They caught up again, they were just a little distance apart. He said, "Now what do I do?" He took the little pottery water jar he'd brought with him and threw it on the ground. He said, "By the truth of the excellent Prophet Solomon I ask that this become a sea[2]

[1] MZ confuses first and second person verbs in this sentence. See below.

[2] /derīyā/, often used in Herātī for gulfs and wide rivers, as well as seas proper.

without head or foot or sides, and they on that side and we on this, so that they can't come."

G.268   It became a sea without head or foot or sides, and these two sisters stayed on that side, and Xasteh Xomār and his wife on this side. Then she spoke up and said, "Xasteh Xomār, dear, Mama's dear, how did you get across this sea, so we can cross, too?"

G.269   He said, "It's nothing, Mama! I took under my arms - I put this mountain on this shoulder and that mountain on that shoulder, and I put a millstone around my neck, and I crossed, I came, I crossed the sea, that way."

G.270   Then those two sisters went and took up this mountain and put it on this shoulder, and took up that mountain and put it on that shoulder, and they went to a mill and each put on a millstone, over her head, and they came and jumped into the sea, to cross it. Xasteh Xomār sat down by the sea, and he said, "If these two - if blood and foam rise out of the water, then my mother and my aunt are dying. But if water and foam rise, then they'll come up and eat me and this human girl."

G.271   After they'd sat there for a long time, they saw that foam rose and blood rose and foam rose and blood rose and foam rose and blood rose, but they themselves didn't rise.

G.272   Then he turned to the girl and said, "See? You saw this kind of treatment from your sister's head - hand, all these bad times! See, I was more of a friend to you! I killed my mother and my aunt and my cousin on your account."

G.273   After that, then, they set off and left there, and went back to that cave that was from before, and all that valuable property came back, all at once and there,

G.274   They were on that side of the stream,
And we lived on this side,

and that's the end of the tale of Xasteh Xomār.

G. 275   [MM: That's very good - it's a long one!]

G. 276   Yes, it is long.

G. 277   [MM: From whom did you learn it?]

G. 278   This story - I learned it a long time ago.

G. 279   [MM: Oh - from when you were little -?]

G. 280   Yes, I was little - and then I told it all the time, and I didn't forget it.

Title: Afsāneh-e Garg [The Tale of Mangy-Head]
Narrator: Adī
Recorded: 3 Aug. 1975
Cassette # E2B-E3A

H.1   There was, there was, there was a king. And this king had a
daughter, and he'd promised her to her husband, and some days,
some while passed, and this girl had a lover.

H.2   So this girl had a lover - (aside) shut up! - so, so then
this girl had a lover, and some days and some while passed until
that night that was set, that day, that would be the night of the
wedding. She would be married. She was to be married, and she
said to her lover, "When the night gets well along, then you come
to the foot of my castle. Because I'll go with you - you take me,
take me to another country. I'll go with you."

H.3   This lover of hers said, "That's good."

H.4   So then - God willed it - there they were, with pipes and
drums, and hither and thither, marching around, having her wedding.
And lights all over the city and the finger cymbals ringing. So
then, dear sister that you are to us, there's this lover and she'd
made this arrangement with her lover.

H.5   Her lover had gone, and this cowherd, who was herding the
cows, just a poor little mangy-headed bastard, this little mangy-
head, he had a little calf of his own, in the herd. So after he's
collected his bread and (   ), and blessed it, and he comes
home - he had a grandmother, one old woman, and she said, "Gram-
ma's darling, didn't your own calf come home, too?" So he puts
down the piece of bread he got from work, and he goes out after
this calf. He goes from alley to alley, alley to alley, till he
comes to the foot of the princess's castle. It gets to be midnight, and he comes to the foot of the princess's castle. So now
he's just standing there, thinking, right there, this poor mangy-
head, thinking "Oh, Lord, where'd my calf go? If I go home now,
my grandma'll hit me, and the calf's lost, I've gone through all
the alleys, what now? What a mess!"

H.6   So then, there he is, right there, leaning on the castle wall,
he just sat down, and she's watching for her lover. She stuck her
head out the window, and she saw someone sitting right there. She
thought it was her lover. So she gathered up all kinds of valuables
and stuff, lots of valuables to take with her, like clothing and
everything, she gathered it up and filled these saddlebags, and

said, "Here, take it." The mangy-head caught it. Again she said, "Take this," and he caught it. So the third time she put herself onto the rope, and said, "Hold on, I'm coming myself." So he caught her.

H.7   He catches her, Margaret, then she says, "You stay right here." She doesn't realize - it's dark, then, it's night, midnight, close to dawn, and there's no moonlight or anything, to see whether this is her lover or not. Yeah, she goes to her father's string of horses, and the sound of her feet (is all there is), running because she's happy. She goes to her father's string, and she gets herself two goood, fast horses, and saddles them, and brings them and ties the saddlebags on behind, and she gets on one and the boy on the other. This grubby little mangy-head. God gave it.

H.8   (   )[1] (laughs) So (she) said, - this boy, put it that his grandmother is expecting him, and the calf.

H.9   OK, so anyway, put it that this girl just mounted up with him, and set off on the road. And this husband - this husband of hers is having his party and his wedding. And she's gone off with her father's cowherd.

H.10   She came, came, came, came, and the night passed. And this mangy-head is in front, and her horse is behind. And it's still dark like that, and day hasn't come yet, it's still a little bit dark. This girl thinks to herself, "Oh, Lord! If this were my lover, by now he would have had a hundred things to say and a hundred jokes and a hundred other things. Now if this is somebody else, what a situation! No matter how far we go, he doesn't say a thing to me. This - what a piece of bad luck this is! I did that, there, and my name is ruined,-" (aside to child) oh, no - get up, don't talk, donkey without a tail! - So from there - he just stays in front. (Whispers, about someone entering the compound) Who was that? If it were your father, he'd tell me 'no' - Can't I see? - One time, Margaret, then, she did this - after a while, they went, and all at once she said, "Wait, if this isn't my father's cowherd, that little mangy-head - what a mess I've made!"

H.11   So from there, like that - he's in front, and she speaks up and says, "Uh - " she saw there were these nice, little green fields, green with hay. She said, "Ayy, how would it be, now, if my father's sheep were here, my father's herds, and the shepherd, the shepherd right here - yeah, herding the sheep, and playing his flute, and the sheep grazing, how nice it would be!" And she saw he didn't say a thing! He didn't answer her at all.

---

[1] Inaudible phrase.

H.12   So she went along, and she saw a field of camel thorn, all
green and growing. He's in front. She said, "Ayy, how would it
be, now, if my father's camel herd was here, and the herdsman
(saying) 'Īlāk, Īlāk'[1] and the camels grazing, wouldn't it be
nice!" And she saw he didn't answer at all.

H.13   So she went along, and she saw - ayy, what a pasture, with
hay, hay that smelled so sweet! She said, "Ayy, how would it be
if my father's string of horses were here, now, and the grooms
were standing here, wouldn't it be nice!" She saw he didn't say
a thing, and she's testing him, to see, "If you're a groom, then
speak, reveal yourself, if you're a shepherd, reveal yourself, if
you're a camel herd, rev - " and she saw he's none of these.

H.14   Finally, then, she came, came, came, and saw - hayyy, a big
reed bed, with reeds, and reeds, thick as grapes. She said, "Ayy,
how would it be if my father's cowherd let his cows loose here,
and herded them around! They'd eat and the cowherd would be
standing here - wouldn't it be nice!"

H.15   So all at once he spoke up, "Ūbais!"[2]

H.16   She said, "Oh, Lord! Didn't I say it was that little mangy-
headed cowherd?! What a mess - what an affliction! I ruined my
name, curse the father of that lover of mine, and look whose trap
I've fallen into!" (But) finally she gave thanks to God, said
"God appointed it, this was on my forehead. I left my proper
husband, and did it for that bastard lover, now, God appointed
this."

H.17   They came, came, came, came, and arrived at a stream. They
arrived at a stream, and this girl, now, she was really done in,
from going on this road all night, from dinner practically to
lunch. She was royalty, and she got tired. When they got to
this stream, she'd had enough, and she spoke up, and said, "I'm
going to get down here for a while. I'm going to get down, and
you do this. You brew a cup of tea, on this stone, here, because
I'm done in."

H.18   He said, "All right."

H.19   So he went over to the girl, and got down, and let the horses
go, there, so "They can graze for a while and get rested, and we
can rest, too."

H.20   So here's this girl, beside this stream. She's going to wash
her hands and face, and her feet, while this stuff was (boiling) -

---

[1] Sound command used for camels.

[2] Sound command used for cattle.

There was a flat stone sitting place there, too. She's by the
stream washing her hands and feet, and she saw that down in the
stream, the water is rolling these pearls along. They're pearls,
and (the water) is rolling them. She called, and he's put on the
tea and lit the fire under it, and so on, and it's after that.
They drank their tea and this and that, and she came back to the
edge of the water. Well, this mangy-head, he doesn't recognize
them - how could his head be opened? All he's seen is cows. Who
learns wisdom and discernment from cows? He's only seen cows.
This girl recognized these jewels herself, though, and after she'd
drunk her tea, and she'd thought it through, she said to him,
"Come here, and take off your clothes, and get down in the water
and pick up some of those jewels." She sent him down into the
water, and he picked up a lot, a lot of those jewels, and put them
in the saddlebags.

H.21   After that he sat down, and this time she (started on) that
mat(ted head of his). She scru-u-u-ubbed that head of his, so
that the dirt and filth and blood went way off down (the stream).
After that she put medicine on his head and wrapped it up and so
on. Then they got back on the horses.

H.22   They mounted. They came, came, came, came, and arrived in
another country. So when they got to this other country, then,
they did this. There was this old ruin, and the girl said, "I -
if I go together with you like this, you won't be able to take me
into town. You'll have to - I'll stay in this old ruin, right
here, and give you money, and you go into this place and (find)
a good, fine house, then come and get me and take me to the house
then. Yeah, now, if people see me, and you, a poor mangy-head -
right then, they'll hit you, kill you, and go their way." [BREAK]

H.23   How did it happen? She gave him money, and he left this girl
right there, in that old ruin, and then he went into the place,
and so he went around, and there - there were people sitting, and
he asked them, "Hey, brothers, who has a house for sale? I want
a house."

H.24   Finally one of them said, "I have a house."

H.25   He said, "Let's go take a look."

H.26   So he brought him into the house and he walked all around it,
and saw that it was a good, fine house, just right, and attractive,
and he said, "How much is it?"

H.27   He said, "Oh . . . " - that is, he said, "So much," and he
gave him him money, and there was a neighbor (living in it), and
he moved him out, and he swept the house clean and prepared it,
and then he got her, that girl, and brought her to the house.

H.28   He brought her to the house, and so a while and some time passed, and when morning comes, he goes to the bazaar, this way and that, and gets some meat and bread, and stuff, and brings it, and so he's sitting with nothing to do until evening, with that woman.[1]

H.29   So finally, (you) see, this, this boy, this mangy-head, this boy spoke up, turned to this other one. He turned to his wife. He said, "I wish you'd take some of those pear- some of those jewels, that I got out of the stream, I wish you'd put a few on a platter, and I'd take them to the king."

H.30   This wife of his spoke up, and said, "DUUUST on your head, you filthy mangy-head, what is it ?! Here you are in a poor country, and these people, and you're poor. You haven't found a poor thing like yourself, to be company, what do you want with the king? You'll cast us into destruction! Half a king's mouth is water, and half of it is fire, now he'll say, 'Bring more, bring more,' you bastard, where will you get them?"

H.31   He said, "Go on, you're a woman, your head can't be opened.[2] I tell you, put them on a plate, and I'll take them. You say, 'This will happen and that will happen'!"

H.32   So he came. This time, she saw that he said that. That is, finally, these two plates - this woman said, "He's my husband, anyway. What can I do? Am I as strong as he is?" She took up the plate and filled it and with a royal cloth - she herself was a princess, anyway - she covered it, and he took it up, her husband.

H.33   He came to the king's audience room. He said "Salām" and they said "Peace" and they put him in a chair next to him.[3] This vizier of his, just, just as he lifted it up, he saw, "Paa! They're pearls! There, now! There's wealth, there's our riches! The king himself doesn't have anything like this!"

H.34   So then, sister dear, after he took it, he did this. He picked it up, and did this with it - the king took it, and gave it to his servant and sent it home, and he sat there for a while, and finally he was dismissed and came home.

H.35   Now this vizier was very knowing. He was very knowing, this king's vizier. He quietly came along behind him. The audience

---

[1] /zan/'woman, wife' : the first indication that she is not a virgin. See next paragraph, where they are man and wife.

[2] /sar-e to wā nemiša/ ; very colloquial expression; "you can't learn a thing".

[3] This text is full of indefinite pronominal references, some of which have been clarified in translation. Irregularities of tense have been preserved from the original.

broke up, and everybody went his own way. Then this vizier didn't go to his own home - he just followed this mangy-head. He came, and followed him, till he came to his compound, and when he came to his compound, and knocked on the gate, this other one, his eye is on the mangy-head, he's watching, and his eyes are at work.

H.36 This woman came, and opened the door. When the vizier saw the woman, and the mangy-head, he said, "Oh, Lord! Look at her, and look at him!" He ran from there, right back to the king. He sa-aid, "Oh, Lord King! That person who brought the jewels, look what he is, sir! He doesn't have a wife, (or anything like that), (he has) one like the moon, like day! He has what should be yours, for you're a king. This bastard has something like that. Strike him, kill him, and go yourself."

H.37 This king spoke up, and said, "Lord Vizier, God gave to him. God gave to him, can I do that? Take it from him?"

H.38 He spoke up, and said, "No, you have to (find a way to do this.)" He turned to the king.

H.39 He said, "What shall I do?"

H.40 He said, "Just this. Tomorrow, with luck, you must send a soldier, to fetch him, and you say, 'These jewels that you brought me, for me, when I sent them home, some of my daughters got a few, and some got a lot, and from early on the day they arrived, till supper time, there was fighting and fussing. Now they're all quarreling with each other. You'll have to bring some more of them.' Like that. Then you'll see what he says."

H.41 Morning came, and he said, "Good, morning has come." He came and sat down in the audience room, and immediately sent a soldier, and he knocked at the gate, and his heart leaped, (thinking) "Now there's a party, and they're taking me to the king" -- (aside) Here, Goldasteh, dear, whenever you go back (home), my child, take your sister's pants with you. [Goldasteh: I'm going.] Are you going right now? Tell (her), "Let me be your sacrifice."[1] Watch out, now, that they don't fall out of your arms - they aren't wrapped in a kerchief. There - she says she's going to the baths tomorrow. Take my child with you, but don't let him cry -- This time, then, he was really happy, (thinking) "Now this soldier has come, he's having a party. Because I took that to the king, now, he's sending for me, he's inviting me."

H.42 When he opened the door and saw this soldier, and this soldier said "The king asked for you, he told you to come," he went off happily, (thinking) "Of course he's invited me, he did something."

H.43 When he went there, he said "Salām" and they said "Peace,"

---

[1] Idiom for polite thanks.

and he put him in a chair next to himself, and he talked, this way
and that, and finally he spoke up and said, "Ahh, my boy, these
jewels that you brought, since I took them home, from morning to
night my hours have become bitter. All my children - one got a
lot, another got a few, and from morning to night they're fighting
and quarreling and fussing and fuming, so I - one says, 'I got
fewer' and another says 'I got fewer.' Now I ask you to do one
thing, (I need) more of them."

H.44   He said, "Lord King, I'm a poor man, downtrodden, and these -
I came from another country like this, and there's this one place,
and I got a few of them, I-so I saw they were fitting for you, but
I'm a poor man, where will I get them?"

H.45   He said, "No, wherever you get them, you've got to, got to
bring them." Yeah, well. It was just power and tyranny. There's
that bastard vizier, there, besides. 'You're fanning the flames,[1]
with this "You've got to do something, to get rid of him, so his
wife will be left to you." Yeahhh. "Now, you don't have a decent
wife. Well -- is an ugly wife any good? Who hasn't any color or
beauty? If it's good, you don't have it!"'

H.46   So then, dear sister that you (are), he came, with his color
all grey, and his head hanging, back to his wife.

H.47   She said, "Eh, what did the king do with you?"

H.48   So he spoke up, and said, "Oh, don't ask."

H.49   She said, "Why, what - what happened?"

H.50   He said, " . . . There, like that."

H.51   "When I told you, you bastard, 'Find someone poorer than yourself, and make friends with him,' you went off to the king, now,
then, go and bring them!"

H.52   He'd given him forty days' permission. "If you haven't brought
them in forty days, all your household and your wife are forfeit."
Fine. He told him.

H.53   So when morning came, he took some bread and water from there
and mounted his little horse. She said, "Go, then, back to that
stream." His wife said it. "Next time, when you don't listen to
what people say - go, then."

H.54   He came, came, came, came, came, and arrived at that stream.
He arrived at that stream, and tethered his horse, and he came, and

---

[1] This and other bits of dialogue here and there seem to be addressed by
the narrator to a character, most often one she is criticizing.

was about to take off his clothes and get into the water, to get
them. All at once he spoke up, and said, "Well, now, this isn't
it. I've got forty days for this. I've got this (time), why not
follow these pearls, and see where they come from? If I go home,
my wife is right (   )[1] there, whatever happens, God will do
it." And this one woman, alone in that compound! Night and day![2]

H.55   He got his horse, and he mounted again, and he went along the
bank of the stream. As the pearls were rolling down from higher
up, like that, he came along the stream bank, came, came, came!
He arrived at the foot of this – thing – he saw a bi-ig walled compound. It doesn't have head or foot. He went all around it, and
he saw that it had no gate, no road, no front side, no <u>nothing</u>.
On this o-o-one side there's this little hole in the wall, and
this, this water coming out, just this much of a hole. This water
is coming out of it.

H.56   So he quietly took his horse way off, and tied it, hid it.
Then he came back to the side of that stream. He said, "Whatever
this is, it's a $d\bar{\imath}v$, and a lair of $d\bar{\imath}v$s. There. He came back
there by himself, beside the stream, right in front of that hole.
Right there he dug himself a hiding place.[3] He threw brush and
dirt on top of it, and he hid inside it, right there. He hid,
concealed himself.

H.57   Evening came. All at once he saw that one, a $d\bar{\imath}v$ came, as
big as a mountain. He came down out of the sky. When he got
there, he sat down by that hole. Then he started a spell. He's
reciting there, and <u>he's</u> down in this thing. Down in – the pit.
He's singing to himself. He sang and sang and sang and sang, and
all at once, he saw this doorway open. The $d\bar{\imath}v$ went inside, into
the compound. Then he sang from the other side, and sang and
sang, and that thing shut again. Yeah. And he, he's singing to
himself, then. Till mo-o-orning, then, he sang there, he's singing. (Aside) The child isn't coming into the house. Where are
you going? -- So he, then, he's singing to himself.

H.58   Morning came. This heathen came out again. He came out,
and came there again, and sang again, there, and the door opened
again, and again he's singing to himself, and he came back to this
side (of the door), and the door shut again, and he took off again
and went off by himself.

H.59   He went off by himself. When he'd gone, and gotten lost, and
a good hour passed, he finally came out of his hiding place. He
came and sat down by the hole, and started to recite the spell.

---

[1] Inaudible word.

[2] The narrator comments on the character's lack of concern for his wife's
safety.

[3] Lit. a pit blind, used in hunting.

He sang and sang and sang, and all at once the doorway opened.
Then he went in, and he sang and sang from that side and the door
shut again. He followed the banks of the stream again and came
and came and came and came, and then he got there! Ayy- he saw
there was a parī with her head cut off her body. When he cut off
her head by the edge of the stream - it's sitting right by her
neck, this parī's head. The drops of her blood roll down the bank,
into the stream, and they become pearls. Yeah. In this water.
The water moved them, so they went. This blood of hers that -
[END OF TAPE]

E3A:

H.60   "I'll carry her gently, in this" - (aside) Lord, then - "What
is this? Shame on him, to do this to her!"

H.61   So then, on this side, right here, he dug himself another
hiding place, and hid there, again. He hid, and again when evening prayer time came, this dīv came and he said, "It's him, then."
He's in his hiding place, again. He's hidden, right there.

H.62   He came, again. He picked up the girl's head, and he washed
the girl's neck and her head clean in the stream, and put it back
on her neck, and started a spell. He started a spell, and he's
right there, reciting it to himself. He's singing here, and he's
singing there, and he sang and sang and sang, and all at once the
girl sneezed and sat up. She came to life.

H.63   She came to life, this girl, then, and sat up, and he put her
on his knee, and started to play and fool around and so on with
this girl. Till -- till morning came.

H.64   Morning came, and it happened again, that he - he left. He
recited the spell again, and separated her head from her body,
and put it there. And he went off by himself. After he went,
when he'd gotten good and lost, he knew he was gone, all trace of
him disappeared. After that he came out of his hiding place.

H.65   He came out, and came, then, and he washed her head again,
and washed her neck, and put her head on her neck and started the
spell and the girl came to life. When her glance fell on him,
first she laughed out loud, then she started crying. He said,
"Oh, Lord, if --" he said, "What did you laugh for, and what are
you crying for?" This boy, the boy spoke.

H.66   She said, "My tears - my laughter was for this, that it's
been so many years since I fell into this heathen's hands, and
I haven't seen a single human. And my tears were for this, that
this even - that when that heathen comes back this evening, he'll
eat both me and you."

H.67   He said, "Eh, Lord, rich and poor are slaves."[1] Just like that.

H.68   So then, these two were there all day, till evening, sitting together and enjoying each other, and it got to be near time for him to come. He recited the spell again, and her neck - from - her head was separated from her neck, and he put it back there again, like that, and he went and sat down in his hiding place again. He spoke up, and said to the girl, "Oh, girl, now tonight you ask him, this dīv, say 'How will you die? Because you take me like this in the morning, and cut off my head, and you yourself leave, what if you got killed over there? I'll stay like this till Resurrection Day. I'll be dead here, like this. I'll be lying here.'"

H.69   So she spoke up. She said, "That's good."

H.70   "So you can see what - what he says. A way to kill this d - this thing. How to kill this thing." This boy said that to the girl.

H.71   She said, "Fine. That's a good plan."

H.72   So then he said the spell, till her head separated from her shoulders, and he put it (down) like that, and the drops of her blood rolled down into the stream. And this dīv came. When the dīv came, he washed her neck again and put it on - put her head onto her neck and recited the spell, and the girl came to life.

H.73   She sat up and turned to him when he put his arm around her, (and he) said, "A smell!" He said that to the girl. He said,

H.74   "A smell, a human smell!
            If a horse comes here, it casts its shoe,
            If a bird come here, it casts its plume.
            What is a human being doing here?"

H.75   She spoke up, this girl turned to him, and said, "All right, what kind of a (Muslim)[2] are you? In the morning, you chop off this head yourself, and put it there. You come back again at evening prayer time and bring me back to life. Where is the human being here? Could a human possibly get over these walls - could even a bird do it? And you --"

H.76   When she answered him like that, this boy - this dīv got to thinking. He got to thinking, "Well, she's right about that. How could a human find a way in here?"

---

[1] I.e. All are subject to God's will.

[2] Lit. "Islām": ungrammatical.

H.77   So after that he's joking with her and fondling her and so
on, then all at once he,says, "A smell, a human smell." This
girl of his had been right next to a human, and she'd gotten it
from him. She'd picked up a human smell. So finally, when they
were go-o-o-od and occupied, and this $d\overline{i}v$'s mood had gotten very
happy, and he was in his best temper, this happened. All at once
the girl spoke up and said, - said, "Well, I have a request. For
you."

H.78   He said, "Speak."

H.79   She said, "Now, I ask you this, that this morning when you go
out, you cut off my head and you go, and maybe sometime your fate
and end will work themselves out, and you'll die, that morning.
Eh, here am I in this living death, then - how would that be?"

H.80   All at once - he (thought) to himself, then "See, she has
some human - making this human smell," and all at once this heath-
en got angry. He got angry, and he slapped this girl on the side
of her face. He hit her, and her face spun around backwards.
After a minute his anger died down, and his heart burned for her.
So he hit her on the other side of her face, and her face came
back where it belonged. This girl doesn't say anything more.
When he came down off his anger, his heart burned for her, thinking, "How - it's quite a while she's been with me, and I haven't
even let the breeze from the flowers touch her face, and now I've
hit her like that." His heart settled down, and he was sorry,
and he sa - a - id, "My death - come, I'll show it to you."

H.81   He took her by the arm, into the compound, the inner compound,
way, far away. She came, and she saw a doorway arch in one corner
of the building. There's a room, and inside the room, there's
this arch. He said, "Do you see? This room - if anyone plasters
it, I - if anyone plasters this room, I become young again. If
anyone plasters this room, I get to be like 14 years old again.
I get young like that. Now do you see that archway?" Here, now,
the top of it was covered. He opened it. He said, "There's the
well. Down in this well, there's a pigeon. The glass of my life[1]
is in the gizzard of that pigeon. Down in this well. If fifty
man[2] of flour are made into dough, and kneaded, and dropped into
this well, all at once this well will boil up like a kettle of
milk, with the pigeon right on top. If it does that, right when
it comes to the top, and boils over, if someone is standing right
there, and makes a lunge and grabs the pigeon, right when it's
boiling up, well and good, but if not, if it doesn't happen and
the foam goes back down, it can't be caught. But if that life-
glass is taken out of its gizzard, then, then I'll die. That's

----

[1] /bīšeh-e omr/ , an external soul.

[2] One _man_ of Herat = approximately 9 lb.

how my death is. Don't you fear a thing! My death isn't as easy as you might think." And this boy is <u>li-i-istening</u> there.

H.82   This girl is right there. When morning came, she said - when he did that, again, when he was going to take off her head again, she said, "I have a request - it would help me pass the time - I ask that I might plaster the inside of that room,"- so that this heathen's heart would be at ease, so he'd be pleased. So then, "I ask that I might plaster that room, so you'll become young."

H.83   He said, "That's a fine idea." That day he didn't kill her. He didn't take off her head. And that day, when he'd gone, then, that girl went down there, with the boy. That day they were making love, till afternoon prayer time, and she put a little plaster on about half the room. This girl. She came and smeared clay on her hands and feet and all over herself, and the boy went back and hid himself down in his hole. And she's all smeared with clay.

H.84   When that heathen came, he saw her all smeared with clay, and pale, as if she couldn't stand the work - she's a *parī*. after all - she couldn't stand the work, and had done this little bit, and gotten very weak. When (he) came, to do (something or other), the girl fell down, and he said, "My soul, my sweetheart, how weak you've gotten, how you're all --"

H.85   She said, "I got tired. There, I was plastering the room of your life."

H.86   He put her arm around his own waist, and picked her up in his arms and put her on his own shoulders, and went to the room. He's going to look, to see how much, and what's going on. When he came, and saw it, he said, "Forget[1] it! I won't allow you to plaster any more. Don't plaster any more."

H.87   She said, "No, I want to plaster it all, all of it."

H.88   "No, just today you've gotten this weak, if you plaster the whole room, I'll lose you." This *dīv* said that.

H.89   She said, "No, I'm doing it. If I go, or if I don't. There, now, I'm doing it."

H.90   So in two, three days, she did the whole room, like that. After two or three days, this other, this heathen, was really happy, that the room was plastered, and his strength was 100 times, 1000 times greater. He was really happy, and he said, "Go on, I'm not going to cut your head from your body again." he said, then, "She's a friend to me, after all. She's a friend, after all, doing this for my sake."

---

[1] Lit. 'lose'.

H.91   So this day came, and right away they got the flour, those two. They quickly wet down the flour, one of them wetting it, one wetting it and the other taking it and dumping it in the well. Till the fifty *man* of flour were finished. All at once. This girl herself just dropped. The boy brings it, and gives it to her and the girl throws it in the well. When all the flour was finished, all at once this well, all at once it boiled up inside like a kettle of milk. As soon as it foamed up, this girl made a lunge. She lunged and caught the pigeon. When she caught the pigeon, she gave it to the boy.

H.92   This boy - just like that, without a sound, he slit its gizzard and threw away its body and picked up that glass. Just as the glass fell into his hand, that heathen arrived from that other side. He said, "Ho, human! Whatever you have in mind, I'll accomplish it for you. Whatever object you have, I'll gain you that object. Hold your hand!" Just as he said, "Hold your hand," he threw it to the ground, all in pieces. He fell out of the sky to the ground like a cannonball, and was smashed to pieces.

H.93   He was smashed to pieces, so his object - God granted their object for these two, and they came, and they passed some days and a while there, then all at once one evening, just lying there, all at once he remembered his wife. And oh, Lord! When he counted up, he saw that there was only the next day and evening left of the forty, and "If I'm not there by day after tomorrow, my wife and child [*sic*] and all my property and things . . ." this boy fell to thinking.

H.94   The boy fell to thinking, and the *parī* spoke up, turned to him and said, "Huh? Why are you so thoughtful? How did you get like this? Why are you looking so ashamed, like this?"

H.95   He spoke up, and said, "I came on account of this."

H.96   Right away she burned some *dīv* hair. This girl. She was the daughter of the king of *parī*s, this one, so she burned some *dīv* hair. The *dīv*s came. She said, "How long will it take you to carry us?"

H.97   This one said, "This long," and that one said, "This long," and one said, "I'll set you down in the time you take to blink."

H.98   Enough. (They sealed) the door with wax and seals. This compound was full of valuables, without end! Not even a bird can get in. So from there, dear sister that you are to me, this little door - both of them mounted on his back. Before you could say, "Lord!", he brought (them) to the foot of the compound, and put them down.

H.99   He knocked, and this girl came, and opened the door, came and saw that this *parī* is with him. She was delighted, delighted, and said, "That's fine. There was one, now there are two."

H.100   Morning came. Morning came. He got a big tray full - this girl's head - very early in the morning he recited the spell and her head came off, and he got a good, big bowl, a big basin, and filled it, then he sang the spell again and this girl sat up and from that, they filled a big tray like that, and put a cloth over it, and picked it up and took it.

H.101   He picked it up and took it, and placed it in front of the *hakīm*.[1] He put it in front of the king, and the king was very happy and so on.

H.102   This bastard vizier was very upset, then. This other one doesn't understand that this bastard is after him. So then, he put it down, and he sent them home and <u>he</u> went back to his own house.

H.103   He came back to his own house, then it got to be afternoon, then, just this time of day,[2] then, and the sitting platforms were in the midst of the garden path, among the pots of flowers, the three were set there, one on this side, one on that side, one for this wife of his, one for that, and one for him in the middle. So they're sitting there together. It's just this time of day. So they're joking and laughing and playing around and things, and then this vizier came again, and is looking from behind the door. His feet did a job from there again.

H.104   He said, "May God wreck your house, King! That, that - that little, mangy-head has the majesty. That little mangy-head has the majesty. He has the life! That day there was one, and now go <u>look</u>! Now there's two, and, and - are these wives fitting for him? They're fitting for <u>you</u>, a king!"

H.105   He spoke up, and said, "Bastard, what can I do? God gave them to him. Can I take them from him?" He said, "I sent him, and he brought me (what I sent him for), what else can I do?"

H.106   He said, "This time, this, this --" this king had a sister, and a *dīv* had carried this sister of his off, like that. A *dīv* took her. Just like that. A *dīv* took her. He said, "He - he's brave, this one, he - he's a hero," he said, "Go on, this" - he has this sister, like, and - " (Say), 'I heard that she's in such and such a mountain valley, and it's been several years, there's this *dīv*, who took her, and she's his captive. Well now, I - could you do this for my sister?' - surely (he'll) go there, it's a *dīv*, and he'll eat him. And the two women will be left for you." This

---

[1] 'Governor, judge, magistrate.'

[2] The storytelling session began in the afternoon.

vizier said that to the king, again.

H.107   Morning came, again, and again someone came to get him - a
soldier came. This soldier came, and called him again, and (his)
heart fell, again, and he said, "Some new trouble for me again,
somewhere!"

H.108   He came and said "Salām" and "Peace," and they talked this
way and that, and then he said, "Oh, friend, I have a request, for
you're a very brave person, and a hero, and I have this sister,
and it's quite a while, several years, that for all my royalty
and all my armies and troops - what have I been able to do? I
wasn't able to do a thing for her. So friend, I'm asking you like
this, because you're brave, a hero, if you could rescue my sister
from this dīv, and bring her back."

H.109   He spoke up, and said, "Lord King! If you finished off all
your armies and troops, and you couldn't do anything, how can I -
one person, alone - go and bring her?"

H.110   He said, "Oh, friend, you can do it. Bring her."

H.111   He said, "I can't, Lord."

H.112   "You don't have any choice. Either you lose your head, or
you do it."

H.113   He got very sad, and came home to his wives, and they saw
how pale he looked. Then this princess called to him, "Well,
what's going on, that you've lost all your color like this?"

H.114   He said, "Well, it's like this."

H.115   She said, "All right, may God make it worse for you! When I
told you, 'Just stretch your legs on your own shawl,[1] because someone who stretches his legs beyond his own shawl gets them cut off,'
- if you had found someone poor like yourself, and made friends
with him - but you went to the king, that's just like a king - just
like that! Didn't I say that half a king's mouth is water, and half
of it fire? OK, go, then, and answer him. Now he's turned away
from men, and he's set dīvs on you!"

H.116   This parī spoke up, and said, "This is easy, don't get upset!"
She turned to her husband, and said, "Be smart, don't worry like
this, this is no problem."

H.117   He said, "What's easy about it?"

H.118   She said, "Go to the king and say, 'I want a cow from you.
Kill the cow. And I need twenty or thirty man of limestone, that

[1] A proverb: 'Don't overreach yourself'.

burns, that they put in snuff,[1] that quicklime, that limestone, I
need twenty or thirty *man*.' Put that in the cowhide, and sew it
up tightly, and tie it on a horse, and take it and put it right
in front of his cave. You yourself go and hide. So then he'll
just - when he comes down out of the sky, and sees this black thing
sitting in front of his cave - there's a stone in front of his cave,
and whenever he - the girl is inside the cave and when he leaves
in the morning, he rolls that big rock into the mouth of the cave,
and then he goes. So you open the mouth of the cave, roll away
the rock." She showed him how, showed him how to recite the
spell for it, so "If you sing this, the rock will roll away. It
will open and when he sees the cave open and sees this black
thing, he'll get furious and when he comes down, he'll eat it at
one gulp. When it gets wet inside his 'basket',[2] this stuff will
start burning, and he'll just be blown to bits. This isn't worth
your worrying about it." This, this *part* said that to her husband.

H.119   So morning came, quietly, and he went and stood before the
king, and said, "I have a petition."

H.120   He said, "Speak."

H.121   He said, "I need a cow, and this much quicklime to put inside,
and on a (pack) animal - a (pack) animal to tie it onto, then I'm
leaving."

H.122   He said, "Good. That's fine." Right away he ordered his
butchers to slaughter a cow immediately and skin it and bring the
limestone and put it inside and sew it up and tie it on a thing -
and (they) led it up and showed him, "There it is."

H.123   He came, came, came, and arrived at the door of that cave.
He recited the spell at the mouth of the cave and the rock moved
away. He saw a girl suspended there by her hair like that, hanging. This girl, just as her glance fell on him, she laughed and
cried, like that, let out a yell.

H.124   He said, "Why were you crying, and why were you laughing?"

H.125   She said, "Ah, it's been so many years, that I - that I was
brought here, from my father's city, and I haven't seen a human.
I haven't seen the sunlight, I haven't seen the day. In the morning I'm hung up like this and in the evening I'm let down. And
this cave is closed in front of me."

H.126   So then he let her down, put her there, until about the time

---

[1] Afghan snuff consists of powdered tobacco and lime, and is placed under the tongue.

[2] Colloquial term for belly.

he realized that - that - he asked this girl, when he would come. She said, "He comes back between late afternoon and evening." So anyway, there he was, playing and fooling around and talking with her. After a while, it got so he knew he'd be coming soon, and he went to a cave in the mountains, and hid himself way off.

H.127   As he came down out of the sky, he saw, "Bau! The door of the cave is open and some huge thing is sitting in the doorway and it looks black." So he got furious, like that, that - "How soon can I get to it? What manner of creature is this, after all these years - is it stronger than I am, to open the door of my cave? What is it?"

H.128   So then, dear sister that I have, when he came down, he just took it at one gulp, this cow with the stuff. And before he c- c- c- c-, before he took a step, the stuff got wet, and he just burst into little pieces, each one not any bigger than his ear, scattered all over.

H.129   So then this boy came and that evening he thanked God and lay down there with that girl till morning came. Until the time when his forty days - put it that the two of them stayed there in (the _dīv_'s) house together. On the evening when he knew that the day after the next would be the appointed time, from there, he burnt these - _dīv_ hairs again. And the _dīv_ came again. To the mouth of this cave, where there's God knows how much wealth and property. He recited this spell again, for the rock, and sealed the door with wax and seals, and the two of them got on the _dīv_'s back. And he came and brought (him) right back to his own house with the girl, and when morning came he took the girl, veiled - and he went in front of her, and the girl behind.

H.130   She came and stood before her brother. She said, "Salām," and he said, "Peace", and he got very happy, and all.

H.131   He said, "There, now, there's your sister."

H.132   He spoke up, then, in that gathering. He said, "Your spoils are your own." Right there in that gathering he betrothed her to him and put her hand in his. That made three, and he brought her home.

H.133   Then some - a few days passed, and again this bastard vizier's heart wouldn't stay home. He came again, at just this time of day. He looked from the doorway again. He saw, "Hmpf! Look! That's the life - this mangy-head has the life!"

H.134   He came back before the king, and he took off his hat and threw it on the ground, and said, "By God! May your lousy throne be overturned! What are you king of? That mangy-head is the king! That mangy-head has the life!"

H.135 He said, "Bastard, God gave it to him! I sent him to the
$d\bar{\imath}v$. There, now. He came back alive. He brought the girl, what
else am I supposed to do? Godd Lord, wherever I send him he's a
hero, and he comes back. Now what?"

H.136 He said, "This time, send him after the Horse of Forty Colts.
All forty of her colts are $d\bar{\imath}v$, and she's a $d\bar{\imath}v$ too. The mare is
a $d\bar{\imath}v$, too. If he manages to do that - if he can't do that, that's
it, then."

H.137 So morning came, again, and again he sent a soldier after him,
and he brought the poor guy. Then he said, "It's this way."

H.138 He said, "Lord King, I'm one person. OK, this is forty -
forty-one $d\bar{\imath}v$s, and I'm a human, well, as soon as they see me,
from far off, (I doubt) if even a drop of my blood will reach the
ground - "

H.139 He said, "No, you're such a hero, you're so brave," and so on
and so forth. No matter how hard he tried, he said, "Either you
bring them, or you lose your head. You'll be killed. Even if you
are my brother-in-law now."

H.140 So sister dear, he came back to his wives. His head is hanging, sad, out of luck. This princess spotted him again. She said,
"Now what happened?"

H.141 "It's like this, again."

H.142 She said, "May God make it worse for you! The end of it will
be that you'll be killed at the hands of those $d\bar{\imath}v$s, in that lair
of $d\bar{\imath}v$s. The end - you'll be a meal for them. Because you - I
told you -"

H.143 Then all at once this - spoke up, this $par\bar{\imath}$ spoke up. She
said, "This is easy. Are you worried again?"

H.144 He said, "They'll take off my head, these forty-one $d\bar{\imath}v$s -
that's easy?"

H.145 She said, "I'll show you something." She said, "Go to the
king. Tell him, 'I want thirty or forty man of fruit from you.
And I want a good, big mirror from you.' Just like that. Take
them along, and there's this tree - you climb up, up in the tree.
Lean (the mirror) against the trunk of the tree. And all the
fruit - there's this pool. Around it - this horse, now, she comes
there with her forty colts to drink. So you spread all that fruit
on the four sides of the pool. And lean the mirror against the
tree-trunk. You climb up into the tree. The colts will come
first. Her forty colts. She'll come last. They'll get busy by
themselves with the fruit, picking them up one by one, and eating
them. When she comes, she'll come slowly up to the water, and

when she's drunk, she'll raise her head, and all at once she'll
see herself in the mirror. When she's seen herself, she'll say,
'Waa - what a fine thing I am!' When she says 'Waa - what a fine
thing, what a fine one I am,' when the mare says that, then you
speak up from up in the tree, and say, 'You're a fine thing now,
but if you were washed and rubbed down and curried, and your coat
were combed, and an English saddle put on you, and an English
bridle, and on this road - on this road, if I were to mount and
ride you a few lengths, then you'd look fine! How fine are you
now? You're all covered with dust, with your mane uncombed, and
your coat all messed up,' and so on and so forth. Then she'll
call out, 'Come down, take me and fix me up.' But don't you
come down till she swears an oath to you."

H.146   He said, "All right."

H.147   He went back before the king and got thirty or forty *man* of
fruit from him, and loaded it on an animal and got a big mirror and
set off on horseback, and came, came, came, - (they told him) "I
heard it was such and such a place - you go that way."

H.148   He came and came and came, and to keep it short - why should
you get a headache? - he came to this pool, and the - he got out
the fruit and spread it around all four sides, and leaned the mirror against the tree trunk like that, and he got up in the tree.

H.149   He got up in the tree, and then, what happened? He saw that
the first of the colts were coming. Her forty colts came then,
and got busy with the fruit. They were pi-i-i-icking them up,
like birds picking up grain. (Aside) Is the tea brewed now? Is
is brewed already? Yeah, get up, let it - go and take it, and put
it on to boil. [BREAK]

H.150   So then he did that. After that, then, he got up in the tree.
All at once their mother came. Their mother came, then, but she
didn't turn toward the fruit and things, she just stopped, and
drank. She drank, drank, drank, drank till she was satisfied,
then she raised her head. When she raised her head, all at once
she spotted the mirror. She saw herself in the mirror, and said,
"Bū! How fine I am! What beauty God gave me!" This horse spoke.

H.151   The boy spoke up from the tree, and said, "Up to now, how could
your beauty show? If you could settle down over there, and be curried and rubbed down, and your coat combed, and an English saddle[1]
put on you, and a bridle, so I could gallop you a few lengths on
these roads, then you'd be fine! (Do you think) you're fine-looking
now?"

---

[1] Afghan admiration for English harness dates at least from the British
military presence of the early 19th century, and perhaps earlier.

H.152   Then she spoke up and said, "Come down, then, are you watching? Fix me up, get up on my back!"

H.153   "He said, "No, I won't do that until you swear to me."

H.154   She said, "By the idol of the right hand, by King Solomon the Prophet, whatever object you have, I'll grant it."

H.155   He said, "Isn't there another oath?"

H.156   She said, "By the idol of the left hand, by King Solomon the Prophet, whatever object you have, I'll grant it. Come down. Fix me up."

H.157   So this boy got down, and the boy got her down into the pool, and washed her clean. He washed her, till "Dear boy, that's enough," and he combed her coat and all and put the saddle on her, and the bridle, and mounted. He mounted on her back.

H.158   He mounted on her, and she'd carried him one or two lengths on the road, and all at once he turned her head toward town. She's in front. He's mounted on her. He's mounted on their mother. All forty colts are following. So he brought them. He called to the colts and to this horse, and said, "If a human comes along, eat him! If an animal comes, eat it! Don't even look around. Anything that comes in front of you, fine - eat it! You're free (to do it)."

H.159   Right through the bazaar, like that - like that, and, and - they're eating people like that, and animals, and all the people started crying for quarter and praying. He emptied the whole city, then he brought them right to court. He said, "Lord King! Here they are!"

H.160   He said, "I repent! I did wrong. For God's sake! My whole populace has been destroyed - let them go!"

H.161   He said, "No, you haven't repented! You say that, that - I'm going to turn you over to them, too." Because he was plenty mad. He still doesn't know that all these things are the work of this bastard - 'What are you doing? Quit it!'[1] - that it's all from this, this vizier. He says, "It must be the king's fault!"

H.162   This dear boy, then, he dismissed her (the horse). He - then, some hair from the horse - the horse said, she pulled out some of her hair, and gave it to the boy. She said, "If ever you get into a tight spot, burn my hair, and I'll be there immediately." Yeah. [M2 screams at children playing noisily in the yard: Curse your fathers, you donkey-cunts! . . .] (AdI and MM look at each other

---

[1] AdI addresses the vizier rhetorically.

in alarm) My little boy was so scared - look how she scared him! Dust on her head - yeah![1] -- Then, after that, he dismissed her.

H.163   He came, to his old [sic] woman's house. Then some more days passed, and again this bastard came to the door of the compound. He looked again. He went back and started complaining, saying, "Do this with him. Send him after - now say, ask him, say this: 'All my children have gotten this "painful disease".[2] This - what the devil[3] is it? I forget. They caught this. This "painful disease". It's shown up in them, and my whole household has become one big "porridge".[4]'" Then he said, "'You have to bring lions' milk, in a lion's skin, on a lion's back,[5] to give them, so they can get well. Now, brother-in-law, God will accomplish it, trust in God, you're a hero, you'll have to manage this.' This next time we'll send him to the lions and leopards, and they'll tear him apart." Watch this. This, - hm - this bastard left.

H.164   Morning came again, and he summoned the poor guy again, and he came again, and he told him that, and again this poor guy was throwing himself to earth and heaven, but he said, "No, there's no way out, you have to."

H.165   He came back to his wives, and this princess reproached him and spoke to him, and said things. And this one spoke up again and said, - then, this *parī* spoke up. She said, said, "This is easy."

H.166   He said, "They'll tear off my head! You said the *dīv*s were easy. If these lions and leopards see me, they'll tear me apart."

H.167   She said, "No, they won't. May God not do it. What are lions and leopards?" She said, "For you it will be easy. There's this mother lion. It's been many years, that there's this reed, like this, stuck through her paw, coming out the top of her paw, out the back of her paw. And it's grown up to the sky. She's lying there lame. She has a number of children. It's been several years that she hasn't been able to get around, and she's lying there night and day, with that reed stuck through her paw, and grown up to the sky. She's just there. You find a sharp saw and do this - you go there by yourself. There's this jungle.

---

[1] Adī voices disapproval of MZ's violent outburst.

[2] /maraz-e āzār/, sometime glossed as tuberculosis.

[3] Lit. 'what death'.

[4] /kāčī/, a pablum given to pregnant women and baby chicks.

[5] A complex word play: /šīr-e šeyr, be post-e šeyr, be pošt-e šeyr/.

H.168   (Aside) There, there's this baby's pacifier - this baby,
it's frightening enough to make talk[1]. This child absolutely
can't stand it without a pacifier. They kept this pacifier all
night and he cried till morning, and till night. There's the
child, and his father says, Mesterī says,[2] "Don't put that pacifier in his mouth." He wasn't raised at his mother's breast, he
had powdered milk. And this pacifier. Now it's like the child is
addicted to it. From morning till night it doesn't leave his
mouth. And from evening till morning. If it isn't there, he
cries till morning. Yeah. And his father says, "Don't do it,
he's big now, don't give it to him." So finally by lunch time he's
cried so much that she goes and takes his cousin's pacifier and
puts it in his mouth for a while, then his cousin's mother gets
upset and makes a big fuss and says it's unfair.[3] So I finally
decided "Go on, when his youngest uncle comes, I'll get some
money from his soldier's salary, from his other uncle, I'll pay
for it. So I got this. Then I tied it (the money) in my skirt,
I said, "It will get lost," --

H.169   So from here, when she did that - This one said, "You (go)
to this - there's this jun-n-ngle, so big it hasn't any head or
foot. And there's every sort of creature in that jungle. Lions,
leopards, wolves, foxes, these - jackals, everything. They're
all together in that jungle. They're way off, in there, and they
all go off by themselves till midday, till noon. Just this one
lion with the foot, that's lame. She stays there. When she's
left there, you go, from under -- she'll go to sleep, and you go
and dig a tunnel up un-n-nder her foot, dig, dig, dig, till you
get to that reed. Then cover the top of it[4] well, then do this -
from - then saw the reed off at the ground. She'll be asleep,
she won't know you're there. So you saw it off like that, saw it
off away from the bottom of her paw. Then back out again, this -
by God, from the back of her paw, as it's grown, out of the back
of her paw, and up to the sky, saw it off. Come back and get into
your hiding place, and cover yourself well. Then all at once, from
under, give it a knock, like this, and it will come out of her paw.
When it comes out of her paw, you'll be in your hiding place, and
she'll let out a screech, loud enough to reach the angels. Everything that flies or crawls will come when she screeches, back into
this jungle. When they come there, when she comes to again, -
she'll faint, and when she comes to again, she'll call out, 'Whatever manner of creature you are, you've done me this kindness,
and freed me from this affliction. Whatever object you have, show
yourself and I'll grant it.' Don't you come out until she swears

---

[1] /az tars goftogū mišah/: tentative translation.

[2] Adī's eldest son, a truck mechanic, married to MZ's half sister.

[3] The two women are sisters, married to brothers, living in the same
household.

[4] The tunnel.

you an oath. Every kind of creature there is, lions, leopards, wolves, foxes, everything will come there. They'll come there. If she doesn't swear you an oath, don't come out. They'll eat you. Once she's sworn to you, you can come out."

H.170   He said, "All right."

H.171   So then he came, and came, came, came, came, and he arrived [1] at this jungle. He came to this jungle, dear sister that you are, like that, then he listened, until it was well toward noon, toward midday. They all went off. On account of their stomachs, they went off to (fill) them. So when everything got peaceful, he came up behind this lion's head, and saw how she was, and dug the tunnel and got down and qui-i-etly cut it off above her paw, so, so – with the saw, without touching her paw. He got down in his hiding place and hit it, so she screeched like that, and every crawling and flying thing came there, together. When a good while had passed, she came to. [BREAK]

H.172   So later, when she came to, she called out. She called out, "Whatever manner of creature you are, who did this kindness for my sake, whatever object you have, I'll grant it. Come out. Show yourself to me."

H.173   He, he didn't move. He didn't move at all. He didn't say a thing. She called again. A third time. She called a third time, and finally she said, "By the left- hand idol of [sic] King Solomon the Prophet, whatever object you have, I'll grant it."

H.174   This boy didn't say a thing. Again she called out, "By the right-hand idol of King Solomon the Prophet, whatever object you have, I'll grant it, for you did this kindness for my sake. As long as I live, I'm a slave of yours with a ring in my ear.[2] For the kindness you did me." After that the boy came out.

H.175   He said, "I have this petition, there's this king, and I'm his subject. He gave this order, that, 'All these members of my household have caught the "little fire",[3] and a lion must -- people did this, they diagnosed that if lion's milk is brought in a lion's skin on a lion's back, for my relatives to drink, and so on, they, they'll be well. That was their diagnosis for me.' So he ordered, and I'm his subject, and I wasn't strong enough - he said, 'You have to bring it, or you'll be killed.' So I came like this, trusting in God, along this way."

---

[1] /keh to dārī/ lit. 'that you have' - she makes this grammatical error persistently in this set phrase, in place of تو داری ‎

[2] A single hoop earring worn in one ear is a traditional mark of slavery, a common image in classical poetry and elsewhere.

[3] /atešak/, see note 2,p. 267.

H.176   Then she sat down and called her children. She said, "Which shall I kill?"

H.177   This child spoke up, and said, "Kill whichever one you want, here we are."

H.178   So she took one of her children, and slaughtered him right there. Look. She just took one of her own children, look at that, they're (just) animals, things like that, but they don't cast their mother down. They didn't say, "We, we - don't give any of us, or kill us." She just took one of her children, and slaughtered him. Right away she skinned him, and took her breasts and milked, milked, milked, milked them into the skin, and filled it. She put it on the back of another one of her children. She sent him in front, saying, "Carry it." She gave him her hair, too. She said, "If ever you get into a tight spot, I'll be there with my children. As long as I live, I'm your servant, for you did me this kindness, about my paw." He and - [END OF TAPE]

E3B

H.179   So then, this one just - then he brought it back, he brought it to the court, and with a push - he said, tog- (stutters) - "Whoever gets in front of you, tear off their heads, eat them." So the - they all - this lion - there's these people, and whoever gets in front of him, he eats them, and this milk is in the lion's skin, and on his back, and the chain around his neck is in this - boy's hand. He brought it. He brought him to a stop there. In front of him.

H.180   He said, "There. Here's a lion, and here's the milk, on his back, right here."

H.181   This king sat with his hand over his mouth.[1] So anyway, he took the skin down off his back, and he said, about the lion, "Dismiss him. I don't need him." So this boy comes, and this lion cub gave him some of his hair and he dismissed him and he left, and came back to his wives.

H.182   Then what? So then ten days or a month passed, and the vizier, again, he came to the door of the compound, and he got heated up again. He came before the king again, and he said, "Bastard, curses on your father, what can I do? It's this way, if I send him to - anywhere, he comes back!"

H.183   He said, "No, send him after the flowers of Laughing Flower." Yeah. "Say this, 'I want flowers from you, from the flowers of Laughing Flower. She's - i-----, - in a mine of $d\bar{\imath}vs$ and $par\bar{\imath}s$. This time he'll go and he won't come back from there."

---

[1] A gesture of amazement or shock.

H.184   Morning came again, and he came and asked for him and he told him that, and again he came back to his wives with his head hanging. Then this wife - this *parī* spoke up, and said, "That's an easy task, don't be upset!"

H.185   He said, "What's easy about it?"

H.186   She said, "It's like this. You go, and say, 'I want forty camels from you.' All forty of them must be loaded with *ḡolūr*,[1] because you'll come to these ants, and every ant is a *dīv*. When you get to the ants, when you get near them, make a hole in one corner of one of the sacks, on one camel, and it will spill out slowly, and the ants will get busy with that, ti-i-ill all forty of your sacks are empty. Then you'll come - after you finish with the ants, you'll come to a lot of lions and leopards and wolves. They'll come and try to get you. They'll be all along the road. Slaughter a camel, and throw it down, and go, and pass by. And whatever comes along, it will get busy with the carcass. You go by, and go on, till these - all these forty camels are finished, and you'll finish with them, too.

H.187   "You'll come to a place where this girl, now - once a week this girl - there's this, this great river[2], and she comes, and she has forty companions, ladies-in-waiting. Right - just when morning comes, - she's the daughter of the king of *parīs*. This Laughing Flower. So just when morning comes, then, this *parī* comes flying to the river, and bathes and goes. Then toward afternoon, she comes back with her forty ladies-in-waiting. Yeah. There's an old woman there, and after she's swum a lot, she won't hold an audience or speak in private or do anything till she goes to see that old woman, she likes her so much. And she has a little house by the river, and this old woman is in her little house, and after she's swum and come out of the water and put on her clothes, and her waiting women are with her, she goes to see this old woman. Now you get a place in that house, with the old woman. Then you gather the flowers when she laughs, in the water, and flowers fall from her mouth. You get them. Keep them safe. We - (stutters) - from this - and you stay with this old woman."

H.188   He said, "All right."

H.189   He came, when it was morning, and came before the king, and (said), like that, "Forty camels and forty camel-loads of *ḡolūr*.

H.190   He said, "Very well." The king said it right away. Right away he arranged it and had it ready.

---

[1] A grain dish which is made of cracked wheat boiled in milk, dried, then boiled again. The dried wheat before the second boiling is also called *ḡolūr*.

[2] /derīyā/.

H.191   And he came and got his food for the journey ready, food and
drink for himself. This poor guy. He set out on the road, and
his three wives stayed there in the compound. He came, came, came,
and came to the ants.

H.192   He came to the ants, and made a hole in the corner of one sack.
The sa - by the time he finished the forty sacks, the ants were
finished, too. Then he slaughtered the camels and threw them down,
till the forty camels were finished, and this danger was over, too.
He went, till he came to the old woman's place. He called out to
the old woman, still mounted on his house, "Eh, old woman, don't
you want a guest?"

H.193   The old woman laughed and said, "How could I not want a guest?
A guest is the friend of God." Then she came out, and took his
horse's bridle and the boy dismounted and she tethered his horse,
the old woman, and she brought him into her house.

H.194   So there she made tea and fixed a water pipe for him, and gave
it to him, and he sat down and asked, "You're just one woman. What
are you doing by this river, out here in the desert?"

H.195   She said, "That's just how it is for me." She said, "I'm just
a person, here. I just landed here, and I stayed."

H.196   So then he asked, like that, and she said, "It's like this,
with me." So it's like now, it's Wednesday night, and the next
evening will be Thursday night, and on Friday she's coming to
bathe.[1] So this evening passed, and the next day came, and the
next evening, and following day came, Friday, and this boy told
the old woman his heart's troubles, "Thus, and thus, and thus."

H.197   She said, "Fine, don't you worry. Before you can say, 'Lord!',
there'll be miles and miles of flowers, and by the time she's
laughed ten times, all the flowers you want will come down, before
she leaves."

H.198   He said, "Fine."

H.199   Now from here, dear sister that you are, then, it was early
Friday morning, that day. They came, and came, one after the
other, these pigeons. They come, and roll over,[2] and they swim,
and jump around, and all. So then, at the end this girl came, she
came. She came, and undressed, and put her clothes beside the
river, and she's laughing with these forty ladies in waiting, and

---

[1] Morning bathing before communal prayer on Fridays ensures one's ritual
cleanliness.

[2] Shape-changing *parīs* assume their anthropomorphic or other forms simply
by rolling over.

the river carries the flowers along. He went, then. Without a sound he picked up her clothes and secured them. He got them, saying, "It would be unmanly of me, after I've experienced all this fear and terror, if I just take flowers from here, and don't take her, too. My manl- my - is this manly of me, or what? Whatever heroic deeds I've done, all the *dīv*-infested places I've gone, for good and ill, God has delivered me, and I've been successful."

H.200   Now he snuck around, and snuck around, and got this girl's clothes. He got them. Once he had her clothes, she swam, and swam, and her forty ladies-in-waiting got out of the water, one by one, and put on their clothes, and she stayed. It got to be her turn, and when she came, no matter how they look around, they can't find her clothes. And the fish [*sic*] have already gotten her annoyed, and she's hollering, this girl, that "Whatever manner of creature you are, deliver my (clothes), and whatever object you have, I'll grant it." The boy didn't give her her clothes, and finally she swore an oath.

H.201   After she swore the oath, he gave her her clothes. When she'd put them on, she went to the house to see the old woman, and she asked her, "All right, where was this boy of yours until now?"

H.202   She said, "Until now he was off at my institute [*sic*][1], - he was off in some other countries and - that's all. This time it was just the will of God. He came along, inquiring, inquiring, inquiring, till he struck my trail. May I be his sacrifice, may I be a sacrifice for this grandson of mine. Just look how many years it's been, that I haven't seen him and he hasn't seen me, now. And now he's done this."

H.203   Well, then. Later on - they're just there. Then she dismisses her ladies-in-waiting - and she's sworn to this boy - and after that she stayed with the boy and when it got to be evening prayer time, that boy burned some *dīv* hair and the *dīv*s arrived. Then this servant (took) them both with this platform - with this gilded platform,[2] that the girl had at home, and these golden birds, and everything this girl had, he picked them all up, and, "Oh, Lord of the Lands!"[3] He came.

H.204   He came, and arrived at his own house. And the day after the next was going to be the fortieth day, and the morning came. He said to this girl, "Laugh, then!" So she laughed, and she filled

---

[1] The old woman pretends that the boy is her grandson, who has been away travelling or studying.

[2] Another form of aerial transport favored by *parī*, in addition to pigeon-disguises.

[3] An invocation of Hazrat 'Alī, used for beginning journeys.

as many platters as she could. Then he took them and put them in front of this king.

H.205   When he put them in front of the king, then, this bastard vizier (said), "Oh, Lord, now, what does it take to kill him? What do I do now, to manage his death?"

H.206   So he brought these in the morning, and it's evening, about this time of the evening, now - and up to now there've been five platforms · ·set up, and now there are six - four wives. And again, he couldn't stand it, this bastard, and he came, and looked in at the door, and she's laughing and flowers are falling from her mouth. Eeeee! (claps once) He takes off running and hollering, and starts banging on the door (of the palace) with a rock, enough to bang it to pieces, and saying, "Right! Your throne and your fortune -" he throws his hat on the ground - [general audience laughter throughout this scene] - cursing this king - "You said, 'Bring flowers,' and he brought the girl herself! He brought her! You go and look!"

H.207   He said, "Bastard, what can I do? God gave her to him. Can I quarrel with God? Whatev— You can see that it's like this - I sent (him to) the lions, and he came back. I sent him to the $d\bar{\imath}vs$, and he came back. I told him to bring the Horse of Forty Colts, and he brought her, and I put unimaginable tasks on his head. If God gave it to him, what can I do?"

H.208   He said, "No. This time, it won't be like that. This time, tell him, 'Go and get me news of my father's mother, how she is' - " [Laughter. MZ: What a wonderful story! It's a wonderful story -] Yeah . . . Now watch this. [Laughter and inaudible comments] To see how they are. In Hell. To Heaven to see what they're doing, and what, what changes there are. OK. [MZ: He's doing very well, Margaret!]

H.209   Now you watch this. He called him again, this poor, out-of-luck guy. So he came, and "It's this kind of a job."

H.210   He said, "All right. For God's sake, how can I go and get news from that world?" 'He's kept to this earth, and now he wants to start with the underworld?'

H.211   He said, "No, you have to bring it." Yeah. "You're brave, you're this, you're that-"

H.212   When he came back from there to his wives, now - up to now there was one $par\bar{\imath}$, now there are two. One spoke up, and said, "There, these things are easy. Go and tell him 'Tell me your father's name and your mother's name, and those of all your courtiers' (relatives), write them down, tell me, so that I can go. If I go there, how do I know what your father's name was, or what your mother's name was, or this one's, or that one's? You must tell me.'"

H.213   Morning came, and he came and stood before the king, and petitioned him, and said, "Lord, your father's mother's name, yours and those of all your officials, whatever there are - tell me them, so I can go. If I go, how will I recognize them?"

H.214   He said, "This was my father's name, and this was my mother's name -" and so he came and told all of this to the *parī*. This *parī* just wrote letters in the style[1] of their mothers and fathers, of the officials' and courtiers' and everybody's there. Just like this, with "Prayers for your well-being," and so on.

H.215   When his forty days were complete, he picked up these letters, and came before him. He said, "Salām", and they said, "Peace," and he sat in a chair and said, "Here. Lord King, here are the letters from your father and mother. They're fine and happy, and - (stutters) better off than in this world." He passed them over to them.

H.216   They read them and said, "For the Lord's sake!"

H.217   He said, "By God, it _is_ my mother's father's handwriting. Yeah. God knows." Yeah.

H.218   "If you ask it, and these others ask it, and you ask it, I'll take you there." [Laughter] "I'll take you there, if these others ask it, because they said, 'If you bring our children, we'll be very happy.' If you ask it, too, I'll take you to see them."

H.219   They said, "Bū! How could we not want it?"

H.220   He said, "Fine." He came back and told his wife, "It's like this."

H.221   She said, "There, tell him, 'I need so many camel-loads of wood from you, and I went into a room - like this.'"

H.222   So, dear sister, he came and said, "Lord King, that is, I need thirty camels, or twenty camels, of wood" - he said - "I need that."

H.223   He said, "It's ready."

H.224   He brought it all into a room, and .filled the room with wood. After that, then, he brought all these officials - the vizier, the *wakīl*[2], the king, and all of them. He came and put them on top of the wood. And he locked the room tightly. He only opened the ceiling vent. This wi- , this wi - , these two wives of his who are *parī*s, are at the vent, one on each side. When he set fire to them, he set it from underneath, struck a match. As soon as he

---

[1] Lit. 'voice'.   [2] Agent, attorney.

struck the match, these two who were *parī*s turned into pigeons and came and lifted up their husband from the midst of it, and carried him out the ceiling vent.

H.225   Put it that he said to them, there, "I fuck your father, King, if I don't take - [MZ: Don't take -] your throne away, and set (myself on it)!" He burnt them all up. He said, "Go on, now, to your father's mother, and get the news!" [Laughter] He said, "Go on, now!" There, there, now, "Give my humble greetings to your father's mother!" [Laughter]

H.226   So then they were completely happy and trouble-free, and he just went and took the king's throne and brought his own wives and children to court and threw their wives and children out in the street. Just as God gave them their object, may God grant the people of the Prophet theirs.

H.227   That's what he did to them. Weeee - God's wrath on you, anyway, - and you started with what was on earth, sending him to the *dīv*s in their lairs, and you sent the poor guy running after the Horse of Forty Colts with her forty *dīv* colts, and she was the forty-first. He brought her. Lions, like that - you said, 'lions' milk, in a lion's skin, on a lion's back,' - [MZ: -bring it-] - this poor guy brought it - 'because my children have the "little fire".' [MZ: As a pretext.] As a pretext. So they would eat him. You said, 'A *dīv* carried off my sister,' and he brought her, too. Look at the *parī* he brought on account of those pearls [MZ: The Tree of Bells] The Tree of Bells and Cats' Claws,[1] he - he brought them, think of it, from the *dīv*s in their lairs, and all these armies and troops were *dīv*s and such. He brought it and set it before you. God's wrath be on you, then, you took all these and he went and - [MZ: This story and the story of the Horse of Forty Colts- the story of 'Alī Zarrin, are really difficult, like this.[2]]

---

[1] Adī has forgotten to tell this episode. See Text I, below.

[2] These two titles refer to one multi-episodic tale from MZ's own repertoire.

Title: <u>Afsāneh-e Garg</u> [The Tale of Mangy-Head]
Narrator: Mādar Zāher
Recorded: 2 Aug. 1975
Cassette # E1A-E1B

I.1   Some things that bear fruit,
           Some bear none,
           Cypress and poplar,
           Pomegranate[1] and quince,
           And pistachio and pomegranate
           The mouse did the (carding)[2]
           The 'mother of mice' the spinning.[3]
           The louse did the tailoring,
           The tick did the dying.
           We went to the house of Mulla 'Abbās,
           And we ate the bread and $m\bar{a}s$[4] [BREAK]
           He put us on that side,
           With a felt rug on top of a mat.[5]
           Night came, we mounted our donkey
           With our water jar behind.
           The wall fell down and our water jar broke.
           The cow gave birth, a female calf.
           (Her) bowl broke and her $m\bar{a}s$ spilled.
           Lord, Lord [that this crop (of events) came to a stop.][6]
           There we stayed.

I.2   When spring comes, the trees blossom - cypress and poplar,
        pomegranate and quince and pistachio and pomegranate and pear and
        china tree[7] and grapes and melons and <u>everything</u>.

---

[1] /nār/ for /anār/. Often /nāk/, 'pear', in other storytellers' opening
formulas.

[2] /mušleh/: tentative translation.

[3] Lit. 'spun the spindle'.

[4] 'yogurt'.

[5] Poor sleeping accommodations follow poor food: the mulla's hospitality
is comically frugal.

[6] /kāsel istād šod/ or kāseleh istād šod/: possibly   که حاصله ایستاد شد

[7] činī/- ?

I.3   There was and there was, there was a king - there should be
no greater king for me and thee than God - there was a king. This
king had one daughter. [Nāder:[1] Ehhh - water!] [MM to Nāder: Be
quiet!] Some days, some while passed and this daughter was well
grown, and people came asking for her. He was about to marry her
off. This poor king didn't know that this girl has a lover, Margaret! (snickers) [MM: (laughs) Oh - I understand.] (laughs) She
has a lover. [MM: I understand.]

I.4   When the people came asking for her, he promised her, anyway!
(smiles) The king promised her, then, and he doesn't know about
this lover, that this girl has a lover. He said, "All right."

I.5   This girl said, "All right, what am I going to do now? My father's promised and I don't want this husband. I'll run away with
this lover, then!" [MM: Yeah.]

I.6   After that some days and some while passed, and they, the ones
who'd asked for her, came, the relatives of the bridegroom and
prepared for the wedding. They prepared sheep and flour and rice
and everything - lump sugar and everything that was needed for the
wedding, and clothes and all kinds of things, because this person
is nice and young and beautiful, she's nice and young. And she
has a lover.

I.7   She said to her lover, "This (very) evening when you hear
that it's my wedding (night), then you come and wait at the foot
of my castle. At twelve or one at night I'll run away with you,
and go."

I.8   He said, "Good."

I.9   Put it that, that evening when the gi- that the princess's
wedding is taking place, there's this mangy-headed cowherd, the
king's cowherd. He went, went to his home, when it was evening
prayer time, and his grandmother said, "May you see no good fortune, you! The calf is lost!" (laughs) - 'gozleh', that's gūsāleh,
anyway![2] [MM: Yeah, OK! (laughs) Yeah, OK!] "Your calf is lost,
and now you come and sit here!"[3]

I.10   He said, "All right, where shall I go?"

I.11   She said, "Go look!"

---

[1] MZ's 3-year-old son.

[2] MZ imitates an old-fashioned, ignorant speaker's pronunciation of the
word 'calf'.

[3] Implies comic incompetence on the part of the boy, who has lost his
own calf out of the entire herd he watches.

I.12   This poor little mangy-head came and looked on this side of
the house, and that side of the house, and the other side, and
searched them all, and went and said, "I don't see it."

I.13   She said, "Death to 'I don't see it'!" His grandmother hit
him, with a stick, and threw him out of the house. After she threw
him out, this poor kid cried and wailed a lot - he didn't have a
mother - and he came along to the foot of the girl's castle and
threw himself down right there. He threw himself down there, but
he didn't realize the gi - that tonight was the princess's wedding.
So after that [Old female listener: Her lover hadn't come?] No,
not yet, her lover hadn't come, he didn't know - I don't know how
it happened, then. Whether he didn't understand (her), or if he
hadn't heard about the wedding, that it was happening, or if he
was coming later.

I.14   So after that he said, "All right" - it got to be night time,
and this bridegroom said, "Come, let's go to bed."

I.15   She said, "You put your head down, go to bed, I'll go and
pray, and do my duty and so on, and then I'll come to sleep."
The princess.

I.16   The bridegroom laid down his head, it was his wedding night,
and he put down his head and went to sleep, he was tired, done in,
and after that this princess - she's not sleeping, she's up - she
came and stuck her head out the castle window, and she saw there
was someone there. Lying down.

I.17   She said, "By God, my lover has come, then." (Laughs) This -
(laughs) - "to the house" - [MM: It was the cowherd?] It was this
little mangy-headed cowherd! (Laughing) She said, (laughing),
"Have you come?"

I.18   He said, "Yes, I've come."

I.19   She said, "Catch this!" (Snorts of laughter) [MM: Laughs.
Children laugh continuously] She filled these saddlebags with
jewels and gold, and she said, "Here!" He took them! She brought
a third saddlebag, and said, "Here!" He took it. After that the
princess said, "Catch --" - about herself, now! She tied a silken
rope around her waist, and lowered herself down.

I.20   She lowered herself down, and this little, bald, mangy-head
caught her. He caught her, but he didn't say a thing! He shut
up, totally silent, thinking, "If I say anything, she'll recognize
my voice, this one - maybe she won't go with me."

I.21   So then, after that, - she went with this - mangy-head. She
went to her father's string of horses and took two good, fast ones.
She took two guns, too. She came, and threw those three saddlebags
of jewels and gold on the horses and she got on one horse, and he
got on the other, and she said, "Let's go, then!"

I.22   So they came, Margaret, came, came, came, came. This princess said, "Hah? He - my poor lover doesn't <u>talk</u>!" [MM: Laughs]
"If he doesn't say anything -- if this is my father's mangy-headed
cowherd, that'll be just great!" [MM: Yeah, yeah!! (laughing)]
She saw he just shut up -- silent. So they came, came, came, they
came a long way, and she saw - she said, "By God, it's nothing
but that mangy-head!" She understood.

I.23   She came, and arrived at a - by a hay field. She saw the
green hay there and she said, "Well, now, how would it be if my
father's herd of sheep were let loose here, and the camel herder
[*sic*] were playing his flute and singing and whistling, and the
sheep were grazing?"

I.24   This mangy-head didn't say a thing. He went. They went,
went, went, went, went - [MM: Does *garg* mean *gong*, 'dumb' - because he doesn't speak?] No! He's not dumb! He just doesn't
<u>talk</u>! He's bald. [MM: Oh, he's <u>bald</u>.[1]] He's bald, yeah - mangy.
His head is that way. [MM: Oh. I understand.]

I.25   As she came and came, she saw this thing, this reed bed. She
said "Well, now! If my father's horses were here, let loose in
this reed bed, and broke them and ate them, and the grooms were
singing here, how good it would be!"

I.26   He didn't say anything, this mangy-head, <u>silent</u>! She said,
"By God, how I've peed in my father's 'flower of speech'[2], and
cursed my own father![3] What have I done, with this little mangy-
head!?" -- This mangy one doesn't say anything! [Suppressed
laughter] He went.

I.27   He went, went, went, went, went. She saw - what was it,
there? Yeah - oh - she saw this - m - green field. Full of hay!
She said, "Well, now! How would it be if my father's camels were
let loose here, and the camel herders were 'striking' the (   )[4]
and they had the bells around their necks and they herded them

---

[1] /kal/, in Herati and standard Persian, 'bald as a result of a skin
disease'. /Garg/, 'mangy', usually applied to animals, was a new word
for MM on hearing this performance.

[2] /gol-harf/ met. 'mouth'. This form of scatalogical obscenity is char-
acteristically used by women, rather than men.

[3] I.e. brought curses on him by disgracing him.

[4] /ǧambūr/ (word unidentified in any dictionary so far)
- probably a musical instrument. *Zadan* 'to strike', is colloquially
used with all musical instruments, including wind instruments.

here! (They planted their staffs.)"(Partly inaudible phrase).

I.28   This mangy-head didn't say anything. So they went and went and went, and she saw a meadow. There was a meadow there, a good, green meadow. She said, "Well, now! What a green meadow! How would it be if my father's cows were let loose here, and that little mangy-headed cowherd were here - m - singing!"

I.29   He said, "Au - au - hūš! Tš! Tš![1]" (claps) (laughs) This mangy-head, from up on the horse, he said, "Eh - au - au - hūš! Baš! Baš! Baš! Baš!" [General laughter]

I.30   She said, "For the Lord's sake! How I've cursed my father! What have I done - I gave up that youth![2] Well, to dust! If this lover of mine, that - this husband of mine, that my father gave me, he was fine, too - what have I done?" [MM: giggles] "I came with this mangy-head, what have I done! I've cursed my father!" So she's cursing herself, and in her cursing, she said - then she said, "Well, thanks be to God, then. Thou'st made him my fortune, Thou."

I.31   After that she came, came, came and arrived at a river. When she arrived at this river, she said, "Get down, then - le- let's drink a copper's worth of tea!" (Laughing) This princess said that.

I.32   He got down, this - she said, "First bring the scrubbing brick[3], so I can wash your head in this stream."

I.33   He went and brought the scrubbing brick, and this princess [saw] there are pearls in the water, and the water is rolling them and they go along. The - pearls! They're valuable jewels, pearls. [MM: Mmm! Yes!] She said, "Get down, and pick up a few of those pearls, then after that I'll wash your head."

I.34   The mangy-head got down, and the pe - the water rolled the pearls along and he got them, and it rolled them and he got them, till he filled up a saddle bag, full! [X, MZ's husband, enters and sits down: Well, now!]

I.35   After that the princess picked up the scrubbing brick, and scrubbed, and scrubbed his head, and rinsed it in the water, and scrubbed and rinsed and scrubbed - [X interrupts: That chocolate cake - MM: Yeah? Oh -] [BREAK IN RECORDING]

I.36   Then after that she washed him, clean. And those jewels just

---

[1] Auditory command used to herd cows.

[2] Her intended husband.

[3] خشت پارچه

went by. After that they cooked their food there and ate. They
ate bread and tea, those two, and night turned to morning, and
they set out. They came and came and came, and they went past
this one city, and arrived at another.

I.37   Here the princess said to this mangy-head, "Now, you should
hide me in this ruin, put (me here) along with all these jewels
and gold, and you go and find an old, run-down house, and buy it."
[MM: Mm.] "Then you come back and take me (there). You take this
sack of 100 tomān.[1]"

I.38   She gave him a sack of 100 tomān and the mangy-head went and
walked around and around, and found a house in this city. He
bought the house, then, and he came and got the princess and took
her to the house. Once he got her there, she gave him more money
and he went and bought pots and bowls and floor coverings and
dishes and everything you need for a house, this mangy-head, then.
He goes every day, and buys a bit of food,[2] or something, and
comes back in the evening.

I.39   This one day, when some days had passed, this mangy-head
said, "Take some of those jewels and fill this tray, and give it
to me, to take to the king. Some of those pearls." [MM: Hmm.]

I.40   This Princess said, "You're a mangy bald-head, a poor thing,
down-trodden, don't you get your ass mixed up with the king's!
(Semi-audible) (I don't like this kind of business)."

I.41   He said, "No, you're a woman, you're foolish, you don't understand!" (Smiles) "M - uh - fill the tray, and give it to me so I
can take it." [Children fuss. MM whispers: Be quiet.] The tray -
she filled it and put a cover over it and gave it to the mangy-head.

I.42   So the mangy-head came into the king's presence, and gave his
greetings, and they took the tray from him, and the king got extremely happy and pleased, and his vizier of the right hand was
very clever and knowing, and he said, "Hah? This mangy bald-head,
with pearls like this? Where did he bring them from?"

I.43   After that the king got very friendly with him, and took the
pearls to his harem, and as soon as his wives saw these pearls and
costly jewels, one says, "Give me this much," and another says,
"Give me this much," all of them. Everyone got a share, got a portion.

I.44   When he went, when the - mangy-head went out, drank his tea

---

[1] Iranian unit of currency, now worth approx. $.14, formerly worth much
more?

[2] Lit. 'bread and water'.

and went out, this vizier went out, (too). When he went out, he came right along, tailing him. When the mangy-head went into his compound and shut the door, the vizier stopped behind the door. As he stood there, he saw there's a woman who's so beautiful that a hand on her face ( ).[1] He came. He came, and said to the king, "King?"

I.45   "What?"

I.46   "Eh, death! The majesty's not yours, it's the mangy-head's! He has a woman who glows like the moon!"

I.47   "Oh, Bastard! What can I do? God gave her to him."

I.48   He said, "God didn't give him anything. Now tomorrow or the next day, when a couple of days have passed, now, you send soldiers after him, and say, 'My children are fighting over those pearls,[2] bring me a few more.' Surely he'll go and get lost, and he won't come back. Then you take his wife."

I.49   He said, "All right."

I.50   When a few days had passed, he told the soldiers, "Go to the house of this person."

I.51   The soldiers came and knocked, and his wife came and said, "Who's there?"

I.52   "It's I, now, his Majesty the King wants this - m -" ' well, he was called 'Mangy-Head'. [MM: Mm.] "He sent for the mangy-head."

I.53   When she went, she said, "Didn't I tell you, 'Don't mix your ass up with the king's'? You, a poor mangy-head? Now go, he wants something else from you."

I.54   He came. When he'd come, he gave his greetings and sat down there, and they brought tea, and he said, "Now you've done a good deed, to bring those pearls, for they were fine, valuable jewels, and we didn't have any, but now my children are fighting. They fight all <u>night</u>! One says, 'I didn't get enough,' and another says 'I didn't get enough.' Now if you'd do one thing; Could you bring a few more of them?"

I.55   He said, "All right."

---

[1] /be zamīn/ or /be oz (h)amīn dār ǧol mīxāst/ - ?

[2] Children, rather than wives, because privacy demands that the women in a household not be mentioned.

I.56   He came back to his house, and sat down all grief-stricken, and his wife said, "What was it?"

I.57   He said, "Nothing, only he said, 'Bring me more of those pearls.'"

I.58   "Didn't I tell you? Not to get your ass mixed up with the king's? Now see what he's done."

I.59   "Well, I'm going, anyway."

I.60   So after he'd slept that night, the next morning this poor mangy-head got up and set out, then, on the road by which he'd come. He untied his horse and mounted, and came.

I.61   He came and came and came and came, came, came by night and came by day, and came by night and came by day, and he <u>arrived</u> at that stream. He got down there. He got down there, and saw those pearls in the water - the water rolls them along and they go. He said, "Ah - hah? I should leave these pearls, and follow them back and see where the water brings them from." [MM: Hmm.] God called[1] to that mangy-head, then.

I.62   As he came, and came, he just followed the water, he came and came alongside the stream. [BREAK for battery check] I should start from right there by the stream, shouldn't I? He came, then, and he saw that the water was rolling these pearls along, and they're coming. He came and the pearls were coming, rolling, and he said, "So now where am I going?" Then as he came, and came, he saw there was a palace there. It reached from earth to Heaven. He said, "Now, then," he remembered his God, and said, "How am I going to get up into that? Come on, then, I'll dig myself a tunnel under it." He saw there was just this much of a hole, and the water is coming out of it, and these pearls are in that water. After that he dug the ground and scraped it out[2] and dug and scraped and dug and scraped and he saw there was a garden there. And there's this *dīv* in the garden. He covered his hole, then. He covered the hole, and he dug himself a hiding place[3] there, dug and dug and dug, and got down in the hole, and covered it over himself. He covered it well, with just one little bit the size of a pea left open, for one of his eyes. He watches to see what's coming.

I.63   After that, when it got to be almost evening, he saw one - it

---

[1] /daraüld/: from درافيرن

[2] /kabš kard/ ; apparently, to scrape loose dirt out of a tunnel as one digs. Not in Steingass, Haim or Fikrat dictionaries.

[3] /korg/, a pit blind, used for hunting.

got dark, the whole world got dark, and something came down like a cannonball. He came down and started to recite a spell. He sang and this mangy-head sang to himself, down in this hole, and he sang and the mangy-head sang to himself, in his hole. And he saw a door open. The lock opened, when he'd sung. After that he started reciting spells again, and with that singing, the door shut.

I.64   Morning came. This *dīv* started reciting spells again, and sang, and sang, and the door opened, and he went out, and sang, and sang, and the door shut. He took flight, and left. So then, this *dīv* - this mangy-head came out. The mangy-head came out, and he'd <u>sung</u> this spell to himself from night until morning, to himself, and he'd <u>learned</u> it. <u>He</u> started to sing. When he started to sing, and he sang and (caught his breath)[1] ⌐⌐. and sang and caught his breath, and all at once the door opened. When the door opened, he went inside, then he started to sing again. When he sang that one spell, the door shut.

I.65   When he went in, he saw the same stream there, and there's a *parī* with her head cut off. She's lying beside the stream. Her blood is dripping, drop by drop, and turning into pearls, and the water makes them roll along. [MM: Yeah.] So then he just sat down, there. He said, "Oh, Lord! It's so red!" [MM: Hmm!] He said, "Now the *dīv* will be coming," then he went and dug himself another tunnel -- hole, dug and dug and <u>dug</u> it well, and got down in it. He covered himself over again, and left a little bitty hole like that. And <u>all</u> at once he saw that he'd come.

I.66   He came and started reciting spells and picked up her neck - her head, and washed off the blood in the stream and put it on her body. On her neck. He started singing. When he started to sing, she sneezed, and sat up, got up and sat. So then he - said,

I.67   "Pah! Pah! A human smell!
        If a horse comes here, it casts its shoe,
        If a bird comes here, it casts its plume,
        What is a human being doing here?"

I.68   She said, "First thing in the morning you <u>killed</u> me! Off you went, and now you've come back, and brought me back to life. What would a human being be doing here?"

I.69   The *dīv* said, "OK, she's ri - she's right, this place scrapes the sky, and keeps her safe inside this garden, where would he be? It must be that I was around humans, and I'm still remembering that." He didn't say any more. Morning came, and this *dīv* left. When the *dīv* had gone, (right after) he disappeared, this mangy-head came out of his hole.

---

[1] /čuf kardah/ ; yet another uncorroborated translation. /čuf/ probably means a sharp intake of breath.

I.70 He came out and went and (took) her little head – God of Repentence,[1] I forgot! In the morning when the *dīv* was about to go, he cut off her head. He cut off her head, and laid her down with her neck by the stream again. He went.

I.71 This mangy-head had <u>sung</u> that spell from the night before to himself, anyway, and <u>learned</u> it. He came, and (took) her little head to the stream and her neck, and washed it and put it back on her body, and started to recite the spell. As he sang, and sang, all at once this *part* sneezed and sat up. She said – first she started to laugh, then she started to weep. He said, "What was your laughter for, and what was your weeping for?"

I.72 She said, "My laughter was for this, that I saw a human. My weeping was for this, that 'Woe for your youth, for when the *dīv* comes , he'll eat you.'"

I.73 He said, "My blood is no redder than yours.[2] It doesn't matter if he eats me."

I.74 After that he stayed there till evening. Then she said, "All right, now what are you going to do?"

I.75 He said, "Nothing. Tonight, when he comes, and you're laughing and talking with him, you tell him this: 'When you kill me like this, and go, what if you don't come back? Somewhere far away, you'll meet your fate, and I'll just be here, dead, with my head cut off.'"

I.76 (Pause)

I.77 She said, "Fine." The *part* said "Fine." He – It got close to evening prayer time and this mangy-head picked her up and cut off her head and laid her down with her neck near the stream, and went <u>back</u> into his hole. He went there and covered himself over, and hid, and just kept a little hole open.

I.78 He came. He came, and her hea – washed her neck and put it onto her body and sang and sang and sang, sang and she sneezed and sat up. He said,

I.79 "Pah! Pah! A human smell!
   If a horse comes, it casts its shoe,
   If a bird comes, it casts its plume,
   What is a human being doing here?"

---

[1] Standard expression for forgetfulness.

[2] This entire verbal exchange, from I.71, is a fixed-phrase formula.

I.80   She said, "You kill me in the morning and revive me at night. Where is the human being here? Where am I going to find a human, and me dead?"

I.81   He said, "She's right, then."

I.82   After that, night came, and they ate, and this *parī* was sitting on his shoul- on the *dīv*'s knee, and talking and laughing, and they're fooling around. All at once she said, "All right. It's been years since you got me from the foot of Mt. Qāf[1], and God made it my fate – I took flight and came here, to look around, and you caught me and imprisoned me here – and if only I were imprisoned <u>alive</u>! In the morning you cut off my head, and leave, and you come at evening prayer, and bring me back to life. Well, what if you went, like that, and didn't come back? Then I'd just be dead, like that."

I.83   He just hauled back, this *dīv*, just as he got angry, like that, he just picked up and <u>hit</u> this *parī* on the face. Her head spun around backwards.[2]

I.84   After a little while, his heart burned, and he hit her on the other cheek, and her face went back where it belonged.

I.85   He said, "You say it's that easy for this (to happen) to me? Killing me isn't like that – I <u>won't</u> die."

I.86   She said, "Well, how <u>will</u> you die?"

I.87   He said, "It's nothing – there's an archway in this very garden. If a person opens that doorway, there's a room. If <u>anyone</u> <u>plasters</u> that room, my life is renewed. Inside this room there's another arch. Under that arch there's a well. In the well there's a pigeon. The glass of my life is in the crop of that pigeon. If anyone takes 100 *man* of flour, and makes dough, and throws it into that well, this pigeon – the well will foam up, and boil, and the pigeon will come up." [MM: Hm!] "If he's quick, and catches it, and takes out the glass of my life, and breaks it, I'll die. If not, and the pigeon goes back down into the well, then I'm still alive." [MM: Hm!]

I.88   So then, the next day the girl said, "If you're like this, then, tomorrow you mustn't kill me, so I can plaster the room and your life can be renewed."

I.89   He said, "It isn't necessary! You'll get tired."

---

[1] The mountain which marks the border of the supernatural world, separating it from the human world.

[2] This event is a commonplace. Cf. G.93.

I.90   She said, "No, by God, you mustn't kill me!"

I.91   He didn't kill her, then, this _dīv_. He didn't kill her, then,
and this - guy - came out. The - this little mangy-head came out
and the girl said, "This is what he said. He said, 'If you plaster
this room, however much you plaster, my life will be renewed, and
this - inside this room, there's an arch, and under the arch,
there's a well, and in the well there's a pigeon, and the glass of
my life is in the pigeon's crop. Now if anyone makes 100 _man_ of
flour into dough, and throws it in this well, the well will foam
and boil up, and the pigeon will come up. If he catches it, and
kills it and takes the glass of my life out of its crop, I'll die,
I'll be broken. If not, and it goes back down, then I'll live.'"

I.92   Then th - they prepared mud and they plastered the room, with
lots of playing and fooling around, and left just a little (to do).
She said, "Bu-- so he won't kill me tomorrow, again! Then we can
finish the room, and make the dough, too, to throw it in the well
so we can get the pigeon."

I.93   So they left that (little bit)[1], and her hands and feet are
all covered with mud, and - it got to be near evening prayer time
and this mangy-head went and hid in his hole, then. The _dīv_ came.
The _dīv_ came, and this girl's hands and feet and clothes were all
full of mud and the _dīv_'s heart burned (for her) and she smiled
and (kissed him)[2] and this _dīv_ jumped for joy.[3] He said, "You've
gotten tired."

I.94   She said, "No, I haven't." She (changed)[4] her clothes, this
parī, and washed her hands and feet, and went, then. She went,
then, and evening became morning, and that day the _dīv_ said, "I'm
not going to kill you any more, myself. I'll just go, like this, to
look around, in the morning, and I won't kill you any more." His
heart burned for her, because "You plastered the room." He
doesn't realize that she's going to kill him, then. [MM: Yes, yes.]

I.95   Morning came, and they hurriedly made the mud (plaster) and
that was finished, then they made all that flour into dough and
threw it in the well, and made dough and threw it in, [MM: Three
xarwār?[5] How much was it?] Dough. [MM: No - three _xarwār_. Was

---

[1] /pīrar/ - ?

[2] Partly inaudible.

[3] /bupond/ - ? (usually used for animals frisking about).

[4] /aleš kard/ - ?

[5] MM tries to elicit the quantity of flour involved from MZ, creates confusion. 1 _xarwār_ = 100 _man_. _xarwār_, lit. "donkey loads",   خَروار

it more? What was it? How much was it?] Mmm - [MM: It doesn't
make any difference, let it go -] This well? There's this well,
under the arch, and - [MM: Yeah, I understand, I understand -]
Then when they opened the top of this well - [MM: Yes -] They
made this 100 *man* of flour into dough, and threw it into the well,
and made dough, and threw it in, and this well - got full. Once it
got full, foam and blood [*sic*] rose and it boiled up. It boils up
like a pot of milk. It came up, and this mangy-head, then, he
was in ambush. He was in ambush, and the moment the pigeon came
up, the mangy-head got it. After he got it, he gave its head a
turn with his hand, and tore it off. After he twisted its head and
tore it off, he tore open its crop with his nails and got the glass.
The *dīv* arrived.

I.96   As he arrived, he said, "Human, stay your hand! Whatever goal
or object you have, I'll accomplish it."

I.97   This *parī* said, "Break it!" He hit it on a rock, and broke
it and the *dīv* fell down. He fell, then, and died, his corpse
just fell out of the air.

I.98   He'd given him forty days' grace, the king. So there, with
that *parī*, playing and fooling around, he forgot! (Claps once)
All of a sudden, it came back to him. He said, "For God's sake!
This evening is the thirty-ninth! The king will declare my wife
single!' He sat down to think.

I.99   When he sat down to think, the *parī* said, "What are you thinking about?"

I.100   He said, "Nothing, only, well, you don't know why I came here."

I.101   "Why did you come?"

I.102   "Nothing, only - they · I was this mangy-head, and I was a
king's cowherd, and then, the king's daughter had a lover and
suitors came for her and he engaged her to someone, her father.
She was going to run away with her lover. One evening, I had a
calf, and my calf got lost, and my grandmother hit me and threw me
out of the house, and I went and lay down below the king's castle
wall. It got to be midnight, and she said, 'Catch', and I caught
it. She said, 'Catch,' and I caught that. She said, 'Catch,' and
she let herself down, and I caught her.

I.103   "We got on two horses, and we came and came and came, and whatever she said, I didn't say anything, whatever she said, I didn't
say anything, and we arrived at a -- m -- er - a thing. A meadow.
She said, 'If only my father's herd of cows were loose here, and
that little mangy-headed cowherd.' I said, 'Ho, oh, būš, dūš, baš,
pāš!'[1] So this, then - we arrived.

---

[1] Auditory command for cows.

I.104   "So when we arrived beside that stream, that had the pearls in it, we got down there. She said, 'Go and bring the scrubbing brick so I can wash your head.' Then she said to me, 'Get down and pick up some of these pearls!' I got down and gathered them, and we went - we spent the night there, and (then) we went to the city of a king, and I bought a house there, and I was there, and one day I said to this woman,' Fill this tray with those pearls, and I'll take them to the king.' My wife said, 'Don't mix your ass up with the king's!' I said, 'No, you're a foolish woman, you don't understand.' I took them. After I took them to (him), when a few days had passed, he sent a soldier after me to say, 'Go and bring more!' So I got forty days' grace, (saying) 'I'll be back within forty days,' - this is the thirty-ninth."

I.105   She said, "Now, old man,[1] don't you grieve. I'll go with you."

      After they'd eaten something, she took a lot of money and precious jewels and good things from this *dīv*'s house, this *parī*. She burned some hair,[2] and a *dīv* came, and she got on this shoulder and he on the other, and she brought the valuables and he picked them up, and took flight, and went. He arrived in front of his own wife.

I.106   They spent the night there, and when morning came, he filled a tray, and went, then, to the king. When he went to the king, he said, "Have you come?"

I.107   "Yeah."

I.108   He saw the jewels, just like those others. The king said, "This came to him from God."

I.109   He drank tea there, and the mangy-head went out. The vizier, this same vizier, followed him again. He came, and when the mangy-head knocked on the door, they opened the door, this *parī* and the princess. When the mangy head went in, this *dīv* [sic] was watching as he knocked on the door. He said, "Hah? We sent him to get killed, for one - and he's brought another?"

I.110   Now when he went back, he said, "King?"

I.111   "What?"

I.112   "Eh, death! The majesty isn't yours, it's the mangy-head's!"

I.113   "Oh, you bastard, what can I do? God gave it to him."

---

[1] /bābā/ - affectionate address.

[2] Supernatural helpers are summoned by burning a bit of their hair or feathers. Cf. sīmorğ in Šāhnāmeh, and note 2, p. 393, below.

I.114   "God didn't give him a thing. Send him after – um – some – er –" –– send him after what? What does he send him after first? After – uh – first he said, "He should go after – mm – after lion's milk." [MM: Lions' milk.] Yeah. He said – [Zāher: Lions' milk, in a lion's skin, on a lion's back.] He said, "Tomorrow a soldier – when some days pass after these jewels, send a soldier after him. Say, 'My children have caught the "little fire"[1]. You must go after lions' milk, in a lion's skin tied on a lion's back, and bring it.'" Do you understand, Margaret? [MM: Mm! Yes!] That is, the milk of lions has to be inside a lion's skin. [MM: Yes, I understand.] And tied on a lion's back. "You bring it." [BREAK]

I.115   This, then – m – when some days had passed, he <u>sent</u> soldiers after him. When they knocked on the door, she said, "Who's there?"

I.116   He said, "Soldiers have come."

I.117   "What do you want?"

I.118   "I came after the mangy-head."

I.119   This wife of his just shook, poor thing. She said, "Now where will he send him?"

I.120   He came, the mangy-head, and went out and came along with the soldiers. He came, and said, "Salām," and the king said, "Peace," and they brought him tea.

I.121   He said, "All right. Lord King, what did you want?"

I.122   He said, "Nothing, only, my children have caught the 'little fire'. You must go after lions' milk, in a lion's skin, tied on a lion's back, and bring it."

I.123   He said, "All right. By my eyes. Give me forty days' grace, and I'll bring it." [MM: Hm!]

I.124   He came. When he came (back) to the house, he sat down, all grief-stricken. His wife said, "Now what did he say?"

I.125   He said, "Nothing, now, he said, 'Go and bring lions' milk, in a lion's skin, tied on a lion's back.'"

I.126   She said, "Fine. (First) he made it a $d\bar{\imath}v$, and now he's sending you into the jaws of lions and leopards and like that!"

---

[1] /ateŝak/: Fikrat glosses this as 'syphilis, venereal disease', Haim as 'mild chancre' – clearly not the meaning intended by the speaker. Native terms for disease merit separate study. See note 2, p. 267. Amīnollāh Azhar, my research assistant, described this as 'a skin disease which can cause paralysis'.

I.127   This *pari* saw that the husband and wife were talking and the mangy-head was grieving, and she said, "What's the talk?"

I.128   He said, "Nothing, now the king's said, 'Go bring lions' milk in a lion's skin, on a lion's shoulders.[1]'"

I.129   She said, "Don't grieve! This is an easy task."

I.130   He said, "What's easy about it?"

I.131   She just said, "It's easy."

I.132   He said, "It's not, either."

I.133   She said, again, "It's easy. There's this sort of a jungle -- you go, go, go, go, - there's lio<u>ness</u> in this jungle. Now it's been <u>years</u> that there's a reed stuck up through her paw. She's pinned to the spot, she can't go anywhere. You go like this ca-a-a-arefully - take a sharp saw with you, and dig in the ground, go from underground. Saw that reed off <u>above</u> her paw <u>carefully</u>, so that her paw isn't hurt. Now when you get through the reed, first she'll let out a screech, so loud the <u>angels</u> will know about it. All the lions and lepards and wolves and foxes, and - snakes, everything there is, will come. After that, she'll say, 'Whatever object or goal you have, I'll accomplish it. Come out, and speak.' You say, 'No.' Now once she's sworn by the right hand idol of the excellent Prophet Solomon,[2] you come out of your hole."

I.134   He said, "Fine."

I.135   This poor mangy-head came, then. The next day he got on his little horse, and came, like that, came by night and came by day and came by night and came by day, and arriiived at that jungle. This jungle - [BREAK]

I.136   So then he arrived at the jungle, and he walked around. When he'd looked all around, walked around, he saw, then, there's a lioness. There's a reed that's come up through the back of her paw, like that. It wasn't a <u>little</u> reed, either, it was a great, big one, like a tree. [MM: Whew!] It had come out through the top of her paw.

---

[1] /keft/ replaces /post/, reducing the density of the word-play. See note

[2] Conflates two oaths binding to supernaturals. In Muslim folk belief, Solomon is thought to have bound the *div* and *jinn* and ruled them, and to have understood the language of birds (and animals?). Solomon was not considered an idol-worshipper. This is a grammatical conflation.

I.137   So after that this poor mangy-head went over that way and dug
        into the ground, like that - and he let his horse go. He dug, and
        dug, and went down into the hole, under the ground, and he took
        his, his saw, and sawed that reed above her paw, and sawed and
        sawed, and went through the reed, so the 'tree' fell over. [MM:
        Yeah.]

I.138   When it fell - it was like a tree, the reed had sprung up and
        grown thick. God knows, if it was twelve years, or thirteen years.
        And this lion was pinned there. On account of this reed. When it
        fell over, she let out a screech like that, so that all the lions
        and leopards and wolves and - foxes and - snakes and everything
        there was, that flew or crawled, arrived when she screeched, came
        there.

I.139   When they came there, after she got over her screeching, then,
        God gave her her object. When it was over, the shock[1] of her foot,
        she said, "Whatever manner of creature or human you are, come out!
        Whatever object or goal you have, I'll accomplish it." And this
        lion has nine children.

I.140   He didn't come out. After that she said, "By the truth of the
        Excellent Prophet Solomon, I swear by the - right hand, come out.
        Whatever object you have, I'll accomplish it." He came out.

I.141   He came out, and said, "I don't have any other object, except
        this - that a king is oppressing me. He sent me, saying 'Go bring
        lions' milk in a lion's skin, tied on a lion's back.'"

I.142   She said to her children, "Which one of you will say I can
        kill you?"

I.143   One of her children said, "Kill me."

I.144   So then she skinned one of her children, and milked her breasts
        and milked, and filled it with milk. She tied up the mouth of the
        skin. Then another of her children said, "I'll carry it." She
        tied it on his back. And she gave this - mangy-head some hair[2], too.
        He went, then.

I.145   She said, "I entrust you to God."[3]

I.146   As he came and came and came, when he got near that city, he
        said to the lion, "Do you know what's going on?"

---

[1] /aulāneh/, possibly from مول /haul/ 'sudden fear, shock'.

[2] Burned, the hair (or feather) serves to summon the magical helper.

[3] Polite farewell.

I.147   "No."

I.148   "If - a horse, or a person, or a camel, or a sheep, whatever comes in front of you, get it! Tear it apart, kill it."

I.149   He said, "Fine."

I.150   So as he came along, he'd come to a person, and eat him. He'd come to a cow, and get it, come to a camel, and get it. So he arrived, and they said, "The mangy-head - he's brought lions' milk, with a lion!"

I.151   He came to the -king's place, then, he was to go to the king's court. He saw, the king saw - that he's eating this one and that one, and he said, "Oh, you bastard! Take him out, out, out!"

I.152   He said, "Bastard yourself, you sent me after lions' milk, in a lion's skin, on a lion's shoulders. So now, you send him away."

I.153   He said, (quickly, semi-audibly) "Takethislionsmilkformychildrenwithoutanymoretyrannyandsendhimaway!"

I.154   This - li - after that he got some hair from the lion's cub and let him go, the mangy-head. He says, "Go on home." This - thing left.

I.155   The vizier went, the next day. He looked in from behind the door, and he saw, ehh! There's these sitting platforms set around, with the parī on one and the woman on the other, and the mangy-head right in the middle [MM: Hm!]

I.156   He went, and said, "King?"

I.157   "What?"

I.158   "Death! The majesty isn't yours, it's the mangy-head's!"

I.159   "Bastard! What can I do, God gave it to him. I sent him to - to the dīv, and he came back. He killed the dīv. I sent him to the lions, and he came back, what can I do?"

I.160   "Nothing, just send him - uh - to do - this. To bring your sister back. From the hands of the dīv. Surely the dīv will eat him, he won't be able to bring her." [MM: Mm.]

I.161   He said, "All right." Some days, some while passed, and he sent soldiers after him. He sent soldiers after him, and this poor mangy-head trembled, (but) he came. He said, "What did you want?"

I.162   "Nothing. Have some tea."

I.163   They brought tea for him, and he drank it, and he said, "Nothing, only my sister is a prisoner in the hands of such-and-such
a *dīv*, and you must go and bring her back."

I.164   He said, "Fine, give me forty days' grace."

I.165   "Go, take forty days."

I.166   He came back. He sat down, all grief-stricken. His wife
siad, "What happened?"

I.167   "Nothing. He said, 'Go bring my sister back from the hands
of the *dīv*.'"

I.168   The *parī* said, "What's up?"

I.169   He said, "It's like this."

I.170   "Eh, old man! You're grieving? This is easy!"

I.171   He said, "Sure, it's easy! You sent me after those lions,
and my heart almost broke in that jungle!"

I.172   She said, "This is easy. You must - go, and tell him to kill
a cow and skin it sack-fashion and take forty *man* - one *xarwār*[1] of
that - lime. He should put it in the cowhide, and you take it and
go. Put it right in front of the door of his cave. When he comes,
in a cloud of dust and smoke, now, he'll see a black thing right
in front of his cave, and he'll eat it. When he eats it, like
that, his stomach will burst, he'll be blown to bits. You take
the sister, just like that."

I.173   After that he went and said, to the king, "Buy a cow and skin
it sack-fashion." He bought a cow and skinned it sack-fashion, and
he said," (Put) a *xarwār* of - lime inside it," and he put a *xarwār*
of lime in it and put it on a horse. The king gave him just forty
days' grace, and he came.

I.174   He came by night and came by day and came by night and came
by day, he came, like that, stage by stage, came night and day,
the poor guy, and he arrived on this desert plain. Once he got
there, he saw there was a cave, with a stone set (in front of it).
He moved away the stone, and he put the cow with the lime right in
front of the cave's mouth, and he went (in). He saw saː her hanging by her hair. First she began to laugh, then she began to weep.
He said, "What was your laughter for, and what was your weeping for?"

I.175   "My laughter was for this, that I saw a human being. It's
been years that I haven't seen a human. I - I'm the sister of such

[1] 100 *man* = 1 *xarwār*.

and such a king. My weeping was for this, that now the *div* will come back and eat you."

I.176   "Don't worry about the *div*."

I.177   So then it got to be about time for the *div* to come, and he got up. He went, then and -- hid. All at once he came down in a cloud of dust and smoke from the sky. He said,

I.178   "Pah! Pah! A human smell!
    If a horse comes here, it casts its shoe,
    If a bird comes here, it casts its plume,
    What is a human being doing here?"

I.179   When he came, he saw that the mouth of his cave was open, and there's a <u>black</u> thing in the doorway. And he made one gulp of it, and ate it. After he ate it, if it was ten minutes, or not, he just <u>burst</u> to bits. Each bit of him fell in a different place, it took him apart like a piece of shot.[1]

I.180   After that, he took her, the king's sister, and left. When he took her and left, the king - he got close to the city, and the talk was flying, that "Now, then, the king's sister and the little mangy-head have come." He <u>went</u> to his audience chamber.

I.181   He said, "Any - anyone who goes hunting, the spoils belong to him. Go. She belongs to you."

I.182   He brought her. That made three. That made three wives, and one morning came, and the - uh - vizier came, (peeking) from behind the door, and saw this mangy-head sitting with his three wives. This one brings him water, that one brings him a water pipe, and the other one washes his hands. He came and said, "King?"

I.183   "What?"

I.184   "Eh, death! The majesty isn't yours, it's the mangy-head's!"

I.185   "Oh, you bastard! What can I do? God gave it to him! What can I do!?"

I.186   He said, "Send him after - eh - after this: after the Horse of Forty Colts, send him. The Horse of Forty Colts, now, she's a *div*, she'll eat him. Along with her forty colts."

I.187   "All right."

I.188   The next day came and he sent soldiers after him. This poor

---

[1] /tup/, Lit. 'cannonball'.

mangy-head went, and said, "What do you want?"

I.189   He said, "Nothing, um -- I want the Horse of Forty Colts, you go and bring her for me. That's a job for you." He's become his _brother-in-law_, he <u>gave</u> him his sister!

I.190   He came back again. He gave him forty days' grace, and she said, "Get an English saddle and bridle and harness, and a full-length mirror along with it, and two sacks of chickpeas and raisins" - this _parī_ told him, "Get it from him, then go. Go, and there's this pool. Spread the chickpeas and raisins on all four sides of the pool and lean the mirror against a tree, and go and hide. When she comes - m - these colts of hers will get busy with the chickpeas and raisins, and she - when her glance falls on that mirror, she'll say, 'My, my what great beauty I have!' You say, 'If someone were to wash you and comb your mane and uh - put an English saddle and bridle on you and mount you for a turn around on - and run around this pool, you'd be greater and more beautiful and younger (looking).' Then she'll say, 'You come and do it.' Once she's <u>sworn</u>, you do it."

I.191   He came, and got two sacks of chickpeas and raisins and a full-length mirror and an English saddle and bridle from the king, and he came, then. He came by night and came by day and came by night and came by day, and came by night and came by day - there was one road, and he went on beyond this road, and he arrived and saw that there was a pool there, and a road running all around it. He spread the two sacks of chickpeas and raisins around and filled the mangers full of sweets and leaned the mirror against the tree, and he went and hid himself. After he hid, <u>all</u> at once she came.

I.192   Her colts went and got busy with the chickpeas and raisins, and when she went to drink, she saw, she happened in that direction, and said, "Well," and "My, my, what great beauty I have!"

I.193   He said, "If someone were to wash you and comb your mane, and put an English saddle and bridle on you, and mount you, and give (you) three turns around this pool, you'd be more beautiful."

I.194   "Come."

I.195   "No, I won't."

I.196   "By the Truth of the excellent Prophet Solomon, by the right-hand idol, I swear, that whatever object you have, I'll accomplish it."

I.197   He went and washed her <u>clean</u> by the pool, and combed her mane, and put the English saddle and bridle on her, and gave her a <u>hundred</u> turns. After that he turned her toward the king's city. And the forty colts were following her.

I.198   He came and when he got halfway there, he spoke into the horse's ear, "Do you know what's going on?"

I.199   "No."

I.200   "When you get to this city, you tell your forty colts, too, that if a man or anything that flies or crawls gets in your way, eat them!"

I.201   When she got near the city, got into the city and some people got in front of them, she ate them, and camels came, and they ate them, and cows came, and they ate them, and word came to the king, that "The mangy-head and the Horse of Forty Colts and her forty colts have come. They haven't let the populace be, and your roads are emptied."

I.202   He got near his audience chamber, and he saw they were laying about with their teeth, this way and that, eating (people). He said, "Oh, you bastard, go, go, I don't <u>want</u> this Horse of Forty Colts' oppression!"

I.203   "Bastard yourself, curses on your own father, that you <u>send</u> me after things like this!" [MM laughs: Yeah!] He took some hair from the Horse of Forty Colts, and let her go. He came to his own house.

I.204   He came to his own house, the poor guy, and after he'd been home for some days and a while, this - m - same one came. This vizier came, and saw from behind the door, "Bū! (claps once). This woman that this little mangy-head, has, nobody has (her like)." He went and spoke to the king.

I.205   The king said, "What?"

I.206   "Eh, death! The majesty isn't yours, it's the mangy-head's!"

I.207   "Bastard! What can I do? Where can I send him?"

I.208   He said, "Nothing, ah - send him after the t-- the Tree of Bells and Cats' Claws.[1] Now, then, he -- at the foot of Mt. Qāf, they'll eat him."

I.209   "All right."

I.210   The next day came. He sent soldiers after him. He came. Shivering and shaking he came, and said, "What is it?"

I.211   "I want one thing, now - you go and bring the Tree of Bells

---

[1] /deraxt-e zang o gorbeh čang/. The object is both noisy and dangerous.

and Cats' Claws from the foot of Mt. Qāf."

I.212   He said, "Fine. I'll bring it. Give me forty days' grace."

I.213   He came and sat down there, all grief-stricken, and the princess said, "What is it?"

I.214   "It's like this."

I.215   "The *parī* - (yawns) said "What's the talk?"

I.216   He said, "Nothing, he said thus-and-so."

I.217   She said, "Eh, are you grieving? That's easy."

I.218   He said, "Sure, it's easy! You say, 'it's easy.' I - me - I - everywhere he sends me, you say 'It's easy.'"

I.219   She said, "It's easy, it's just like this, you go, and there are seven *dīv* brothers. It's with the first brother - he has a test, of wrestling. If you beat him," she said, "You can --" [X, MZ's husband: Have you made tea?] Yeah. Come, drink. "If not, if you don't beat him, then you can't do it -- (can't) bring it back." [BREAK FOR TEA]

I.220   Yeah. So when he came, then, the next day came, and entrusted the fate of the three women to God and he got on a horse, and took his things and came. He came by night and this poor guy came by day, and came by night and came by day, and he came, on this one road, night and day. As he came, night and day, he arrived at a desert plain, and the Messenger of God met him. He said, "Where are you going?"

I.221   He said, "I'm going to the foot of Mt. Qāf, there, for a tree, the Tree of Bells and Cats' Claws. To the -- brothers."

I.222   "The Tree of Bells and Cats' Claws -- just this <u>one</u> *dīv* brother could knock you to the ground with his finger. You'll never get to the foot of Mt. Qāf."

I.223   "I'm obliged to go. The king sent me."

I.224   After that the Messenger of God gave him a flask of kohl and he put some on his eyes, and he gave him his walking stick, and he slapped him on the back between the shoulder blades,[1] and said, "Go, and let no sword, no lance, no *dīv*, no *parī*, let nothing overcome

---

[1] Magical kohl provides protection, often invisibility; the walking stick provides magical transportation, and the slap on the back confers a protective mark.

you. You shall be stronger than any."

I.225   Then he came (along). As he came, and came and came and came, he came to a gre-e-e-een field of hay, and he let his horse free in it. He let his horse free, and the sister of this very *dīv* said to her serving maid, "Go, for the sake of God! What a youth he is - [Crash of kettle. X whispers] " - My brother will be coming now, and he'll eat him. Go, then, and send him away! Tell him, 'My dear brother, whatever way you came, go back!'"

I.226   The servant girl came, and this mangy-head was so young and beautiful,[1] as soon as she saw him, she gasped and fell over. She lay there for some minutes, unconscious. After that she said, "Oh, dear brother, aren't you afraid of being eaten? The *dīv* is coming, and he'll eat you. Get your horse out of this field, go!"

I.227   He said, "I'm not one of those people who came on this road (only) to turn back. Let the *dīv* come and eat me. My sister, you go back the way you came!"

I.228   She came and said, "He said thus-and-so to me."

I.229   She said, "How could he say that?"

I.230   After that the sister herself came, and said, "Oh, dear brother! Aren't you afraid for your youth? Go back the way you came, because my brother's a *dīv*, and he's coming now, he'll eat you."

I.231   "Mother, sister! I'm not one of those people you've seen, who came on this road (only) to turn back. Let him eat me."

I.232   Just a bit later, the *dīv* came. He said,

I.233   "Pah! Pah! A human smell,
If a horse comes here, he casts his shoe,
If a bird comes here, he casts his plume,
What is a human being doing here?"

I.234   He said,

"I drank raw milk.
I go about everywhere.[2]"

I.235   He said, "Come, I'll wrestle (with you). Come, let me get

---

[1] Perhaps the effect of the prophet's blessing, perhaps an artifact from another story.

[2] A fixed phrase exchange. The answer implies, "I am a human who nursed at the breast, and I go where I please."

a grip."[1]

I.236   They began to wrestle, and they twisted and turned, and when the mangy-head called on his god, he threw the *dīv* to the ground. When he was about to kill him, he said, "What good is one drop of my blood to you? Uh - I - uhm - you can be one brother, as we are seven. We'll be your brothers, too. You'll make eight."

I.237   After that he let him go. He let him go, then, and he stayed there that night, and morning came. After that he gave him a letter. He said, "If you just go a little farther on like this, (you'll come to) my brother's."

I.238   He gave him a letter, and he came and came and came (sips tea), and arrived and again he saw a field of hay, and a fort[2] there. He came, and a woman said, "Oh, brother, go! If this *dīv* comes, he'll eat you. Don't let your horse go here."

I.239   "He won't eat me. Go back, mother, don't worry, go."

I.240   After she left, the *dīv* came. When this *dīv* came, he showed him the letter, and his eyes lit up, and he took him (in). [X whispers in background. MZ pauses to listen.]

I.241   He took him (in). He took him, and he stayed there that night, and it was morning, and he wrote a letter, and (gave it to him to deliver)[3]. He said, "Go, like this, till tomorrow night, then, there's my other brother's fort."

I.242   Another morning came, and he came, and came, and came, and he saw a field of hay there, and he let his horse go and sat down. After that this servant girl came again, and said, "Brother, dear, go, if this *dīv* comes, he'll eat you!"

I.243   "Go back, he won't eat me, I'm his brother."

I.244   That *dīv* came, and he showed him the letter, and he took him on his shoulders, and carried him to his house. He had a good, long talk with him that night. Morning came again, and he set out again. Again he came. That evening he came to the fourth brother's place. Again he spent the night there, the poor guy, and in the morning he gave him a letter, and he went, again.

---

[1] Starting position for Afghan-style wrestling has the two opponents leaning forward, gripping each other with both hands on the shoulders or upper arms.

[2] /qal'eh/: In Afghanistan, often indicates a fortified private home.

[3] Lit. 'posted it'.

I.245   Here again - he let his horse go and - a girl came and said, "Go, brother, this *dīv* will eat you."

I.246   He said, "He won't eat me. I'm his brother."

I.247   He came, and he showed him the letter. He took him home. He gave him a nice time. Again the next morning he gave him a letter. The next evening came, and he came, then.

I.248   When he came there, that evening, then, they were sitting and talking and chatting. He said, "Now, when you go, tomorrow, you'll arrive at the foot of Mt. Qāf. There's a fort there, and it reaches from the earth to the sky. You won't be able to go in, but there's this cat. The keys are hung around this cat's neck. So then, (put) an arrow to the bow, and if you can hit it, so it falls and is killed, take the keys from its neck, and go, then. Then you go - you'll be able to bring the Tree of Bells and Cats' Claws."

I.249   This young boy came and came and came, and he sat down right there below the palace, and he saw a cat with keys around its neck like that, forty keys, jingling and jangling, going back and forth, back and forth. He sat there and sat there, and sat there for a long time, till - [prolonged rattle of tea kettle drowns out speech] - he hit it, then - [MM to X: Think, that makes noise! X: OK.] He - he went. The - cat fell down, fell down, there, below. He said, "If it falls down inside that garden, that's it, then. You'll have to turn around and come back. If not, if it falls outside in the alley, it's done, then, you unfasten the keys from its neck and take them."

I.250   When he hit it, the cat fell outside in the alley. When the cat fell into the alley, he unfastened the keys from its neck, and went. He went, and (there were) forty stairs with a *dīv* and a *bārzangī* asleep on each. He opened (a door) and went, and opened, and went, and opened and went, and when he got to the fortieth room, he took the golden lampstand from her[1] head and put it at (her) feet, and took the silver lampstand and put it by (her) head, and ate her roasted chicken, and put her ring on his own finger, and kissed her cheek, and put her shawl on his own shoulders, and went out.

I.251   He came out, and came, and he took the Tree of Bells, too. And he'd written a letter, and put it under her pillow, saying, "If you have a quarrel, bring it to such-and-such a city. Such-and-such a person was here."

I.252   So he came out, and he found another cat, he looked here and

---

[1] A *parī* is asleep in the room from which the tree is to be taken. The events of this scene are a commonplace, including all the boy's actions which later lead to his reunion with the *parī*. Cf. K.36, and discussion,

there, for a cat, and put the keys around its neck, so that it
went back up on the palace (wall), ran up there, again.

I.253   He came, then. That evening he came and stayed at the house
of that _dīv_. He said, "Now you've got to go immediately, because
if she finds out, she'll have it out with <u>us</u>."

I.254   The next night he came to this one's house, and the next night
he came to that one's house, so that he went on past those seven
brothers, again. He came. He comes by night and he comes by day,
and he comes by night and he comes by day. He got near the king's
city - [END OF TAPE]

ElB

I.255   So then, someone saw that this Tree of Bells, with forty bells,
like that - [MM interrupts to check tape recorder: (It's) OK -
from the start?] This, this Tree of Bells has forty bells ringing,
like that, and when it reached the king's ears, he said, "What
luck! He brought the Tree of Bells and Cats' Claws, the mangy-
head didn't get killed!" [MM: Yeah - yes!]

I.256   When he brought it, he said, "Have you brought it, then?"

I.257   "Yes, I brought it."

I.258   When sh - when morning came, when this daughter of Shãhgol
the _Parĭ_ King work up, she saw, when she got up, she saw the golden
lampstand at her feet. The silver one was at her head. She said,
"Hah? Who's this, who's come to my palace?"

I.259   She went to wash her face, and she saw that her ring wasn't
on her finger. She went and looked in the mirror, and saw a wound
on her cheek.[1] She looked at her shawls, and she saw one was missing. She said, "Bring me my chicken, so I can eat." There <u>was</u> no
chicken.

I.260   When she looked <u>all</u> around, she saw her pillow, and there's
this letter under it. She read the letter, (that said) "Such-and-
such a person in such-and-such a city. If you have a quarrel with
me, come."

I.261   After that she got out artillery and ammunition and planes,
and everything. She got them out, then, (but) let that go and put
it that this - a few days passed, after he brought the Tree of
Bells and Cats' Claws, and the vizier went and said, he saw that
he's sitting there with company and (   )[2], and all, and he

---

[1] She is so delicate that even a kiss leaves a mark on her face.

[2] /ma'awā/ - ?

came and said, "King?"

I.262   "What?"

I.263   "Death! The majesty isn't yours, it's the mangy-head's!"

I.264   "Bastard! What can I do?"

I.265   "Nothing, just - hm - uh - send him after 'laughing flowers'!"

I.266   "Bastard -" [MM: Hmm - (writing) - laughing flowers?] Yeah!
He said, "Bastard, I sent him to the foot of Mt. Qāf! He came
back! Now I should send him to that 'Laughing Flower'?"

I.267   "Yes."

I.268   They sent soldiers after the mangy-head. When they sent soldiers after him, he went, and they brought tea, and he drank it,
and then he said, "What did you want?"

I.269   "Nothing. I just want Laughing Flower[1] from you - you must
go and bring Laughing Flower for me." - The king said that.

I.270   "That's fine. Give me forty days' grace, and I'll go and
bring Laughing Flower."

I.271   They gave him forty days' grace. He came, that evening, and
said, - he sat down again, grief-stricken. His wife said, "What
is it? Didn't I tell you not to get your ass mixed up with the
king's? You, a poor mangy-head?" [MM laughs]

I.272   This parī said, "What is it?"

I.273   "Nothing. He said, 'Go bring laughing flowers.'"

I.274   "Eh, and you're grieving? It's easy to bring laughing flowers."

I.275   "Sure, it's easy! That other was easy, too!"

I.276   "This is easy. Laughing flowers are easy, like this, (just
get) forty camels and make wheat ǧolūr[2], and load up the camels,
and you'll get to a plain, where dīv ants are everywhere. These
cam--- just poke the (corners) of these bags with a bodkin. It'll
tri_-i-i-ickle out and the ants will eat it, and you go on. Till

---

[1] The narrator seems uncertain whether a proper name or an object is being requested. Here she uses the definite object marker, singular noun.
At I.265 and I.273, she uses the indefinite plural.

[2] See note 1, p. 371.

you get to the 'Laughing Flower(s)'[1]. When you go there, it's beside a great river[2], and water flows by, and Laughing Flower comes
to swim. You pick up the flowers, and bring a few laughing flowers, then, for him. It's easy."

I.277   "Fine. Easy."

I.278   After that, this poor little guy went out, then. He went out,
and came and said to the king, "Forty camels - and make wheat *ǧolūr*,
and load it on (them), so I can go and bring you laughing flowers."

I.279   "Very, well, by my eyes."

I.280   He sent and they made forty camel-loads of *ǧolūr* and loaded
it into sacks and put it on the camels, and they let him lead them
off, and he came. He came, came, came like that, night and day he
came, night and day he came, night and day this poor guy came, and
he came to these - ants. When he got to the ants, he stuck the
needle in, and made a hole in one of the sacks. This sack was
finished, and he let the camel go. He went on. Then he stuck another sack. So that way, he came (along) and made holes in all
forty sacks and finished the *ǧolūr* and let the camels go. Until
they were finished. When the forty camels were finished, he arrived, and saw the river. And there's an old woman there, with a
house.

I.281   He said, "Old Mother, I'm a traveler, give me a place to stay
tonight!"

I.282   She said, "Fine, I'll give you a place, Mother's dear."

I.283   He came into the old woman's house, and gave her a purse of
one hundred *tomān*, and the old woman was very happy. He said,
"Mother, what a fine river this is!"

I.284   She said, "Mother's dear, this river belongs to those girls,
the forty girls who come to swim, and to Laughing Flower. She's
always coming to swim. Now you stay, Mother's dear, till afternoon
prayer time today, and I'll show you how beautiful this Laughing
Flower is - what can (I) say!"

I.285   He said to her -- [MM: Is 'laughing flower' a flower, or a
person?] No, she's a *parī*, of course. [MM: Oh, I understand, yes.]
A *parī*. So now, when he stayed, then, these forty girls came, and
they swam and went (away), and this Laughing Flower came (last),
then. After that she came, the girl, to swim, and she went, and
this one came to swim, and left, and this one came to swi - and

---

[1] Ambiguous. See note 1, p. 404.

[2] /derīyā/.

<u>every</u>one who comes is a *parī*, besides. To swim, and goes. So it got to be afternoon, got toward afternoon prayer, <u>then</u> he saw that one came, <u>in</u> front of forty others, (now they came)[1]. They came and they started to swim and this mangy-head went and took Laughing Flower's clothes, and hid them! [MM: Hm!]

I.286   He hid them, and when she got up to put on her clothes, she swam and these flowers went down -down the river. After that she came to - put on her clothes, and she saw her clothes weren't there. She said, "Eh?" - She was a *parī*, anyway, she was clever, she said, "Whatever manner of creature or human, what<u>ever</u> you are, whatever desire you have, I'll accomplish it. Reveal <u>yourself</u>! By the Truth of the Excellent Prophet Solomon, by the idol of the right hand, I swear I have no quarrel with you. Come, come out."

I.287   He came out, and said, --- he came. This Laughing Flower thought in her heart, "This is an amazing human, who took the clothes and hid them."

I.288   She came to the old woman's house. She said, "Old mother, make a little tea."

I.289   She made the tea, (sips tea), and she drank it with him, and said, "All right, tell me your object, so that I can accomplish it."

I.290   "My object is this, the king said, 'Go and bring laughing flowers.'"

I.291   "Fine, I'll go with you. He said, 'Bring laughing flowers,' I'll go <u>myself</u> with you."[2]

I.292   After that, then, they - there was a *dīv* and Laughing Flower summoned him and they mounted on his shoulders - put it that when this daughter of Shāhg̈ol the *Parī*King, found out, she came, and when she got close to his city, no matter <u>who</u> was sent, her *dīv*s ate them. [MM: Yeah.] He's gurgling on the end of a rope, this king.

I.293   (He) came and came, and got close to the city, and people said, "The little mangy-head has come with Laughing Flower herself!"

I.294   "Eh! Curses on the little mangy-head's father!"

I.295   He came, and he said, "Oh, bastard! Since you went, like

---

[1] Semi-audible.

[2] "Laughing flowers" indefinite plural, again. Non-ambiguous contrast with the girl's declaration.

that, after the Tree of Bells and Cats' Claws, <u>you</u> go, and give her an answer."

I.296 "Bastard yourself! You sent me - first you sent me after those pearls. Then you sent me, saying, "Go and get my sister from the *dīv*'s clutches.' Again, you sent me after the Tree of Bells and Cats' Claws and you said, "Go, bring laughing flowers.' You're a bastard, yourself! You go answer her yourself."

I.297 "May God protect me! May the Holy Qor'ān protect me! Don't do that, may God look on your face, they've eaten my sons! They <u>ate</u> my vizier and *wakīl*! They've finished off my entire populace - go and give her an answer."

I.298 After that the mangy-head summoned the Horse of Forty Colts, and threw that shawl around his shoulders and spoke into the horse's ear, "Let me direct you - you go just like this -- " The whole plain was covered with silken carpets[1] - "Right on top of these carpets, so they're torn to bits under your feet."

I.299 This horse came like that, in a cloud of dust and smoke, and the daughter of Shāhg̈ol the *Parī* King said, "My friends, he was the one, then! This is the one!" And no matter who came she knew it wasn't he. Whenever <u>his</u> horse put a hoof down, the carpet was torn in two, and the wind blew it away. She said, "He's the one."

I.300 He came, and when he came into her presence, she gave her greetings and gave him her hand, and said, "Now, then, sit down." Whoever they sent, she'd say, "Come and give a sign that you've been to the foot of Mt. Qāf."

I.301 They'd give a sign, saying, "It was like this, and like this, "but they wouldn't give her the right sign, and she'd give them to the *dīv*s to eat.

I.302 She said, "All right, now, given me a sign that you've been to the foot of Mt. Qāf."

I.303 "I'll give you this sign - I came, and there were seven *dīv* brothers. I wrestled with the first brother, and I threw him to the ground. For the next six nights I stayed at the houses of the other six brothers. I came, and you had a great castle like that, and a cat was walking around on top of the walls. I struck it and knocked it down, and got the keys from around its neck. You had forty rooms, with forty stairs. There was a golden lampstand at your head, and a silver lampstand at your feet. There was a roasted chicken there for you to eat when you woke up. I ate the chicken. I put your ring on my finger. I took your shawl. I

---

[1] The *parī* has carpeted the ground between her encampment and the city.

kissed your cheek. There, those are my signs. I found a cat and put the keys around its neck, and let it go, and it ran up on the castle wall, and I came back."

I.304   She said, "Go, then, I'll marry you." And she took him, too.

I.305   So Laughing Flower, too, here - she went, too, along with this little mangy-head. Laughing Flower and the daughter of Shāhǧol the *Parī* King, and that *parī* who was in the hands of the *dīv* who cut off her head, she and the sister of the king, and the princess - how many does that make? The sister - m - the daughter - [MM: It's a lot] - of the king - [MM: Yeah.] and then - the one who was in the hands of the *dīv*, makes two. The - king's sister, three. [MM: Yeah.] Then - Laughing Flower is four, the daughter of Shāhǧol the *Parī* King is five. Five of them. Five, and this one[1] makes six. He was sitting there and this - vizier came. [MM Laughs] (claps once)

I.305   He went, and said, "King?"

I.306   "What?"

I.307   (Heatedly) "Death, dust! Curses on your father, and on your kingship! The majesty isn't yours, it's the little mangy-head's. You said, 'Go get laughing flowers,' and he brought Laughing Flower herself - yeah! Bastard! Go, take Laughing Flower from him!"

I.308   He said, "Oh, you bastard! God gave her to him! What can I do? The *dīvs* ate my sons! They ate up my entire city, what am I supposed to do?!"

I.309   "Nothing, just send him to bring news from the dead!" (Snickers) [MM: laughs] Whatever road they put (him) on - [MM: What?] From the dead, he should go to bring news from the other world - [MM: From - from the world of the dead?] (laughing) From the world of the dead! [MM: laughs]

I.310   They sent the soldiers after the poor mangy-head. This poor mangy-head, he came, and they brought tea for him, and he drank the tea and then he said, "What did you want?"

I.311   He said, "Nothing, just - look, you've done all these things, you've (managed all these heroic tasks)[2], you're a clever person, able and skillful, now you must go and (laughing) bring news from my mother's father." [MM laughs]

---

[1] The boy himself.

[2] /sarwardūnīar bekešīdī/ - سرووانی طارا بکشیری

I.312   He said, "All right, by my eyes. Give me forty - forty days' grace."

I.313   He came back and sat down, all grief-stricken, and sat there with his forehead all in lines. His wife said, "What happened? I told you, 'Don't get your ass mixed up with the king's, you're a mangy-head, a poor thing!"

I.314   He said, "Don't ask. He said, 'Go bring news from the dead.'"

I.315   She said, "You see? He made it (   )[1], then he made it lions and leopards, then he made it *dīvs*, then he made it the foot of Mount Qāf, and now he's sending you to the other world. Now go - now your friend has set you a good task!" [MM: laughs] "Now go."

I.316   This *dīv* [*sic*] said, "What did he say?"

I.317   He said, "He said thus-and-so."

I.318   She said, "Don't you grieve! You just sit here at home, don't go out, for the forty days. I'll give you a way out."

I.319   So after that, when forty days were almost up, they - they made five, clever and wise, these *parīs*. They wrote, "This world is such a good place, Heaven is like this, it has these wonderful fruits, and it's such a fine place, if you're my offspring, if you're my child, you must come to this world, for I think of you a lot, and I love you. You must come, that's all there is to it." They wrote a letter from the vizier's father and mother, and from the *qāzī*'s[2], and the *moftī*'s[3], they wrote five or six letters. [MM: To take them to the world of the dead?] Yeah - no! He's not going to the world of the dead, anyway! [MM: Yeah.] These *parīs* write them themselves, they just know how, anyway. They write some letters. [MM, in background: OK . . . I understand, yes.]

I.320   So then after forty days, it's the fortieth day, then, and they gave him those letters that they'd written, all well and correctly. He came. He came and they said, "Oh! The little mangy-head has brought news from the other world!" They took the letters, and they said, "You have to take us there!"

I.321   "Fine, by my eyes, I'll take you there!"

I.322   He came, and said, to the *parī*, "They just said, 'You have to take us there.'"

---

[1] /sandehār/ - ?

[2] The judge, who administers Islamic law.

[3] The interpreter of the law.

I.323   She said, "Nothing to that – just go and tell him, 'This – unload <u>seven</u> truckloads of firewood, and put it all in one room, and pour <u>seven</u> gallons of petrol over it, and I – you come into the room, and sit on the wood, and I'll light the fire, with you – I'll take you to the other world!'" [MM laughs] (laughing) The *parīs* said that. "As soon as you strike the match – leave the roof vent open. As soon as you strike the match, we'll come down through the vent, and pick you up, and bring you out, and they can stay there and burn."

I.324   "Fine."

I.325   After that he came and said, "King?"

I.326   "What?"

I.327   "Nothing, only, I (put) seven truckloads of firewood in a room, poured seven gallons of petrol over it, and lit the fire, and that's how I went to the other world.[1] (laughing) I brought news from your mother and father." [MM laughs] "I say, you must do the same (laughs), so we can go to the other world."

I.328   "All right, do it, then. You know how, you do it. We'll go. You take us with you, yourself."

I.329   So they came, and unloaded seven truckloads of firewood, and filled a bi -i-i-ig room with it, and poured the petrol over it, and they fastened <u>all</u> the doors and windows up tightly. So then, the *parīs* were standing above by the vent. The mangy-head struck a match, and the *parīs* came right down into the heart of this (burning) petrol, and picked up the mangy-head, and the room was dark, and they <u>went</u>! So then, it went, hau! hau! and the wood, and the vizier and *wakīl* and *qāzī* and *moftī* and the king were <u>all</u> burned up!

I.330   So then God gave the little mangy-head his desire, and so he went, and took the king's crown and put it on his own head, and he became king and stayed there, and that's the end of the story. This story. [MM: Very beautiful!] – very goo- [MM: The tale of – what?] This – the Tale of Mangy Head. [MM: (writes) Mangy-Head.] Yeah. [MM: The Tale of Mangy-Head.] Yeah. The name of the tale is "The Tale of Mangy-Head." [MM: It was <u>very</u> long!] Now, Margaret, I told it <u>quickly</u>! She takes – [MM: Yes, I know.] She takes up most of an afternoon. She says, "But," "Of course," and (laughs) so on – [MM: It was correct, it was complete.] It was correct. And Adī's language, when she talks, she forgets, then she remembers, <u>then</u> there's her language, it's different. I talk

---

[1] Prof. Annemarie Schimmel has observed that burning as a medium of transportation to the other world suggests connections of this aspect of the story with the Indian subcontinent.

like this, quick, quick - and I told it to these (children) two or
three times. [MM: Two or three?] Yeah. For them. [MM: Before
this.] Yeah. [MM: How many days ago might it have been, when you
heard it from her?] After you left,[1] she stayed that next night,
too - [MM: Oh.] - she stayed that night. But she didn't tell
stories that night, anyway. She came here later on, one day when
I was washing Rick's[2] clothes, she came here because she'd gotten
a little unhappy. [MM: That same week that I left for Kabul?] Not
that same week - a few days later. [MM: Later on.] My mother
said, "Adī, come, let's go," and she said, "No, if I - Mādar Zāher
will have to put me out, I'm not coming tonight." I said, "No,
stay for two or three nights, and eat, (or) I'll be sad."

I.331   So that evening, I said, "Adī, I've learned those stories
that you told. Let me tell them."

I.332   She said to me, "I know one story, it's very long, but I know
it."

I.333   I said, "You've got to tell it."

I.334   She said, "All right, I'll tell this one. If I'm (still)
here, I'm here, but if I'm not, you can tell it to Margaret."
[MM: Oh -]

I.335   So the poor thing told it, and the next day, I told it, that
evening, for them. [MM: Oh, very good!] Then I told it twice
more, and I (would) sort of like it, if I don't forget this one.
[MM: (inaudible) ... I like this one-] [MZ to Zāher, her fourteen-
year-old son:] Are you going to record your story now? [MM to Z:
Do you know one?] He knows this one. Tell the "Tale of the
Sheikh". [Z: No . . .] [MM: No~? It has gotten late, tonight.]
[MZ to Z:] To dust with you! [MM: Well - did you learn this
story?] [Z: Yess - (mumbles).] They learned a little of it.
[END OF TOPIC]

---

[1] About one month before this recording session.

[2] A Peace Corps English teacher residing in the neighborhood.

Title: <u>Afsāneh-e Garg</u> [The Tale of Mangy-Head]
Narrartor: Mādar Zāher
Recorded 14 February, 1976
Cassette # F3B-F4A

J.1   [MM: And also, do you remember any of those things that you
           learned from Adī last summer? One was <u>Mār Čučeh</u>. What else was
           there? There was a lot -] Mm - [- sixe or seven -] - one other,
           what was it? - [MM: That one about the mouse. The guy who falls
           in love with a mouse.] Yeah. Yes - the mouse. I know the <u>Mouse</u>,
           and I know that <u>Mār Čučeh</u> , too, but my own stories are better,
           now - [MM: Don't you like it?] I'll tell it. I'll tell those,
           too.   There's plenty of time, and I'll tell those, too. [MM:
           What else was there? About the - what?]   There was the tale
           of <u>Mār Čučeh</u>, and one was the tale of the thing - the tale of
           the lions, I learned that one, too, that one with the lions'
           milk in a lion's skin on a lion's back - [MM: About that, or
           about - (inaudible) . . .] That's from Adī.   From Adī. [MM:
           Good. Tell that.] (MZ converses with children in muffled
           tones) [Zāher: Tell it - that that person wasn't there, and -
           there's a castle, and in the - in the river, as it flows, those
           things - (s/he) says -] All right, you go and fix the qorut[1] and
           I'll tell it. So then. later, I'll tell some (now) and I'll tell
           some more afterwards. Margaret will be going with these -
           [Background comment] Yeah. She's going - there. Their name is
           on the tip of my tongue. Let me just get the beginning of it
           right, get it straight. Oh -(tiredly) - this - uh - (pauses) -
           what (task) was it? -(pauses)

J.2   Some things that bear fruit,
           (Some that) bear none,
           Cypress and poplar,
           Pomegranate and quince and pistachio and pomegranate,
           The mouse did the (carding),[2]
           The mother of mice the spinning,
           The louse did the tailoring,
           The tick the dyeing.
           We went to the house of Mulla 'Abbās
           (There) we ate bread and mās[3]
           He (put us) over there, with a donkey blanket on top of a mat.

---

[1]Dried yogurt which is reconstituted by rubbing with hot water, used
as a sauce.

[2]/mušleh/ - ?

[3]yogurt

> Morning came, and we led out our donkey,
> With our water jar on behind.
> The wall fell down and our water jar broke,
> And the cow gave birth, a female calf.

J.3   There was, there was, there was a king, and God (be) my king and thine, there is no one better (than He.)

J.4   There was a king. This king had a daughter. This king's daughter was playing around with a lover. In the old days, long ago — [[MM to kids talking loudly in background: Don't talk, like that — the sound of it-(inaudible)]] Nabī dear, don't talk, now. No matter what your mother did, you wouldn't go home. Look at the baby, look at Nāder, he (coughed)[1], so we fell (in) and did this and that so that he got better and went to sleep.

J.5   Put it that these suitors' go-betweens came and the girl didn't accept. [MM: Yeah?] Go-betweens came and she didn't accept, and go-betweens came and she didn't accept, and one day, they forced her father and he gave in to them. When he gave her away, this girl, she said to her lover, "Now you come on such and such a night, and I'll run away with you." [MM. Yeah.]

J.6   Her lover said, "Fine."

J.7   Put it that this bald cowherd had brought his herd of cows to the foot of the princess's castle, he saw that there was something going on at the princess's castle that day. She says, "Now what can I do? This suitor's people came and I told my father, 'I don't want (this one),' and he didn't give me to him, and that suitor's people came, and he didn't give me, and now the go-betweens forced him, now that he's answered (for) me, you come on such-and-such a night, and we'll run away. I'll go with you."

J.8   He said, "Fine, I'll come."

J.9   "I'll take everything I'm going to want, from the house."

J.10   Let that be, and listen to this, that her lover left, and he hadn't made his way back yet, this — s — evening, this poor bald cowherd, he had this little calf, in the herd, and his calf got lost that day. Evening prayer time came. His grandmother said, "Au, bald-head!"

J.11   "What?"

J.12   She said, "The calf didn't come back! Go find the calf!"

J.13   He said, "Where should I go, Grandmother, to find it?" He

---

[1] /čoɣ zad/ - ?

went and walked all over the plain, and didn't see the calf, and came back home. His grandmother beat him, and (threw him) out. She hit him and threw him out, and he came along in the heat of anger and came down below the princess's castle. That talk was still in his ears, that "(Sleep is going to be impossible here, anyway.")[1]

J.14   He put his head down right there, and when the night got well along, all at once one - he saw someone stick a head out of a window, and say, "Have you come?"

J.15   And the bald boy was scared, but he got up from his place, and said, "Yes, I've come."

J.16   She said, "Come here, then."

J.17   So she tied up a saddlebag and lowered down a bunch of jewels, and loaded up saddlebags and lowered them, and tied up saddlebags and lowered them, and he saw that she came out. She said, "Catch (me),", she tied the rope around her own waist and the rope - a silken rope, she tied it to the bedpost and slowly, slowly she came down. She came down, and untied the rope, and the bald boy saw that the king's daughter had come down.

J.18   The princess went to where her father's horses were, to the stables, she went and got a good, spirited horse - untied two fast horses and came and loaded the saddlebags on them and gave him a gun, and gave (him) a gun, and the bald boy did all this with his back turned and without saying anything, mum! And the night is dark and the princess can't see whether this is her lover, or the bald boy, or what or who it is, or isn't.

J.19   So after that they got on the horses, and she said, "Hah? If this were my lover, he would be talking so much - wh - why doesn't he talk, this one? What happened?" She said, "All right, you just wait - " she was intelligent, this princess, she came and came, came, came, and (then she) said, "Aleyyy! What a fine place this is, what fine hay it's got! How would it be if - my father's grooms were here and my father's horses were loose, and they ran around and played."

J.20   This bald boy didn't say anything. They went on, and passed by that place. They passed by there, and went, and she saw, heyyy! A fine plain. Right there, there was this fine field of hay. She said, "Aleyyy! How would it be, if this -- if my father's sheep were loose here and wandered around and the shepherd whirled his stick and sang and held his hand up to his ear!"[2]

---

[1] Semi-audible.

[2] Traditional position for singing: the hand is cupped forward behind one ear.

J.21   He didn't say a <u>thing</u> - mum! He came, and came, and they arrived at a -- river, and they saw that there were reeds along the river, and grass, and everything growing well, like that, around the river. She said - this princess said, "How would it be, if that little cowherd of my father's were to let his cows loose along this stream, here, and those cows were rustling around in the reeds and eating them, and that little cowherd were singing, now."

J.22   He said, "Au, bā-'št, bā'št!"[1] (muffled laughter)

J.23   (Whispers) She said, "For God's sake! How I've peed in my father's mouth![2] What have I done!? What kind of a thing have I done!? This is my father's cowherd!" She said, "Fine, the one - that my father gave me to, even he was <u>better</u>!" [MM giggles] (giggles) "Now <u>this</u>!" She was cursing herself there and quarreling with herself, and still he didn't say anything. "To dust, then, by God!" [MM to noisy children in audience: Enough, now!] Yeah. "God did it. God did it, what can I do?"

J.24   She came, came, alongside a great river, and they came to this place, hungry and thirsty. First the princess took the thing - the scrubbing brick. And she pulled the bald cowherd down (giggles) and scrubbed and scrubbed and scrubbed and scrubbed his head, till the skin wore off it. The skin wore off it in places - (aside) - lift that up, it's from the <u>korsī</u>[3] - After that she had some medicines in her bag, and she put them on his head, after that, for him, and she came, and saw - the princess saw that the water is carrying precious stones along, as it flows. She said to - to this bald boy, "The (water jug)[4] - the tea won't be ready for a while, nor the food. Get down and gather up a few of these." The princess knew they were precious stones. The bald boy got down and picked them up and picked them up and picked them up, and she filled a saddlebag with them. This princess. After that they had their bread and tea, and they set out.

J.25   They came by night and came by day and came by night and came by day, and came to a city. This princess. They went there, and there was a little, old, broken-down fort and they got down there. After that she gave him money, and said, "First you go and walk around and ask, 'Who has a house for sale?'"

J.26   He went this way and that way and this way and that way, and

---

[1] Auditory command for cattle.

[2] I.e. wilfully shamed him. A woman's obscenity.

[3] A low table with a charcoal brazier beneath it and a quilt over it, around which people sit in winter, to keep warm.

[4] Semi-audible.

said, "Who has a house for sale? I was sent in advance - one for lease or rent or sale."

J.27 This one guy said, "I'm selling." And the price of his house was twice what it was worth.

J.28 He said, "I'll buy it."

J.29 He came, and told the princess, "It's like this." The princess put good clothes on him, and gave him money, and he went and bought the house and they went to that house, and settled down there. After that he started in on floor coverings and carpets and pots and bowls and household equipment and beds and this and that, he bought them and brought them and put them in the house. Filled it.

J.30 One day came, and this bald cowherd said to the princess, "Mistress?"[1]

J.31 "What?"

J.32 He said, "Put a few of those pearls in a tray, and give it to me to take to the king. (Maybe) the king will toss me something or other."

J.33 This - this one said, this princess said, "Your profit (from that) will be worse than an injury. You shouldn't take them."

J.34 He said, "No, you're a woman, you're foolish! I'm going to take them. Come! Fill up a platter, or a tray, and put a cover on it."

J.35 The princess brought them and filled the tray, and put a cover on it, and gave this bald boy good clothes, and he came, and called out. "Where is the king's audience held?"

J.36 He brought them, and this king - they saw that - m - it's a person in royal clothes, with a tray in his hand. They said, "Someone's brought a gift of honor." He brought it in.

J.37 They put in a chair, and the king, when he uncovered the tray, he said, "Oh!?", he said, "In my whole kingdom, not one of these was to be found, these are precious pearls!" He took them off to his private quarters, and his little women got so happy, got (   )[2]. The king's right-hand vizier was very knowing. He was knowing, and when this bald boy had eaten some food and

---

[1] A mode of address usually used by servant to employer, or child to elder woman.

[2] /ăčĭ(z)/ or /ăčez/ - ?

things and that is to say, this king was very pleased with these things, the bald boy was excused, and he came home. He took up his tray and the cover, and brought them back. The king didn't give him anything, either.

J.38   Put it that, after that, this vizier said, "King?" He said, "Do you know what this is all about?"

J.39   "No."

J.40   He said, - this vizier had kept sight of him, and come, and come and come and come, when the bald boy went home, the vizier went and stood behind the door. There were these holes, and he was looking (through them). He <u>saw</u> that <u>all</u> at once a woman came out of the house, and she's like the sovereign of all lights, glowing. He came back to the king's audience. He said, "Eh, may your lousy throne be overturned![1] He has a wife, who's fit for <u>you</u>!"

J.41   He said, "Bastard! God gave her to him. How can I - I, eh - what am I to do? God gave her to him. Can I take the guy's wife? He brought me all those pearls!"

J.42   After that, put it, Margaret dear, that he said, "Nothing, only - you send for him, and say, 'My wives and daughters fought over those jewels, now, bring a few more."

J.43   Put it that - this soldier went after the poor bald boy, and said, "The king has sent for you."

J.44   His wife said, "Now, then, go and give him an answer. I told you, '<u>Don't</u> take him those pearls,' but you didn't listen, now go, and give him an answer! You'll have to see those pearls in your sleep!"

J.45   "Now, woman, you're foolish - I'll go back there, and find them." God had given to this little bald cowherd.

J.46   He came and the king said - said "Salām," and acted very pleased, the king, and said, "Now, friend, you did a fine thing, to do that, but you also did a bad thing. You did well to bring those things to us, we didn't have any, but now <u>all</u> my children are fighting over them. Now you'll have to bring me a few more."

J.47   He said, "By my eyes!"

J.48   He gave him forty days' grace. He came back. He got food

---

[1] An approximation. The original is /pox-e lebax-e pādšāhī-to čapah šayeh/, which is probably mildly scatological, but I have not succeeded in translating it.

and things for his wife, and hired a little servant, and then he
set out, and came, just the way he came the first time, to that –
into [*sic*] the river. He hadn't come to the thing yet – (this very
grace is leading him to the *parī*.[1] Put it, Margaret, that this
road – he mounted his horse and came, and came, and came, and came,
and came, and came, and came, and found that river, and saw that
the water is rolling these same jewels along, those pearls. He
said, "I'll let these jewels be, and go after the place (they come
from)."

J.49   He came, and came, came, and saw a thing like a castle, there,
and there's a hole. These jewels are coming rolling out of the
hole. After that he quit following the stream and went over by
the wall, and dug a tunnel under the ground, and dug and pushed
the dirt out behind him, and dug and pushed the dirt out behind
him, and dug and pushed the dirt out behind him, and he came and
saw he was in a thing – a garden. It was a garden. He saw that
in this garden, a thing – m – saw – it was a garden. Nothing more.
It got to be evening. As evening came, suddenly he saw the sky get
dark, and something came down. When (he) came down, (he said),

J.50   "Baaa! Pah! Pah! A human smell,
               If a horse comes here, it casts its shoe,
               If a bird comes here, it casts its plume,
               What is a human being doing here?"

J.51   He went everywhere, this way and that, and didn't see anything.
There's nothing. He said, "Good, there's nothing here. I was
around humans, myself."

J.52   All at once he saw that he started singing. He set to reciting spells, and sang and sang and sang and sang, and when he'd
rea-l-l-ly sung a lot, there was a door, locked, and the door
opened. When the door lock opened, he was inside the walls.[2] As
he went, he saw that beside the stream, then, he, he's recited
this spell, and beside this stream, there's a *parī* with her head
cut off. Lying there. Her blood is dripping, drop by drop, into
the (stream), where it turns into pearls, and the water carries
them along.

J.53   He picked up this *parī*'s little head and washed it in the
stream, and placed it on her body and set to reciting spells. He
sang and sang, and she sat up. After she sat up, he stayed there,

---

[1] Semi-audible: /amī (taufer / taufek) b-am parī(d) mīboreh/
Could also be /Hamītau fe(k)r b-am parīd mīboreh/, 'his thoughts are
all scattered and torn, like that'

[2] Pronoun ambiguity persists throughout this section. 'He' here refers
to the *dīv*.

that night, and in the morning the $\widetilde{div}$ left. He set to reciting spells, and sang and sang and sang, and the door closed on her. The bald boy recited that spell to himself until morning, and he learned it. So in the morning, when he went out, he recited the spell, and sang, so that it locked, he - sang.

J.54   He[1] went out. He[1] came out of his hole, and started the spell, and sang and sang and sang, and pulled on the door lock, and it opened. He went (in). When he went (in), he saw the $\widetilde{pari}$, there. So after that, once he got inside the door, he sang the spell, and sang, and the door shut and locked.

J.55   He went and dug there, again, and dug and dug a hole in the ground, and got down in the hole and pulled dirt over himself, and kept a little hole, and he saw that there's someone there with their head cut off. Lying by the stream. He looks out of his little hole, there, and he saw - evening came, it got dark, the sky got dark and something came down. He saw, hoo! in a cloud of dust, it's a $\widetilde{div}$! He came, came and said,

J.56   "Pah! Pah! A human smell,
        If a horse comes here, it casts its shoe,
        If a bird comes here, it casts its plume,
        What is a human being doing here?"

J.57   He saw there was nothing there, again, no human there, just the person lying there with no head, and he said, "Old man,[2] this one with no head isn't a human, either, where's the human?'"

J.58   Her head - the bald boy watched, and saw that he picked up her head and washed it in the river, and the blood from it - it just turned into pearls. The water carried them away.

J.59   Put it that he put (the head) on her body and set to reciting spells, and when he set to reciting and sang and sang, all at once this $\widetilde{pari}$ sneezed and sat up. He said,

J.60   "Pah! Pah! A human smell!
        If a horse comes here, it casts its shoe,
        If a bird comes here, it casts its plume,
        What is a human being doing here?"

J.61   She said, (Angrily) "You cut off my head in the morning, and put me here, where's the human?" When the $\widetilde{pari}$ sat up, she noticed the human smell, too. She didn't say anything to him. She said, "Maybe God will deliver me." (inaudible phrase) Now . . . he's

---

[1] Typical ambiguity. The first pronoun refers to the $\widetilde{div}$, the second to the boy.

[2] Addressing himself.

talked about that . . . [MM laughs] (resumes normal tone) After that, he said, - after that, this happened. He - after he's spent the night, this *dīv*, after he'd spent the night, in the morning he cut off her little head, and put her back beside the stream, and he left.

J.62   After he left, (yawns) put it that - this bald boy took - up her head and washed it by the river, got out of his hole, then, and washed off her head and put it back on her body, and set to reciting the spells. He sang and sang and the *parī* sneezed and sat up. First she laughed, and after that she began to weep. She said, "What is a human being doing here?"

J.63   "God brought me," he said, "Now what shall I do?"

J.64   She said, "Nothing, now - you, last night - when did you come here?"

J.65   "I was in the garden the night before last. Last night I came here."

J.66   She said, "But where were you?"

J.67   "I was down in a hole." He said, - "This will never do. Now, he - you must ask (him), 'Where is the glass of your life?' Then see what he says, so I can kill him, and take (you) away, then."

J.68   So it's evening again, and he stayed till evening, and in the evening this - bald boy cut off her head, again, and put her back there and went back down in his hole. When the *dīv* came, he said,

J.69   "Pah! Pah! A human smell!
       If a horse comes here, it casts its shoe,
       If a bird comes here, it casts its plume,
       What is a human being doing here?"

J.70   She said, - "Human? And you go, a hu-" - he picked her up — her head, and washed it and put it on her body, and set to reciting the spell, and she sneezed and sat up, and said, - "You cut off my head. OK, you come back, and wash my head, and put it back, and bring me back to life, is that a good thing to do?" She said, "It could be that you'll cut off my head like this," - this girl got powerfully angry, (sniffles), and said, "You cut off my head, and leave ! OK, here I am, like that, and if you die - I'll just stay here with my head cut off, how will that be?"

J.71   He said, "Eh, woman! You've spent all these years with me!" He was in love with her, anyway, though she wasn't his woman - he was a *dīv*, and this *parī* couldn't sleep with him. He said, "I won't die, like that, killing me isn't that easy."

J.72   She said, "How is it, then?"

J.73   He said, "I can be killed like this, you see this chamber, whose door is locked? Inside this room there's an arch, and under the arch there's a well, and in the well, there's a pigeon. If someone makes a *xarwār* of flour into dough, and throws it into the well, the well will foam up. The pigeon will spring up, and rise up. If anyone catches the pigeon and kills it, the glass of my life is in the crop of this pigeon." [MM: Hm.]

J.74   Put it, Margaret, that she didn't say anything more. She said, "Well, all right, now that you've let me know."

J.75   He said, "Now, if anyone whitewashes this room, my life will be lengthened." [MM: Yeah.]

J.76   She said, "How would it be, if you don't kill me tomorrow, and I whitewash that room?"

J.77   "It's not necessary! You'll get tired!"

J.78   "To dust with it, if I get tired! I'll whitewash it."

J.79   Put it, then, (she made) lots of excuses to him, and that day he didn't cut off her head, and just left her there, because if you don't cut off her head - he could have cut off her head, anyway, because the bald boy knows the spell. He's sung it. He didn't cut off her head and [child coughs] - this - (sighs) he came, and - s -, - m -, when he'd gone, this bull-sized *dīv* set to reciting the spell, and went, and the door shut. The bald boy came out.

J.80   When the bald boy came out, put it that - here - they opened the door to that room. and they saw the arch. They opened [*sic*] the arch, and saw the well. When they looked into the well, they saw that there's a flat stone over the well-head. They didn't disturb the stone, they (just) brought the hundred *xarwār* of flour, - [Māhgol: They whitewashed the room, a little and then, the next day -] Oh, you've got it. Whitewashed the r - they did that. First they took and whitewashed the room. The wa- [Māhgol: They whitewashed <u>half</u> of it.] - they plastered them, the walls of this room. They whitewashed half of it. So then she kept back a bit of the - a little of the (   )[1], and whitewashed (it) and after that, she enjoyed herself for a little while with this bald boy. This girl's clothes and her body were all smeared with clay. So then, the bald boy went down in this - hole, and the *dīv* came in a cloud of dust, and saw the *parī* smeared with clay, and he was pleased with her and hugged her and put her on his knee, saying, "You got tired today."

J.81   "Come, Look."

---

[1] /čuk/ or /čük/ - ?

J.82   He came, and looked, and saw that one room was whitewashed.
He said, "Now my life has been lengthened."

J.83   Put it that he was very pleased. When morning came, the next
day, the *dīv* did't cut off her head, now, then, her head - he said,
"After this, it would be too strong, I'm not going to cut off your
head any more. I'll just go, like that." He didn't cut off her
head. He left.

J.84   They got up, and came and got out the flour. They opened
the top of the well, and they kneaded[1] and threw (it) in, and
kneaded, and threw (it) in, and made dough, kneaded it, and threw
it in, and all at once - he was sitting, then, in ambush, this
bald boy. The pigeon, this place - well foamed up. Boiled up.
Came up. When it came up, the pigeon, to the top, he made a lunge
and caught the pigeon. Just as he lunged and caught it - [Māhgol,
semi-audibly: That - thing - was torn open, that -] - m - he tore
open its crop. Just as he tore open its crop, the glass of his
life was in his hand, and the *dīv* arrived.

J.85   He said, "Human, stay your hand!" Just as he said, "Human,
stay your hand," he just threw it on the ground. And the *dīv*
fell right out of the air, his corpse, to the ground. [child cough-
ing] He was smashed to pieces. After that he - God gave them their
desire, and (may) he give my desire and thine - and that of the community of Islam. Everyone who has a desire. Our desire is in the
hands of Ḡolam Nābi, that we can get Zāher married.[2]

J.86   Let that be. This, this difficulty of his was solved, when
this difficulty of his was solved, it was evening, and he said, -
huh? - he was playing and fooling around, the bald boy started in[3]
with this *parī* and forgot his own wife. He said, - "You m-" at the
moment when he was about to fall asleep, he got to worrying about
his wife, and said, "Huh? What have I done? It's almost forty
days - " he said, "You haven't asked me why I came here."

J.87   "OK, why did you come here?"

J.88   "The king sent me after those pearls. I have a wife," and so
forth and so on, he told the whole story from the beginning, that
"There was this king's daughter, and she was playing around with a
lover, and one evening, my calf got lost and I went to the foot of
her castle and fell asleep, and at midnight she said, 'Have you
come?' I said, 'Yeah.' She handed me (things) and I took them, I

---

[1] /nāleh kardam/ - from context.

[2] A reference to the land dispute which has complicated Zaher's engagement to the daughter of this man, who is his father's cousin. Cf. Text
N, and discussion, Ch. V.

[3] /lagah be gard kard/.

gave, and she took [*sic*], and I took them. She herself came down, and so we came, and she said, 'If my father's horses were here -' I didn't say anything. She said, 'If my father's sheep were grazing here,' and I didn't say anything. She said, 'If my father's cows were here, rustling and feeding in the reeds, the reeds are sweet - and that little bald cowherd were here, striking the (   )[1] and singing.' And after that I spoke, and she recognized me. She didn't run away from me, though, and we came, that evening, to this stream where the jewels were, and she sent me down into the stream to pick up some of them. We took them and went to such-and-such a city, and bought ourselves a house there. I took (them) to the king, and the king said, 'Go bring more.'"

J.89   She said, "You've had a lot of grief. I'll go with you tomorrow."

J.90   Morning came, and the *parī* immediately summoned a *dīv* and filled a saddlebag with those jewels and said, "Take us to such-and-such a city immediately."

J.91   He delivered them to the city - right to his wife. His wife saw (them), and said, "Thank God, for I was alone, now we are two."[2] The princess gave abundant thanks, that the *parī* was there, she was happy, then.

J.92   Put it that he filled a little tray, then, and went, and took it to the king.

J.93   The king, the vizier said, "Huh? Didn't I tell you?"

J.94   This poor little bald boy ate and drank tea there, and went out, and the vizier tailed him <u>again</u>. He tailed him out, and came. He came (and stood) behind the door of his compound and looked, "Buuu! He's <u>brought</u> one who's better than the other!" He came and said, "May you catch fire and burn, King! May your rule be overturned! This woman - this bald cowherd, he has a wife fit for you. Now he went after those jewels, and he's brought one even better than her!"

J.95   "Bastard! What can I <u>do</u>? <u>God</u> gave her to him! Can I kill him? Now, I sent him after pearls, and this *parī* had her head cut off, he brought her and killed the *dīv*." After that, what did he send him after, the second time? [Mahgol: The second time, after his own sister. The king sent him after his own sister.] (undertone) After his own sister. Yeah.

---

[1] /ǧambūr/ - a type of musical instrument? See note 4, p. 380.

[2] An unusually exemplary attitude in a co-wife.

J.96   This, this time when some days and some while had passed, he sent soldiers after him again. When he sent soldiers after him, he said, - they came, and said, "We came after the bald boy, his Majesty the King sent us."

J.97   This bald b - his wife said, "Now he's sent for you again, now look -" the princess - "where he sends you this time, this one."

J.98   The *parī* overheard, and said, "What's the talk?"

J.99   He said, "Nothing, the king sent for me."

J.100   "Don't you worry a <u>bit</u>! <u>Any</u> place - no <u>matter</u> where he sends you, I'll untie the knot of his tasks."

J.101   This poor bald boy got dressed, came, and he said, "It's like this, now, I have this one difficulty, and (you) must (do) it - now it's several years since a *dīv* has carried off my sister, now, you go and get news of her."

J.102   He said, "Fine."

J.103   He came back. She said, "What did he say?"

J.104   "Nothing, he just said, 'It's some years since a *dīv* carried off my sister, now you have to go, and bring - bring news of her.'"

J.105   She said, "Fine." Pu-u-u-ut it that she said, "Now, get forty camels from him and make wheat *ǧolūr*, forty sacks of it, and load it on the camels. Now there's a place where there are ants, and all of those ants are *dīv*s. Pou-ou-our out that *ǧolūr* and go un- til - [Mahgol: Wheat!] Whea- [Mahgol; Pour out wheat! Pour out wheat, and come, and pour, and come . . .] (Heatedly) No, God of Repentence! That's from another layer.[1] It's nothing (like that). She said - m - the *parī* said to him, "You go, like this, to a plain, there's a plain, and a cave, and in (front of) the cave, there's a flat stone, placed in the mouth of the cave, and that sister of his is in the cave. When the *dīv* comes back at night, he picks up the stone, and goes (in). Then when he comes out for the day, he puts the stone back." Now, then, how do I know, how he killed him, this *dīv* - ahhh - God of Repen- [Mahgol: A cow, he skinned a cow -] Yes. He skinned a cow. I remember that, too. She said, "Go and tell him, 'Skin a cow, and put forty *man* of - lime inside the cow- hide.'" [MM to child, about microphone: Don't (touch) -] "'Then give it to me, so I can go.'" [MM: (Leave it) like that]

J.106   Put it that this cow, now, he went and had a cow skinned, and put forty *man* of lime inside the cowhide, and he left, then. He left, and came to that plain, and came, came, came, came, came,

---

[1] /lāy/ لَی - 'fold', ply'.

came, - (yawns) - this, this plain, and the cave, like that, and the door of the cave, he lifted the stone and went and spoke to her and let her know, "I've come to ask about you, but I'm going to take you (back), my [sic] brother sent me."

J.107 She said, "How will you take me?"

J.108 (stutters) "This - by the door - (I'm) putting this by the cave. The door of the cave," he said - "will be open." He left the d - door of the cave open and dragged the cowhide up and put it right, smack in the way[1] of the mouth of the cave. Then this $d\bar{\imath}v$, when evening came, as he came down all in a cloud of dust and smoke, he saw a <u>black</u> thing in the mouth of his cave, like that - [Mahgol: He went for - to that thing. MM: Where? Mahgol: He hid in the hole.] He himself had <u>gone</u>, anyway, and hid. The $d\bar{\imath}v$ got really burned up, as he came down, and said, "What's this in the door of my cave?" That instant he made <u>one</u> bite of it, ate it. Just as he made one bite of it, and ate <u>it</u>, it wasn't ten minutes, till his stomach burst, and he was <u>blown</u> all to bits. (inaudible phrase)

J.109 He took the sister and left. He went and took her, took the sister and let her go to the king's private quarters, and went back to his own wives.

J.110 This $d\bar{\imath}v$ said, this vizier said, "Now, did you see?"

J.111 He said, "All right, what can I do? How can I do anything to him? (The) guy set out traveling, came here from another country, bought himself an old house - God gave it to him."

J.112 After that, they said, "Where shall we send him?"

J.113 He said, " - After the - say, say, send for him and say, 'My children have caught the "little fire". Go after lions' milk, in a lion's skin, on a lion's shoulders, and bring it.'" [Mahgol: "Bring it!"]

J.114 When some days had passed, they sent soldiers. When they sent the soldiers, they said, "His Majesty the King has sent for you."

J.115 This wife of his said, "Now what are you going to do?" This princess. [Mahgol, brusquely: He married off his sister, <u>gave</u> her to him! MM: Hm.] So he (gave) his sister, then, he'd brought the spoils, and after a few days passed, he said, this - "Anyone who goes hunting, his spoils are his own." He gave her to him, anyway. What could he do with his sister? That made three wives.

J.116 After he brought her, he said, "Do you understand? Although you've become my brother-in-law, now, even though you've become

---

[1] /b-am rau berī/

part of my household,[1] these children of mine have caught the 'little fire'. You'll have to go, they said - the doctors said, 'It must be lions' milk, inside a lion's skin, on a lion's back,' you bring that."

J.117   He said, "By my eyes."

J.118   He came back. He came, and this *parī* said, "What's the talk?"

J.119   He said, "It's like this. Even you can't do it."

J.120   She said, "Don't you worry a bit. Now, there's this lion, in such-and-such a jungle, and it's been ye-e-ears since a reed got stuck up through her paw. Now, she hasn't been able to walk around, or get anything to eat, just what God - now if someone appears, to cut off that reed, so that it will fall away from her paw, now, for him, she'll - more difficult -- [END OF TAPE]

F4A:

J.121   He - I was there, at the place with the - lion's milk. [MM: Yeah.] (He) sent (him) for (it). He said, "Go, you have to bring a little lions' milk, in a lion's skin, on a lion's back, because my children have the 'little fire,'" The king said that.

J.122   This - mangy-headed cowherd said, "By my eyes."

J.123   When he came back, the *parī* told him, she said, the *parī* told him [child coughs continuously] "Now, you go, there's a lioness in this one jungle, it's been ye-e-ears that a reed has been hurting her. It's in her paw. It's this reed, that - it's with this, that if her desire is accomplished, and this reed is cut off, she'll accomplish your desire, too. You go, and dig a tunnel, dig,dig,dig, under the ground, carefully, and saw off that reed, above her foot. Then when the reed falls over, then, all at once she'll let out a screech. When she screeches, all the lions and leopards and wolves, all the creatures will come, to see, 'What was that?' After that, she'll say, 'Whatever manner of creature, human, *parī*, *dīv*, whatever you are, come out, and I'll accomplish your goal and desire.' Now you make her swear by the idol of the right hand, and on her mother's milk, an oath, and after that, then, go." [MM: Oh.]

J.124   Now, Margaret dear, put it that he, then he went out. He went out, and came, and came, and came, came, came, came, came, like that, and saw the jungle black in the distance. When he came there, he saw, yes, there was no one in this jungle, they'd all gone. When day comes, they go, then, the lions and leopard and those kinds of things. He saw there was one lion, with this reed

---

[1] Reading ميروان for /mīrewān/. Could also be مهربان /mehrebān/, 'kind, generous', hence 'though you've been kind to me'.

growing out of her paw. From - from - from - the bottom of her
paw, it had sprung up through the top of her paw, wounded it.
She's pinned, there. Put it that, from underneath - the ground,
he dug a tunnel, dug, dug, dug, like a tomb, and went down into it
and dug out the tunnel, right under the (   )[1] of this lion.
Then he slo-o-owly, slowly sawed through the reed, so she wouldn't
know, sawed it away from the top of her paw, sawed, sawed, sawed,
and when the reed fell over like that, she let out a screech. This
person hid hims- went and hid in his own hole.

J.125   These, all the lions there were - and she had <u>seven</u> children -
her children and lions and leopards and wolves and foxes, they <u>all</u>
came (back) to the jungle, (saying) "What was that? What happened
to her? Our friend who was here, and (couldn't) walk around, did
they kill her, or what?!" After that, when she stopped wailing,
she saw that she could lift her foot off the ground, (the reed) had
fallen over.

I.126   She said, "(Whatever) manner of creature, human, *parī, dīv*,
whatever you are, come out. I'll accomplish your desire and your
goal, whatever desire you have."

J.127   After that he said, "No, I won't come out, You'll eat me."

J.128   She said, "I swear by the idol of the left hand, come out, I
won't eat you."

J.129   "No."

J.130   "By the idol of the right hand, I won't eat you."

J.131   "No."

J.132   "I swear on my mother's milk, I won't eat you."

J.133   When she swore on her mother's milk, he came out. He said, "I'm
compelled, now - I accomplished your desire and your goal, like that,
and cut off the reed in your paw, - my goal and desire is this, that
the king sent me after lions' milk in a lion's skin, tied on a lion's back - I have to take it to him."

J.134   Immediately these children - this child of hers said, "Kill
me," and that child of hers said, "Kill me," and the other child
said, "Kill me," She killed one of her children herself and skinned
it and prepared the skin and took her own breast, and milked, milked,
milked, milked, milked, and <u>filled</u> the lion's skin with milk, and
tied it on the shoulders of one of her children, on his back. She
sent him in front, saying, "Take it."

---

[1] /čatan/ - ?

J.135   After that, when he got to the plain, this lion – when a murmur started going around the city and people said that – now, when they go out, he – this one jumps back into his house, and that one jumps back into his house, and the other one jumps back into his house, and he brought him to the king's private quarters.

J.136   The king said – when the king saw this lion, he was scared, he grabbed (the boy), this vizier – this king, and said, "Go! Take him away!"

J.137   He said, "Where shall I take him? Death to 'take him away'! You said, 'Go bring lions' milk in a lion's skin on a lion's shoulders,' now you go, take your lions' milk in a lion's skin on a lion's shoulders, and drink it! If your children have caught the 'little fire'!"

J.138   After that he said to the vizier, "Oh, you bastard, you've brought a monster down on me, now what do I do? If I let him go, now, he'll eat my whole army!"

J.139   He said, "Take him away, let him go!"

J.140   After that they [sic] took some of the lion's hair, and let him go. They let him go, and he went back to his own home. He came to his own home, and some days, some while passed, and this vizier of the right hand said, "King –"

J.141   "What?"

J.142   He said, "This time send him to a place that he won't come back from again."

J.143   "Where shall I send him?"

J.144   "After laughing flowers![1] He won't come back. They'll eat him."

J.145   When some days had passed, he sent soldiers, saying, "Go bring the mangy-headed cowherd."

J.146   He came, the soldier knocked on his door and he came, and his wife said, "Who is it?"

J.147   "It's I, now, me – the king sent me after the mangy-head."

J.148   After that his wife went and said to him, whispered,[2] "Now go,

---

[1] Ambiguous whether this is a singular, personal name, or an indefinite plural, common noun. See note 1, p. 404.

[2] /busukīd/ - a verb, /sukīdan/, is deduced from context.

and give him an answer!"

J.149   She saw, this *parī*, that the husband and wife were whispering, and the *parī* said, "What's the talk?"

J.150   He said, "It's this - the king has sent for me."

J.151   She said, "I understand - he's going to send you after laughing flowers. Be smart, don't worry, (get) seven camels from him, and (have him) make *ǧolūr*, load forty camels with forty sacks of it, then go, after laughing flowers. Come back, and I'll tell you (how) - go on."

J.152   After that, put it that, Margaret dear, he went, and he gave his greeting, the king, and he sat, on his - on his chair, and said, "It's just this, you must go and bring laughing flowers, for my wives and children."

J.153   "Fine, by my eyes."

J.154   He came back, and (she) said, "What did he say?"

J.155   "Nothing, he just said, 'Go bring laughing flowers.'" He was fretting and worrying (about it), the bald boy.

J.156   The *parī* said, "Don't you worry and fret. Don't you worry and fret, this is nothing!"

J.157   So it was that he said to the king, he went and said, "You make forty camel-loads of *ǧolūr*, and tie them up. Tomorrow I'll come and load them, and go after the laughing flowers for you."

J.158   That night he came and stayed (at home), and in the morning they committed each other to God, he and his three wives, and he went out. He went out, and came, and they loaded the forty camels and gave him the lead, and he came. He came, like that, came, came, came, came, came, and came to the ants. He made a little hole in one camel('s sack), like that, and went along, pouring, pouring, until this sack was finished, and he let the camel go. They were *dīvs*, these ants were *dīvs*. It poured out for them to eat, and when the camel (loads) of *ǧolūr* poured out, they would get busy (with that), and they'd let the camel go. So he got away from them.

J.159   He got away from them, and came - the *parī* had given him directions - and he saw an old woman there, and a river. He went to the old woman's house, and she said, "Eh, Mama's dear, where have you been?"

J.160   He said, "Mother dear, don't ask - I've had all sorts of difficulties, I'm a traveler, I wander around." He gave the old woman lots of money and said, "It's nothing, now - I - m - I, now, old Mama, now, you're a mother to me, don't tell anyone, (but) I've come after flowers, laughing flowers."

J.161   She said, "There's plenty of laughing flowers, now, she comes tomorrow, this – Laughing Flower, with forty ladies-in-waiting, to swim in the river, and I'll get <u>all</u> the laughing flowers you want, just like that." The old woman said that.

J.162   After that, Margaret dear, the *parī* had given him directions – she'd told him, given him directions, (so) they, when the next day came, these forty girls came and swam, came and swam, came and swam, came and <u>swam</u>, and it finally got to Laughing Flower('s turn). Laughing Flower came, and said,

J.163   "Pah! Pah! A human smell!
         If a horse come here, it casts its shoe,
         If a bird comes here, it casts its plume,
         What is a human being doing here?"

J.164   This old woman said, "No, Nanny's dear, there's no human being here."

J.165   Laughing Flower took off her clothes, and went to the river to swim. The mangy-headed cowherd went and stole her clothes. He stole them, and hid them. Laughing Flower swam, and flowers fell from her mouth and the water carried them down the river, and she swam, and swam, and when they got out of the water, the forty girls got out slowly, one by one, and put on their clothes, and her turn came, to come out last of all, and she came (and saw) that the place was there and nothing in it, her clothes weren't there. <u>Thirty</u> were still there. After that, she was ashamed to go among the little women, she was naked, and she said, "What can I do?" She said, "Whatever," she said 'it is, now, it's – whatever it was, it was in the old woman's house. A human, or whatever, that's what." She said, "Whatever manner of creature, human, *parī*, *dīv*, whatever you are, come out. Your desire and goal – whatever desire or goal you have, I'll accomplish it. Give me my clothes."

J.166   "I won't come out."

J.167   "I swear by the idol of the left hand, I won't quarrel with you."

J.168   "No!"

J.169   "By the – the idol of the right hand, I don't have a quarrel with you. Come out! I'll accomplish your desire and your goal."

J.170   "No!"

J.171   "On my mother's milk, I swear, whatever manner of creature, human, *parī*, *dīv*, whatever you are, come out. I – whatever desire you have, I'll accomplish it. Give me those clothes."

J.172   After that this mangy-headed cowherd came out and gave back her clothes, and she put them on. He said, "It's like this, a king is oppressing me, the king sent me, saying, 'Go and bring Laughing Flower.' So I came after you."

J.173   She said, "That's fine, by my eyes, I'll go." She'd <u>sworn</u>, already! If she hadn't <u>sworn</u> – but it was all right, she'd sworn, and she couldn't refuse to go. [MM: Yeah.]

J.174   Put it that they spent that night in the old woman's house and the next day Laughing Flower put the mangy-headed cowherd on her own shoulders – she summoned a $d\bar{\imath}v$, and they mounted the $d\bar{\imath}v$'s shoulders, and he <u>took off</u>, and left with Laughing Flower.

J.175   When he left there, then, it had come to the evening of the thirty-ninth day, and he – said, "Let's go to the door of his house and see, if he still hasn't come. Whether he's come or not." So he came – the king hadn't remembered. So the king's vizier came, and looked from behind the door, and (saw), "Bau-au-au!" The whole compound is drowning in <u>flower</u> petals! (claps once) He went, and said, "King!"

J.176   "What?"

J.177   "Eh, death! Eh, you don't have anything worthy of royalty! The mangy-head has it!"

J.178   He said, "Bastard! What am I to do? God gave it to him."

J.179   "Go, look! You sent him after laughing flowers, and he brought Laughing Flower herself!"

J.180   He – they sent for him, and he put the laughing flowers on a tray with a cover over it, and they brought them. He brought them. They said, "Good. May you see good fortune.[1] It's very good that you brought laughing flowers." He didn't take her, herself, there, just the flowers.

J.181   Put it that several – again, some days and some while passed, and once (again) this – one said, the vizier of the right hand said, "Lord King, this won't do. This time send him, tell him, 'Go, bring news from the dead!' Now he <u>can't</u> bring news from the dead, that will kill him, he'll die, then. Where are the dead, that he could go and get news from that world?" [MM: Yeah – yeah.]

J.182   He – they sent soldiers after him. They came, and knocked on the door, and (she) said, "What do you want?"

J.183   He said, "Nothing, I just want that – I want the mangy-head.

---

[1] Polite thanks.

His Majesty the King sent for him."

J.184   The mangy-head went out, and went. He went, and came to - they said, "Salām," and put him in a chair and said, "Welcome! You're very welcome!" They brought him tea, and food, and he ate, and after that they said, "It's just this - that, that, since you're my brother-in-law," - he'd given him his sister - "now, you've solved all these difficulties, and brought (everything), now there's one more - you must go and bring news of my mother and father, from the other world!" (laughs) [MM: Yeah!]

J.185   No, he said, - m - "That's fine, Lord King, I'll bring it!"

J.186   He came, came back home, (and said), "This king lifts off one stone, and puts on another! His father! His dead! His living! How can I go to the other world, to get the news?"

J.187   This *parī* said, "Don't say a thing, not a thing! You just keep mum! I'll fix it up. You just go, and tell him, say, 'Write a letter and give it to me, so I can go and bring news of the other world, from your - for you.'"

J.188   He came, the next day, and said, "Lord King, write a letter and give it to me, so I can take it and give it to them, and bring news from your (people), and a letter." The vizier wrote a letter, too, and the *wakīl* wrote, and the king wrote, and the *qāẓī* wrote. Four, five, six letters, they wrote, and gave them to him.

J.189   He came. He came (back), then, this *parī* and his three wives, (she) didn't let him go outside the house. She said, "You just sit here."

J.190   Now this *parī* knew (   )[1], and she wrote out answers to all their letters, saying, "This world is such a good place, Heaven is thus-and-so, there's no bother in Heaven, everyone just sits around, with the fruits of Heaven, everything is good here, this is the world, what use is that world? You come to us, here, too!" [MM laughs] "Let that world go!" She wrote all kinds of good things like that in the letters. After that, when the fortieth day arrived, then, she gave him the letters.

J.191   He took them, and when he took them (there), the king and vizier and *wakīl* got extremely happy and pleased, and said, "We'll go, too! You must take us to the other world!"

J.192   "Fine, I'll take you, Lord King, I'll take you (there)!"

J.193   He came (back) to the house, and said to his wife, to the *parī*, "Now, they're saying, 'You have to take us, too!'"

---

[1] /tajdewer/, with fahmīdan?

J.194   She said, "Don't you say a thing. Everything's fine, now!" (laughs) After that she said, "Fine, you go and tell them, say, 'You can't be taken <u>there</u>, unless you fill a room with firewood, and pour petrol over it, and all the doors and windows must be shut and locked, with just one ceiling vent open, like that, then I'll light the fire, myself, then we'll go to the other world, then you'll see, about that other world. I got there <u>just</u> that way.'"

J.195   Put it that he came. He came, Margaret dear, he came and said, "Lord King, now you must fill a room with wood, and pour petrol (over it). Now, then, I'll come, and you all come, too. Then we'll go, I'll light the fire in the room, then, and I'll take you to the other world. I'll go with you to the other world. I'll show you how, and we'll go."

J.196   This *parī* said, "We'll be sitting on top of the roof." This wife of his. She's a *parī*, like a pigeon. M - at home she's like a human, but when she goes out, she can fly, like a dove, and come down to earth, or go up to the sky. She said, "Just as you've lit the fire, I'll come down through the vent, and pick you up and carry you out. Those others can stay there (laughs) and burn."

J.197   After that he sent, and trucks full of wood came and they put it in the room, and filled the room, and after that they poured oil over it, and the mangy-headed cowherd went and - <u>all</u> of them went into the room, and they fastened the door and windows and locked them and the ceiling vent is open just a bit. Then after that, just as the bald boy struck the match, just as the smoke curled around the room, they couldn't see, and the *parī* came and from right in the midst - he said, "You sit around the four sides, and I'll stand right in the middle." He was standing in the middle, and she came down from above, the *parī*, and picked him up and left. That's all. They <u>burned</u>, then! Along with the (laughs) wood, they, the vizier and *wakīl* and the king, and the *qāzī* burned. There, those kinds of fortunes, that was the story, this story. [MM laughs] This was from those people of the - what? from those 'valley folks',[1] it was!" [MM: From - whom did you learn it?] From Adī! I learned this story from Adī! [MM: Before that, you never heard it from anyone else?] No, no, now, Margaret dear - [MM: It was new to you?] Yeah, it was new to me. The idea is, that if someone tells a story around me, and there's not any uproar, or anything, - how long has it been since Adī told it? The time of - a long time ago, it was harvest time.[2] I didn't forget it, though [MM: Yes.] It doesn't go out of my mind. [MM: Did she tell it once, or twice?] <u>She</u> told it <u>once</u> - she told it once. She told it once, because it didn't work out for her to tell it, because

---

[1] Adī is from Anār Darreh, "Pomegranate Valley."

[2] Late June.

for her - she left, then. [MM: Yeah. Yeah.] I said, "Adĺ, tell
it," after you (left) she got a little unhappy with her son, and
she came here, then, she was - here for three days. Yeah - Now he
sent my mother[1] after her. That same day that you went --
[END OF TOPIC]

---

[1] Adĺ's 2 sons' mother-in-law.

TEXT K

Title: Alī Zarrīn [Ali the Golden]
Narrator: Māder Zāher
Recorded 14 April, 1975
Tape CXL - CXLI

      Portions of the text have been synopsized and are enclosed in
brackets. The translated portions are not entirely verbatim: some statements have been abbreviated.

K.1   [A poor woman gives birth to forty sons at once, and puts them
under the cow basket.[1] Her husband returns from cow herding and
runs away when he learns he has forty children that he cannot support. The boys grow up, and the fortieth, Alī Zarrīn, is called
before the king, who has heard of his unusual birth and prodigious
strength. The king's vizier sees Alī's fate written on his forehead, that he will kill and succeed the king. The vizier advises
the king to send Alī somewhere, from whence he will not return.]

K.2   [The first task set for Alī is to dig a pool in the king's
garden, which he does with the help of his brothers.]

K.3   [The second task is to fetch the Horse of Forty Colts. Alī
sets off, with no guidance. Finally, lost and hungry in the
desert, he prays and is met by the Messenger of God:]

K.4   He said, "Oh, God, where shall I go? Where will I find it?"

K.5   The Messenger of God, a good person, and wise, with a white
beard and white clothes, and a walking stick, appeared before him,
and said, "Alī Zarrīn, where are you going?"

K.6   "I'm going after the Horse of Forty Colts."

K.7   "She's a *dīv*. She'll eat you."

K.8   "I have to go, because the king sent me. Either I bring her,
or I die."

K.9   "All right." He slapped him on the right shoulder, and said,
"Alī Zarrīn, wherever you go, may God see to it that no *dīv* eats

---

[1] /gau sabad/ a dome of woven wicker, up to four or five feet in diameter,
which is put over milk jugs, etc., to keep animals out of them.

you, and no lion, and no leopard, and that no sword should come down on your head. May you meet with good fortune."

K.10   "Fine."

K.11   "If you go along like this, you'll come to a plain, and a reed bed, with two springs. Drain the water out of the springs and plug them with cotton, and make two mangers and fill them with chickpea candies,[1] and set up a full-length mirror, and hide a new saddle and bridle, and hide under there. The horse will come, and go, and come, and go, and the third time she comes, she'll say, 'My, my! What beauty I've got!' You say, 'If some human would saddle and bridle you, and mount you, you'd be even more beautiful.' She'll say, 'Come here.' You say, 'No, you must swear.' She'll say, 'By the left hand, I swear.' You say, 'No.' She'll say, 'By the right hand, I swear.' Say, 'No, I won't come.' She'll say, 'On my mother's milk, I swear I won't eat you.' After that, go."

K.12   Alī Zarrīn went and went and found the reedbed and drained the springs and put the cotton in them, and made two mangers and filled them with chickpea sweets and set up the full-length mirror, and hid himself under a thorn bush.

K.13   The Horse of Forty Colts came with her forty colts and whinnied, and came again, and a third time, and her glance fell on the mirror. She said, "My, my, how beautiful I am."

K.14   [Alī Zarrīn carries out the exchange with the Horse according to directions.]

K.15   When he placed his foot to mount her, she whinnied once and her forty colts arrived. When the forty colts arrived, he threw down a bunch of walnut meats and the colts got busy with them, and he hit her with the whip and the horse took off through the air, and they went.

K.16   When they came near the city, the horse whinnied and caused the earth to shake, and the king heard her whinny. [Xairuddīn prompts MZ, inaudibly] I forgot - yes. After Alī Zarrīn left, they took his forty brothers and put them all in a place where the work was hard and dirty, and the food scanty. When Alī Zarrīn reappeared, they took these forty - thirty-nine brothers, and sent them to the baths, and dressed them in new clothes, and sent them to meet Alī Zarrīn with guns and artillery [salutes] and marching bands. They brought the Horse of Forty Colts and let her loose in the garden.

K.17   [The vizier tells the king that Alī Zarrīn is a great *dīv*, who will kill him, and persuades the king to send him after the head of

---

[1] /noql/.

the White *Dīv*. There are forty *dīv* brothers. Alī Zarrīn agrees to go and bring it, within forty days. His mother tries to dissuade him. He takes the Horse of Forty Colts with the king's permission. The Horse warns him against the *dīv*s, but delivers him to a plain between two mountains, and gives him directions as follows:]

K.18   She said, "As you climb these mountains, in the midst of these mountains there's a house, locked. Break the lock, and go in. There's a well inside, with a flat stone on top of it. Lift the stone, strike with your whip [*sic*], and one will come out, strike again, and again, - don't let your hand falter."

K.19   [Alī Zarrīn goes and finds everything as the Horse described, and the well with a millstone on top of it. He lifts the millstone and beheads the *dīv*s one by one with his sword as they emerge, except for the last:]

K.20   Of these forty brothers, one was left, and he'd killed forty, and the last came up (out of the well), but when Alī Zarrīn struck with his sword, his hand faltered, and one drop of blood fell to the ground. That drop of blood became a pigeon and flew up into the air. It said, "No matter how long you live, one day I'll have business with you."

K.21   [Alī Zarrīn takes the head of the White *Dīv* and, lost in thought, summons the Horse of Forty Colts with a burning hair and returns home. The king assembles his brothers to greet him as before. The Horse and the *dīv*'s head are placed in the king's garden.]

K.22   [The vizier tells the king to send Alī Zarrīn after the Tree of Forty Voices. Alī Zarrīn agrees to go, as before. His mother tries to dissuade him, but he takes food and the Horse of Forty Colts and leaves. The Horse agrees to take him as near as possible to the house of the *parī* who has the Tree, but she explains that she cannot enter the *parī*s house because she, too, is a *parī*.

K.23   [As they are flying toward their destination, Alī Zarrīn looks down and sees the Messenger of God walking along. He descends and pays homage to him.]

K.24   He said, "Alī Zarrīn, where are you going?"

K.25   "To the foot of Mount Qāf."

K.26   "Oh, my son, they're all *dīv*s and *parī*s at the foot of Mount Qāf. Whoever is sending you there, is sending you so you won't come back."

K.27   "I have to go, or die."

K.28   "All right, if you're going, then put this kohl on your eyes, so no *dīv* or *bārzangī* or *parī* can see you. When you get down by the wall, there's an old woman *bārzangī* asleep, there, sleeping the sleep of forty, with her breasts thrown back over her shoulders. You go and suck at her breast,[1] and suck, then <u>bite</u>! You make her swear an oath, and when she swears by her own mother's milk, let go of her breast."

K.29   "Fine."

K.30   [Alī Zarrīn flies off again and seeing the old ogress asleep, follows directions.]

K.31   She said, "All right, now, when you climb up on this wall, be careful not to touch the branches of the trees with your head or your shoulder, but get up on the wall, and you'll find a cat. Pet the cat and play with it. It has forty keys hung around its neck; you take them and go, then, and take a branch from the Tree of Forty Voices."

K.32   "Fine."

K.33   He went and climbed the wall, but as he got to the top, his head touched the branches of the Tree of Forty Voices, and forty voices broke out from the Tree, and the earth shook and all the *parī*s and *dīv*s and *bārzangī*s woke up at once. She[2] said,

K.34   "Pah! Pah! A human smell!
If a horse comes here, it casts its shoe,
If a bird comes here, it casts its plume,
If a human comes here, it leaves its head,
What is a human being doing here at the foot of Mount Qāf?"

K.35   [The *dīv*s and their *parī* mistress argue about whether a human is present. They can't see him on account of the magic kohl which he has applied to his eyes, but she insists that she can smell him.]

K.36   After that he went and took a limb from the Tree of Forty Voices (undetected), and caught the cat and played and played and played with the cat until it was almost asleep, and took the keys. There were forty rooms, and in each room there was a *dīv* couple asleep, servants of the Daughter of Shāhḡol, the *Parī* King. Finally, he got to the fortieth room, where the Daughter of Shāhḡol the *Parī* King was asleep, and he took her roasted chicken that was set by her, and ate it, and moved the golden lampstand by her head down to her feet, and the silver one by her feet up to her head. He took her ring and put it on his own finger. She had on seven pairs of pantaloons, and he untied six of her pantsbands and left the seventh, and kissed her twice on the face, and took one of her best, most

---

[1] Thereby becoming her foster child.

[2] The *parī* who owns the garden.

beautiful shawls and put it on his own shoulders, and left.

K.37   He came back toward the old woman's house [*sic*], and burned hair to summon the Horse of Forty Colts, and quickly returned to the king's city. Once again the king recalled Alī Zarrīn's brothers from their work and sent them to meet Alī Zarrīn with pomp, when he heard the sound of the Tree of Forty Voices.

K.38   [The king greeted Alī Zarrīn cordially, although he was even more frightened. They planted the branch of the Tree of Forty Voices by the pool which Alī had dug in the king's garden.]

K.39   [That evening a man came looking for the woman who gave birth to forty sons at once. This man was Alī's father, who had fled on first seeing his 40 offspring and not been seen since. He came and announced his identity, and was well received by his wife and forty sons.]

K.40   [Alī Zarrīn tells his mother that he has an enemy, and that the (fortieth) White *Dīv* will be trying to catch him by night, so someone must stand watch. Alī Zarrīn's father insists on standing watch, despite his age, and falls asleep, at which point the *dīv*, who has been watching through the vent in the roof, flies down and snatches Alī Zarrīn, and carries him up into the sky. He carries him up until Alī Zarrīn says that the earth looks no larger than the point of a pin, then says:]

K.41   "If I drop you from here, will even your pieces[1] fall to earth?"

K.42   He said, "No," he said, "All right, I killed the forty because a king oppressed me, and if I hadn't killed them, he would have killed me. The tyranny is from the king. If you kill one, what will the other thirty-nine do? My blood is no redder than the blood of those forty. We are forty brothers, you can be the forty-first."

K.43   Alī Zarrīn and the White *Dīv* made friends there, and gave each other their hands, and the *dīv* brought him down. Alī Zarrīn's heart was great, and it grew greater. He was very happy, and came home.

K.44   [Once again the vizier tells the kings to send Alī Zarrīn away, in pursuit of the 'Cat Meynaqā'[2] which is also a *dīv*, and will tear him apart. Alī Zarrīn agrees to go, and goes home and tells his mother to prepare food for the road. He says goodbye

---

[1] /čokke'ā/

[2] I cannot find any plausible translation for this word. Turkish, perhaps?

to his mother and father and prepares to ride off on the Horse of Forty Colts.]

K.45   The White *Dīv* said to him, "Do you know what, Alī Zarrīn?"

K.46   "No, what?"

K.47   "When you come to such-and-such a desert plain, you must take a cow and skin it sack-fashion and sew up the tail end of it. Cook milk rice[1] by the plateful and load it into the skin. That Cat comes and goes on that plain, and he'll say,

K.48   "Pah! Pah! A human smell,
        If horse comes here, it casts its shoe,
        If a bird comes here, it casts its plume,
        What is a human being doing, in <u>my</u> desert plain?'"

K.49   He said, "Fine."

K.50   [Alī Zarrīn and the Horse of Forty Colts set out, come to the plain, and carry out the *dīv*'s instructions, leaving the cowhide full of milk rice 'cooked like cheese', with one end of the sack open, lying in the plain. The Cat appears.]

K.51   It said,

        "Pah! Pah! A human smell,
        If a horse comes here, it casts its shoe,
        If a bird comes here, it casts its plume,
        What is a human being doing here, in my desert plain?"

K.52   He said, "I drank raw milk,
                I go about everywhere."

K.53   The Cat said, "All right." He went and looked at the sack, and walked this way, and that way, and this way and that, and looked in, and finally went inside it to see what was there, and started to eat the milk rice. Then Alī Zarrīn went right up to it, and tied the end of it closed <u>tight</u> with a rope. Then he burned some of the Horse of Forty Colts' hair, and the Horse arrived, and he picked that up and I don't know if it was an hour or just half an hour, till he got to the city. And this cat was meowing and carrying on and raising a fuss, and the king heard it.

K.54   First the king was happy, and then he got very upset, (thinking), "Alī Zarrīn has brought all these things. What's going to happen in the end?" And besides, when morning came - just the night before, a letter had come from the foot of Mount Qāf, saying, "I have a quarrel with you. Who was it that came from you to the

---

[1] An unsweetened dish of rice to which milk is added in the last stages of cooking.

foot of Mount Q̄af?"

K.55   This Alī Zarrīn - the king gathered all Alī Zarrīn's brothers
and sent them to meet him with artillery (salutes), and Alī Zarrīn
came and greeted the king, and the king said, "Alī Zarrīn, do you
know what's happened?"

K.56   "No, what?"

K.57   "A letter has come from the foot of Mount Q̄af, saying that
the Daughter of Shāhg̈ol the *Parī* King has a quarrel with me. Since
you went to the foot of Mount Q̄af, you'll have to go and fight her."

K.58   He said, "Fine, yes, I'll go and fight her."

K.59   The next morning, Alī Zarrīn wrote a letter and sent it (to
her) with the White *Dīv*, saying, "Yes, I'm back, and I'll fight
you."

K.60   Now this desert, from here to - what do they call it -? The
Pashtu Bridge, like from here to there, two or three times that
far, it was desert plain, and she'd covered it __all__ with silken
carpets, and Turkoman carpets, and tents. Alī Zarrīn said to the
Horse of Forty Colts, "Do you know what?"

K.61   "No, what?"

K.62   "Now, when you go that way, stamp with your hooves so that
all these carpets and tents will be torn in __four__ pieces under your
feet."

K.63   "Very well."

K.64   After that, when the dust and smoke was whirling up, the
Horse of Forty Colts was coming, and the Daughter of Shāhg̈ol the
Parī King said to herself, "This is a fine, able man. I'll have
to marry him."

K.65   Then when he got close to the tent of the Daughter of Shāhg̈ol
the *Parī* King, and he was about to greet her, Alī Zarrīn, the
Daughter of Shāhg̈ol the *Parī* King, who was stronger than he, she
greeted him. She greeted him and rose from her chair and took her
handkerchief out of her pocket, and wiped away Alī Zarrīn's sweat,
and took him by the right shoulder and put him in a chair. She
said, "All right, you sit here crossways, but tell me straight,
whether it was you who came to the foot of Mount Q̄af, or someone
else."

K.66   "I myself came." Her shawl was on his shoulders, too, and
her ring on his finger.

K.67   He said, there, "All right, I came to the foot of Mount Q̄af,
like this: I came with the Horse of Forty Colts."

K.68   "Fine. The Horse of Forty Colts is my sister."

K.69   [A full recapitulation by Alī Zarrīn follows, recounting all
the events of K.28-36, and explaining how the magic kohl of the
Messenger of God had made him invisible.]

K.70   Alī Zarrīn and the Daughter of Shāhğol the *Parī* King gave each
other their hands, there, and agreed to marry. He said, "We'll be
married."

K.71   She said, "How many days from now?"

K.72   "Ten days from now." He said, "I have one job to do, and when
I'm through with it, I'll be married."

K.73   "Fine."

K.74   The Daughter of Shāhğol the *Parī* King took her leave, with her
*dīv*s and *parī*s and troops of *parī*s and armies and troops and tents
and all, and set out, and - no, God of Repentence, excuse me, I
forgot. That evening, Alī Zarrīn went, and the king had invited
them. [After that the Daughter of Shāhğol the *Parī* King returned
the invitation. The whole party arrived, but saw no sign of fires
or cooking. When they'd come, a tablecloth came and spread itself
and was covered with platters of rice and roasted chickens, and
they couldn't tell whether it came up from the earth, or down from
the sky.]

K.75   After that the invitation were over, and she took her leave
and the White *Dīv* saud to Alī Zarrīn, "Alī Zarrīn, do you know
what?"

K.76   "No."

K.77   "Tonight, you bring the Cat, and play with it, and tell it
this one thing."

K.78   "What?"

K.79   "Tell the Cat, 'Tomorrow, the king has invited (us) to his
garden. You play with the king, and play and play and play, and
get up on his shoulder, and tear his head off.'"

K.80   "Fine."

K.81   [The next day, Alī Zarrīn got permission from the king to take
the Cat home for the evening,] and he played with the Cat and
played with it - excuse me, I forgot one thing, that Alī Zarrīn's
brother came and said, "Excuse me, Alī Zarrīn, but you've never
asked us, how he oppresses us when you're off traveling."

K.82   He said, "All right, I'm asking you now, what troubled you when I was off traveling?"

K.83   He said, "As soon as you left town, the king took these clothes away from us and put us all in a place where we were troubled, and hungry, and worn out. After that, when he heard (you were coming), he took us and sent us to the baths and got us shaves and haircuts-and gave us new clothes and sent us to meet you."

K.84   He said, "That's just fine!"

K.85   [Alī Zarrīn brings the Cat home and explains what he wants the Cat to do, and it agrees. Alī Zarrīn invites the king for the next evening, and regales him and the other members of the court with food and drink.]

K.86   The Cat Meynaqā jumped onto the qāzī's shoulder, and played, and jumped onto the wakīl's shoulder, and played, and jumped onto Alī Zarrīn's shoulder, and played, and jumped onto the White Dīv's shoulder, and played, and then jumped onto the king's knee, and sat. He played there, and played and played, and got closer and closer to his neck, and then tore his head off. He threw his head away, but he took the crown and put it on Alī Zarrīn's head.

K.87   He[1] said, "Now you can applaud, Brothers!" So there they were, they had to clap, and Alī Zarrīn got to be king and his forty brothers all around him as viziers and wakīls and qāzīs and moftīs.

K.88   [After ten days have passed and the king has been decently buried in a shrine and mourned, Alī Zarrīn celebrates his marriage to the Daughter of Shāhgol the Parī King.]

K.89   He said, "I've become king, (now) I'll marry you."

K.90   He gathered his forty brothers, and all his relatives, and invited his mother and father and everyone, and

K.91   For seven days and nights they beat the sticks on the drum,
            and the drum on the sticks,
        They gave the Hindu raw food and the Muslim cooked,[2]
        And we didn't get a thing,
        Not one burnt bit off the bottom of the pot!

---

[1] Speaker unspecified - probably the cat.

[2] The sense is that even non-Muslims were entertained, but with inferior provisions. Interestingly, Brahmins in Indian villages regularly receive their share of a communal feast in raw form, because lower-caste people (including Muslims) cannot cook their food for them without polluting it. This detail seems to belong to an Indo-Muslim setting.

K.92   And he married the Daughter of Shāhğol the *Parī* King, and Alī
Zarrīn was very happy and fortunate and comfortable, and everything
was peaceful with him and his *dīv*s and *parī*s, all there together,

K.93   And they lived there,
And we here,
They stayed on that side of the sea[1]
And we on this.
And the sea is big, we can't cross.... (laughs)

K.94   Now the story of Alī Zarrīn is finished.

---

[1] /derīyā/.

TEXT L

Title: Šīr o Palang [Lion and Leopard]
Narrator: Mādar Zāher
Recorded 3 Aug. 1975
Cassette E1B-E2A

L.1   Some things that bear fruit,
            (Some that) bear none,
            Cypress and poplar,
            Pomegranate and quince,
            Pistachio and pomegranate.

L.2   There was one - uh - leopard. [MM: Yeah.] A leopard - he had
    no house or place. He always wandered the plains and mountains and
    desert. He went, searched, searched, searched, searched, and fixed
    himself a house, fixed a den in one place and was living there.
    While he was living (there), after some days and some while passed,
    he was in the den, and he noticed like the sound of a lion, moan-
    ing and coming (along). This leopard came out of his den, and saw
    a lion, sick, coming along the road, moaning. He came and ques-
    tioned the lion. It said, "I'm sick."

L.3   "All right, please come into my house." He brought (the
    lion)[1] to his own house. After he brought her home, he treated
    her with medicines and drugs and did everything, and she got well.
    [MM to storyteller's husband and daughter, who are talking near
    microphone: OK, be quiet, then, you understand what we're doing
    here? Both (of you), quiet.]

L.4   - It got well, this lion. After the lion got well, the leopard
    and the lion stayed there together. Some time and some while passed,
    and this lion went off - somewhere, to walk around, look around.
    The leopard was right there, in his own room. He was in his own
    room, and then he noticed - he went outside. The leopard said,
    "What am I doing here? I'm hungry. I'll go some place and find a
    sheep or a cow or something, and eat."

L.5   He went and wandered around the plain, and he caught a good
    (big) cow, and he ate and was satisfied, (then) he went - to the
    mountains. He saw a nice, fat female leopard (coming along). He
    made friends - he was a male - with his female. After they made
    friends, they came back to the house. After that, evening came,

_____

[1] The sex of the lion remains unclear until paragraph L.20, below, where
    it is described as female. The ambiguity seems to be one of language
    and not of the storyteller's meaning, so I have not tried to preserve
    it in translation.

and the lion came back. They didn't say any more. This lion came back, and three people were living there, in one room.

L.6   After some time had passed, this leopard had babies, this female. This leopard - male said to the lion, said, "All right, the three of us, it would be better if we'd build[1] another house for ourselves."

L.7   This lion got angry, got angry at what the leopard said. The lion said, "They don't like me, then."

L.8   She left. Went out, and left. Went out, and left, and some days and some while passed, and the leopard gave birth, had maybe eight or nine (cubs), like that. These cubs got bigger, little by little, and (each) day one (leopard) would go and one would stay, and one day these cubs got pretty big. The father and mother both left. To go hunting. This lion is out to get them (thinking), "Whenever she has cubs, I'll go and eat them."

L.9   After that, this lion came, and saw, listened carefully and saw that there was no sound from the mother or the father leopard. She came (in), (MZ speaks in undertone, indicating stealth) came to the room, and (voice rising) ate all her cubs.

L.10   After she'd eaten them, first this - uh - male leopard - came. He came, and got close to the house, and he saw there was no squalling and crying, there's nothing. He came inside the room, and saw there was nothing. He thought all the cubs had gone with their mother.

L.11   "Good," he said, "They've gone with their mother." Then he said, "If she didn't take them before, (it was because) they weren't big enough for her to take them with her, so now what? Today they went out."

L.12   He came out of the house and lay down on the road, the poor thing, then, and he's thinking,[2] then. All at once, he saw the (female) leopard coming alone - the lion came - this leopard came alone, their mother. When she got close to him, he said, "Where are the kids?"

L.13   "The kids are in the house."

L.14   "There's not a one!"

---

[1] /tîâr mîkonîm be xo/ - ambiguous in Herati. Either 'let us build for ourselves' or (polite) 'you build for yourself'.

[2] /fekr mîkoneh/ - this verb regularly means 'to worry' in colloquial Herati. The leopard's soliloquy indicates concern, too.

L.15   She said, "All right," she said, "You know what this is about?"

L.16   "No."

L.17   "That lion has eaten all my cubs."

L.18   "No, she won't have eaten them."

L.19   "No, I know she's eaten them. She's eaten them, because you said, 'You build another house,'[1] and she thought you didn't like her, she got angry and left, and she came and ate my cubs."

L.20   Then he said, "All right, if she ate your cubs, them, don't you worry. I - now, when - I'll go and sleep with her,[2] she'll have cubs and you can go and eat all her cubs. Don't quarrel!"

L.21   (She) came - they went, the two of them, and these two, these two leopards were really - quarreled, quarreled, quarreled. Morning came, and the male leopard went out. He came to the mountains. He knew where the lion was living, then. She prowled, prowled, found a good place, this lion, said - the leopard said, "What are you doing?"

L.22   She said, "Nothing. I'm just lying around here, living here. you put me out of your house, and I live here."

L.23   "No, I didn't put you out, you came here yourself."

L.24   She said, "All right, how are those cubs of yours?"

L.25   "They're fine, I think my cubs are in your stomach." (laughs)

L.26   [MM: He said that?] Yeah, he said it, then, "They're in your stomach."

L.27   "No, I didn't eat them. I don't (even) know whether you've had cubs or not."

L.28   (He) said, "No." He said, "All right. Better than this would be for you and me - (you were) like a sister to me - I'll find a good fellow for you, a lion, so you can get married. With this lion."

L.29   "No."

L.30   This leopard said, "No."

---

[1] Not ambiguous: /Dīgeh otāq jor ko/, second person singular imperative.

[2] This strange plan is the first direct indication of the lion's gender.

L.31   The leopard went out, and went to a forest, a big forest that he knew of, where there were a lot of lions. He prowled, prowled, and found a good, <u>big</u> lion, and spoke to him, said, "I have a friend, a lion, and you could live together."

L.32   "All right."

L.33   He came, this lion, this female is like a child, and this (male) lion is as big as an ox. He came there, the leopard left the two of them in that house and he left. When they'd been there for some days and some while, the two lions, this lion got pregnant. The leopard, then, he was thinking and he knew (it). Besides, he doesn't (show) that he's upset, this leopard. He doesn't get upset. He's happy[1] with this lion. He went, and came to her house, and went, and came, till he knew the time was near that she would give birth to these kids. He didn't go again. Some days passed after that, and he said – to his wife – he said to the female lion [sic], "All right, now, she's borne these cubs, and if you go and eat them, it's up to you, but the sin will be yours, not mine."

L.34   She said, "I'm going to eat them. Because she ate mine, I'm eating (hers)."

L.35   This time when she came she saw that she was there with the cubs, (whispers dramatically) she left. She went back. She left, this lion – (pause) (whispers) – eh – this lion, ah – understood. She understood, that it was the sound of her feet. When she came out, she saw the leopard, going off. She said, "By God, this, this – I ate this leopard's children, and she'll eat mine."

L.36   When her husband came, the lion came, she said, "(Let's) give up this house!"

L.37   "Why should we give it up?"

L.38   "This is a bad place." She didn't say, 'I did this thing, I ate this leopard's children,' and so on. Just, "It's bad here. Let's go somewhere else."

L.39   This – male lion – said, "No. If I go anywhere else – I went to a lot of trouble for this place, I made a good home, it's better here."

L.40   He didn't do what she wanted. So he didn't do what she wanted, and this female lion didn't go <u>any</u>where. After this, when some days had passed after this, all at once, she got very – her skin got enflamed. So she got warm, this lion. She went off to swim. Now this leopard's ears are at work, she's coming all the time. This leopard came, and saw no one in the house, and she

---

[1] /xoš/ – 'pleasant'?

ate all her babies and went home. She went to her own home, she went in the evening, and this (lion) went to a good (big) river, and washed, washed, washed.

L.41   After that, she sunned herself, then went back toward home. Right - the - (stutters) - when she came, she saw there wasn't a single child. She said, "Well this - what shall I do? She ate my children, then."

L.42   This (male) lion came, and said, "Where are the cubs?"

L.43   She said, "The cubs got lost."

L.44   "No, they didn't. You have to tell me the truth. If you don't, I'll kill you."

L.45   "Why would you kill me?"

L.46   "I'll kill you, because you said, 'Let's move out of here. Let's go live somewhere else.' I said, 'No, this house is better,' - You must have done something to someone, for these cubs to disappear. If they weren't stolen, some other animal must have eaten them."

L.47   She said, "I did like this, with a leopard - " [END OF TAPE]

E2A: [First 45 seconds of tape were recorded over with extraneous material. Story begins after the lioness has recapitulated the quarrel with the leopards.]
[Male lion speaks:]

L.48   " - (and) she ate your cubs, (so) you're quarreling."

L.49   "No, I'm going."

L.50   "It would be better not to go."

L.51   "I'm going."

L.52   "All right."

L.53   This male lion is very intelligent, has a good brain. He stayed (behind). He sat down, this female lion went out, went to (the leopard's) door and called. She called (her), this female - lion - [sic] came out. She said, - "What do you want?"

L.54   "I came (because) I want my babies."

L.55   "Where are your babies?"

L.56   "You ate my babies. They're in your stomach. (In a flat, nondramatic tone of voice) I'll rip open your stomach, and take my babies."

L.57   "If it's like - I'm just the same - I'll tear open your stomach first! You ate mine first! [MM: Muffled laughter] But - I'll tear (yours) first, and you mine second - that's better."

L.58   So after this, this lion got very angry, and she came toward home. That night, she (cried), a lot, cried, cried, cried, and came (home).

L.59   Morning came. Morning came, and she said, "All right, then, what shall I do? I'll either kill myself, or - like this."

L.60   She went and sat on the leopard's path. When the male leopard came (along), she said, "All right, look. This wife of yours came and ate all my cubs, all at once."

L.61   "No, she won't have eaten them."

L.62   "No, by God, she did eat them."

L.63   "All right, there was that time, when I said, '(Let's) build[1] another house,' and you got angry. You came back, and ate all of her cubs. If she ate yours, too, well, she ate them, that's all. That's all there is to say."

L.64   He left. He came, this leopard, came home, to his wife. He said,"You went and ate those cubs."

L.65   "Yeah."

L.66   "She came today, (and met me) on my way, and she was like my own sister to me. If you ate her cubs, I feel like you ate my sister's cubs."

L.67   This leopard got good and mad - (laughing) - at her husband. [MM laughs] She said, (shortly and sharply), "If she's your sis- ter, let her come and live with you - I'm leaving." [MM: short laugh]

L.68   She ran away! She ran away, left, and went off to the deserts, (stutters) - a wee - for a week, she stayed. This leopard came and said to the lion, "All right. I quarreled with her. I got very angry. If you would, go and ask pardon so that my wife will come back."

L.69   The lion went out. The lioness. She went out, went - well, she prowled, prowled, prowled, prowled, prowled, lots of places, and found one little leopard cub. Whe- she found it, she brought it, she carried it and came close to the leopard, found where she was. She went, and saw that she was lying in a reed bed, really angry and weeping, and her eyes all full of dust, and dirt, and

---

[1] Ambiguous /konĩm/.

sore. She said - she came, and greeted her, and kissed her cheek, and said, "Don't worry, I brought you a leopard cub, (to have) until you have (more) cubs. Now come, let's go home."

L.70   "No, I'm not going."

L.71   "No, you must, so come."

L.72   She took her and brought her and reconciled her with her husband, and they on that side of the stream and I on this. It's just a little story. And after this I'll tell that story - of the king - I've got to bring it to mind -

L.73   [MM: Was this one from your own heart, or from someone else?]

L.74   This story of the lion and the leopard? From my own heart. But this one that I'm telling now is from Maryām . . .

TEXT M

Title: Šīr o Palang [Lion and Leopard]
Narrator: Mādar Zāher
Recorded 13. Feb. 1976
Cassette F1B

M.1   [MM: And that story of the lion and the leopard that you made
up, do you still remember it?]

M.2   Yeah. Isn't it finished?[1] (You mean) that story that I just
told? Or no, (the one) before.

M.3   [MM: No, that other, about the lion and the leopard, who made
a - house, - then they quarreled -]

M.4   (doubtfully) Oh - yeah.

M.5   [MM: The lion (sic) got married and -]

M.6   (Comprehending) Oh, yeah! Yeah, yeah. Sure, I remember it.
Do you want me to tell it?

M.7   [MM: Yes, I like it a lot.]

M.8   What time is it now? Because you have to go, to Azīzah's
house.

M.9   [MM: A quarter to ten.]

M.10   (laughs) Oh, good, there's time.

M.11   [MM: Wait a minute, I think - (interrupts recording to check
batteries)]

M.12   [Māhgol, MZ's 10-year old daughter, whispers inaudibly]

M.13   (to Māhgol, heatedly) She's going to eat! She's going to
eat something - I wish she would eat something!

M.14   [Māhgol: She's going to eat at their house, then?]

M.15   Yes, she's going to. If your grandmother comes after her -
if not, then let her stay here. Four o'clock - [Break in record-
ing]

M.16   [MM resumes recording: Please go ahead.]

_____

[1] Referring to the story she just told, which also concerned a lion.

M.17   There was, was, this - there was a leopard. This leopard, some days and some while passed, and he was going around by himself like that, in the plain and mountain and desert, then he went to (this) one place, and his heart was pleased, so he said, "I'm going to make myself a den right here."

M.18   He dug himself a little den, and fixed it up there, and right there - days he would go to the plains, and nights he'd come and lie in his den. One day on this plain, (there's) a lion lying there, sick, moaning. [MM laughs quietly] And after that - lions and leopards are friendly with one another - he came, and said, "Lion!"

M.19   "What?"

M.20   "Why are you lying here?"

M.21   "I'm not well."

M.22   He said, "Come, let's go, you and I, we're brothers to each other."

M.23   "All right."

M.24   He brought this little lion back to his own den, brought (her), and days he would go, this leopard, hunting, he'd (prowl) [Child coughs into microphone] and whatever food would come into his grasp, he'd bring and give to the lion. So they made ends meet, and went along. When some days and some while had passed, this leopard was wandering around on the plains, he was a male leopard, and a female leopard came his way. He made friends with this female leopard. He made friends with the female leopard, and brought her, brought her to the den. When he brought her to the den, this lion - she was female - she got a little angry. So then, it troubled this one's heart,[1] and this leopard said, "This same house, let's all live here together." Just that.

M.25   Some days and some while later, put it that this female leopard and male leopard mated, then. When they mated, this female got pregnant. This is just one den, with three people, and it's narrow, this den. The male leopard said to the lion, "You'd better make another house for yourself, dig one out."[2]

M.26   This leopard - this lioness got angry. Got angry, and left. She said, "By God, one day, the day will come . . ." this lioness said, "And (see) if I don't eat his children."

---

[1] Ambiguous. Either 'it bothered the lion' or 'the leopard felt badly' - probably the former.

[2] Unambiguous second person verb.

M.27   When some days and some while had passed, this lion (sic)
whelped. She had cubs. After she had the cubs, she was lying up
in the den. Lying - [MM: The leopard?] This leopard whelped.
The leopard whelped. This lion had gone, by then. To another
place. The lion had gone to another place, some place (or other)
when the leopard whelped and the cubs were lying there, and she
was lying there too.

M.28   Some days and some while passed, and these cubs got bigger.
Like they were being weaned. This leopard - their mother, is
going (out). The father was (always) going, and whatever came into his grasp, he would bring and give to the female. He would eat
with her. As these cubs got bigger, the mother would leave, too -
she'd gotten a little tired.

M.29   So put it that this male lion (sic) knows, then, counting
nights and days, when she gave birth, and when she'll be going
out, so as to come and eat the cubs. One day this leopard heard
the sound of feet. She said, "Oh, Lord, what is it?" The sound
of feet came, but (on one) came into the den. Since no one came
in, she didn't get up, then, she was still zāj,[1] and lying there
like that, and she didn't get up. She said, (whisper, then rising
volume) "Who is it - (I hope) they go!" Then she said, "Whoever
it was, if it were a hunter, he would have come in on me. He would
have come into the den, shooting with arrows and guns, and if it
were my husband, he would have come (in) - so it was nothing, then,
it's gone."

M.30   When her husband came in the evening, she asked, "Didn't you
come (here) earlier today? To the house?"

M.31   He said, "No, I didn't come in the morning."

M.32   She said, "Well, there was the sound of feet, but then,
nothing."

M.33   So two, three days passed, and the female leopard went out,
too. When the female leopard left, that lion - female - came and
saw that - she went around and stuck her head in on all sides of
the house, and saw that their mother wasn't there, and she came
(in). She ate them, and left. She ate these little ones, and
left.

M.34   After that, this little lioness (sic) to her - this little
leopardess, on account of her little ones, she came back early.
She got back early, and saw the place, and nothing there. She
said, "It could be that this female - male - leopard has come,
and taken them off with him." She thought to herself. Said it.
She went into the den, and didn't worry, (but) said, "Their father

---

[1] 'Recovering from the birth,' the forty-day period of restricted movement
which follows childbirth.

must have come and taken them."

M.35   This female leopard - as it got later, this male leopard came back. She said, (emphatically), "Where's the kids?"

M.36   "What do I know about the kids? I left this morning. What would I know?"

M.37   "Well, I came, and here's the place, and nothing in it."

M.38   "Now, what happened to them? Some hunter or other must have come and taken them." (Aside to MM) Some people bring back leopard cubs. [MM: Yeah.]

M.39   Said - this female leopard said, "No! That lioness came and ate the children!"

M.40   "She wouldn't have eaten (them)."

M.41   "No, she ate them. As God is One, she ate them, she ate them." [Kids whisper in background. MM: Go out and play. Go on!]

M.42   "She ate them."

M.43   After she said, "She ate them," then, he said, "Don't you grieve! Don't say a thing . . ." [Changed batteries] He said, "Don't you worry. If that lioness has eaten your cubs, I - she'll have cubs, too, and I'll send you to eat hers." He said, to his wife, "I - she was sick and lying in the desert and I brought her here, - eh - and every day I went and stole a sheep or something, and brought it and gave it to her, and I ate, too, and we were together in the den for some time, she was like my sister. We were like sister and brother - would she come and eat my cubs?"

M.44   Nothing more, then. He didn't get angry. He (just) went off to the plains, this leopard, prowled, prowled, prowled, prowled, and found a big male lion. He said, "Lion!"

M.45   "What?"

M.46   "I have this sister, I'll give her to you (in marriage). Do you want her?"

M.47   "Yes! How could I not want her? (Here) I am, prowling around, and I can't find a female, not one comes into my grasp!" (laughs) [MM laughs]

M.48   So he came, right away, and found the lioness, and he didn't get angry at all, he didn't say, 'My cubs are lost, what happened?', he said, "Sis! Sis!"

M.49   "Heart of your sister!"

M.50   "Come on, I want to make you a bride."

M.51   "How do you mean, bride?" (Shouting, smiling)

M.52   "By God, I found a good, big, clever, intelligent lion, what can I say? You've <u>got</u> to mate with him, so mate with him!" (smiles)

M.53   So they argued, that way (till she said), "All right!"

M.54   So he showed them, and said, "In such and such a place, on the mountain, we'll dig you a den." So all four went up on the mountain, and they dug a den for those two, this male - lion - and lioness mated, and she got pregnant. This leopard was doing (all) this, so the female leopard could eat her cubs, to make an end of it.

M.55   So it was, that some days, some while passed, normally, and counting nights and days, he knows - this lioness has whelped. When she whelped, had her babies, then, the male (lion) would go, days, and bring some food to sustain them, and the lioness was lying up there, and this (other one) didn't go, saying, "Let it be, she's in the den."

M.56   So (s)he[1] is counting nights and days, till one day the lion went out, to hunt. And the - female - leopard (<u>sic</u>) said, "Now, then, it's your turn." To his wife. The male leopard said, "Go, then."

M.57   (heatedly, shouting). So now she went, and she <u>ate</u> her cubs (claps once) and came back. When this lioness came, she saw the cubs weren't there. She said, "By God, the - eh - female leopard came and ate (them.)"

M.58   So now, they came. These - to the - lions and leopards came together, (and) the lion said, "I have a quarrel with you."

M.59   "What quarrel do you have with me?"

M.60   "I have this quarrel, that you ate my cubs."

M.61   "You and I are even. Why should you eat (mine), if I should(n't) eat yours? So now, you ate (mine) and I ate (yours), and I did a <u>good</u> thing, so (laughing as she speaks) if you're a <u>man</u> (<u>sic</u>), come and fight with me. If you're not, (then) go about - about your business." So then, they said, "It was <u>manly</u> of me to eat (them), so if you're a man, come and quarrel with me, if (not), go to your face[2] - on your way! You came <u>first</u> to my house, and stole and

---

[1] Ambiguous.

[2] Slip of tongue, ᴄⱱᴊ / ᴏᴊ,

ate my children. I, who came after - if you hadn't eaten (mine),
I wouldn't have eaten yours! For years I was sick - you were sick
- I cared for you here, and fed you, and for you I went and stole
people's sheep, (and that's) forbidden! I brought them and gave
them to you so you would get well, and have a bit of a mouthful
of meat!

M.62   "I mated, (and) you - I said to myself, 'The house is small,
come, let's dig a good den,' you got angry and left, and were digging a den. So when you got angry and left, my wife had cubs, and
you came and ate her cubs. So now you've eaten, and I've eaten,
and I did a good thing. Your strength (recourse)[1] is with the
government, so go (to them)."

M.63   So the lion's teeth were left on edge, and she got up with her
husband and left. There, that's the end of the tale of the lion
and the leopard. So she left, and if the lion would have eaten the
leopard's cubs again, (instead) she said, "If I go and eat the
leopard's cubs, the leopard will come and eat mine." So they
didn't do that sort of thing again. (smiling)

M.64   [MM, smiling: That's a good story.]

---

[1] /zūr-e to b'am hokūmat ê, būro!/.

TEXT N

Title: [History of Dispute between Xairuddīn and Ğolām Nabī]
Narrator: Mādar Zāher
Recorded 14 Feb. 1976
Cassette #F3B

N.1   [Leads in from lengthy discussion of MZ's half sister's divorce
       and remarriage]

N.2   MM: Marriage in Afghanistan is very difficult.

N.3   MZ: It is difficult.

N.4   MM: How many times is it that you've found fiancees for Zāher?

N.5   MZ: Until -

N.6   MM: - How many fiancees have they given him, before this?

N.7   MZ: Before this, Margaret dear, we haven't (really) given him
       any other fiancee, just this - Setām, who was here yesterday? His
       brother had brought a daughter.

N.8   MM: Yeah?

N.9   MZ: He - they always said it, in words, like that - we didn't
       give him anything, and we didn't say anything. They would say,
       "We'll give this one to Zāher." She died.

N.10   MM: Oh, poor thing.

N.11   MZ: This Ğolām Nabī who's given his daughter now, he had one
       daughter who was, maybe, bigger than Shāhgol.[1] If she were still
       alive, he would have given her long before this. We would have
       brought her here, and the trouble would have been over. He always
       said, "She's Zāher's." We didn't give her anything, or make her
       any clothes, nobody ate any sweets,[2] or anything. He was just say-
       ing, like that, "I'm giving this one to Zāher."

N.12   MM: What (relation) is Ğolām Nabī to Xairuddīn? The son of -

N.13   MZ: His father's brother's son!

---

[1] Zāher's nine-year-old sister.

[2] Refers to /šīrīnī xorī/, the party to announce an engagement, at which
   sweets are distributed to the guests.

N.14   MM: His father's brother's son.

N.15   MZ: He's his father's brother's son. She died. Gŏlām Nabī's
brother - Gŏlām Nabī's brother, who was called - called Amīd, his
wife gave birth to a daughter -

N.16   MM to fussing child: Go outside! (To his sister) Take him
outside.

N.17   MZ: When Zāher's father went (there), she said, "Cousin,"[1]
- his wife, she called him 'cousin,' "I'll give this daughter of
mine to Zāher."

N.18   Zāher's father said, "Truly?"

N.19   (She) said, "Yes, by God, I'll give (her) to your son." That
is, 'If you brought a kerchief and tied it on her, or if you didn't,
she's yours. If I haven't given her (to you), I'm no woman, with a
veil on my head.' (But) she died.

N.20   Put it that Zāher's father said, "The wo - " he came and said,
"Amīd's wife has gone, like that." When he came from the city, he
got a scarf, and ten sīr[2] of sweets. He took that (there). The one
that he took, it was silk, with a pattern of plants, he sent that.
But then her daughter died, too, (went under the breast.)[3] That kind
of - we didn't make any gathering.

N.21   Then, right here, there was a girl, of his father's brother's
son, and Zāher's father said, "I'll give her to Zāher." Margaret
dear, he sent them, and after that his wife came, and stayed here
for seven or eight nights. Gail[4] was - uh - Gail - it was that -
Bill,[5] it was. I don't know if Bill was here, or if he'd come back
from travelling.[6] This Bill said, "May God grant good fortune!"
Bill said, "Xairuddīn, be smart, don't do like this. Now, now -
if this girl is grown up and Zāher is little," - the girl was grown.

N.22   And when Zāher's father went to - to that Ziāratjāh,[7] when he

---

[1] "Father's brother's son" - she calls him "cousin" by the designation
her husband would use, implying that she is not so related to Xaruddīn
herself.

[2] In Herat, 1 sīr = 1/10 kilogram.

[3] /be zīr-e sīneh šod/ - ?

[4] P.C. English teacher who rents part of X's house.

[5] A former Peace Corps employer of X.

[6] Out-of-country leave.

[7] Village to the south of Herat city where X's cousins live.

went to Ziāratjāh, he had this sister, an old lady, if only she
were alive! She said, "Oh, Lord! Come on! Be smart, don't do
like that, if your boy is little, don't you see? - Don't give her
to him."

N.23   Put it, Margaret dear, that he came (back). He came (back),
and said, - this - this other person had also said, "Don't do it,
because the girl is grown, and your boy is little, don't be oppres-
sive, what do you want to do? Go on, now, take care of your own
interests."

N.24   I - my heart turned bad, then. My heart turned bad, and for
ten days, this woman[1] was in my house, for a visit. Her husband
came after her, to take her (home). Her husband came after her,
and took her, then. And we didn't go after her, or follow up what
was said, or say anything, or anything. [Child cries over record-
ing] So it didn't happen. So that's how it was, that a year passed,
a while passed, and someone from the village - he was headman before, now he's not. Maybe - fifteen years ago, he was headman.
Now he's fallen from the headship. He was a good person, he had
two wives, too, and a good life, if someone came to his place with
ten people, he could handle it, - that daughter of his. And Zāher's
father, his heart drank it up. It drank this up, he said, "He's a
good person, he's not ignorant, he's not hungry, he's got property,
his daughter, if he gives his daughter, makes (her over) in Zāher's
name, " - and his daughter was little - [MM: Yeah.] - "by the time
his daughter grows up, God has doors,[2] maybe I'll be able to lift
the burden of it.[3]" He was going to give this man's daughter to
Zāher.

N.25   So it was, Margaret dear, that he'd said to him, one time, that
guy had said, "This (other) daughter of mine that's engaged, - I'll
not give her to you first, but after they take that daughter of mine
that's engaged (to her husband's family), after that we can see to
our others."[4]

N.26   My heart just drank (that up). When the boy came to our house,
Zāher's father is the kind of person who - if he has to go begging,
that is, if he had ten guests in his house day and night, he doesn't
raise an eyebrow. That is, if he eats dry bread on other nights,
this one evening when he has guests, he'll put out everything (he

---

[1] Mother of the girl in question.

[2] ʼthat He can open' - a proverb.

[3] I.e. Pay the brideprice.

[4] Because in the event of her death, her sister may take her place.
This was the circumstance of MZ marrying X, who is 15 years older than
she.

has), and nothing (stutters) - to face - then he calls - he's a person like this, Margaret dear, he says, "A friend can't - wealth is easy to find, but not a friend! Wealth is like this, you should pour a lak[1] of rupies over a friend's face, (if you must), so the friend won't turn his face away!" There are people, like that, who are friends with someone on account of his wealth, (and) that makes unhappiness.

N.27   Zāher's father and we are all one kind. I say, "The world may pass, my (life) may pass, but don't let my friends pass away." So it was, this person spoke like that. This, this same cousin, G̃olām Nabī. - We went - "Eh, old man! If your boy wants a wife, what's he going to do? I'll give him my daughter! I'll give him my daughter," he himself said, "I'll give her."

N.28   His (Zāher's) father finally said, "Mādar Zāher, it's the wish of his heart that we should give his daughter to Zāher."

N.29   I said, "Oh, Lord, what do I know? It's your choice!"

N.30   He said, "Well, my heart doesn't drink to give her to Zāher, but to Tīmur,[2] I'll give her to Tīmur."

N.31   Put it, Margaret dear, that after some days passed, about a month, or forty days passed, and his wife had one little daughter, she'd gotten sick, and they came to the city. They'd brought her to the doctor. I - I tied a kerchief on her head, just like that one, a new kerchief, that they'd brought from the pilgrimage,[3] I tied it on her head, and - Henny[4] had brought two velvet weskits. One for Tīmur, one for Nāder. I put one of those velvet weskits on her, too. There wasn't anything else in the house, (but) I said, "This is in the name of Tīmur."

N.32   Her father said, "Yes, I'm going to give her." Her mother said, "Oh, go on, die, your liver and heart be under the dust![5] Will you see anyone better than the child of a father's brother?" They left, and it was settled. Put it that I - it was in my heart, I said, "Let it be like this till they grow up, if this other guy says he wants our son, we'll give him, if he doesn't, that's all right, that's all."

---

[1] 100,000.

[2] Zāher's seven-year-old brother.

[3] This gives the kerchief curative powers, as well as the symbolic value of engagement, which any kerchief so bestowed would have.

[4] A female P.C. teacher of whom MZ was very fond.

[5] Good-natured.

N.33   Margaret dear, a month or a month and a half passed. Zāher's
father is starting in, said to this one, "I've given Ǧolām Nabī's
daughter to my son, let's do the 'eating of the sweets,'" and he
said to that one, "I've given Ǧolām Nabī's daughter to my son, let's
put on the 'eating of the sweets.'" So they were saying that,
"We've given Hanīfeh to you," and Tīmur would <u>bawl</u> so <u>much</u>[1] (laughs,
stutters) - that what - [MM laughs]. He got as thin as a reed.
Finally, I said, "Mother, Sister, don't talk about this stuff any
more." I told Zāher's father, "If you're going to take Ǧolām Nabī's
daughter in Zāher's name, do it, (but) <u>this</u> boy of mine is ready
to <u>die</u>! If you don't do it, it's all right, that's all, may disaster stalk him, everyone says, 'They've given Tīmur a wife,' and he
cries." I - I don't know, if he got scared - he was <u>little</u>, after
all. Now he's six and a half, then he was five or four and a half,
not more.

N.34   Put it, Margaret dear, he sent for him. He sent for them, and
I sewed a suit of clothes for Zāher, we got an undershirt, socks,
shoes, and bought two suits of clothes for the girl. Socks, shoes,
everything, nail polish, earrings, a locket, we bought all that sort
of stuff. They said, "Let's have the 'eating of the sweets.'" He
picked it up, answering what we'd said, he said something. He said,
"You do it, and then you give me an accounting."

N.35   At this sweet-eating that we put on, there were forty or fifty
people, and first they did the Qor'ān reading, then they brought the
sweets and they took the kerchiefs and handed them out. There
weren't a lot of women, Maryām was there, and I was, but nobody
else, just men. [Māhgol: My grandmother.] My mother came, too, at
the end. Put it, Margaret dear, that the next morning came, and
Wendy came, and Veronica[2], and they played the hand-drum a little,[3]
and this and that. Her ma - her mother went, too, these ones - the
children's mother left.

N.36   So this, nine months, maybe eight months passed. And we - this
house - fate ran, then - we didn't have that kind of money, in a
lump sum. We bought this house, anyway. Well, God has doors, and
He opened them, anyway. There was this four <u>jerīb</u>[4] of land, and he

---

[1] Tīmur was considered a fearful child by the family, and in fact tried to
run away during his circumcision party, etc.

[2] Wendy: a former PC volunteer. Veronica: V. Baily, an ethnomusicologist.

[3] A further announcement to the community that the 2 families are celebrating an alliance. Cf. H. Baghban, 1977, on the ceremonial place of music
(and more especially drama) in Afghan wedding of circumcision observances.
See also Slobin (1976) on music for the Turkic culture of Northern Afghanistan.

[4] 1 jerīb = 0.4 acre.

sold one jerīb, and gathered up a little change, here and there, and we had some household stuff that we sold. If we had a radio, or a small carpet, or this or that, anything in the house that had any value, we sold that, too. And we had a little change, and we sold that one jerīb for 25,000 rupies,[1] and we bought the house.

N.37   After we bought the house, we moved into it, (but) John[2] had said, "Xairuddīn, until I'm back (from leave), you have to stay here." [MM: OK.] But first we'd brought all the (household stuff),[3] and come (here). After that Zāher's father had said, "John, I'll come (back). I'll find someone and put them in this house, because I've just bought this house, and if I don't occupy it, or nobody does, it could happen that the (former) owner[4] will say, after four or five months, 'I didn't sell it.'"

N.38   Put it, then, that he went and - said to Golām Nabī, "If you could come to the city, and get yourself some wage labor, because we didn't give anything to you for - it's this, that you gave your daughter to our son."

N.39   He said, "I'm not coming to the city."

N.40   "If you're not coming, that's fine, let it be."

N.41   And I said, "Let's move our household stuff into the house, just a bit of it" - he said, [MM: That Golām Nabī said 'I'm not coming to the city -']

N.42   Yeah. "I'm not coming to the city. You put stuff in the house, we'll find someone for you."

N.43   Put it, Margaret dear, that it's - four, five days passed, and all at once we saw, Golām Nabī had come, and they were knocking on the door, one night - "Oh, Lord, what's that?" Zāher's father, he got up, and it's "Give your cousin the key!" His wife and kids were trailing after him, and he'd left them right there in front of the door and come after the key.

N.44   "May you burn, you said 'I'm not coming to the city.'" So there, put it that they came, anyway. After they came, they stayed here, this past winter. And he went before the qāzī and said, "He's given half this house as the brideprice for my daughter." And he came before this (other) one, and said, "This house is the

---

[1] 'rūpī': Afghānī, = approx. 2¢ at that time.

[2] X's current P.C. employer.

[3] /res-e pādšah/ -?

[4] Who is married to X's 1/2 sister, and lives next door.

brideprice - he's given half of it for my daughter." [MM: What?!]
"He gave me half the house! As brideprice for my daughter." [MM:
To whom did he talk like that?] Lies, he told that to everyone.
He told Abd al Rasūl, Abd al Rasūl's brother, and this one, and
that one. [MM: Didn't he give anything to, to buy the house? Two
or three -] Margaret dear, God knows that we didn't get a 'six-
teener',[1] a dīnār, a qur'ān[2] from him! Your God knows, we wanted
five - twenty-five hundred Afghānīs from him, and if he - came
(here), he'd get 100 rupies, or fifty rupies, or 50 'papers',[3] to
get this or that for his own (use). For the love of God, Margaret,
I'm always saying, saying, "Oh, Lord, lay that 5000, or that 500
up to him, because you said," - my children (are) like this, look,
this one's been sick since yesterday, and Zāher went and got two
oranges from the shop (on credit)" - If I get (together) 5 qur'ān
that comes my way,[4] you -" my 5000 rupies, what had come to me,
ten 'papers,' 20 'papers,' he took it. It was never added up.
They didn't add it up, those greybeards, all together, they[5] said,
"We want 5000 Afghanis from you." He said, "I want 10,000 from
him." As a lie. He (just) lied, to do that.

N.45   But it that this happened, then. Zāher's father heard about
it. Talk gets back, anyway! This one and that one said, "Golām
Nabī is talking like this." My heart was broken, and Zāher's
father was going to go two or three times, and throw his household
stuff out in the alley. I said, "Don't do that." John was traveling. I said, "I'll go. I'll go to - I'll go and tell him, and
he'll leave."

N.46   I came, came here to the house, and we have guests that very
evening, his God knows, Margaret dear, I went to the house, and
put the pot on, and got food for the children, and took a light
from the fire, and I came. I came here, and I said, I told his
wife, "Mother of Sargol, Zāher's father's boss is in Kabul, and
he telephoned and said, 'Xairuddīn -' we were in debt besides!
From the price of the house, we owed 25,000 Afghānīs - rupies -
there was that! "So his boss has telephoned, 'Xairuddīn, I found
someone (to rent the house).'[6] So - if I rent out these two rooms
of the house, now, whatever you (decide to) do, you have to go!
Because we'll be in two of the rooms, and that person in the

---

[1] pūl = 0.16 Afghānī.

[2] 0.5 Afghānī.

[3] 1 "paper" = 5 Afs.

[4] MZ makes some money doing laundry for P.C. volunteers.

[5] Xairuddīn.

[6] Gail, a P.C. English teacher who had been assigned to Herat.

other two."

N.47   She said, "Why are you coming into the house, when you didn't before?"

N.48   I said, "Now I just told you (a while ago), I've gotten permission from the Master,[1] and on some days, if God makes it work out, two or three or four women come, or a man, or whatever, for me to open a (- - - -),[2] OK, that's a foreigner's house. If - if - a woman - mustn't come to a foreigner's house. They'll start talking about me, g(o) to the government - if I don't go (sic), it's better if I come (here) and sit in my own house. When no one came here, and Zāher's father, here, if he stays here night and day, what have they got against me? I just ended up here with my children." [MM: Yeah.]

N.49   (She) said, "Give me one room!" [MM: Yeah.]

N.50   I said, "You can't live with the foreigner!" They fight, like that - the father and the kids, and hit each other, and slap each other around, what can you say!? (smiling) The point is, this day I spoke (to them), and this day they put it off, and the day after, and I said, "Whatever you do, they're coming tonight, and you've got to go today, whatever!"

N.51   So then he left the house. When he left the house, and we put him out, he got burned up about that [MM: Yeahhh-] When the land was ready to harvest, it was (on/about) this very same land, that - when we bought this land from him, I was carrying Tīmur. [MM: Tīmur.] Just carrying him. [MM: That makes it seven or eight years ago.] Yeah, of course. I was carrying Tīmur, like that, Margaret dear, maybe two or three (months along), not more. We bought the land from him - they were two brothers. When Zāher's father bought this land, he[3] went, then, to Kabul. After that his[4] brother died. He went and stood on the land that we bought from him, and said, "I didn't sell it. Iff - he comes, this Xairuddīn, I'" the crop, our tenant farmer had salt, that he should harvest it,[5] (but) he said, "This is my land, I didn't sell it to him! The land was mortgaged to him. And I gave the mortgage money back." [MM: Yeah, yeah!] "And I gave back the mortgage money."

---

[1] Said Alī Shāh, a pīr or religious leader and healer in Herat, who died in June, 1975, gave MZ permission to divine and dispense religious charms (/ta'awīz).

[2] /dūtāl/ -?

[3] Xairuddīn.

[4] Ğolām Nabī's.

[5] I.e. had a rightful interest in the harvest.

N.52   This guy came and said, "Ǧolām Nabī won't let me harvest."

N.53   Zāher's father said, "What do you mean, he won't let you?"

N.54   "Nothing, only he says, 'I - If you harvest, I'll kill my child on this land, and I'll kill myself, you - by myself, what can I do, we -'" - and he's[1] a sister's son, too.

N.55   Zāher's father left here. Since he'd said that, he didn't harvest. Then he came back to the city, and this half jerīb of land that was mortgaged, the mortgage holder went with Zāher's father. They'd come to Ǧolām Nabī's village, and he said, "I won't allow you to harvest."

N.56   Zāher's father had said, "When I go, I'm going to harvest. It's my property. I bought it from you. I have a (- - - - -)[2] from - from you. If you're coming, come and kill me."

N.57   He'd gone, Margaret dear, now, and he'd harvested it. He came there. With his shovel. - This shovel was in his hand. He'd come, and he says, "Right in the harvest, I was harvesting. (sic)" They[3] said (heatedly), "You came with a shovel. You came with a shovel, come on, then. Just cross -" he said, - "that ditch."

N.58   (Imitates slower, deeper-voiced speaker) "May God (- - - - - -), if I don't kill you, son of Ǧafūr, if I don't hit your 'bowl' with this shovel, I'm not Ǧolām Nabī." [MM giggles]

N.59   Zāher's father says, "I said, if you're a man, come on, then, oh, you bastard, oh, you liar, oh, greybeard! All right, beard, come on, then!" He says, "I put down the 'bird's beak'[4] I said, I won't hit you (first), you come on, and hit with that shovel!"

N.60   So then, he says, people come from that side. This one said, said, "Bastard, you sold the land, how come you're barking like a dog -" [from outside: Aunt! Aunt!] Hah? [Where are you?] (shouts) The door is open!

N.61   So any way, they cursed each other, and he harvested it. Once he harvested it, Margaret dear, then when they got it harvested, he went again, and gathered up the sheaves, my father's brother[5]

---

[1] The tenant farmer who is relating the story.

[2] /ǧawali/ - perhaps from قول "promise, word".

[3] Xairuddīn: The third person plural is used to show respect.

[4] A pointed tool of some kind, probably a sickle.

[5] Who is also MZ's step father.

picked them up and loaded them on a donkey. [Nāder, 3-year-old, speaks inaudibly] (answering Nāder) How should I know? There isn't any (   )[1], but we'll do something, there's my mother, Abdullah's mother - [MM: OK -]

N.62   So, my uncle gathered up the sheaves, and it went to the people who handle grievances, then, he'd made a formal complaint, in the summertime, and [Visitors, entering: Peace be on you!] [BREAK IN RECORDING]

N.63   [Later] After he harvested it like that, <u>he</u> lodged a complaint against him. Čolām Nabī lodged a complaint. So then, he, the complaint was made and they went running and cursed him to the <u>hakīm</u> and the <u>qāzī</u>. Zāher's father said, "You yourself, if you like this land (so much), I'll give it to you."[2]

N.64   He went, to the village, and the greybeards and the headman and these others - he gave a written note to - gave a written note, and after that, this person and that person said, "You gave him a written note, and you should have taken a note from him for yourself, from what he said."

N.65   So then, from - about four months passed after that, I don't know how long, then the note - then he went,[3] and made a complaint. So he paid out a certain amount of money, then the qāzī said to him, bawled out Golām Nabī, and said, "Go on, you settle it together. You settle it together," that is, (with) a written note. "He should get a note, you give him a note. Give him a note, and (for us) - and seal it with your finger, with your thumbprint, and that's the end of it."

N.66   So they went, and the greybeards at the village again, and again he[4] wasn't satisfied, and Zāher's father came back again, and the headman came after him, again, and they went. So he got a note from him. And - when he went before the qāzī, the qāzī said, "Fine, this note - now that he's put his thumbprint on it, it's correct."

N.67   So now, the girl is there, and since he liked that land, we gave it to him. And he's keeping his daughter until she grows up. She's little still. She's only seven - if she's even that. If Shāhgol is nine, then she's seven or seven and a half - Sh - Shāhgol was still in my arms, eight months or so, and her mother was three

---

[1] /iškeh/ - ?

[2] /hamīn zamīn az to/ - not 'it belongs to you,' but 'I give it to you.' Cf. No. 67.

[3] Xairuddīn.

[4] Xairuddīn.

months along. She's a little over a year behind Shāhgol. [Shāhgol:
She was six-] [MM: So it happened, anyway.] Oh, yeah. He's co -
then, once - uh - once (while) Zāher's father was in Kabul, he came.
He went, and wanted to get some money from somewhere else, so he
went. I told him,[1] later on, "He's come so you (can) go after
him." Everyone does what he can for himself.

N.68   So he came, and he ate here that night, and slept over. And
another time, after that, he came.

N.69   [Child coughing] [MM:...That sweet-eating that you held with
them, was that with a mulla and all?] Oh yeah! The mulla was
here! [- was it all correct?] The mulla 'tied ' the contract![2]
[MM: Oh, OK]. Then again, when we gave him the land, then they
'tied' the nekāh a second time. [MM: Yeah.] Yeah. The contract
is settled now. Now, if - m - [MM: So after that, did you settle
the argument about the land?] (You mean) the first complaint,
that came up? [Yeah.] They contracted, when Zāher's father gave
the land, they contracted a second time. Now, if we don't perform
the marriage, and Zāher goes - uh - when that girl grows up, and
they put them together,[3] there's no sin to it. Because it's contracted. It's contracted two or three times over. If we do it
(i.e. the wedding), fine, we do it. If we don't do it, he'll be
happy with that, coming, and coming. (laughs) God knows (what will
happen), till she grows up.[4]

N.70   [MM: What sort - do you know the girl, now?] Zāher's seen
her. She's a regular rascal, nice and fat, in the Name of God,[5]
she's like - [MM: What's her personality like? Does she help
around the house? What does she do?] She's still little. What
can Shāhgol do now? She's just the same. She's ignorant, still,
she doesn't know anything. But anyway, she's good and fat, she's
pretty, no ailments. She's like this, that - in a year, I'd say,
she doesn't get a headache. We and these kids - it must be close
to four, five, six times, maybe ten times, (we're) at the doctor's.
and it happens again and again. No. She's got no ailments. They

---

[1] Xairuddīn.

[2] /nekāh/.

[3] A form of bundling. The engaged couple is left alone together, sometimes overnight in bed, but fully clothed.

[4] There is a veiled threat in this, in that Zāher's family need not perform the wedding until they want to. They have a certain power over
Golām Nabī, in that he cannot now give his daughter to anyone else, unless they release her, and he pays back the bride-price.

[5] Pronounced to ward off evil eye from the person or thing which is
praised.

just sent her to the mosque school. [MM: Good, good.] We - she's going to the mosque. She's reading the 'alhamdeh'[1], that time when your father [to child] and Zāher's father went there, he told me, "She's going to the mosque, reading the 'alhamdeh.'" Yeah, she's learning that. [MM: That's good. If she's intelligent -] That's fine, anyway, we'll see - till she grows up, if they get along together, and are happy - right now, it's good. There was and there was, - there was a king . . . (MZ launches into a folktale)

---

[1] First book in instruction program of village religious schools.

TEXT O

Excerpt of a letter from Zāher to M. Mills, dated 10. Hamal, 1356 (30 March, 1978):

0.1   ". . . I would like to answer the question you asked me.[1] Feel free and don't worry about asking [me] any questions you may have. If I can't answer it myself, I'll find you an answer from elsewhere.

0.2   My dear friend, this wife of Ǧolām Nabī's is related, but very distantly. She's the father's brother's daughter of my grandfather.[2] Now she can't manage it any other way,[3] (and) she says, "You have to furnish my daughter's house, like (with) mattresses, [for sitting and sleeping], pillows, carpeting, dishes, pots and pans, trays, bowls, and that sort of thing, and you have to get [her] everything that's necessary for housekeeping."

         And my father told her, "I'm old now and I don't have anything else, and I'll have to sell this house of mine to get these things for you, and put my children out on the street." My father said, "Everything is prepared and correct for Zāher's house. These things that are already here, belong to your daughter."[4]

0.3   She said, "No. You must get new things from the bazaar."

0.4   Ǧolām Nabī and his children are silent. His wife is not silent. My father's thought is to have the wedding in four or five months, if God wills. Because I now understand a bit about having a wife, I told my father, "Try to have the wedding. The sooner it is, the happier I'll be." My father thinks now that he will hold the wedding sooner. And if we hold the wedding, we'll let you know. We'll send you work if we don't hold it, too.

0.5   During the month between the feasts of Rowzeh and Qorbān[5]

---

[1] In a March, 1978 letter, I asked what relation Zāher's prospective mother-in-law was to the rest of the family, and whether plans were progressing for his wedding.

[2] Probably on his father's side, but perhaps on both sides, since his father and mother are first cousins.

[3] *Hālā digar šekl nemītavānad resānd.*

[4] Implying that Z. and his wife will live at his father's house.

[5] I.e. the end of Ramazān and the feast at which hajjīs of previous years sacrifice animals and give away the meat as alms. This period is regarded as inauspicious for certain ceremonies, including weddings.

and at New Year, too, I take three or four dresses, and shoes, and veils, and tea and tea sweets and fruit [to them]. And if I go to the village once or twice a month, I buy tea and tea sweets and fruit and candy from a shop and take them to the village, and they're still not happy. And I never saw such a family before. They don't understand kindness or humanity. Whatever I do for them, they treat me badly. Now, my dear, kind friend, I don't want to use up your time . . . (letter closes)

SELECT

BIBLIOGRAPHY

Abrahams, R.D..

    1969 "The Complex Relations of Simple Forms," _Genre_ 2:2, pp.104-128.

Adams, R.J.

    1967 "Folktale Telling and Storytellers in Japan," _Asian Folklore Studies_ 26:1, pp.99-118.

Alder, Garry J.

    1974 "The Dropped Stitch," _Afghanistan Journal_ 1:4, pp. 105-113, and 2:1 (1975), pp.20-27.

Armstrong, R.P.

    1959 "Content Analysis in Folkloristics," in I. de Sola Pool, ed., _Trends in Content Analysis_, Urbana, Ill., pp. 151-170.

Asadowskij, Mark

    1926 _Eine Siberische Märchenerzahlerin_ (= Folklore Fellows Communication #68), Helsinki: Suomalainen Tiedeakatemia, 70 pp.

Babcock-Abrahams, Barbara

    1975 "A Tolerated Margin of Mess: The Trickster and His Tales Reconsidered", _Journal of the Folklore Institute_ 11:3, pp. 147-186.

Baghban, Hafizullah

    n.d. "An Overview of Herat Folk Literature", mimeograph, 16 pp.

    1972 [Bibliography on Middle Eastern Folklore, untitled], _Folklore Forum_ Bibliographic and Special Series, No. 9, 43 pp.

    1975 "Afghanistan", in R.M. Dorson, _Folktales Told around the World_, Chicago: University of Chicago Press. pp. 209-242.

    1976 _The Context and Concept of Humor in Magadi Theater_, unpublished PhD Dissertation, Folklore Institute, Indiana University. 4 volumes.

Bartlett, F.C.

    1932 _Remembering_, New York: MacMillan, x,317 pp.

Bascom, W.

    1975 _African Dilemma Tales_, Hague: Mouton, xiii,162 pp.

Başgöz, I.

   1970 "Turkish *Hikayeh*-Telling Tradition in Azerbaijan, Iran," Journal
       of American Folklore 83:330, pp. 391-405.

   1975 "The Tale Singer and His Audience", in Ben-Amos, D. & Goldstein,
       K., Folklore: Performance and Communication, Hague: Mouton,
       pp. 143-205.

Bauman, R.

   1975 "Verbal Art as Performance," American Anthropologist 77:290-311.

Beidelman, T.O.

   1961 "Hyena and Rabbit: A Kaguru Representation of Matrilineal Relations,"
       Africa 31, pp. 61-17.

   1963 "Further Adventures of Hyena and Rabbit: The Folktale as a Socio-
       logical Model", Africa 33, pp.54-63.

   1966 "Swazi Royal Ritual", Africa 36, pp. 373-405.

   1967 "Kaguru Folklore and the Concept of Reciprocity," Zeitschrift fur
       Ethnologie 92:1, pp. 74-88.

Ben-Amos, D.

   1969 "Analytical Categories and Ethnic Genres", Genre 2:3, pp. 275-301.

   1971 "Toward a Definition of Folklore in Context", Journal of American
       Folklore 84, pp. 3-15.

Boratav, P.N.

   1963 Le Tekerleme, contribution á l'ètude typologique et stylistique
       du conte populaire turc, (Cahiers de la Societé Asiatique, No.
       XVII), Paris: Imprimerie Nationale, 209 pp.

Bremond, J.

   1970 "Morphology of the French Folktale", Semiotica 2, pp. 247-276.

Cejpek, J.

   1968 "Iranian Folk-Literature", in J. Rypka, History of Iranian Liter-
       ature, Dordrecht: Reidel, pp. 607-710.

Centlivres, P.

   1972 Un bazar d'Asie Centrale, Wisebaden: Reichert, 226 pp.

Cermak, L.S.

   1972 Human Memory: Research and Theory, New York: Ronald Press, viii,
           294 pp.

Child, I.L., Storm, F.S., & Veroff, J.,

   1958 "Achievement Themes Related to Socialization Practice," in Atkin-
           son, J., ed., Motives in Fantasy, Action and Society, pp. 479-
           492.

Clouston, W.A.

   1890 Flowers from a Persian Garden and Other Papers, London, xii, 368
           pp.

Crowley, D.J.

   1976 "'The Greatest Thing in the World,' Type 653A, in Trinidad," in
           Dégh, L, Glassie~, H., & Oinas, F., eds., Folklore Today (Fest-
           schrift Dorson), Bloomington: Indiana University Press, pp. 93-
           100.

Da Matta, R.

   1971 "Myth and Anti-myth among the Timbira," in Maranda, P., & Köngas-
           Maranda, E., Structural Analysis of Oral Tradition, Philadelphia:
           Univeristy of Pennsylvania Press, pp. 271-291.

Dégh, L.

   1969 Folktales in Society: Story-Telling in a Hungarian Peasant Community,
           Bloomington, Indiana: Indiana University Press, xviii, 430 pp.

Dégh, L., & Vaszonyi, A.

   1975 "The Hypothesis of Multi-Conduit Transmission in Folklore," in Ben-
           Amos & Goldstein, Folklore: Performance and Communication, Hague:
           Mouton, pp. 207-254.

Devereux, G.

   1948 "Mohave Coyote Tales," Journal of American Folklore 61, pp. 223-255.

   1971 "Art and Mythology: A General Theory," in Jopling, C., ed., Art and
           Aesthetics in Primitive Societies, New York: Dutton.

Dorson, R.M.

   1975a "African and Afro-American Folklore", Journal of American Folklore,
           88;348, pp. 151-164.

   1975b "Oral Styles of American Folk Narrators," reprinted in Folklore:
           Selected Essays, Bloomington: Indiana University Press.

1975c <u>Folktales Told around the World</u>, Chicago: University of Chicago
  Press, xxv,622 pp.

Douglas, Mary

1970 <u>Purity and Danger</u>, Baltimore: Penguin (Pelican Books), 220 pp.

Drummond, Lee

1977 "Structure and Process in the Interpretation of a South American
  Myth: The Arawak Dog Spirit People", <u>American Anthropologist</u>,
  79:4, pp. 842-868.

Dundes, A.

1962 "From Etic to Emic Units in the Structural Study of Folktale,"
  <u>Journal of American Folklore</u> 75, pp. 95-105.

1963 "Structural Typology of North American Indian Folktales", <u>Southwest
  Journal of Anthropology</u> 19. pp. 121-130.

1964 <u>Morphology of North American Indian Folktales</u> , Helsinki: Suomalainen
  Tiedeakatemia (= Folklore Fellows Communication # 195).

1969 "The Devolutionary Premise in Folklore Theory", <u>Journal of the Folklore Institute</u> 6, pp. 5-19.

1971 "The Sherente Retellings of <u>Genesis</u>", in Maranda, P., & Köngas
  Maranda, E., <u>Structural Analysis of Oral Tradition</u>, Philadelphia:
  University of Pennsylvania Press.

Eberhard, W.

1976 "The Impact of Modernization upon Chinese Folklore", in Dégh, L.,
  Glassie, H., and Oinas, F., eds., <u>Folklore Today</u>, Bloomington:
  Indiana University Press, pp. 139-144.

Farnham, W.E.

1920 "The Contending Lovers," <u>PMLA</u> 35:3, (n.s. 28:3), pp. 247-323.

Fernea, E.W. & Bezirgan, B.Q.

1976 <u>Middle Eastern Muslim Women Speak</u>, Austin: University of Texas
  Press.

Finnegan, R.

1977 <u>Oral Poetry: Its Nature, Significance and Social Context</u>, Cambridge:
  Cambridge University Press, xiii, 299 pp.

Fischer, J.L.

1971 "Art Styles as Cultural Cognitive Maps," in Jopling, Carol F., <u>Art
  and Aesthetics in Primitive Societies</u>, New York: Dutton, pp. 171-

192.

Friedl, E.

1975 "The Folktale as Cultural Comment," Asian Folklore Studies 34:2,
      pp. 127-144.

1977 [unpublished texts: 'Gedulak';'Ali Pazanak and Ali Marak'; mimeo-
      graphed, n.d., no pagination]

Georges, R.

1969 "Toward an Understanding of Storytelling Events", Journal of Amer-
      ican Folklore, 82, pp. 313-328.

Goldstein, K.

1967 "Experimental Folklore: Lab vs. Field," in Wilgus, D.K., ed., Folk-
      lore International (Festschrift Wayland Hand), Hatboro, Pa.:
      pp. 71-82.

Gregorian, V.

1969 The Emergence of Modern Afghanistan, Stanford: Stanford University
      Press, xii, 586 pp.

Greimas, A.J.

1971 "The Interpretation of Myth: Theory and Practice" in Maranda, P., &
      Köngas Maranda, E., Structural Study of Oral Tradition, Philadel-
      phia: University of Pennsylvania Press, pp. 81-121.

Grønhaug, R.

1972 "Scale as a Variable in the Analysis: Reflections based on field
      material from Herat, Northwest Afghanistan," Advance Paper for
      Burg Wartenstein Symposium # 55, July 31-Aug. 8, 1972, Wenner-
      Gren Foundation, New York (mimeograph), pp.43.

Grötzbach, E.

1974 "Anardarreh - das verborgene „Tal der Granatäpfel", Afghanistan
      Journal 1:4, pp.114-117.

Gurgāni, F.

1972 Vīs and Rāmīn, G. Morrison, trans., New York: Columbia University
      Press, pp. xix,357.

Hackin, Ria, & Kohzad, A.

1953 Legendes et Coutumes Afghanes, Paris: Imprimerie Nationale (Publi-
      cations du Musée Guimet, Bibliotheque de Diffusion, Tome LX),
      xxvi, 204 pp.

Hanaway, W.

1970 Persian Popular Romances before the Safavid Era, New York: Columbia University unpublished PhD dissertation.

Hankiss, E.

1972 "Meaning as a Source of Aesthetic Experience", Semiotica 6, pp. 201-211.

Haring, L.

1972 "Performing for the Interviewer: A Study of the Structure of Context," Southern Folklore Quarterly 36, pp. 383-98.

Haymes, E.R.,

1973 A Bibliography of Studies Relating to Parry's and Lord's Oral Theory, Cambridge, Mass: Harvard University PUblications of the Milman Parry Collection, 45 pp.

Hendricks, W.O.

1973a Essays in Semiolinguistics and Verbal Art, Hague: Mouton, 210 pp.

1973b "Methodology of Narrative Structural Analysis", Semiotica 7, pp. 163-184.

1973c "Linguistics and Folkloristics," in Sebeok, T., ed., Current Trends in Linguistics, Vol. 12, pt. 3, Hague;Mouton, pp. 127-151.

1973d "Verbal Art and the Structuralist Synthesis", Semiotica 8, pp. 239-262.

1975 "The Work and Play Structures of Narrative," Semiotica 13.

Heuscher, J.E.

1974 Psychiatric Study of Fairy Tales, 2nd ed., Srpingfield, Ill.: Chas. A. Thomas, vi, 295 pp.

Honko, L.

1968 "Genre Analysis in Folkloristics and Comparative Religion," Temenos 3, pp. 48-66.

Hrdličkova, V.

1969 "Japanese Professional Storytellers," Genre 2:3, pp. 179-210.

Hymes, D.

    1964 Language in Culture and Society, New York: Harper & Row, xxxv,
          764 pp.

    1971 "The 'Wife' Who 'Goes Out' like a Man," in Maranda, P. & Kōngas
          Maranda, E., eds., Structural Analysis of Oral Tradition, Phila-
          delphia: University of Pennsylvania Press, pp. 49-80.

    1972 "The Contribution of Folklore to Sociolinguistic Research", in
          Paredes, A. & Bauman, R., eds., Toward New Perspectives in Folk-
          lore, Austin: University of Texas Press, pp. 42-50.

    1975 "Breakthrough into Performance", in Ben-Amos, D. & Goldstein, K.,
          eds., Folklore: Performance and Communication, Hague: Mouton,
          pp. 11-73.

Jacobs, M.

    1966 "A Look Ahead in Oral Literature Research," Journal of the American
          Folklore Society 79, pp. 413-427.

Jason, H.

    1972 "Jewish-Near Eastern Numskull Tales, an Attempt at Interpretation",
          Asian Folklore Studies, 30:1, pp.1-39.

    1973 "The Genre in Oral Literature," Temenos 9, pp. 156-160.

Kerenyi, K.

    1956 "The Trickster in Relation to Greek Mythology," in Radin, P., The
          Trickster, pp. 173-191.

Kiefer, E.E.

    1947 Albert Wesselski and Recent Folktale Theories, Bloomington: Indiana
          University Press, 84 pp.

Klatzky, R.L.

    1975 Human Memory: Structure and Process, San Francisco: W.H. Freeman,
          276 pp.

Levi-Strauss, C.

    1958 "The Structural Study of Myth," in T.A. Sebeok, ed., Myth, a Sympo-
          sium, Bloomington, Ind.: Midland Books, pp. 81-106.

    1959 "La Geste d'Asdiwal", Ecole Pratique des Hautes Etudes, Section des
          Sciences religieuses, Annual (1958-59), Paris.

Levy, R. (trans.)

   1959 Tales of Marzuban, Bloomington: Indiana University Press, 254 pp.

Littleton, C.S.

   1970 "The 'Kingship in Heaven' Theme," in J. Pühvel, Myth & Law among the
        Indo-Europeans, Los Angeles: University of California Press, pp.
        83-121.

Lord, A.B.

   1960 The Singer of Tales, Cambridge, Mass: Harvard University Press, 308 p

Lüthi, M.

   1969 "Aspects of the Märchen and the Legend," Genre 2, pp. 162-178.

   1976 "Goal-Orientation in Storytelling," in Dégh, L., Glassie, H., & Oinas,
        F., eds., Folklore Today, Bloomington: Indiana U. Press, pp.357-68.

Malleson, G.B.

   1880 Herat: The Granary and Garden of Central Asia, London: Allen, 248 pp.

Maranda, E. Köngas

   1971 "The Logic of Riddles," in Maranda, P., & Köngas Maranda, E., Struc-
        tural Analysis of Oral Tradition, Philadelphia: U. Penn. Press,
        pp. 189-232.

Maranda, P. (ed.)

   1972 Mythology, Baltimore: Penguin, 320 pp.

   1974 Soviet Structural Folkloristics, Hague: Mouton, 198 pp.

Maranda, P., & Köngas Maranda, E. (eds.)

   1971 Structural Analysis of Oral Tradition, Philadelphia: University of
        Pennsylvania Press, xxxiv, 324 pp.

Mathiot, M.

   1972 "Cognitive Analysis of a Myth: An Exercise in Method," Semiotica
        6, pp. 101-141.

McKean, P.F.

   1971 "The Mouse-Deer (Kantjil) in Malayo-Indonesian Folklore: Alternative
        Analyses and the Significance of a Trickster Figure in Southeast
        Asia," Asian Folklore Studies, 30:1, pp. 71-84.

Meletinsky, E.

    1971 "Structural-Typological Study of the Folktale", Genre 4:3, pp. 249-
         279.

    1974a "Marriage: Its Function and Position in the Structure of Folktales."
         in Maranda, P. ed., Soviet Structural Folkloristics, Hague: Mouton,
         pp.

    1974b "The Problem of the Historical Morphology of the FOlktale," in
         Maranda, P. , ed., Soviet Structural Folkloristics, Hague: Mouton,
         pp. 55-72.

    1974c "Problems of the Structural Analysis of Fairy Tales," in Maranda, P.,
         ed., Soviet Structural Folkloristics, Hague: Mouton, pp. 73-139.

Ministry of Planning, Kingdom of Afghanistan

    1972 Statistical Pocketbook of Afghanistan, 1350, Kabul: Government
         Printing Office, pp. 203.

Mitchell, R.E.

    1968 "Genre and Function in Eastern Carolinian Narrative," Asian Folklore
         Studies 27:2, pp. 1-15.

Morgenstierne, G.

    1975 "Volksdichtung in Afghanistan", Afghanistan Journal 2:1. pp. 2-7.

Nathhorst, B.

    1968 "Genre, Form and Structure in Oral Tradition," Temenos 3, pp. 128-137.

Norman, D.A.

    1969 Memory and Attention, New York: John Wiley & Sons, ix, 201 pp.

Oinas, F.

    1976 "The Notion of Soviet Folklore" in Dégh, L, Glassie, H., & Oinas, F.,
         eds., Folklore Today (Festschrift Dorson), Bloomington, Ind.:
         Indiana University Press, pp. 379-397.

Opler, M. E.

    1938 Myths and Tales of the Jicarilla Apache Indians, New York: American
         Folklore Society, Stechert, pp. xxiii, 408. (Memoirs of the Ameri-
         can Folklore Society, vol. 31)

Ortutay, G.

    1959 "Principles of Oral Transmission in Folk Culture (Variations, 'Affin-
         ity'), Acta Ethnographia 8, pp. 175-221.

Peacock, J.L.

  1971 "Class, Clown, and Cosmology in Javanese Drama," in Maranda, P.,
       & Kongãs Maranda, E., eds., Structural Analysis of Oral Tradi-
       tion, Philadelphia: University of Pennsylvania Press, pp. 139-
       168.

Pop, M.

  1970 "La Poetique du Conte Populaire," Semiotica 2, pp. 117-127.

Prizel, Y.

  1974 "Evolution of the Tale from Literary to Folk," Southern Folklore
       Quarterly 38:3. pp/ 211-222.

Propp, V.

  1968 Morphology of the Folktale, Austin: University of Texas Press,
       pp. xxvi, 158.

  1971 "Generic Structures in Russian Folklore," Genre 4:3, pp. 213-248.

  1972 "Transformations in Fairy Tales," in Maranda, P., Mythology,
       Penguin, pp. 139-150.

Radin, P.

  1956 The Trickster, London & New York: Routledge and Kegan Paul, xi,
       211 pp.

Reaver, J.R.

  1972 "From Reality to Fantasy: Opening-Closing Formulas in the Structures
       of American Tall Tales," Southern Folklore Quarterly 36, pp. 369-
       382.

Reichard, G.

  1950 Navaho Religion: A Study in Symbolism, New York: Bollingen Founda-
       tion (Pantheon Books), Bollingen Series # XVIII, 2 vol., xxxvi,
       800 pp.

Roberts, J.M., Sutton-Smith, B., & Kendon, A.

  1963 "Strategy in Games and Folktales," Journal of Social Psychology
       61, pp. 185-199.

Rosenberg, B.

  1975 "Oral Sermons and Oral Narratives," in Ben-Amos & Goldstein, eds.,
       Folklore: Performance and Communication, Hague: Mouton, pp. 75-103

Rypka, J.

    1968 <u>History of Iranian Literature,</u> Dordrecht: Reidel, xxvii, 928 pp.

Sebeok, T.A.

    1957 "Towards a Statistical Contingency Method in Folklore Research,"
         in Richmond, W.E., ed., <u>Studies in Folklore</u>, Bloomington, Ind.:
         Indiana University Press, pp. 130-140.

Segal, D.M.

    1972 "The Connection between the Semantics and the Formal Structure of
         a Text", in Maranda, P., ed., <u>Mythology</u>, Baltimore: Penguin,
         pp.130-140.

Seiler, H.

    1969 "On the Interrelation between Text, Translation and Grammar of an
         American Indian Language", <u>Linguistische Berichte</u> 3, pp. 1-17.

Slobin, M.

    1976 <u>Music in the Culture of Northern Afghanistan</u>, Tucson: University of
         Arizona Press, xiv, 297 pp.

Smith, H. H. et al.

    1973 <u>Area Handbook for Afghanistan</u>, 3rd Edition, Washington, D.C.: U.S.
         Government Printing Office, lvi,454 pp.

Swahn, J.O.

    1955 <u>The Tale of Cupid and Psyche</u>, Lund.

Sykes, P.

    1940 <u>History of Afghanistan</u>, London: MacMillan, 2 vol., vii,411 & ix, 414
         pp.

Tedlock, D.

    1972 "On the Translation of Style in Oral Narrative", in Paredes, A. &
         Bauman; R., eds., <u>Toward New Perspectives in Folklore</u>, Austin:
         University of Texas Press, pp. 114-133.

Toelken, J.B.

    1969 "The 'Pretty Language' of Yellowman: Genre, Mode and Texture in
         Navaho Coyote Narratives," <u>Genre</u> 2:3, pp. 211-235.

Turner, V.

    1964 "Betwixt and Between: The Liminal Period in <u>Rites de Passage</u>",
         <u>Proceedings of the American Ethnological Society</u>, Symposium
         on New Approaches to the Study of Religion, pp. 4-20.

    1968 "Myth", <u>Encyclopedia of the Social Sciences</u>, New York: MacMillan
         & Free Press, Vol. 10, pp. 576-582.

Wescott, J.

    1962 "The Sculpture and Myths of Eshu-Elegba, the Yoruba Trickster,"
         <u>Africa</u> 32, pp. 336-354.

Wilson, D.

    1969 "Afghan Literature: A Perspective," in Grassmuck, G., Adamec, L.,
         & Irwin, F.J., eds., <u>Afghanistan: Some New Approaches</u>, Ann
         Arbor: University of Michigan Press,

Yen, Alsace,

    1974 "Thematic Patterns in Japanese Folktales: A Search for Meanings",
         <u>Asian Folklore Studies</u> 33:2, pp. 1-36.